ENTREPRENEURSHIP AND BUSINESS DEVELOPMENT

FGF Entrepreneurship-Research Monographien

Band 3

Herausgegeben von Prof. Dr. Heinz Klandt, Jünkerath
für den Förderkreis Gründungsforschung

Förderkreis Gründungs-Forschung e.V.
Entrepreneurship-Research

c/o Universität Dortmund, Postfach 50 05 00, D-4600 Dortmund 50

Entrepreneurship and Business Development

Edited by
DR HEINZ KLANDT
University of Dortmund

Ashgate

Aldershot • Brookfield USA • Singapore • Sydney

© Dr Heinz Klandt 1993

Published by
Ashgate Publishing Limited
Gower House
Croft Road
Aldershot, Hants
GU11 3HR
England

Ashgate Publishing Company
Old Post Road
Brookfield
Vermont 05036
USA

Reprinted 1997, 1998

A CIP catalogue record for this book is available from the British Library and the US Library of Congress

ISBN 1 85628 416 6

Printed in Great Britain by Biddles Limited, Guildford and King's Lynn

Contents

Preface   ix

Authors   x

Part 1: New conceptual frameworks and paradigms in entrepreneurship

1   Paradoxes of entrepreneurship
    Bengt Johannisson, Knuth Senneseth   3

2   In search of entrepreneur: business environment contingencies
    Asko Miettinen, Nina Hedberg   21

3   The process of becoming an entrepreneur: a theoretical framework
    of factors influencing entrepreneurs' start-up decisions
    Visa Huuskonen   43

4   Venture teams start-ups: an undiscovered field of research
    Detlef Müller-Böling   55

5   Entrepreneurs', competitive definitions: evidence from
    computer-software start-ups
    Michael Levenhagen, Howard Thomas   67

Part 2: Special methodological approaches in entrepreneurship research

6 Entrepreneurship: some lessons of social anthropology
Peter Rosa, Alison Bowes   87

7 Real and potential entrepreneurs playing a business
simulating game
Heinz Klandt   101

Part 3: Survival and exit of enterprises

8 The owner-managers exit route
Sue Birley, Paul Westhead   123

9 Survival, entrepreneurship, growth: which relationship?
The Milanese area's case
Giuliano Mussati, Andrea Fumagalli   141

10 New firm and plant survival in United States manufacturing
David D. Audretsch   161

Part 4: Factors influencing entrepreneurial intentions and activities

11 Entrepreneurial interest among business students:
results of an international study
Hermann J. Weihe, Frank-Rainer Reich   179

12 'Ecological' basis for the analysis of gender differences
in the predisposition to self-employment
Daphne Hamilton   199

13 Social continuity and change: the contextual environment
of self-employment
Dieter Bögenhold, Udo Staber   211

Part 5: Factors influencing entrepreneurial performance

14 Factors associated with relative performance amongst small firms in
the British instrumentation sector
Graham Hall, Sally Fulshaw   227

15 Intensity of planning conviction among entrepreneurs:
differences between zealots and non-believers
Harold P. Welsch, Gerhard R. Plaschka   239

Part 6: Entrepreneurial versus administrative behaviour

16 Profiling entrepreneurs: multiple perspectives and
consequent methodological considerations
Elizabeth Chell, Jean M. Haworth   251

17 A new perspective of entrepreneurship: a dialectic process of
transformation within the entrepreneurial mode, types of flexibility
and organizational form
Henk W. Volberda, Hock-Beng Cheah   261

Part 7: Entrepreneurship and government policy

18 Towards an effective subsidizing policy
Hermann Frank, Gerhard Plaschka, Dietmar Rößl   289

19 Incentives for the venture capital industry in Finland
Juha Auer, Kai-Erik Relander, Heikki Westerlund   299

Part 8: Entrepreneurship and innovation/technology

20 Manager participation in innovation activities of small
and medium-sized industrial enterprises
Liisa Hyvärinen   325

21 Creating an entrepreneurial management system in large
corporations: the STK innova case
Birgit Helene Jevnaker   335

22 Introduction of information technology to small firms:
a network perspective
Mette Mønstedt   359

Preface

Entrepreneurs, business start-ups, new ventures, venture capital, intrapreneurs, spin-offs, MBOs: these terms represent a wide range of topics, which are most important for many nations today, industrial, developing and transitional economies.
Academics engaged in these fields have done lot of empirical research, but more research is needed, the state of the art reached in these fields is not satisfying; for example:

* In most nations we have weak statistics about the dynamics of market entries and exits, and the reasons behind these dynamics.
* We are not sure about the set of characteristics and abilities entrepreneurs should posess to be successful.
* We do not know what characterises efficient behaviour of entrepreneurs in their firms.
* We need better instruments to support entrepreneurs, bankers or venture capitalists and to evaluate the expected performance of a venture etc.

This book is based on papers presented at the meeting of some 60 academics at the RENT IV (Research in Entrepreneurship) conference in Cologne in November 29 - 30, 1990, organized by the Foerderkreis Gruendungsforschung e.V. (FGF), Cologne-Dortmund and the European Institute of Advanced Studies in Management (EIASM), Brussels in cooperation with the European Council on Small Business (ECSB).
My special thanks go to the FGF which sponsored the publication of these proceedings which will also form volume 3 of the 'FGF- Entrepreneurship Monographien'.
As the editor of these proceedings I have to give many thanks to all people engaged in the RENT IV conference and preparation of this publication: beside the authors of the contributions who revised their original presentations, especially to Jochen Struck, Olaf Kurpiers, Pea Koglin, Martin Pfennig and Sabine Seiler.

Heinz Klandt

Authors

Audretsch, Dr. David D., Forschungsschwerpunkt Marktprozeß und Unternehmensentwicklung, Wissenschaftszentrum Berlin für Sozialforschung, Germany

Auer, Juha, Finish National Fund for Research and Development, Helsinki, Finland

Birley, Dr. Sue, Professor, The Management School, Imperial College, Science, Technology and Medicine, UK

Bögenhold, Dr. Dieter, Research Fellow, Department of Sociology, University of Bielefeld, Germany

Bowes, Alison, Scottish Enterprise Foundation, University of Stirling, UK

Cheah, Dr. Hock-Beng, Department of Economics and Management, University of New South Wales, Australia

Chell, Dr. Elisabeth, Director Centre for Small Business Research, University of Salford, UK

Frank, Dr. Hermann, Universitätsassistent, Institut für Betriebswirtschaftslehre der Klein- und Mittelbetriebe, Wirtschaftsuniversität Wien, Austria

Fulshaw, Sally, Manchester Business School, University of Manchester, UK

Fumagalli, Andrea, Centro di Studi sull'Imprenitorialita Furio Cigogna, Universita Commerciale Luigi Bocconi, Italy

Hall, Graham, Dr., Manchester Business School, University of Manchester, UK

Hamilton, Daphne, Scottish Enterprise Foundation, University of Sterling, UK

Haworth, Dr. Jean M., Senior Lecturer, University of Salford, Centre for Small Business Research, UK

Hedberg, Dr. Nina, Lappeenranta University of Technology, Finland

Huuskonen, Dr. Visa, Tuurku School of Economics and Business Administration, Finland

Hyvärinen, Liisa, Lic. Tech. Assistant, Lappeenranta University of Technology, Department of Industrial Engineering and Management, Finland

Jevnaker, Birgit Helene, Centre for Research in Economics and Business Administration, Bergen, Norway

Johannisson, Dr. Bengt, Professor for Entrepreneurship and Business Development, Institut of Economic Research, Lund University and Växjö University, Sweden

Klandt, Dr. Heinz, Professor for Empirical Research, Faculty of Business, Economics and Social Sciences, University of Dortmund, Germany

Levenhagen, Dr. Michael, Lecturer in Marketing and Strategic Management, Warwick Business School, UK

Miettinen, Dr. Asko, Professor, Department of Industrial Engineering and Management, Lappeenranta, University of Technology, Finland

Mønsted, Dr. Mette, Center for Innovation and Entrepreneurship, Copenhagen Business School, Denmark

Müller-Böling, Dr. Detlef, Professor, Director Betriebswirtschaftliches Institut für empirische Gründungs- und Organisationsforschung e.V., Universität Dortmund, Germany

Mussati, Giuliano, Professor, Condirettore Centro di Studi sull'Imprenitorialita Furio Cigogna, Universita Commerciale Luigi Bocconi, Italy

Plaschka, Dr. Gerhard R., Professor of Mangement, College of Business Administration, Butler University, USA

Reich, Frank-Rainer, Fachbereich Wirtschaft, Fachhochschule Nordostniedersachsen, Germany

Relander, Kai-Erik, Finish National Fund for Research and Development, Helsinki, Finland

Rößl, Dr. Dietmar, Universitäts Assistent, Institut für Betriebswirtschaftslehre der Klein- und Mittelbetriebe, Wirtschaftsuniversität Wien, Austria

Rosa, Dr. Peter, Scottish Enterprise Foundation, University of Stirling, UK

Staber, Dr. Udo, Associate Professor, Faculty of Administration, University of New Brunswick, Canada

Senneseth, Knuth, Centrum för Smaföretagsutveckling, Högskolan i Växjö, Sweden

Thomas, Howard, Department of Business, College of Commerce and Business Administration, University of Illinois at Champaign-Urbana, USA

Volberda, Henk W., Assistant Professor of Strategic Management, Rotterdam School of Management, Erasmus University Rotterdam, Netherlands

Weihe, Dr. Hermann J., Professor, Fachbereich Wirtschaft, Fachhochschule Nordostniedersachsen, Germany

Welsch, Dr. Harold P., Professor, Endowed Chair in Entrepreneurship, Department of Management, DePaul University, Chicago, USA

Westerlund, Heikki, Finish National Fund for Research and Development, Helsinki, Finland

Westhead, Dr. Paul, The Management School, Imperial College, Science, Technology and Medicine, London, UK

Part 1
New conceptual frameworks and paradigms in entrpreneurship

1 Paradoxes of entrepreneurship

Bengt Johannisson and Knut Senneseth

Abstract

Conceptual and empirical research on entrepreneurship is characterized by absence of interstudy comparability. Possible explanations can be found in the emerging status of the research field and the ensuing less rigorous methods. We argue that the character of entrepreneurship in itself generates ambiguity. We replace the hitherto vain ambitions to create a consensus model of entrepreneurship with a perspective that focuses paradox - paradox defined as dual statements, which, taken one by one, are equally true but, if combined, are contradictory. A famous paradox with implicit dual interpretations (true/false) is the Liar who states: 'I always lie'.

Elaborating on five paradoxes of entrepreneurship - independence vs. dependence, process vs. personal attributes, revolution vs. evolution, vision vs. action, social vs. business orientation - we introduce four ways of approaching the paradoxes: live with them; change level of analysis; give sequential attention to the contradictory parts; and reframe the paradox. The lessons are illustrated with the help of the design of an ongoing research project into 'contextual entrepreneurship', where surveyed contexts for (semi)autonomous entrepreneurs include a local community, a science park and one or two corporations.

Vain search for harmony

Management researchers are often accused (by sociologists e.g.) of displaying a bias for consensus and evolutionary development in their interpretation of social phenomena. This bias is understandable in the light of the management thinking of the 60s and 70s which was founded on systems theories and normative planning of organizational change. Variations in conditions for different industries and individual businesses were dealt with by way of contingency models. In the 80s however, organization theorists and management thinkers have recognized the need for a completely different perspective in order to deal with the increasing environmental complexity and turbulence.

Tom Peters has been one of the most influential management writers in the 1980s. In the last of a triology of monographs on management for excellence he identifies 18 'paradoxes' that make up the foundation for new leadership. These all relate to need for flexibility and the combination of small- and large-scale advantages; here we quote - and comment - the six paradoxes which are most obviously related to entrepreneurship (Peters 1988:474-476):

* 'More stability of purpose/employment is necessary to deal with less stability in the environment' - the entrepreneur is guided by vision and recruits personnel that fits his/her own personality;
* 'Success will stem from more love of the product - and less attachment to it' - the entrepreneurial career is characterized by parallel, overlapping or subsequent ventures;
* 'Accelerating the success rate comes only from accelerating the failure rate' - the entrepreneur realizes that trial--and-error is the only way to bring about innovative change;
* 'We must be wary of the economies of scale - but create more complex alliances' - the entrepreneur uses resources episodically by way of his/her personal network;
* 'Tighter adherence to policy is accomplished when less time is spent in the office' - the entrepreneur personifies the business' basic values and makes them visible 'by walking around';
* 'Success will come to those who love chaos - constant change - not to those who attempt to eliminate it' - the entrepreneur scans the changing environment for opportunities and adds to change by implementing innovations.

Peters' definition of paradox follows Webster's New World Dictionary: 'A statement that seems contradictory, unbelievable or absurd but that may actually be true in fact.' The American Heritage Dictionary provides another phrasing in the following definition: 'An assertion that is essentially self-contradictory, although based on valid deduction from acceptable premises.' Quinn & Cameron (1989:2) identifies paradox as 'the simultaneous presence of contradictory, even mutually exclusive elements'.

While the Schumpetarian entrepreneur represents the revolutionary in the economy, Kirzner (1973) sees him/her as an organizer of resources who alertly exploits available opportunities. Most present-day researchers into entrepreneurship attempt to reconcile the entrepreneur's anarchic and disciplined actions. Writers such as Peter Drucker (1985) expand without hesitation the realm of management to include both innovation and entrepreneurship. In the 1980's book titles and articles on corporate entrepreneurship have welled up, generally arguing that individual initiative can be stimulated and tamed to the benefit of the organization, cf. e.g. Pinchot III (1985), Kanter (1983) and Burgelman (1983).

Still other contemporaries are intrigued by the existential and aesthetic dimensions of entrepreneurship and focus its creative and artistic dimensions. However, pretentious book titles such as 'The Art and Science of Entrepreneurship' (Sexton & Smilor 1986) leave the reader with no conclusive answer. Art is rather juxtaposed to practice. The editors 'more effectively (want to) link theory with practice and more completely appreciate the art and science of entrepreneurship.' (Op. cit. 1986:xvi). Drucker (1985:viii) states that 'Entrepreneurship is neither a science nor art. It is practice. It has a knowledge base....' But if this knowledge is tacit? What then? If one accepts that there always exists a tension between convergent scientific and divergent artistic reasoning (Schön 1983), then Drucker in the field of entrepreneurship appears to be a normative and wishful management thinker.

It seems to have become a ritual at conferences on small business and entrepreneurship to debate the definitions of the founding concepts, whith outsiders or newcomers to the field desperately trying to reconcile the different opinions. One argument is that the research field has not yet settled, that it is a matter of following through a maturing process, another that the research field is filled with opportunists who have an interest in an ambiguous concept whose content can be changed to serve their own interests.

A quite different interpretation of the 'state of the art' would be to recognize that the ongoing debate on definition and conceptualization reflects the inherently contradictory character of entrepreneurship as a phenomenon. In this paper we will argue for the recognition of the paradoxical character of entrepreneurship. Our purpose here is to contribute to a framework that proposes that the management of paradox in the marketplace is the entrepreneur's main task.

In the following section we introduce a set of paradoxes concerning entrepreneurship. Some strategies for dealing with paradox are presented in Section 3 and these are applied to the stated paradoxes of entrepreneurship. Section 4 introduces the theoretical and methodological lessons which can be learned through the application of these strategies to an ongoing project concerning appropriate contexts for entrepreneurship. In the final section areas for further research are indicated.

Paradoxes identified

We look here at 'paradox' as dual statements which, taken one by one, are equally true but, if combined, are contradictory. - Below five paradoxes associated with entrepreneurship are introduced and briefly commented below.

Entrepreneurs are both independent and dependent

Need for independence is considered to be an important determination of the initiation of the venturing process, whether it concerns iberation from a dominant father figure or an employer (Collins & More 1970). On the other hand, due to liability of newness and/or uniqueness, the would-be entrepreneur is dependent upon different kinds of support, including role models, e.g. a father who is also in business (cf. e.g. Shapero & Sokol 1982).

The ventures being launched take advantage of an opportunity and claim a niche in the market. However, territories occupied by entrepreneurs with limited owner-controlled resources can only be defended through the creation of strategic alliances with others, e.g. supplementary market suppliers. The enlarged resource base and legitimacy achieved thereby means increased dependencies but are also prerequisites for the realization for strategic ambitions.

Entrepreneurship reflects both an organizing process and a set of Personal attributes

A chronic debate within the literature on entrepreneurship concerns whether entrepreneurship is about creating new patterns of activities (Shapero & Sokol 1982, Gartner 1989) or is epitomized by individuals with specific personal qualities, cf. e.g. Hornaday (1982), Carland et al. (1988). Supporters of the former view argue that entrepreneurship can appear on any level in the organization, from the shop floor, cf. the notion of 'team entrepreneurship' (Stewart 1989) to the founder/leader. Within such a perspective entrepreneurship is obviously mainly the outcome of organizational design, cf. the discussion on corporate entrepreneurship above. This provides support for the belief that entrepreneurship can be taught and managed, that entrepreneurship is externally controlled.

Although the research on personal attributes of entrepreneurs does not always manage to discriminate between entrepreneurs and non- entrepreneurs, it continues to produce reports. It seems that while certain personal characteristics are not unique for entrepreneurs, they are significant for the initiation and carrying out of innovative ventures. The notion of the entrepreneur as egocentric is supported by findings that suggest that self-confidence is the most important attribute of the entrepreneur (Hornaday 1982). High internal locus of control implies that venturing is internalized by the entrepreneur. This view, supported by Schumpeter's (1934) emphasis on entrepreneurial will-power, suggests that it is difficult to teach entrepreneurship, cf. Gibb (1987).

Entrepreneurship implies both evolution and revolution

Along a Schumpeterian line Mintzberg (1973) introduces the entrepreneurial mode of strategy making as characterized by discontinuous and radical changes guided by a tunnel vision. Stevenson and Gumpert (1985) also argue that an entrepreneurial culture is characterized by revolutionary exploitation of opportunities in contrast to the administrative culture where changes in the environment are recognized successively.

As indicated above, Kirzner (1973) suggests instead that the entrepreneur successively creates new ways of organizing economic activity. Along the same vein others argue that entrepreneurs are experiential learners cf. e.g. Lessem (1984). This implies that ventures are realized step by step, balancing small winnings and mistakes, cf. Weick (1984).

Entrepreneurs are both prophets and (wo)men of action

Entrepreneurs are designers of new realities, whether in terms of creating a genuinely new image (such as the effect the introduction of fast food had on restaurant habits) or introducing a new concrete product or process, cf. Drucker (1985). In contrast to managers' rational-linear logic, entrepreneurs apply a intuitive-holistic approach to challenges. Swedish research suggests however that managers, surprised by radical environmental changes and the need for strategic flexibility, apply intuition more than rational-linear reasoning to identify and implement responses (Kylén 1989). The act of entrepreneurial creation has neither prototypes nor any methodology to copy. The entrepreneur's mission is highly internalized and implicit.

Bias for action makes entrepreneurs outward oriented and visible. The action orientation itself does not differentiate them for other managers, cf. Mintzberg (1973a). However, due to the successive creation of the venture, most actions mean exchanges with other external actors. The objective, the evolving innovation, and the restricted means to achieve the objective, limited own resources, suggest persistent and frequent actions: initiatives to convince others about the unique qualities of their product and the successive procurement of means for production.

Entrepreneurial action is driven both commercially and socially

It is not surprising that entrepreneurs are associated with the creation of wealth, both for themselves personally and for society. Even if the functions of the capitalist and the entrepreneur may be conceptually separated, in practice most entrepreneurs end up as owner-managers. This, if nothing else, reflects the kind of society they operate within. With price as the generic governing mechanism in the market it is natural to measure entrepreneurial action and success in pecuniary terms.

Although intrinsically motivated, entrepreneurs as high achievers also appreciate feedback on their capability in terms of increased wealth. To many immigrants for example, an entrepreneurial career is the only road available to recognition in their new community. In both cases the emerging entrepreneur will need social support from fellow countrymen, peers and like-minded. Furthermore, the marketplace is not the only arena for entrepreneurship; it may be applied to e.g. the political arena and the community sphere, cf. e.g. Casson (1982) and Johannisson (1990b).

This list of paradoxes could easily be extended. Elsewhere we e.g. argue that entrepreneurship means both small-scale operations and growth (Johannisson 1990) and that entrepreneurs are both anarchists and organizers (Johannisson 1987). It could also be argued that entrepreneurs are both professionally and emotionally driven, considered to be both marginal and in the limelight in contemporary society. Entrepreneurs can not solely be considered to be 'creative destructors' and introducers of uncertainty into the marketplace but must also, along with leaders, be seen to be managers of meaning and thereby as reducers of uncertainty, cf. e.g. Smircich & Morgan (1982), Bennis (1984) and Czarniawska-Joerges & Wolff (1989). However, we here restrict our discussion concerning different strategies for dealing with paradox to the five entrepreneurial paradoxes introduced above.

Dealing with paradox

The different strategies for approaching paradox span between attempts to re-inject consensus and the acceptance of contradiction as a point of departure - and return. Contingency theories and classificatory models represent defensive approaches to entrepreneurship that basically, at least to begin with, revoke the paradox's contradictory element. These approaches include different ways of classifying proprietors/entrepreneurs, usually by way of dichotomies, e.g. craftsman vs. opportunist (Smith 1967) and farmer vs. hunter (Gorb 1978). These, however, all imply 'either/or' approaches, not 'both/and', i.e. they escape the challenges of including both problems and opportunities embedded in the paradox concept. Contingency theories (e.g. suggesting that the character of entrepreneurship depends on context, cf. below, or industry) in our mind also appear as defensive approaches to an understanding of the entrepreneurial phenomenon. - Van de Ven and Poole (1988) suggest four generic strategies to deal with paradox and organizational change that to different degrees take this criticism into consideration:

I. Learn to live with paradox: it is an intellectual challenge to recognize and actively deal with the fact that the world may not be consistent and is only understood if at least two interpretations are simultaneously applied. It can be argued that entrepreneurs epitomize the management of situations which (thus far) have been considered to include contradictory or unrelated elements. Tension energizes the entrepreneur (Stevenson & Gumpert 1985) Cf. also the pivotal role of the entrepreneur as a broker and intermediary (Barth 1963).

II. Resolving paradox by shifting level of reference: the analysis of relationships between e.g. micro/macro and parts/wholes is a common strategy within the social sciences. With respect to entrepreneurship this can be illustrated by the fact that while risky operations imply that ventures and firms fail, a high turnover of individual entrepreneurial events is a pre-requisite for the development of a viable population of firms.

III. Resolving paradox over time: within a process perspective, different mechanisms may succeed each other as the sequence' unfreezing, moving and refreezing' e.g. is applied in organizational change. In the field of entrepreneurship this is illustrated by the process that is expected to make a new venture: stimulating creativity (idea generation), establishing a (tunnel) vision and implementing it through planning.

IV. Resolving paradox by introducing a new logic: a new conceptual framework may dissolve the taken-for-granted paradox and even become the a foundation for a new theory. Einstein found inspiration for his theory of relativity through observing that two falling objects when dropped simultaneously remain stable in relation to each other: they would be moving and at rest at the same time (Quinn & Cameron 1988:5).

Below, we approach each of the five paradoxes concerning entrepreneurship introduced above by way of the four generic strategies given in Van de Ven & Poole (1988).

The contradiction independence and dependence can be accepted since it reminds the strong-minded entrepreneur that (s)he always has to listen to the environment. (S)he has to be aware that the freedom of action originally created through the uniqueness of the venture is transient. - Even if individual ventures may appear to be generated ad hoc, also without any direct interconnections, they may accumulate into a linear entrepreneurial career (Driver 1988), where the social context defines the outcome. Thus, by changing level of analysis from that of the individual venture to that of his/her overall career, independence turns into dependence. The entrepreneur may within a transitory career pattern also balance individual ventures which, taken one by one, are not very creative. By oscillating between proactively- and reactively-initiated ventures, the entrepreneur can solve the independence/dependence paradox over time. Finally, by recognizing the personal network of the entrepreneur as his/her major resource, the whole paradox can be reframed. As stated in Johannisson & Peterson (1984), the personal network is voluntarily created by the entrepreneur but, once established, reciprocity of exchange will tie the entrepreneur to mutual commitments.

The contrasting views of entrepreneurship as an evolving new pattern of activities or a personal attribute can be accepted, arguing that a spontaneous flow of actions and incidents can be serendipitously organized into a venture only by an alert and strong-willed entrepreneur. If the level of analysis is changed, various initiatives taken by resolute individuals may generate a collective pattern of interrelated activities that is agreed upon. It can however also be argued that cycles of personal initiatives and making of an entrepreneurial process combine in sequences over time: an individual initiates action and the sedimented outcome will stimulate him and others to continue the process. Finally, following Bouwen & Steyaert (1990), it can be argued that individual action and collective structure combine into a web of warp och weft. Obviously the setting of the paradox then has been reframed and the contradictory elements reconciled.

The evolution/revolution paradox can simply be accepted and dealt with by encouraging awareness that minor changes initiated by chance may initiate revolutionary change, cf. chaos theory and the notion of 'lateral thinking' (de Bono 1967). By changing the level of analysis from organizational to industrial, radical, innovative, ventures will successfully sediment into a smooth change of the whole industry. Change within the individual firm can in turn be characterized by crisis management or management by exception. In that case steady-state periods and abrupt reorientations will alternate over time, cf. e.g. Greiner (1972). However, following e.g. Mintzberg & Waters (1981), strategy and changes thereof, whether incremental or radical, can basically only be stated retrospectively through interpretation of a stream of activities. What is evolution and revolution respectively then becomes less relevant. The new framework has resolved the paradox.

The contrasting concepts vision and action can simply be reconciled by stating that fantasy and imagination energize people and make them capable to act. Relating to learning theory, it can alternatively be argued that vision implies a review of choice criteria. Thus, going from action to vision implies a change in a level of analysis, from single-loop learning to double-loop learning, cf. Argyris & Schön (1978). The periodical statement and review of the business strategy, the overt side of the vision, suggest that patterns of activities - some logically, some intuitively, initiated -are rationalized periodically. If, however, reality is considered to be socially constructed, entrepreneurs appear as superb enactors and creators of meaning. Such a paradigmatic reframing makes vision and action complementary.

The business/social issue can be dealt with by arguing that we have to accept both social and autonomous entrepreneurship, cf. e.g. Johannisson & Nilsson (1989). The literature on industrial marketing suggests that personal exchanges between business friends, when considered on the interfirm level, appear as trust relationships which are instrumental in the conduct of business and even promote innovation, cf. e.g. Håkansson (1982, 1987). Our research into emerging entrepreneurial networks suggest that the social vs. business orientation of entrepreneurs changes over time. Initially entrepreneurs are dependent upon the social dimension of their personal networks in order to overcome marginality; during the growth stage networks are used to acquire additional operative resources. Stanworth & Curran (1973) propose that entrepreneurs' social orientation is activated again later in their careers and now aiming at communicating success. Changing choice criteria from decision rationality to 'action rationality' (Brunsson 1985) in business venturing means reframing. Social forces, such as motivation and commitment, are then recognized as conditions for the implementation of non-routine choices - the true character of entrepreneurship. - In Table 1 above we summarize the arguments.

Researching paradox - The case of contextual entrepreneurship

In Subsection 4.1. we present current research into entrepreneurship and supportive 'organizing contexts' while we in Subsection 4.2. report on the methodological implications of applying a framework based on paradox.

Organizing contexts for entrepreneurship

Considering that the entrepreneur's generic function is to organize resources, including people, into new ventures, the individual/collective dichotomy is crucial in entrepreneurship research focusing contradiction. In an ongoing research project our endeavour is to contrast an egocentric perspective of entrepreneurial activity with a collective, an organizational, approach to change and renewal. On the one hand the foundation of entrepreneurial initiative in individual action must considered; on the other the need for a collective view, encompassing non-entrepreneur members of collectives as well, has to be recognized. Such an 'entrepreneurial' collective may e.g. be an innovative corporation, a local community with a favourable business climate or a dynamic science park. If we are successful the paradoxes of entrepreneurship introduced above can then be jointly dealt with.

Our concern for the immediate surroundings of (young) entrepreneur's is based on previous research that indicates that they, by way of personal networking, to a considerable extent are locally oriented (cf. e.g. Johannisson 1983, 1990a). Others have, using concepts such as 'texture' (Lorenzani & Ornati 1988) and 'milieu' (Lecoq 1990), pointed out that co-location of entrepreneurs will promote further venture development within a collective structure. Elsewhere we have defined such a supportive structure as an 'organizing context' that

'... provides ends and means for the enactment, selection and retention subprocesses. It may operate as a springboard (supporting ecological change/enactment), a gearbox (supporting selection), and as a shock-absorber or defence wall (supporting retention) between the entrepreneur and environments beyond the context.' (Johannisson, 1988:88)

Entrepreneurial contexts are not the only structures that provide entrepreneurs with support, cf. e.g. franchising or qualified subcontracting systems (Peterson 1981). However, here our concern focuses on contexts where exchange is basically non-hierarchical. We believe that physical and social proximity is needed in order to create the needed dialogue between the leaders of the context and the leaders of individual ventures. This calls for a kind of meta-entrepreneurship. More precisely we define 'contextual entrepreneurship' as the dualistic organizing processes initiated by individuals and the context that jointly defines the terms for - individual and collective - innovation and renewal.

Thus, in order to study contextual entrepreneurship as defined, the context itself must be scrutinized, using entrepreneurial concepts. Just as individual ventures are deliberately launched and managed, contexts may, albeit within limits, be planned and managed. Promotion of corporate entrepreneurship within formal structures can either be initiated top-down as an innovative strategy, cf. e.g. Miller (1983), Burgelman (1983), or created from below by providing potential entrepreneurial units with a formal support structure, cf. e.g. Jonnergård et al. (1981), Johannisson (1988). Contexts encompassing ventures that are independent in terms of ownership may be either spontaneous (e.g. the local community favourable to entrepreneurship) or induced (e.g. the science park or the development corporation).

Table 1
Paradoxes of entrepreneurship and their resolution

APPROACHES

PARADOX	Accept it	Change level of analysis	Solve it over time	Reframe it
Independence/ Dependence	Initiative and listening	Venture vs. career management	Oscillating in venture and career	Voluntary reciprocal networks
Organizing/ Personal attribute	Process enforced by alert individuals	Organizing individual action	Actions as antecedent and outcomes of action	Action embedded in social webs
Evolution/ Revolution	Recognition of serendipitous change	Venture vs. firm vs. industry level	Management by exception	Retrospective framing of minor changes
Vision/ Action	Fantasy empowering people	Double-loop learning	Periodic rationalization of action	Social construction of reality
Business/ Social orientation	Different kinds of entrepreneurship	Trust as instrumental in network ties	Initial social support	Action rationality

When studying contexts as arenas for individual action in general and entrepreneurial initiatives in particular, alternative approaches are employed. The local community as a business context can be modelled after an organization (Gustafsson & Johannisson 1984) and vice versa the organization after a community (Butler 1983). Ouchi (1980), referring to transaction-cost theory, suggests different governing metaphors: the bureaucracy, the market and the clan. Various contingencies, such as goal congruence, will define which metaphor applies. Johannisson (1988) argues that the three governing principles should be applied simultaneously in order to generate the variability needed for successful contextual entrepreneurship. However, all of these approaches, applied one by one or in combination, presuppose consensus and are thus opposed to the view based on paradox promoted here. Consequently these models do not suffice in the search for the basic mechanisms of contextual entrepreneurship. They do however remain useful inasmuch as they provide fundamental descriptions which are needed in an analysis based on paradox.

There is an abundance of models of contextual entrepreneurship that are ensnared by the illusion that entrepreneurship can be organized. Such a 'management approach' is implicit in contributions by e.g. Miller (1983), Kanter (1983) and Burgelman (1983) in their inquiry into corporate entrepreneurship. It seems obvious that we can have little faith in managerial approaches to entrepreneurship if management is associated with formal structuring to achieve stated goals. If, on the other hand, management is associated with 'organizing', some propositions can be made. Varying conditions for business venturing in the local community, the science park and the (innovative) corporation are reflected in the different ways the entrepreneurial context is managed.

We propose that contextual management in the local community primarily appears as spontaneous. Such an organic mode uses the social networks sprung out of a common culture. The science park, in Sweden usually established by public and private parties jointly, needs a management that recognizes its pluralistic structure and thus adopts an adaptive mode. The corporation, characterized by monolithic management, can manage innovation according to a planning mode. Within each mode, variations appear suggesting e.g. that corporations in dynamic environments allow for a highly decentralized and spontaneous development. Strong leadership in a science park would allow for a planning mode. A local community may supplement spontaneous processes with collective projects, e.g. the creation of educational programs and technology centres.

In order to match the proposed conceptual outline as well as demonstrate the basic features of organizing contexts as intermediary structures in the entrepreneurial process, a broad empirical base must be provided. Our need for both holistic and detailed reports implies that only a limited number of case studies are appropriate. With our research agenda, it is natural to select contexts which are in basic respects contrasting. In the innovative corporation, contextual leadership and management is formalized while venture responsibility is sometimes ascribed, sometimes self-chosen. In the local community with a favourable entrepreneurial spirit it is the other way around: the local culture guides tacitly, formal co-operation is minimal while entrepreneurship is incorporated into owner-managed firms. In most science parks, management is formalized but marginal while entrepreneurship, as in the local community, achieved and institutionalized.

Methodological implications

Our conceptual framework focuses the interface between the organizing context and entrepreneurial activity. This, to begin with, calls for definition of entrepreneurial activity, through, as has been stated above, both psychological measures and identification of concrete entrepreneurial records. Secondly, entrepreneurship on both the contextual and the venture level must be recognized. Our focus, though, is the venture per se, whether in the form of incorporated businesses (the science park and the local community) or projects (the corporations). A major challenge will thus be to separate entrepreneurship from other (small-scale) activity, i.e. to define and apply indicators that are independent of the venture structure (project, incorporated firms).

The ventures/individual entrepreneurs studied within each context will be chosen according to different criteria. These include, among others, contextual data on entrepreneurial networks that are analyzed by way of multivariate analytical models aiming at, e.g., identification of central and peripheral actors. Egocentric entrepreneurial networks, encompassing the context as well as the wider environment, can be successively mapped. Cf. Hull & Hjern (1987) for a report on such a methodology.

The local community being studied is Anderstorp, with approximately 5,200 inhabitants and almost 150 manufacturing firms. Our earlier research there shows that the community provides a very favourable context for small- and medium-sized firms, proven e.g. by dense business networks.

The science park being studied is IDEON on the Lund University campus in Southern Sweden. The park has about one hundred tenants, including four subsidiaries of major Swedish public companies.

The corporation being researched because of presumed internal entrepreneurship is TELUB Service, a former division within a state-owned high-tech enterprise operating on both public (military) and private markets. It has over the years generated many spin-offs and the TELUB Service division was recently bought out by the management. Several lines of business within TELUB Service are organized as operative adhocracies, but like IDEON it also contains professional bureaucratic structures.

In an earlier research strategy, dialectics was scrutinized as a means of approaching paradox (Johannisson & Senneseth 1990). Contributions include e.g. Benson (1977), Jonnergård et al. (1981) and Ford & Backoff (1988). However, further inquiries into dialectics and its philosophical foundations revealed considerable ambiguity. We refrained therefore from applying (any version of) it explicitly. What basically remains from that effort is Mason's (1969) practical rationale for designing a 'dialectic' inquiry. Applied to our research problem, that methodology means, first, that a joint data-base is established from descriptions of each one of the three contexts. Secondly, the three members of the research team will be assigned to different tasks. One is expected to one-sidedly interpret the joint database given the assumption that individual action explains the course of entrepreneurial events. A second team member will equally dogmatically adopt the perspective that the entrepreneurial sequence of activities is due to features that can be ascribed the context as a collective only. These two team members will thus each provide 'primary' interpretations of the origin and character of entrepreneurial venturing. The third, and more senior member of the team will compare the two 'biased maps' being provided for each case. His task is to identify a conclusive 'secondary' interpretation that hopefully will go beyond each separate case as it is being mapped in either primary analysis.

In Table 2 we try to summarize our approach. At the point of departure are the two primary descriptions. One reflects the collective, organizational view of change, the other the individual, entrepreneurial perspective. Each one of these descriptions are pursued by way of a 'paradoxical' approach as presented above in Section 3. The five paradoxes introduced there and possibly supplemented will guide the making of the 'entrepreneurial perspective'. The ingredients for a corresponding 'organizational perspective' will mainly be retrieved from Van de Ven and Poole's (1988) seminal work. The outcome of the primary analysis is expected to provide a set of strategies for dealing with paradox. Table 1 presents, in the case of the 'entrepreneurial perspective', hypothetical ingredients in such strategies. It is up to the empirical research to verify or dispute them. Analogously, approaches for dealing with paradox suggested by Van de Ven and Poole (1988), possibly supplemented, will be empirically tested concerning their 'organizational perspective'.

The 'secondary' analysis aims at reconciling individual and collective ways of dealing with change and renewal. The appropriate set of concepts and models needed will be generated inductively within the project. However we assume that only part of the tensions studied in the primary analysis will be resolved. Along with Normann (1977) we argue that tensions within the organization and between the organization and the environment are not always dysfunctional. They energize the organizations and initiate learning processes, cf. also Stevenson & Gumpert (1985).

Concluding remarks

Limiting research resources and limited access indicate that some issues will have to be selected for further studies. That is, besides a general description of entrepreneurial activity and publicly stated policies by way of documents, only partial analysis can be made. Such issues may include:
- contrasting successful and failed ventures with respect to how they interact with the context;
- tracking the history/strategy of the context (e.g. by way of critical incidents) and studying implications of strategy changes for individual ventures;
- studying how exchange between the ventures/entrepreneurs and the context varies over the venture cycle/entrepreneurial career;
- studying the context as an intermediary structure in longdistance operations which are beyond the reach of the entrepreneur's personal enactment.

Nevertheless, the research agenda outlined here is rather pretentious and its confrontation with data is obviously needed. The outcome may very well be that only some of the paradoxes of entrepreneurship can be dealt with through the introduction of the notion of 'context'. However, as several of the contributors to Quinn & Cameron (1988) state, the very idea of contrasting perspectives, as paradox invites to, is fundamental to any social research that strives for insight. Whether the paradox is cemented or resolved the road to such a finding per se will add to the further understanding of entrepreneurship.

Contradictory 'facts' concerning entrepreneurship are abundant. At 1990 Rencontre St Gall, data on Belgian entrepreneurs were presented that are in conflict with what is considered to be a must for small businessmen: sticking to the knitting. Almost half of the entrepreneurs argued however not only that they would depart from business plans once made but also from areas where they had a unique competence. Learning from paradoxical methodology, this seemingly self-suicidal strategy reflects the entrepreneurs' ability to not only create ventures based on opportunities but also to build an absorption capacity (Collin & Levinthal 1990) or 'strategic flexibility'(Kylén 1989) that is always needed. However privileged the current position in the market may appear to be, business venturing is always associated with risk-taking. We may hypothesize that a generic instrument

Figure 1
Contextual entrepreneurship - modelling out of paradox

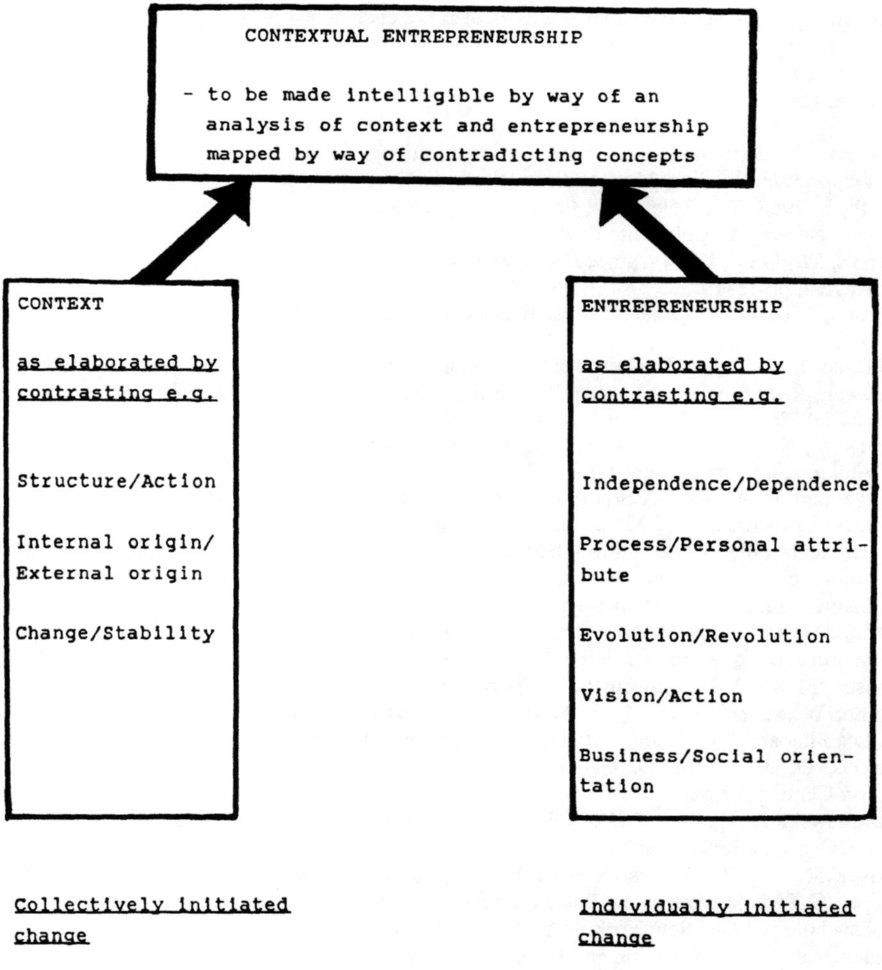

CONTEXTUAL ENTREPRENEURSHIP

- to be made intelligible by way of an
  analysis of context and entrepreneurship
  mapped by way of contradicting concepts

CONTEXT

as elaborated by
contrasting e.g.

Structure/Action

Internal origin/
External origin

Change/Stability

ENTREPRENEURSHIP

as elaborated by
contrasting e.g.

Independence/Dependence

Process/Personal attri-
bute

Evolution/Revolution

Vision/Action

Business/Social orien-
tation

Collectively initiated
change

Individually initiated
change

15

for creating needed strategic flexibility in entrepreneurial firms is preparedness to accept paradox.

We have here refrained from discussing the mechanism for and consequences of transition from one extremity of the paradox to the other. These transitions are certainly most intriguing, just as the dawn and twilight zones enchant everyday life.

References

Argyris, C. & Schön, D.A. 1978 Organizational Learning: A Theory of Action Perspective. Reading, Ma.: Addison Wesley.

Barth, F. 1963 The Role of the Entrepreneur in Social Change in Northern Norway. Bergen: Norwegian University Press.

Bennis, W. 1984 'The 4 Competencies of Leadership'. Training and Development Journal. August, pp 15-19.

Benson, J. K. 1977 'Organizations: A Dialectic View.' Adminstrative Science Quarterly, Vol 22, pp 1-21.

de Bono, E. 1967 The Use of Lateral Thinking. London: Jonathan Cape.

Bouwen, R. & Steyaert, C. 1990 'Construing Organizational Texture in Young Entrepreneurial Firms.' Forthcoming in Journal of Management Studies.

Brunsson, N. 1985 The Irrational Organization. Irrationality as a Basis for Organizational Action and Change. New York, N.Y.:Wiley.

Burgelman, R. A. 1983 'Corporate Entrepreneurship and Strategic Management: Insights from a Process Study.' Management Science, Vol 29, pp 1349-1364.

Butler, R. J. 1983 'Control through Markets, Hierarchies and Communes: A Transactional Approach to Organisatinal Analysis.' In Francis, A. et al. (Eds.) Power, Efficiency and Institutions. London: Heineman.

Carland, J. W. & Hoy, F. & Carland J. A. C. 1988 'Who is an Entrepreneur?' Is a Question Worth Asking.' American Journal of Small Business, Spring, pp 33-39.

Casson, M. 1982 The Entrepreneur. Oxford: Robertson.

Collin, W. M. & Levinthal, D. A. 1990 'Absorptive Capacity: A New Perspective on Learning and Innovation.' Administrative Science Quarterly, Vol 35, pp 128-152.

Collins, O. & Moore, D. G. 1970 The Organization Makers. New York: Appleton-Century-Crofts.

Czarniawska-Joerges, B. & Wolff, R. 1989 Leaders, Managers, Entrepreneurs on and off the Organizational Stage. Research Paper 6389. Stockholm: EFI, HHS.

Driver, M. J. 1988 'Careers: A Review of Personal and Organizational Research.' In Cooper, C. I. & Robertson, I. (Eds.) International Review of Industrial and Organizational Psychology 1988. New York, N.Y.: Wiley. Pp 245-277.

Drucker, P. 1985 Innovation and Entrepreneurship. New York: Harper & Row.

Ford, J. D. & Backoff, R. H. 1988 'Organizational Change in and out of Dualities and Paradox.' In Quinn, R. E. & Cameron, K. S. (Eds.) Paradox and Transformation. Toward a Theory of Change in Organization and Management. Cambridge, Mass.: Ballinger. Pp 81-121.

Gartner, W. B. 1989 'Who is an Entrepreneur?' Is the Wrong Question.' Entrepreneurship Theory and Practice. Summer, pp 47-68.

Gibb, A. A. 1987 'Enterprise Culture - Its Meaning and Implications for Education and Training.' Journal of European Industrial Training.' Vol 11, No 1, pp 1-38.

Gorb, P. 1978 'The Management Development Needs of Small Business: Farmers and Hunters.' Management Education and Development, Part 2, August.

Greiner, L. 1972 'Evolution and Revolution as Organizations Grow.' Harvard Business Review, July-August, pp 37-46.

Gustafsson, B. Å. & Johannisson, B. 1984 'Local Business Cultures A Network Perspective.' Paper presented at the First International Conference on Organizatonal Symbolism and Corporate Culture. University of Lund, Sweden, June 36-30, 1984.

Hornaday, J. A. 1982 'Research about Living Entrepreneurs'. Kent, A. A. & Sexton, D. L. & Vesper, K. H. (red) Encyclopedia of Entrepreneurship. Englewood Cliffs, N.J.: Prentice Hall.Pp 29-38.

Hull, C. & Hjern, B. 1987 Helping Small Firms Grow. An Implementation Approach. London: Croom Helm.

Håkansson, H. (Ed.) 1982 International Marketing and Purchasing of Industrial Goods. An Interaction Approach. Chichester: Wiley.

Håkansson, H. (Ed.) 1987 Industrial Technological Development - A Network Approach. London: Croom Helm.

Johannisson, B. 1983 'Swedish Evidence for the Potential of Local Entrepreneurship.' European Small Business Journal, Vol 1,2, pp 11-24.

Johannisson, B. 1987 'Anarchists and Organizers - Entrepreneurs in a Network Perspective'. International Studies of Management and Organization, Vol. XVII, No. 1, pp 49-63.

Johannisson, B. 1988 'Business Formation - A Network Approach.' Scandinavian Journal of Management. Vol 4, No 3/4, pp 83-99.

Johannisson, B. 1990 'To Grow and Not To Grow - On the External Growth of Small Firms.' Forthcoming in the International Small Business Journal.

Johannisson, B. 1990a 'Building an Entrepreneurial Career in a Mixed Economy: Need for Social and Business Ties in Personal Networks. Paper presented at the Academy of Managment Annual Meeting, San Francisco, USA. August 12-15, 1990.

Johannisson, B. 1990b 'Enterprising in Different Organizational and Societal Contexts. Forthcoming in Internationales Gewerbearchiv.

Johannisson, B. & Nilsson, A. 1989 'Community Entrepreneurship Networking for Local Development.' Journal of Entrepreneurship and Regional Development, Vol 1, No 1, pp 1-19.

Johannisson, B. & Peterson, R. 1984 'The Personal Networks of Entrepreneurs'. Conference Proceedings, ICSB - Canada. Toronto Ryerson Polytechnical Institute.

Johannisson, B. & Senneseth, K. 1990 'Entrepreneurs in Context - A Generic Approach to Venture Management.' Paper presented at the 6th Nordic Research Workshop on Small Business. Copenhagen, Denmark, June 14-16 1990.

Jonnergård, K. & Lagnevik, C.-M., Svensson, C. & Wijk, G. F. 1981 Beslut i kooperation. Ansatser till en federativ, dialektisk organisationsteori (Decision in Cooperation. Towards a Federative, Dialectic Organization Theory). Lund: Studentlitteratur.

Kanter, R. Moss 1983 The Change Masters. New York, N.Y.: Simon and Schuster.

Kirzner, I. M. 1978 (1973) Competition and Entrepreneurship. Chicago, Ill.: The University of Chicago Press.

Kylén, B. 1989 Hur företagschefer beslutar innan de blir överraskade (How CEOs Decide Before Being Surprised). Dissertation (English summary). Stockholm: Stockholm School of Economics.

Lecoq, B. 1990 'Industrial Organization, Technological Change and Regional Development: A Network Approach'. Paper presented at the 30th European Congress of the Regional Science Association. Istanbul. Turkey, September 28-31 1990.

Lessem, R. 1984 'The Gestalt of Action Learning.' In Cox, C. & Beck, J (Eds.) Management Development: Advances in Practice and Theory. New York, N.Y.: Wiley. Pp 223-250.

Lorenzoni, G. & Ornati, O. A. 1988 'Constellations of Firms and New Ventures.' Journal of Business Venturing. Vol 3, No 1, pp 41-57.

Mason, R. O. 1969 'A Dialectic Approach to Strategic Planning.' Management Science, Vol 15, No. 8, pp B 403-411.

Mintzberg, H. 1973 'Strategy-Making in Three Modes.' California Management Review, Vol XVI, No. 2, pp 41-53.

Mintzberg, H. 1973a The Nature of Managerial Work, New York, N.Y.: Harper and Row.

Mintzberg, H. & Waters, J. A. 1981 'Tracking Strategy in an Entrepreneurial Firm. Academy of Management Journal, Vol 25, No 3, pp 465-499.

Miller, D. 1983 'The Correlates of Entrepreneurship in Three Types of Firms.' Management Science, Vol 29, pp 770-791.

Normann, R. 1977 Management for Growth. Chichester: Wiley.

Ouchi, W. G. 1980 'Markets, Bureaucracies and Clans.' Administra tive Science Quarterly. Vol 25, pp 129-141.

Peters, T. 1988 Thriving on Chaos. New York, N.Y.: Harper & Row.

Peterson, R. A. 1981 'Entrepreneurship and Organization.' In Nystrom, P.C. & Starbuck, W.H. (Eds.) Handbook of Organizational Design. Vol. 1. Oxford: Oxford University Press. Pp 65-83.

Pinchot III, G. 1985 Intrapreneuring. New York, N.Y.: Harper & Row.

Quinn, R.E. & Cameron, K.S. 1988 'Organizational Paradox and Transformation.' In Quinn, R.E. & Cameron, K.S. (Eds.) Paradox and Transformation. Toward a Theory of Change in Organization and Management. Cambridge, Mass.: Ballinger. Pp 1-18.

Schön, D. 1983 The Reflective Practitioner. How Professionals Think in Action. New York. N.Y.: Basic Books.

Schumpeter, J.A. 1934 Theory of Economic Development. Cambridge, Mass.: Harvard University.

Sexton, D.L. & Smilor, R W (Eds.) 1986 The Art and Science of Entrepreneurship. Cambridge, Mass.: Ballinger.

Shapero, A. & Sokol, L. 1982 'The Social Dimension of Entrepreneurship'. In Kent, C.A. & Sexton, D. L. & Vesper, K.H. (Eds.) Encyclopedia of Entrepreneurship. Englewood Cliffs, N.J.: Prentice-Hall. Pp 72-90.

Smircich, L. & Morgan, G. 1982 'Leadership: The Management of Meaning'. Journal of Applied Behavioural Science. Vol 18, No 3, pp 257-273.

Smith, N. R. 1967 The Entrepreneur and his Firm: The Relationship between Type of Man and Type of Company. East Lansing: Michigan State University.

Stanworth, M. & Curran, J. 1973 Management Motivation in the Small Business. London: Gower Press.

Stevenson, H.H. & Gumpert, D.E. 1985 'The Heart of Entrepreneurship'. Harvard Business Review, March-April, pp 85-94.

Stewart, A. 1989 Team Entrepreneurship. London: Sage.

Tucker, D.J. & Singh, J.V. & Meinhard, A.G. 1990 'Organizational Form Population Dynamics, and Institutional Change: The Founding Patterns of Voluntary Organizations.' Academy of Management Journal, Vol. 33, No 1, pp 171-178.

Van de Ven, A.H. & Poole, M.S. 1988 'Paradoxical Requirements for a Theory of Change.' In Quinn, R.E. & Cameron, K.S. (Eds.) Paradox and Transformation. Toward a Theory of Change in Organization and Management. Cambridge, Mass.: Ballinger. Pp 19-63.

Weick, K.E. 1984 'Small Wins. Redefining the Scale of Social Problems.' American Psychologist, January, pp 40-49.

2 In search of entrepreneur: Business environment contingencies

Asko Miettinen and Nina Hedberg

Background

Contingency theory is a code of many colors. Having originally begun with sosio-technological theory, which combined the technological emphasis of earlier classical organization theory with later human relation school's attention to people in a system-based all-inclusive approach to organization of work, it now covers a wide variety of issues on fitting design to situation. Contingency actually means that one thing depends on another thing, or that one characteristic depends upon another characteristic.

In organizational analysis open system theory and information processing recognize environmental input, but the contingency approach goes one step further and relates this environment to specific organization structures. After the pioneering research conducted at England's Tavistock some further major contributions in the field were done by Burns and Stalker (1961) and Joan Woodward (1969), followed by the refining efforts of Thompson (1967), Lawrence and Lorsch (1967), and the Ashton group (1969) and Charles Perrow (1970). The work of Woodward and Lawrence and Lorsch is often still considered to be the most significant of contingency organization research.

More recent organization theorist like Galbraight (1977), Pfeffer (1982) and Minzberg (1983) build on the pioneering work of the earlier scholars. They continue conclusions drawn from the large cross sectional comparative studies. Galbraight stresses that there is no best way to organize, but not all the ways to organize are equally effective. The contingency theory actually suggests that one can observe a wide range of differences but these differences are not random. To specify under what conditions what type of organization is preferred the nature of the organization's task should be taken into account. Different tasks require different types of behaviour for effective performance. Furthermore, organizations, due to their artificial nature, cannot rely on employees' voluntary adoption of goal-related behaviours, but must undertake the design and administration of a reward system. Presumably the most effective reward system depends on the behaviours required the task (Galbraight, 1977, 291).

Jeffrey Pfeffer relates contingency management to the behaviour-consequence connections to understand organizational behaviour (Pfeffer, 1982, 86-87). This particular linkage has become an important target of attention for managers. In general terms the focus on the external determinants of behaviour represent an example of external constraint on behaviour perspective. The very phrase, contingency management, has become a part of the language encapsulating the idea that contingent reinforcement of behaviour is the key technology for managing and changing the behaviour.

Minzberg (1983, 121-156) concludes as well that most of the contemporary research on organizational structuring has uncovered a set of what are called situational or contingency factors, organizational states or conditions that are associated with the use of certain parameters. He mentions these factors in four groups: the age and size of the organization, the technical system it uses in its operating core; various aspects of its environment, notably stability, complexity, diversity and hostility; and certain of its power relationship.

As the environment becomes more complex, an organization must adjust both internal structure and process to maintain effectiveness. Environmental uncertainty (lack of specification) inevitably has a major impact upon the core of technological specification. This impact is buffered by various structural and administrative devices. Especially under conditions of great uncertainty or great technological specification, one may expect elaboration of structure and devices to protect the technology. An elaborated contingency hypothesis like this needs further investigation in variety of technological settings joining multiple environments and multiple technologies.

Alongside this kind of elaborated structural parameter combinations, some other contingency approach applications should not be forgotten. Fiedler's Contingency Theory of Leadership goes back behavioural scientists' notion about the importance of situational factors explaining leader effectiveness. The contingency model of leadership effectiveness grew originally out of comprehensive programme by Fred E. Fiedler (1967) indicating very clearly that effective leadership depends on the leader, his followers, the situation and the situation between them. Much recent research has concerned moderator (contingency) variables. This research has focused on identifying and specifying moderator variables. Most popular leadership paradigms include at least one moderator, usually several of them. Examples include task structure, quality of leader-member relations, leader's position power (Fiedler, 1967, 1978); role clarity, formal organizational rules and procedures, the nature of primary work groups (House & Michell, 1974; Evans, 1979; Jago & Vroom, 1980); subordinates' job maturity and psychological maturity or readiness (Hersey & Blanchard, 1988); and the availability of support service and the quality of the organization of the work unit (Yukl, 1981).

Another application of contingency approach can be found in person-environment (P-E) congruence or fit. The idea of P-E fit has been around a long time in psychological literature and provokes a great deal of research in the field of organizational and occupational psychology as well (Cooper, 1983; Furnham & Shaffer, 1984). Considerable evidence has been found suggesting that career change, labour turnover, performance and motivation are associated with. The P-E fit perspective also forces to pay more attention to the process of coping with various types of P-E 'misfits'. Job satisfaction measures might be too static and, in fact, tend to disguise and distort the whole process of man's adaption to, and his coping with, the discrepancy between needs and satisfaction of those needs by the work environment.

Van Harrison (1978) has suggested that there are two kinds of P-E fit: the extent to which an individual's skills and abilities match the requirements of the job he or she is doing, and also the extent to which the job environment provides the resources to meet the needs of the individual. The coping strategies that may be employed by an individual to reduce his/her job stress include changes in the objective person or environment in order to improve the fit between the two. The individual may also use defence mechanisms to distort the individual's perception of P-E fit, or to deny the experience of job stress altogether. Use of these coping procedures may reduce strain and overcome the problems involved, but if the measures are unsuccessful, the stress effects which are additive, may lead to long term problems such as low self-esteem and job dissatisfaction, and even poor health.

Several examples showing the adverse effects of P-E misfit on health and well-being have been reported which highlight the importance of the individual's personality being congruent with his work environment. This need for congruence between a person's interests and abilities, and the factors inherent in his environment forms the basis for a theory of vocational choice. In addition to the core idea of P-E fit some secondary concepts can be used to determine more efficiently the goodness of fit between P and E. Firstly according to Holland (1973), within a person or environment some pairs or types are more closely related than others, and that relationship within (which yields a measure of consistency) and between (which yields a measure of congruence) personality types of environments can be ordered according to a model, in which the distances within and between the personality profiles and job codes are inversely proportional to the theoretical relationship between them. These degrees of relatedness are assumed to affect job satisfaction and general well-being.

A second concept is differentiation, which means that some people and environments are more clearly defined than others; for example, a person or environment may be dominated by a single type (well differentiated), or may resemble many types equally well (undifferentiated). The better the environment or person is differentiated the more likely the person is to find congruent job, and the more likely he will be to have high job satisfaction and well-being as a result.

Building on the concepts by Holland, Furnham and Schaeffer (1984) suggest that the third and maybe most important measure is congruence or compatibility referring to a personality and job type which are very similar. They argue that it is strictly speaking only congruence and not consistency of differentiation that measures person environment fit. Consistency is characteristic of either a person's profile or of an environment, but says nothing about the relationship between the two.

Contingency theory is recently related to key success factors, which are important concepts in the strategy area (Vasconcellos, 1988). Several authors have suggested the propositions that different contexts possess different key success factors; and that the more similar two contexts are, the more similar their key success factors will be. More generally the theory states that in order to outperform competition, an enterprise should look for a context in which the prerequisites for success match its strengths (Aaker, 1984; Ansoff 1984).

Strengths are those attributes in which an enterprise is superior to its competition. Key success factors are those tasks or variables which must be performed particularly well for a firm to outperform its competition. The importance for organizational performance that organizations possess strengths which match the key success factors, does not by itself imply that key success factors will differ from context to context. Hypothetically, the same set of attributes could be critical for performance in all types of contexts, as

Vasconcellos (1988) states. In such case one would have an universal theory of key success factors.

Such a universal theory of key success factors is not, however, suggested by literature. Indeed strategy literature suggests a contingency theory for success factors. It suggests once again that what is critical for performance in one context differs from what is critical for performance in another context (Yavitz & Newman 1982, Aaker 1984, Porter 1987).

Purpose of the study

The aim of this study was to analyze business environment - entrepreneur relationship to find out if there were contingencies or fit between them. Business performance was also addressed to focus on more explanatory issues.

The implications of contingency approach was further discussed based on the findings of this investigation.

Methods

Subjects

151 petrol station dealers were tested. Subjects were of both sexes and ranged from 23 years to 58 years. In all there were 130 males and 21 females. They came from two different companies (or marketing chains) having slightly different strategies and different visual image.

Some notes about petrol dealer branch in finland

In early 1990 there were 1937 petrol stations in Finland in six chains. The number of entrepreneurial/owner based stations were 1700. The total sales of the last Fiscal year were a bit more than one billion US dollars. The major cash flow came from petrol and diesel oil covering about 3/4 of the sales and a half of the contribution in average. Spare parts, lubrications and other items account about 10% of the sales and some 20% of the contribution. Cafeteria and kiosk activities brought about 5% of the sales and 7-8% of the contribution.

The dealer branch is at very mature stage with 'price wars' occurring every now and then. The branch is very labour intensive. Labour costs is very critical issue in this particular business. There are too many stations in the field at the moment. Decreases in term of the number of the stations are expected in the near future.

The growth of this branch has been low equalling roughly to annual inflation rate of 5-6% during the last few years. The entrepreneurs/dealers of the two companies studied (Alfa & Beta) have grown faster than the branch average indicating aggressive marketing and reasonable entrepreneurial skills. The market share of the Beta dealers grew from 15,3% to 16,8% in 1988-1990, demonstrating a growth rate of 12-13% last year. Kesoil gained less in terms of the market share growth, but has been on the winners' side as well with the growth of some 7.8% during last fiscal year. In terms of economic results have been good at the company level in both cases. The fiscal year 1989 was very good one with lower expectations for the year 1990.

Questionnaires

The Career Orientation Inventory (COI) The Career Orientation Inventory was developed by Edgar H. Schein. It is based on his theory about career anchors, by which he means a set of self-perceptions pertaining to one's (1) motives and needs, (2) talents and skills, (3) personal values, which one would not give up if one is forced to make a choose. The nine career anchors: Technical/Functional Competence, Managerial Competence, Autonomy, Organizational Security, Geographical Security, Service/Dedication, Pure Challenge, Style of Life and Entrepreneurship are described in the Appendix 1.

The Achieving Style Inventory (ASI) Achieving Styles are the preferred strategies, or characteristic styles, individuals use to accomplish tasks. They are implementation strategies or personal technologies for achieving goals. They describe how individuals accomplish their goals, regardless of the specific nature of those goals. The Achieving Styles Inventory of Leavitt and Lipman-Blumen identifies three major orientation toward achievement: Direct, Instrumental and Relational orientations.

The current Achievement Styles model (ASI, Form 13) has been refined from the first model 1973. The reliability of the model by Cronbach's Alpha Model is from 0.61 to 0.91. The model and the scales are described in Appendix 2.

Self-Concept Inventory (SCI) The purpose of this instrument is to measure one's conscious view about himself/herself. Self-concept is a sort of miniature model of the relationships between oneself and one's environment, including personal coping expectations, action codes and personal identifications. Self-concept changes over time.

Used Self-Concept Inventory is developed by Häyrynen (1970). It consists of 11 Osgood's semantic differential type of contrasting attributes. The respondent places himself or herself between the attributes. (Appendix 3)

Procedure

The three standardized tests were administrated as a part of a management development programme specially designed for the Alfa and Beta dealers respectively. The participating dealers filled the questionnaires in a group situation after the first day classes of the programme. The instruction was given by one of the authors. Personal feedback was employed the next morning. The test profiles were studied together with the instructor.

There were 15 participants in average in each programme. The data was gathered in 1988-1990. A small amount of regional managers from both companies attended the programme as well. The same tests were administrated in their case. This particular sample totals about 20 regional managers so far representing an essential group of people serving in multiply roles from the point of view of the dealers. The manager-dealer relationships may constitute a major situational/contingency factor to be further analyzed as a moderator variable.

Expert Panel

Two expert panels were constituted, one for each company. The members of the panels were regional managers with sales directors responsible for organizing the activity. The members of the panels were asked to rate the type of the petrol station, from 'City Station' to 'Travellers' Station' and to 'Country-side Station' respectively.

Without any considerable problems the panels could classify the petrol stations into three categories as follows:

Table 1
The station types according to the expert panels

	N	%
City Stations	79	52
Travellers' Stations	49	33
Country-side Stations	23	15
In Total	151	100

The expert panels were further asked to make another evaluation effort according to the business performance of the stations. Business performance is a multidimensional, complex concept to operationalize. The panels agreed about to make their evaluations based on the economic outcomes of the stations combined with an assessment about how well the stations had carried out the strategy of the company/market chain in their own business operations. After some negotiations the distribution of the business performances of the stations included in the sample were rated by the panels as follows:

Table 2
The business performances of the stations by the expert panels

	N	%
Good	48	32
Acceptable	75	50
Inappropriate	28	19
In Total	151	100

By cross tabulating the evaluations according to the two criteria of station type and business performance it is possible to see (presented in percentages) that there is generally speaking no strong relationship between the station type and the business performance: in each class there are roughly 20-30% of the cases in category 'Good', about a half in 'Acceptable' and 10-20% in the category 'Inappropriate'.

Table 3
The business performances on the different types of stations
in percentages

	Good	Acceptable	Inappropriate	In Total
City Stations	30%	52%	18%	100% (79)
Travellers' Stations	29%	47%	24%	100% (49)
Country-side Stations	48%	43%	9%	100% (23)

Results

From preliminary inspection of the results inspection of the results it was noted that in terms of means and rankings of the used 33 variables the petrol station dealers/ entrepreneurs were much like other entrepreneurs and unlike the managers in bigger firms (Miettinen, 1984). They rank highest in Creativity and Entrepreneurship and Sense of Service/ Dedication to a Cause and low in Managerial Competence compared with their counterparts in bigger firms (Career Orientation Inventory); they were generally both Direct and Relational in their achieving styles (indicating that their goal was not only to take responsibility but share it as well to a certain extent), but not very instrumental; and in terms of their Self-Concept they considered themselves more Extrovert than Introvert, rated themselves less Intelligent, more Energetic, Practical and People Oriented than the managers in bigger companies. These findings contradicted the old folklore and stereotype seeing entrepreneurs as selfish, egoistic money makers, difficult to cope with and poor in their interpersonal relations.

Table 4
The means, standard deviations and t-values of the COI, ASI and SCI variables

Variable	City-Stations (N=79) Mean	S.D.	Travellers' Stations (N=49) Mean	S.D.	Countryside Stations (N=23) Mean	S.D.	t-Value City vs. Travellers'	t-Value City vs. Country-side	t-Value Travellers' vs. Country-side
1. Technical Competence	3.61	0.82	3.58	0.99	3.79	1.00	0.21	0.88	0.84
2. Managerial Competence	3.53	0.68	3.48	0.64	3.45	0.90	0.39	-0.67	0.16
3. Autonomy/Independence	3.82	0.83	3.69	0.80	3.96	0.94	0.85	0.85	-1.23
4. Organizational Security	3.81	1.03	4.01	1.12	3.85	1.14	-1.05	-0.18	0.55
5. Geographical Security	3.05	1.51	3.53	1.52	3.51	1.44	-1.75	-1.30	0.06
6. Service /Dedication	4.51	0.75	4.40	0.83	4.37	0.90	0.79	0.77	0.14
7. Pure Challenge	4.03	0.83	3.79	0.82	4.06	0.94	1.62	-0.15	-1.26
8. Life-Style	4.10	0.68	4.22	0.69	4.13	0.94	-1.02	-0.19	0.48
9. Entrepreneurship	4.84	0.80	4.63	0.69	4.90	0.69	1.46	-0.33	-1.50
1. Intrinsic Direct	5.09	0.78	4.93	0.74	4.98	0.97	1.46	0.54	-0.25
2. Competitive Direct	4.44	0.95	4.59	1.06	4.90	1.02	1.14	-0.09	-1.18
3. Power Direct	4.99	0.99	4.87	0.96	4.74	0.78	1.62	1.10	0.58
4. Personal Instrumental	4.56	1.13	4.31	1.16	4.66	1.08	0.64	-0.39	-1.23
5. Social Instrumental	4.58	1.02	4.29	1.05	4.55	0.93	1.19	0.15	-0.99
6. Reliant Instrumental	4.56	1.05	4.53	0.94	4.81	0.86	1.54	-1.04	-1.18
7. Collaborative Relational	4.71	1.05	4.70	1.01	5.14	1.06	0.13	-1.72	-1.69
8. Contributory Relational	4.46	0.87	4.57	0.67	4.62	1.20	0.05	-0.69	-0.21
9. Vicarious Relational	4.77	0.98	4.87	1.02	5.11	1.04	-0.76	-1.47	-0.94
1. Direct Domain	4.99	0.73	4.80	0.73	4.84	0.94	1.40	0.81	-0.18
2. Instrumental Domain	4.56	0.85	4.39	0.82	4.67	0.71	1.15	-0.56	-1.42
3. Relational Domain	4.56	0.80	4.71	0.64	4.96	0.94	-0.40	-1.54	-1.32
4. Test Item Mean	4.73	0.60	4.62	0.58	4.83	0.70	0.95	-0.71	-1.32
1. Conventional vs Original	15.49	2.87	15.96	4.00	14.70	3.44	-0.76	1.12	1.30
2. Unstable vs Stable	17.71	3.58	19.04	2.89	19.00	2.99	-2.20*	-1.58	0.06
3. Energetic (little - much)	20.51	2.45	20.47	2.59	20.65	2.31	0.08	-0.25	-0.29
4. Introversive vs Extrovert	17.59	3.48	17.04	3.72	16.74	3.03	0.85	1.07	0.34
5. Self-rated Intelligence (little - much)	12.86	2.68	13.24	2.71	12.22	2.07	-0.78	1.06	1.61
6. Extensive vs Narrow	14.96	3.13	15.71	3.01	15.57	2.15	-1.34	-0.87	0.21
7. Submitted vs Dominant	16.68	2.20	16.51	2.08	16.09	1.51	0.44	1.22	0.87
8. Practical vs Theoretical	8.53	2.34	9.02	2.53	9.26	1.69	-1.11	-1.39	-0.41
9. Object vs People Oriented	14.39	2.63	14.41	2.64	13.91	2.39	-0.03	0.78	0.76
10. Worried vs Well-being	10.33	2.42	10.41	3.12	10.48	1.95	-0.16	-0.27	-0.10
11. Intuitive vs Rational	15.42	3.44	16.22	4.05	16.48	2.76	-1.21	-1.36	-0.27

When the differences between the three subgroups (the type of the station on the other hand , and their business performance on the other hand) over 33 variables were analyzed (Table 4), only a few significant differences were found. The dealers/entrepreneurs representing travellers' stations considered themselves more Stable (or less Unstable) than their counterparts in at city stations. This finding might be due to the different task environment: city stations usually have more munificence, complexity and dynamism in their environment.

Table 5

The means, standard deviations and t-values of the COI, ASI and SCI variables

Variable	Good (N=48) Mean	S.D.	Acceptable (N=75) Mean	S.D.	Inappropriate (N=28) Mean	S.D.	t-Value Good vs. Acceptable	t-Value Good vs. Inapprop.	t-Value Acceptable vs. Inappropriate
1. Technical Competence	3.75	0.89	3.54	0.86	3.64	1.03	1.31	0.50	-0.49
2. Managerial Competence	3.59	0.75	3.44	0.69	3.51	0.64	1.15	0.46	-0.49
3. Autonomy and Independence	3.88	0.91	3.74	0.77	3.84	0.90	0.94	0.20	-0.56
4. Organizational Security	3.64	1.03	3.92	1.05	4.19	1.16	-1.47	-2.14*	-1.11
5. Geographical Security	3.01	1.38	3.30	1.52	3.67	1.67	-1.08	-1.86	-1.16
6. Service /Dedication	4.42	0.87	4.38	0.79	4.68	0.65	0.22	-1.40	-1.79
7. Pure Challenge	4.06	0.81	3.88	0.92	3.98	0.71	1.09	0.44	-0.50
8. Life-Style	4.00	0.74	4.14	0.70	4.38	0.72	-1.07	-2.14*	-1.50
9. Entrepreneurship	4.95	0.76	4.72	0.75	4.65	0.71	1.63	1.70	0.43
1. Intrinsic Direct	5.14	0.86	4.95	0.78	4.99	0.71	1.25	0.77	-0.23
2. Competitive Direct	5.01	1.05	4.64	0.97	4.81	0.96	1.96	0.80	-0.79
3. Power Direct	4.99	0.91	4.88	1.00	4.86	0.91	0.62	0.59	0.07
4. Personal Instrumental	4.54	1.21	4.51	1.09	4.37	1.14	0.17	0.60	0.55
5. Social Instrumental	4.54	1.15	4.44	1.02	4.49	0.74	0.50	0.20	-0.24
6. Reliant Instrumental	4.63	1.06	4.51	0.93	4.74	1.03	0.70	-0.41	-1.08
7. Collaborative Relational	4.71	1.14	4.73	0.98	5.00	1.03	-0.08	-1.10	-1.24
8. Contributory Relational	4.52	0.96	4.51	0.83	4.54	0.85	0.04	-0.07	-0.11
9. Vicarious Relational	4.92	0.99	4.81	1.01	4.85	1.03	0.60	0.30	-0.18
1. Direct Domain	5.04	0.85	4.83	0.76	4.89	0.61	1.43	0.81	-0.39
2. Instrumental Domain	4.56	0.92	4.49	0.80	4.54	0.70	0.48	0.11	-0.31
3. Relational Domain	4.71	0.87	4.68	0.75	4.80	0.70	0.20	-0.44	-0.70
4. Test Item Mean	4.78	0.66	4.66	0.61	4.74	0.49	1.01	0.27	-0.61
1. Conventional vs Original	15.50	3.51	15.57	3.13	15.43	3.82	-0.12	0.08	0.20
2. Unstable vs Stable	18.83	3.06	18.03	3.27	18.32	3.92	1.37	0.63	-0.39
3. Energetic (little - much)	20.46	2.46	20.44	2.33	20.82	2.86	0.04	-0.59	-0.69
4. Introversive vs Extrovert	16.88	3.25	17.36	3.81	17.79	2.99	-0.73	-1.21	-0.53
5. Self-rated Intelligence (little - much)	12.81	2.46	12.99	2.57	12.75	3.06	-0.37	0.10	0.39
6. Extensive vs Narrow	15.42	2.84	15.19	2.97	15.39	3.27	0.43	0.03	-0.31
7. Submitted vs Dominant	16.38	1.95	16.65	2.07	16.50	2.30	-0.74	-0.25	0.32
8. Practical vs Theoretical	9.06	2.34	8.72	2.43	8.57	2.01	0.77	0.93	0.39
9. Object vs People Oriented	14.25	2.72	14.35	2.39	14.39	2.96	-0.21	-0.21	-0.08
10. Worried vs Well-being	10.52	2.44	10.19	2.58	10.64	2.91	0.72	-0.20	-0.77
11. Intuitive vs Rational	15.81	3.31	16.12	3.35	15.14	4.49	-0.50	0.75	1.20

In Table 5 the entrepreneurs/dealers were classified according to the business performance into three groups from good to acceptable and inappropriate. There were two significant t-values: the dealers/entrepreneurs with inappropriate business performance ranked Security and Lifestyle considerably higher than their counterparts with good business performance. This seemed to relate not only to their careers but to their work orientation in general. To be an entrepreneur still means hard work and certain risk as 'condicio sine qua non'.

One more t-test was administrated: the dealers were grouped by the years they had worked as an entrepreneur 6. As result more significant differences were found. The new dealers (who had worked only 1-3 years as an entrepreneur) considered themselves more Extrovert and Intelligent, and less Well-being (or more Worried) than 'the mature dealers' with 10 or more experience in the field. These differences in terms of SCI-variables could indicate that the newcomers are better educated and represent more modern type of people working in this particular service industry branch, but with more obstacles and challenges to be faced compared to their more settled down and mature counterparts. Maybe that is why they indicated more Object Orientation than People Orientation in their Self-Concept.

The new dealers scored also significantly higher in Social Instrumental achieving style possibly emphasing the meaning of network formation, which can not yet be ready after a few years as an entrepreneurs.

The mature dealers (with 10 or more years of experience) were significantly higher in Technical/Functional Competence, which can be partly explained by the changes in selection criteria during last 10 years towards more emphasis on the functional quality issues.

There were two more significant differences based on 'entrepreneurial life-cycle'. The middle group of dealers having 4-9 years of experience in the field were the most People Oriented group of all. This may indicate that after the first very hard years there is a period of working less, and possibly delegating more than during the first years as an entrepreneur, or perhaps hiring more people to work for them. The middle group of dealers seemed to be the most relational group in its achieving styles as well, but not to statistically significant extent.

Table 6
Standard deviations and t-values of the COI, ASI and SCI variables

Variable	1-3 Years (N=41) Mean	S.D.	4-9 Years (N=55) Mean	S.D.	over 10 years (N=39) Mean	S.D.	t-Value 1-3 vs. 4-9	t-Value 1-3 vs. over 10	t-Value 4-9 vs. over 10
1. Technical Competence	3.75	0.95	3.45	0.88	3.85	0.81	1.58	-0.48	-2.20*
2. Managerial Competence	3.44	0.68	3.45	0.66	3.54	0.82	-0.05	-0.59	-0.61
3. Autonomy/Independence	3.86	0.81	3.71	0.75	3.79	0.99	0.99	0.34	-0.50
4. Organizational Security	3.78	1.10	3.84	1.09	3.92	0.98	-0.27	-0.60	-0.36
5. Geographical Security	3.12	1.62	3.31	1.62	3.64	1.36	-0.59	-1.55	-1.08
6. Service /Dedication	4.54	0.77	4.41	0.77	4.10	0.83	0.73	1.20	0.51
7. Pure Challenge	3.84	0.81	3.90	0.80	4.29	1.03	-0.38	-1.28	-1.06
8. Life-Style	4.04	0.73	4.15	0.71	4.97	0.78	-0.55	-1.50	-0.91
9. Entrepreneurship	4.65	0.84	4.70	0.70	4.87	0.79	-0.32	-1.74	-1.73
1. Intrinsic Direct	4.92	0.84	5.06	0.71	5.02	0.92	-0.91	-0.53	0.25
2. Competitive Direct	4.80	0.99	4.67	0.67	4.87	1.13	0.67	-0.28	-0.93
3. Power Direct	5.00	0.93	4.74	1.03	4.88	0.86	1.26	0.59	-0.69
4. Personal Instrumental	4.57	1.13	4.24	1.12	4.66	1.12	1.42	-0.38	-1.81
5. Social Instrumental	4.73	0.93	4.27	1.17	4.44	0.85	2.07*	1.46	-0.76
6. Reliant Instrumental	4.58	0.84	4.70	1.06	4.43	0.91	-0.60	0.79	1.31
7. Collaborative Relational	4.74	1.10	4.85	1.05	4.61	1.00	-0.52	0.54	1.12
8. Contributory Relational	4.42	0.90	4.60	0.82	4.38	0.91	-1.03	0.17	1.20
9. Vicarious Relational	4.80	1.06	4.99	0.97	4.72	1.04	-0.91	0.33	1.27
1. Direct Domain	4.91	0.67	4.83	0.77	4.90	0.92	0.51	0.05	-0 38
2. Instrumental Domain	4.61	0.70	4.41	0.96	4.51	0.74	1.12	0.57	-0.58
3. Relational Domain	4.66	0.80	4.81	0.74	4.56	0.82	-1.01	0.51	1.55
4. Test Item Mean	4.72	0.52	4.67	0.66	4.66	0.66	0.36	0.42	0.08
1. Conventional vs Original	15.54	3.39	15.89	3.68	14.90	2.62	-0.48	0.94	1.44
2. Unstable vs Stable	18.22	3.03	19.02	3.12	17.87	3.64	-1.26	0.47	1.64
3. Energetic (little - much)	20.66	2.39	20.24	2.55	21.00	2.27	0.82	-0.65	-1.50
4. Introversive vs Extrovert	17.88	3.44	17.36	3.37	16.21	3.53	0.73	2.15*	1.61
5. Self-rated Intelligence (little - much)	13.68	2.75	12.78	2.40	12.21	2.55	1.71	2.49*	1.12
6. Extensive vs Narrow	15.07	2.62	15.25	3.02	15.92	2.92	-0.31	-1.37	-1.07
7. Submitted vs Dominant	16.27	1.95	16.40	2.09	16.79	1.79	-0.31	-1.26	-0.96
8. Practical vs Theoretical	8.98	2.19	8.87	2.33	8.54	2.23	0.22	0.88	0.70
9. Object vs People Oriented	13.85	2.55	15.07	2.39	13.72	2.78	-2.41*	0.23	2.53*
10.Worried vs Well-being	10.07	2.32	9.85	2.42	11.15	2.57	0.45	-1.98*	-2.50*
11.Intuitive vs Rational	16.34	3.77	15.56	3.30	16.08	3.48	1.07	0.33	-0.73

The explorative analysis was further employed in terms of simply rankings in the three subgroups (Appendix 4). When looking at the first career orientation rankings in different station types, no systematic variation was seen. Taking the other classification based on business performance, one interesting difference was found: those dealers with good business performance ranked Autonomy and Independence on the fourth place compared to the other two groups ranking Organizational Security that high respectively. There were no differences seen, however, between the first three rankings.

When moving on achieving styles there were some differences in terms of rankings in the subgroups. The city station dealers ranked the Power Direct style first, while in the case of other two subgroups it was not at all ranked among the first four. The travellers' station dealers ranked the Vicarious and Intrinsic Relational achieving styles first, and the country-side station dealers Collaborative and Vicarious Relational achieving styles respectively

In the case of including the business performance issue it can be seen that the combinations of some direct and relational styles were there with the systematic variation of the ranking of the first Direct Style: the higher it is, the better the business performance.

One further analysis, discrimination analysis, was performed for each station type, while the business performance was the discriminating variable. Ten significant correlations were found between the two discriminating functions and independent variables: the most significant correlations were negative ones for variables Independence, Submitted vs Dominant and Entrepreneurship. In Table 7 are the results of classification by the discriminating functions: 67 % of all the city-station cases were classified correctly and particularly in case of the dealers with 'good' or 'inappropriate' business performance the classification came off very well.

Table 7

Classification results for city-stations classified by business performance

No. of Predicted Group Membership			
Actual Group	Cases	Good	Acceptable	Inappropriate
Good	23	18 78.3%	1 4.3%	4 17.4%
Acceptable	42	9 21.4%	24 57.1%	9 21.4%
Inappropriate	14	1 7.1%	2 14.3%	11 78.6%

Percent of "grouped" cases correctly classified: 67.09%

The classification succeeded even better for the travellers' station and countryside station dealers (Tables 8 and 9). 88 % of the cases of travellers stations dealers were correctly classified. Significant correlations for the business performance of travellers' station dealers were Organizational Security (negative) and Autonomy (positive).

Table 8
Classification results for travellers' stations classified
by business performance

No. of Actual Group	Predicted Group Membership Good	Acceptable	Appropriate
Good	14	13 92.9%	1 7.1%	0 .0%
Acceptable	23	4 17.4%	18 57.1%	1 4.3%
Inappropriate	12	0 .0%	0 .0%	12 100.0%

Percent of "grouped" cases correctly classified: 87.76%

Table 9
Classification results for country-side stations classified by business performance

No. of Actual Group	Predicted Group Membership Cases	Good	Acceptable	Inappropriate
Good	11	11 100.0%	0 .0%	0 .0%
Acceptable	10	0 .0%	10 100.0%	0 .0%
Inappropriate	2	0 .0%	0 .0%	2 100.0%

Percent of "grouped" cases correctly classified: 100.00%

The countryside station dealers were all classified correctly. The only significant correlation was positive correlation between the discrimination function and Self Concept variable Submitted vs Dominant.

32

Summary and discussion

The empirical evidence on type of business environment - type of entrepreneur fit or match was not strong in this study. By administrating discrimination analysis over all 33 predictor variables it was possible to group 60 % of the cases correctly in relation to the criteria variable, the type of station. This indicates considerable overlapping between the station types. Much better prediction can be made based on business performance as the criteria variable: 70 - 100 % of the cases were correctly grouped. A closer look indicates that some of the variables have clear 'negative' predictive power in terms of inappropriate business performance. This type of negative prediction has practical value for example for the selection procedure of new dealers.

Another situational/contingent predictor variable in relation to business performance was the career stage of the entrepreneur/dealer. The share of correctly grouped cases varied from 70 % to 95 %. Best predictions were made with 'young' (1-3 years of experience) entrepreneurs and 'mature' (10 or more years) entrepreneurs. (95 % of correct groupings in each class)

Simple explorative or descriptive ranking analysis gave some more interesting details. In terms of the achieving styles (by most favored styles) it was recognized that direct achieving styles indicate the city stations, whereas in the case country-side stations relational styles dominated the first rankings. Thus the city station dealers/entrepreneurs were more characterized by a propensity to select, initiate and/or seek out activities which permit more direct confrontation with one's environment and entail the use to accomplish goals compared to their counterparts at the country-side stations. The latter group of entrepreneurs was more characterized by the propensity to seek success or achievement trough relationships. The travellers' station dealers/entrepreneurs stayed in the middle down this issue. To sum up, the city station dealers/entrepreneurs were closer to the traditional managerial idea emphasing control and strong personal task oriented efforts.

The same seemed to be true in relation to business performances: direct styles predicted Good performance in a systematic way. The higher the ranking of some direct achieving style was the better the business performance seemed to be. This finding relates indirectly also to the strategy employed by the two companies with their somewhat aggressive and growth oriented strategic behaviour in the market place.

In terms of career orientation variables there were hardly any contingencies. Entrepreneurship seemed to be the dominating orientation or personal preference to the extent it had no differential power among the dealers/entrepreneurs investigated. Organizational security functioned in a reverse way: the higher the score the worse the business performance. The difference was statistically significant between good and inappropriate cases, and almost significant between acceptable and inappropriate ones.

In the case of self concept variables only one dimension, Unstable-Stable was recognized to indicate statistically significant difference. The dealers/entrepreneurs working in the local country-side and at the travellers' stations respectively were more stable in terms of the group means compared to their counterparts at the city stations.

To conclude, there were less contingencies than the naive observer would expect. There are no doubt certain issues needing more careful analysis. The first one is the issue of environmental variation. Only three different type of business environments were postulated. Researchers search usually for structure, stability and pure types rather than the sources of variability and disharmony. The concept of variation, because it refers to variation in both organizations and environments, requires a careful examination of both sides of the organization-environment relationships in order to understand contingencies an probable changes. Predictions about the effect of environmental characteristics cannot be made without knowing more about the organization population in question, and predictions about the adaptiveness of organizational structure cannot be made without knowledge of environmental contexts.

Contingency approaches reflect an attempt by researchers to take account of contextual differences. There is the danger, anyway, about incomplete conceptions of the environment and its variation and diversity. Contingency researchers' typical focus on cross-sectional studies of fairly large, stable organizations, was avoided in this study, but the question remains, if this particular sample of petrol stations was still a highly selected (and possibly biased) sample, compared to the total population of new start ups, successes, and failures. Furthermore, longitudinal studies of representative populations in varying environments are badly needed. The study of successful enterprises - those still available for investigation - maybe quite misleading it blinds the analysts to essential differences between these successful enterprises and those that are no longer in existence.

The issue of the complexity and multidimensionality of business performance was left to the hands of the expert panels in this study. They were working on their own based on the inaccurate quest from the investigators. No cross checking was employed in order to guarantee the scorer reliability. Both panels indicated some cases where the dealer/entrepreneur was doing excellent business from his personal point of view, but was doing not very well at all from the standpoint of the company. Criteria lead from the strategy of the host companies were employed in these few cases.

Most petrol stations are very much what is traditionally called simple structures. According to Minzberg (1983, 157-162) they are characterized by little or no technostructure, few support staffers, a loose division of labour, and a small managerial hierarchy. Little if any of its behaviour is formalized to the extent simple structure can be considered nonstructure.

Coordination in the simple structure is effected largely by direct supervision, and power over all important decisions tends to be centralized in the hands of the entrepreneur-manager. Many simple structures want to remain like this. For them , informal communication is convenient and effective.

In simple structures like most petrol stations in this study, leadership related factors are the most correlated with entrepreneurial activity in terms of the leader's personality, power, and his/her knowledge of markets, products and services. According to Miller (1983, 783) even environment did not seem to matter. Entrepreneurship seemed to be much more a function of leader's goals and character than external events.

However it would be naive to assume that P-E fit is the only, or indeed the most important, factor predicting further outcomes like business performance. One of the many problems associated with this type of research is that numerous additional factors may confound the relationship. A more differentiated analysis of the task environment is needed. The dynamics between leader-follower interaction (e.g. the entrepreneur/dealer - regional managers) might provide some further moderator variables also relating to the developmental phase of the petrol station. Too little is known about many other possible moderators like formal organizational rules and procedures; the nature of primary work groups; quality of leader-member relations inside the station etc.

It would be interesting to analyze the failures in the petrol dealership as well. Why an entrepreneur leaves or gets fired or how a poor business performance is managed in a longer run? It is mainly due to the incongruent occupational setting? An entrepreneur can leave an incongruent occupational setting to improve his or her setting, but the coping process can occur in the opposite direction, namely entrepreneurial types can be modified possible by their environment. People may adjust to a lower challenging work situation, with an accompanying change in their personal value and need structure. That is, there may be both adaptive and non-adaptive reactions to poor entrepreneur-business environment fit. And furthermore, coping with unpleasant state of affairs is not solely affected by the individual concerned or the P-E fit but may again be mediated by many outside events, e.g. life events, financial situation and support from others (emphasizing the role of regional managers and other significant persons).

The present research is also constrained by its rather small amount of variables and insufficient data about promising issue of life cycle stages of the business studied. With partial confrontation to the hypothesis concerning the relationship between entrepreneur-business environment congruence it raises many more questions relating back to the very general point of contingency theory, 'it depends'.

References

AAKER, D.A.(1984). Strategic Market Management. New York: Wiley.

ANSOFF, IGOR H.(1984). Implanting Strategic Management. Englewood Cliff, N.J.: Prentice Hall.

BURNS, T., and STALKER, G.M. (1961). The Management of Innovations. London : Tavistock.

EVANS, M.-G. (1979). Leadership. In S.Karr (ed.), Organizational Behavior. Columbus, Ohio. Grid.

FIEDLER, FRED E. (1967). A Theory of leadership effectiveness. New York: McGraw-Hill.

FURNHAM, ADRIAN, and SCHAEFFER, ROSEMARY (1984). Person-environment fit, job satisfaction and mental health. Journal of Occupational Psychology, 57, 295-307.

GALBRAITH, JAY R. (1977). Organization Design. Addison-Wesley.

HARRISON, R. VAN (1978). Person-environment fit and job stress. In C.Cooper & R.Payne (Eds), Stress at Work. New York: Wiley.

HERSEY, P. and BLANCHARD, K. (1988). Management of Organizational Behavior. (5th ed.). Englewood Cliff, N.J.: Prentice Hall.

HOLLAND, J. (1973). Making Vocational Choices: A Theory Of Careers. Englewood Cliff, N.J.: Prentice Hall.

HOUSE, R.J. and MICHELL, T.R. (1974). Path-goal theory of leadership. Journal of Contemporary Business, 5, 81-97.

HOWELL, J.P., DORFMAN, P.W., and KERR S. (1986). Moderator Variables in Leadership Research. Academy of Management Review, Vol.11, No.1, 88-102.

HÄYRYNEN, YRJÖ-PAAVO (1970). The Flow of New Students to Different University Fields. Suomalaisen Tiedeakatemian Toimituksia. Helsinki.

JAGO, A.G., and VROOM, V.H. (1980). An evaluation of two alternatives to the Vroom/Yetton Normative Model. Academy of Management Journal, 23, 347-355.

LAWRENCE, PAUL R., and LORSCH, J.W. Organization and Environment. Homewood, 111.: Irwin.

LIPMAN-BLUMEN, JEAN (1989). Individual and Organizational Achieving Styles: A Handbook for Researchers and Human Resource Professionals. Achieving Styles Institute, California.

MIETTINEN, ASKO (1984). Small Business Managers: Are They Different? A paper presented at the Small Business Management Conference 'Perspectives into European Small Business Research', St.Michel, October 19-20.

MILLER, D. (1983). The correlates of entrepreneurship in three types of firms. Management Science, 29, 770-791.

MINZBERG, HENRY (1983). Structure in Five. Design Effective Organizations. Prentice Hall.

PERROW, CHARLES (1970). Organizational Analysis: A Sociological View. Belmont, Calif.:Wadsworth.

PFEFFER, JEFFREY (1982). Organizations and Organization Theory. Pitman.

PORTER, M.E. (1987). From Competitive Advantage to Corporate Strategy. Harvard Business Review, May-June, 43-59.

SCHEIN, EDGAR H. Career Anchors.

SMITH, M.R., and MINER, JOHN B. (1983). Type of Entrepreneur, Type of Firm, and Managerial Motivation: Implications for Organizational Life Cycle Theory. Strategic Management Journal. Vol.4, 325-240.

THOMPSON, JAMES D. (1967). Organizations in Action. New York: McGraw-Hill.

VASCONCELLOS, JORGE A. (1988). Some Empirical Evidence on a Contingency Theory of Success Factors. European Management Journal. Vol.6, No.3, 236-249.

WOODWARD, JOAN (1965). Industrial Organization. London: Oxford.

WURTMAN, MAX S. Entrepreneurship: An Integrating Typology and Evaluation of the Empirical Research in the Field. Journal of Management. Vol.13, No.2, 259-279.

YAVITZ, B. and NEWMAN; W.H. (1982). Strategy in Action. The Free Press.

YUKL, G.A. (1981). Leadership in Organizations. Englewood Cliff, N.J.: Prentice Hall

Appendix 1

Career orientations inventory (COI)

The Career Orientation Inventory includes ones observations of (1) motives and needs, (2) talents and skills and (3) personal values. Most people has numerous talents, motives and values but in here the most important ones are selected. Career Anchors tend to develop around following kinds of dominant themes:

1. Technical or functional competence

Some people discover, that they have strong talent and high motivation for a particular kind of work. (e.g. engineering). Such people develop in their self-concepts the dominant theme that they are specialists and craftsmen, that they have certain talents around which their identities revolve. To be anchored in ones technical or functional competence means that one would not give up that area of work even if one had to sacrifice a certain amount of security or autonomy to remain in it. These people may be able to manage within the function in which their talents lies, but they usually are not interested in managing.

2. Managerial competence

Some people, but only some, find themselves interested in management and competent in it. This group of people wants high level of responsibility, opportunity to contribute to the welfare of their organization, leadership opportunities and high income. These job values becomes their criteria of success. In order to function as a good general manager it is necessary to be able to identify, analyze an solve problems under conditions of incomplete information and uncertainty, as well as to be able to influence, supervise, lead, manipulate and control people at all levels of organization toward organizational achievement. These people should have capacity to bear high levels of responsibility without to be paralyzed and the ability to exercise power and make difficult decisions without guilt and shame.

3. Autonomy and independence

Some people discover that they cannot stand to be bound by other people's rules, by procedures, by working hours and other kind of norms. They have need to do things in their own way, at their own pace and by their own standards. Independence should not be understood as entrepreneurship.

4. Organizational identity and security

Some people seek jobs in organizations which provide job tenure, which have the reputation of never laying off people, which have good retirement plans and generous benefits, and which have the image of being strong and reliable in their industry. Such people obtain some selfgratification from identifying with the organization even if they do not have very high ranking or important jobs in organizations.

5. Stability and geographical security

Some people links themselves to a geographic area, putting down the roots in a community, sting in a house and a way of life. He or she would shift jobs or companies whenever it is necessary in order to avoid being uprooted.

6. Service / dedication

Some people are more oriented to values embodied in their work than the actual talents or areas of competence involved. The most obvious examples are doctor, teacher and social worker whose self-image is developed around the inter-personal helping activities. These people would organize their entire career and the sequence of job decisions around the ability to work in a setting in which these values could be met.

7. Pure challenge

For these people the most important thing is to solve extremely difficult problems win adversaries. The competition is the more important than e.g. some specific area in the job. For some people this is a competition between different persons. The variation and challenges will become the aim. If something is easy, it is also boring.

8. Life-style

These people find their identity based on whole life. They try to balance all the components of their lives into a harmonic entirety. They oppose even promotions if it could break the harmony of their life.

9. Entrepreneurship

Some people want to create a new organization or develop a new business around a product or service which they may or may not have intended themselves. Entrepreneurial activity means an overriding pre-occupation, for some people even obsession, with creating something of their own and proving to the world that they have done it.

(Edgar H. Schein)

Appendix 2

Definitions of sets and styles

The direct set

The direct achieving styles include three styles which are primarily oriented toward accomplishing or mastering the task. These styles are characterized by a propensity to seek out, select and initiate activities which permit direct confrontation with the task. They represent a self-reliant orientation, entailing personal efforts of mind and body to accomplish goals.

1. Intrinsic Direct One is highly task oriented, confronting the task directly pitting one against it and working intensely to complete
2. Competitive Direct One seeks or selects activities which permit evaluation of ones performance against others or by rank ordering own contribution to a task in relation to the contributions of others.
3. Power Direct One takes charge controlling and organizing other individuals, resources, tasks and situations related to task accomplishment.

The instrumental set

The instrumental achieving styles is characterized by a propensity to seek out, select and initiate activities which permit the use of personal attributes, accomplishments relationships with others as conduits to still other achievements.

4. Personal Instrumental One uses ones direct accomplishments as gateways to further ends, evaluating personal achievement in terms of its instrumental value in gaining recognition, relationships or other success.
5. Social Instrumental One uses ones relationships with others as a mechanism to gain access to achievement arenas. Developing relationships in a primary or intervening step toward accomplishments.
6. Reliant Instrumental One seeks or initiates situations in which others assume part of the responsibility for ones success. One perceives self in need of help in order to meet achievement goals.

The relational set

The relational achieving styles is characterized by a propensity to seek out, select and initiate activities which permit achievement by contributing actively or passively to the tasks and goals of others.

7. Collaborative Relational One achieves through participation in groups and expects and appropriate share of both responsibility and rewards of group accomplishment.
8. Contributory Relational One achieves by contributing by another's achievement, accepting the goals and means defined by the others, acknowledging own contribution as helpful but secondary to the accomplishment.
9. Vicarious Relational One experiences achievement through identification with one or more others or with an institution, perceiving the other's accomplishments as if they were ones own.

(Jean Lipman-Blumen 1987)

Appendix 3

Self-concept inventory (SCI) scales

1. Conventional vs Original
2. Unstable vs Stable
3. Energetic (little - much)
4. Introversive vs Extrovert
5. Self-rated Intelligence (little - much)
6. Extensive vs Narrow
7. Submitted vs Dominant
8. Practical vs Theoretical
9. Object vs People Oriented
10. Worried vs Well-being
11. Intuitive vs Rational

(Häyrynen, Y-P, 1970)

Appendix 4

First ranking analysis for career orientation and achieving styles

Table 10. The Favored Career Orientations by Station Type

Rank	City Stations (N=79)	Travellers' Stations (N=49)	Country-side Stations (N= 23)
Rank #1	Entrepreneurship	Entrepreneurship	Entrepreneurship
Rank #2	Service / Dedication	Geographical Security	Pure Challenge
Rank #3	Geographical Security	Organizational Security	Service / Dedication
Rank #4	Organizational Security	Service /Dedication	Geographical Security

Table 11. The Favored Career Orientations by Business Performance

Rank	Good (N=48)	Acceptable (N=75)	Inappropriate (N=28)
Rank #1	Entrepreneurship	Entrepreneurship	Entrepreneurship
Rank #2	Service / Dedication	Service / Dedication	Service / Dedication
Rank #3	Geographical Security	Geographical Security	Geographical Security
Rank #4	Autonomy and Independence	Organizational Security	Organizational Security

Table 12. The Favored Achieving Styles by Station Type

Rank	City Stations (N=79)	Travellers' Stations (N=49)	Country-side Stations (N= 23)
Rank #1	Power Direct	Vicarious Relational	Collaborative Relational
Rank #2	Vicarious Relational	Intrinsic Relational	Vicarious Relational
Rank #3	Competitive Direct	Personal Instrumental	Personal instrumental
Rank #4	Reliant Instrumental	Competitive Direct	Competitive Direct

Table 13. The Favored Achieving Styles by Business Performance

Rank	Good (N=48)	Acceptable (N=75)	Inappropriate (N=28)
Rank #1	Competitive Direct	Vicarious Relational	Vicarious Relational
Rank #2	Collaborative Relational	Power Direct	Intrinsic Relational
Rank #3	Vicarious Relational	Reliant Instrumental	Competitive Direct
Rank #4	Personal Instrumental	Collaborative Relational	Reliant Instrumental

3 The process of becoming an entrepreneur: A theoretical framework of factors influencing entrepreneurs' start-up decisions (preliminary results)

Visa Huuskonen

'[...]Although much research in the nature of the entrepreneur has been done, he or she still remains an enigma, his motivations and actions far from clear, a state of affairs aggravated because of contradictory theoretical and research findings.' (Sexton - Bowman 1983, 214)

Synopsis

The aim of this study was to provide new views on the phenomena of becoming an entrepreneur. Secondly to give improved conceptual tools for describing entrepreneurs and small businesses. As a result a holistic process model was developed. This model contributes as a decision making theory of becoming an entrepreneur.

No empirical evidence for the study was gathered at this stage of the research project. The study will be continued with an empirical part.

The purpose of the paper

The objective of the theoretical part of the study was to create a framework that could then be used in the future. The research problem was to find out what kinds of motivational and decision making processes lead to the decision to become an entrepreneur.

This study is based on literature analysis. Its approach is hermeneutic and it has connections to the 'Verstehen'-school (The 'understanding' tradition). No attempt was made to produce any statistical generalizations.

Theoretical background

Career involves a sequence of interrelated decision situations. The decisions that are made restrict future choice alternatives. Entrepreneurship and career mobility are thus understood as decisions that can occur at any stage of a person's career. They can be repeated several times during the entire career. Each career decision involves basically similar decision process.

The career decision process is consistent with the pattern of practical syllogism. It incorporates three sets of choice determinants: general background factors, personal factors such as the person's abilities, values, beliefs and duties, and the contingency or situational factors. It should be noted that career behavior is not based on objective information but on subjective, situational comprehension. A person's behavior is thus directed by situational perception and its interpretation.

The studies that have dealt with entrepreneurial motivation and initiating businesses have usually been statistical. They have not been examining this phenomenon from the level of an individual entrepreneur. In addition, the studies also have concentrated on a single section of the start-up process that however is holistic by nature.

Entrepreneurship has very different meaning to the individual in different stages of the work career. Social environment changes and influences one's freedom of choice and patterns of behavior.

It is commonly agreed that going into business is a consequence of entrepreneurial motivation. In practice only a small portion of those people who have the motivation do really establish new firms or otherwise set up businesses. Why is that? Traditional theories of entrepreneurship have no answers to this question. From this we can draw the conclusion that there is an inconsistency between 'entrepreneurial motivation' and 'going into the business'. Describing the start up-process and trying to fill this gap is the main idea of the whole research project. An attempt will be made to find out how this motivational and decision making process works at individual level. That is, what is the subjective logic behind the decision to initiate a firm of one's own?

The entrepreneur

The ideas of the entrepreneurial manager dominate strongly the choice of strategy, organizational form, and other major decisions in small businesses. In previous research it has been found that the entrepreneurs usually aim to create either a very big successful firm or a small firm. Small firm is easier to manage and simple in its operations (Liles 1981, 35-36). This is consistent with Chandler's categorizing ideas of 'craftsman' and 'opportunistic entrepreneurs' (Chandler 1983, 35).

It seems that the main motive for creating one's own firm is to seek autonomy and personal freedom (Mäkinen 1977, 18-20, 1982, 42). Also; self-fulfilment, achievement, pride of craftsmanship, money etc. are among the most often mentioned positive arguments for entrepreneurship. There is also much entrepreneurship, which has been started to avoid unemployment or other negative imperatives.

In broader terms; the reasons for entrepreneurship have been classified into push-factors and pull-factors. The former refers to environmental imperatives that have forced people to become entrepreneurs involuntarily. On the other hand; the 'pulled' entrepreneurs have been seeking for some positive rewards instead of just trying to cope somehow.

According to the classical typology created by Stanworth and Curran, an 'Artisan Entrepreneur' seeks to reach independence and autonomy through his firm. Making money is not as important as getting satisfaction from the work. His firm is usually small, and he does not try to make it any larger. For an entrepreneur of the 'Traditional Type', it is important to earn money. His firm is bigger than was the artisan's firm and he tries to make it grow. For the 'Managerial Entrepreneur' it is important to earn a good income and get a higher social status through managing a successful firm. He also tries to make his firm grow bigger and bigger. (Stanworth - Curran 1977 & 1981; Mäkinen 1982, 10; Paulsson 1986, 463-464)

Even from these two typologies we can presume that people become entrepreneurs for miscellaneous reasons in diverse situations.

The process of becoming an entrepreneur

General background

The 'General background' means person's social background and earlier experiences. They influence personality and the way one is prone to observe the environment.

Beginning entrepreneurs are often described to be 25-40 years old first-born males who have achieved necessary skills and self-confidence. During this phase there is a time, when they are mature personalities and not yet so bound with social-, family- and economic ties into their present status. (Brockhaus 1982, 53; Miettinen 1986, 26. Mäkinen 1982, 79-90; also Hébert - Link 1989, 39; Hauta-aho 1990, 44)

The person's reference groups have a strong effect on entrepreneurial values. This is confirmed by the fact that present entrepreneurs have very often been working in small businesses. There has often been entrepreneurs in their family, too (DuBrin 1984, 89-90).

As potent entrepreneurs have often been working in small firms they are more aware of the advantages entrepreneurial career has to offer. On the basis of their previous experiences they are able to weight entrepreneurship in a more concrete level in the present context. (Cooper - Dunkelberg 1986, 66; Bowen - Hisrich 1986, 400; Shapero - Sokol 1982; Brockhaus 1982, 52; Hauta-aho 1990, 43-45, 148-149)

Values of the potential entrepreneur are personal ideas about what is right or wrong, and what is good or bad. Values together make up a value system, which has a direct effect on the attitudes toward entrepreneurship. (Katz - Kahn 1978, 363; Robbins 1983, 50-51)

People are more likely to form favourable beliefs and values if they have acted in a small business or if they have followed their parents' small business activities. In more general terms; rationality is affected by the common attitudes towards risk, risk taking and wealth in the social group one identifies with.

Bowen - Hisrich (1986, 399) make a summary of several independent studies. Almost in all of the studies it was found that entrepreneur's father or some other close relative had been an entrepreneur. In any case, entrepreneurs have entrepreneurial parents more often than their proportion in the general population would suggest. Similar findings were presented earlier in Shapero and Sokol (1982, 84).

Personal factors

Personal factors mean different dimensions of the personality of the potential entrepreneur.

Personal factors act like a 'mental filter' which filtrates knowledge about business opportunities and other environmental factors. These factors also guide behavior in various circumstances. The same business opportunity can be seen and taken in an entirely different way, depending on the observer.

Personality and other personal characteristics are shaped by genetic and milieu (see also 'General Background'). Earlier learning processes are behind the entrepreneur's knowledge base and his capabilities. Knowledge and capabilities are roused by motivation to steer miscellaneous acts and activities. There are also certain learned and inherited, relatively permanent patterns of behavior which can be called 'traits'.

The most important personality factors in the entrepreneurship literature are:

Locus of Control It has been generally believed that entrepreneurs have exceptionally strong feeling of being masters of their own destiny (Internal locus of control). In later studies, no difference has been found between E:s and other compared groups. (Brockhaus 1982, 43; Robbins 1983, 58; Chad et al. 1986, 56; Kulik - Rowland 1989, 361; Scheinberg - McMillan 1988, 673)

Need for Achievement McClelland stated that NAch is the striving force behind entrepreneurs. It has been thought that E:s differ from other groups in this sense. In consequent studies this has not been proven. Entrepreneurs are high in NAch, but so are many other groups as well (e.g. managers). (McClelland 1971, 110; Chad et al. 1986, 55-56; Brockhaus 1982; Gartner 1985)

Attitude to Risk E:s have often been regarded as apt risk-takers. Later findings prove that they are neither seeking for small or big risks. They resemble more or less the general population. (Brockhaus 1980, 1987; Bowen - Hisrich 1986, 398; Carle 1980, 17-18)

Need for autonomy and

Need for Power It is important for the E:s 'To be One's Own Boss'. They have also been characterized to be difficult and rebellion personalities, who cannot adapt into a normal working environment. Therefore they have to tailor a suitable job for themselves. (Stanworth - Stanworth et. al. 1989, 12-13; Low - MacMillan 1988, 147; Bowen - Hisrich 1986, 403; Carle 1980, 17-18; Laitinen 1982, 20-22; Scheinberg - McMillan 1988, 671; Hamilton 1987)

General attitudes

and values Attitudes or values are not direct causes for entrepreneurship by themselves, but they affect perception and different reasoning processes. Weberian hypotheses of protestant values and entrepreneurial behavior are often cited. These explanations are often questioned now.

Taken together, personal characteristics have failed to distinguish entrepreneurs from other groups of reference. In spite of this there is a connection, although not directly deterministic by nature. Values, attitudes, personality and needs have an influence on the kinds of observations that the person makes on business opportunities. The interpretations that one gives to the observations is also based on prior knowledge and value system (cognitive map). The person's earlier views will be supported in daily life by selecting, classifying and generalizing incoming information. These mentally screened observations will be associated to the cognitive map. The resulting subjective knowledge-base will guide the person's behavior and ideas of various phenomena.

Perceptions in their context

Behavior and perceptions are very strongly guided by the fact that consistency is sought between behavior and all these personal factors that have been mentioned earlier. For example, favourable attitudes make it more likely to start a business of one's own and vice versa.

There are several ways to avoid cognitive dissonance, which can result from inconsistency between ideals and perceptions. The two major ways are: 1) *Adapting behavior* (e.g. to become an entrepreneur) or 2) *Changing opinions* (having new ideas about entrepreneurship which are consistent with the thought behavior).

Figure 1
Perceptions in their context

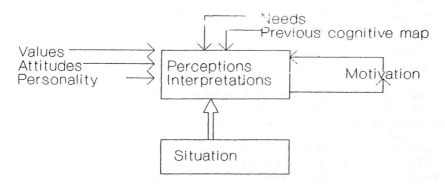

Perceived idea of the environment

Neither the motivation or the behavior of the potential entrepreneur are directly influenced by external environmental factors. Situational influences are linked to decision making through the perception or 'cognitive map' of the person (Vroom 1964, 13; Weiner 1972, 273). This means that the person who is thinking of becoming an entrepreneur has only a limited subjective impression of the business environment and its quirks.

The judgement of business opportunities is rarely based on accurate and reliable information. As it is well known, forecasting the future is difficult. The sense of business possibilities is influenced by personal characteristics like tendency to seek risk, self perception, and business experience. (McClelland 1971; Kilby 1971, 7-8)

The cognitive map of the potential entrepreneur consists of more or less incomplete and distorted information. This information can be classified into three broad categories: knowledge of situations, knowledge of means and knowledge of goals.

The mental states

Motivation

The strength of motivation depends on a) personal need and b) the capability of the thought target to satisfy that need. Hence, motivation is a combination of the tension created by the need and the valence of the satisfying target (Campbell - Pritchard 1976, 68). The stronger the need and the more attractive the target, the stronger becomes motivation (Robbins 1983, 58). Similarly, the strength of the entrepreneurial motivation goes in proportion to the perceived attractiveness of being an entrepreneur. Running a business can look like an excellent alternative for various reasons.

Entrepreneurship can be either extrinsically or intrinsically motivated, like any other activity. *Intrinsically motivated* entrepreneurship is steered by the mental satisfaction one is getting from it. The target of *extrinsic entrepreneurial motivation* is a (material) means to satisfy some other need. (Staw 1985, 227-229; Robbins 1983, 141)

Generally speaking, motivation is a group of internal forces which originate from outside and inside of the individual. These forces construct and regulate activity, and give form, direction, intensity and duration to it. (Pinder 1984, 8; Mitchell 1982; 81, Leontjev 1975, 39) Likewise, entrepreneurial motivation is formed as a result of mental processes (Leppäalho 1981, 24-25). These motivational processes are centrally affected by 1) Personal factors and 2) Situational factors.

Reasoning

In terms of common business thinking, it can be assumed that the person considering entrepreneurship does strategic planning of his own life. The potential entrepreneur has a rough idea of his odds. He estimates his strong and weak sides, the opportunities and threats that affect the business he is thinking of. After evaluating these questions more or less carefully he sets his own goals and ranks different procedures to reach them. The very basis for this reasoning is the strategic 'S-W-O-T' analysis which he has been doing somewhat intuitively. (Strengths - Weaknesses - Opportunities - Threats)

Figure 2
Background of the reasoning process

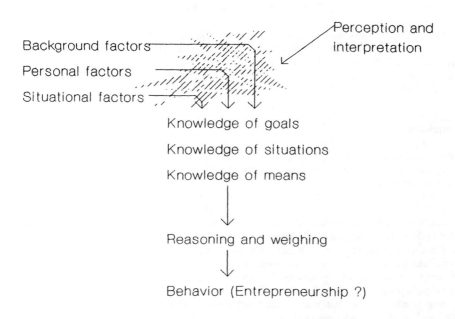

Entrepreneurship is a way (means) of reaching a goal or at least of taking a small step towards it. There is no one general concrete reason for entrepreneurship. Anyhow, it can be said that the goal is something that is important or desirable for the person in question.

As a result of the reasoning process it may look obvious that the best personal strategy, in this given situation, is to become an entrepreneur. Maybe one cannot see (right or wrong?) any other alternatives that could be as good as this is. It must be stressed that the weighing of the alternatives (reasoning) is done on the basis of subjective knowledge. (Simon: Bounded rationality)

Intentions

Becoming an entrepreneur is explained most directly by behavioral intentions which are on the cognitive level (This Aristotle's idea of intentional behavior has been advanced by philosopher G. H. von Wright). In fact, there is no direct environmental imperative that could explain entrepreneurship by itself, unless entrepreneurs are taken as inactive puppets, which they are not.

First, entrepreneurial intention is possibly created by entrepreneurial motivation. Second, this intention may in turn lead to entrepreneurship. The connection is not as clear as it looks like, though.

The intention to become an entrepreneur will only be realized, if the situational factors are still favourable enough at the starting time. Situational factors must *look* good enough to the potential entrepreneur, even if a long time has run from the original business idea.

Proceeding towards to the new venture is not linear or steady at all. The plans can come to a halt for different reasons. Unexpected changes in circumstances can return the process to earlier stages or stop it permanently. The business idea can be given up any time. In essence, it is an iterative process which' speed varies. This time period has sometimes been called the 'Pre Start-up Phase'.

Conclusion

From the discussion above we can draw the conclusion that entrepreneurship consists of many (balanced) components. It takes a lot more than just a signal from the market to make an entrepreneur start:

Background factors give potential entrepreneurs a set of values, knowledge, attitudes and abilities which affect their orientation on the career path. If there is previous nearness to entrepreneurship, it seems to have a strong positive influence on the likelihood of becoming an entrepreneur (one learns behavioral scrips and patterns).

Personal factors explain why different people evaluate entrepreneurship in different ways and have different interpretations of their business environment. As a result of learning and socialization processes they have internalized those norms, ideas and behavioral patterns (scripts) they follow.

Situational factors have not as direct influence to the behavior as often is thought because the same environmental context has broadly different meanings to different persons. Situational factors have an effect on intentions only after the perceptions of the conditions have been 'screened' to fit into the prevalent cognitive map.

Figure 3
The resulting model of 'becoming an entrepreneur'

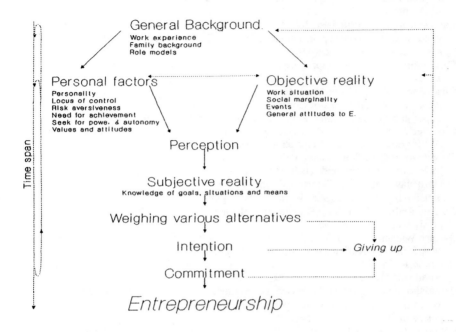

Entrepreneurial decisions are therefore best explained with the person's cognitive perceptions and interpretations of the present situation and its causal relations related to one's own person. Entrepreneurship develops if it is perceived as the best alternative. This in turn depends on what kind of perceptions the actor has about obtainable occupational strategies in the perceived situational context.

Thus, becoming an entrepreneur cannot be explained simply by referring to a few environmental imperatives or one or two personal characteristics. Becoming an entrepreneur involves contingent background-, personal-, and situational properties.

References

Bowen Donald D., Hisrich Robert D. (1986), The Female Entrepreneur: A Career Development Perspective. Academy of Management Review 1986:2, 393-407.

Brockhaus Robert H., (1982), The Psychology of the Entrepreneur. In Kent Calvin A., S-exton Donald L. Vesper Karl H (eds.). Encyclopedia of Entrepreneurship. Prentice-H-all 1982.

Brockhaus Robert H. (1980), Risk Taking Propensity of Entrepreneurs. Academy of Management Journal 1980:3, 509-520.

Brockhaus Robert H. (1987), Entrepreneurial Folklore. Journal Of Small Business Management 1987:July, 1-6.

Campbell John P., Pritchard Robert D. (1976), Motivation Theory in Industrial and Organizational Psychology. In Dunnette Marvin D. (1986) (ed.), Handbook of Industrial and Organizational Psychology. Chicago 1976.

Carle Göran (1980), Entreprenören: Vem är han? Affärsekonomi Management 1980:1, 16-2.

Chad Perry, Ross Macarthur, Meredith Geoffrey, Cunnington Bert (1986), Need for Achievement and Locus of Control of Australian Small Business Owner-managers and Super-entrepreneurs. International Small Business Journal 1986:Summer, 55-64.

Chandler John S., Trone Thomas, Weiland Michael (1983), Decision Support Systems Are for Small Business. Management Accounting, Apr. 1983.

Cooper Arnold C., Dunkelberg William C., Woo C. Y. (1986), Optimists and Pessimists: 2994 Entrepreneurs and Their Perceived Changes for Success. In Ronstadt Robert, Hornaday John A., Peterson Rein, Vesper Karl H., (eds.) Frontiers of Entrepreneurship Research 1986. Wellesley Massachusetts.

DuBrin Andrew J. (1984), Foundations of Organizational Behavior, an Applied Perspective. Prentice-Hall Inc.

Gartner William B. (1985), A Conceptual Framework for Describing the Phenomenon of New Venture Creation. Academy of Management Review 1985:4, 696-706.

Hamilton R. T. (1987) Motivations and Aspirations of Business Founders. International Small Business Journal 1987:1, 70-78

Hauta-aho Seppo (1990) Yrityksen perustamisen vaiheet - Työsuhde-lähestymistavan teoreettista analysointia ja perustamisen konkretisointi. Vaasan korkeakoulun julkaisuja, tutkimuksia No 146.

Hébert Robert F., Link Albert N. (1989), In Search of the Meaning of Entrepreneurship. Small Business Economics 1989:1, 39-49.

Katz Daniel - Kahn Robert L. (1978), The Social Psychology of Organizations. New York.

Kilby Peter (1971), Hunting the Heffalump. In Kilby Peter (ed.), Entrepreneurship and Economic Development. London.

Kulik Carol T., Rowland Kendrith M. (1989), The Relations of Attributional Frameworks to Job seekers' Perceived Success and Job Search Involvement. Journal of Organizational Behavior 1989, 361-367.

Laitinen Erkki K. (1982), Mistä on kiinni yrittäjän työmotivaatio? Yritystalous 1982:4, 20-23.

Leontjev A.N. (1975), Toiminta ja persoonallisuus. Psykologia 1975:5, 17-53.

Leppäalho Markku (1981), Yrityksen menestyminen, toiminta-analyyttinen tutkimus. Yrityksen taloustieteen ja yksityisoikeuden laitoksen julkaisuja. Sarja A1: Tutkimuksia 19. Tampere.

Liles Patrick R. (1981), Who Are the Entrepreneurs? In Gorb Peter, Dowell Philip, & Wilson Peter (eds.), Small Business Perspectives. London.

Low Murray B., MacMillan Ian C. (1988), Entrepreneurship: Past Research and Future Challenges. Journal of Management 1988:2, 139-161.

McClelland David C. (1971), The Achievement Motive in Economic Growth. Kilby Peter (ed.) The Entrepreneurship and Economic Development. London.

Miettinen Asko (1986), haastattelu artikkelissa Kilgast Riitta, Sulaako jää yrittämisen tieltä. Kehittyvä kauppa 1986:1.

Mitchell Terence R. (1982), Motivation: New Directions for Theory, Research, and Practice. Academy of Management Review, 1982:1, 80-88.

Mäkinen Vesa (1982), Yrittäjyyden edellytykset ja niiden toteutuminen, empiirinen vertailututkimus. Tampereen yliopisto, Yrityksen taloustieteen ja yksityisoikeuden laitoksen julkaisuja A1: Tutkimuksia 22. Tampere.

Mäkinen Vesa (1977), Yrityksen perustaminen, teoreettinen tarkastelu. Yrityksen taloustieteen ja yksityisoikeuden laitos, julkaisuja A:10. Tampere.

Paulsson Margareta (1986), Entreprenörskapets kulturella bakgrund. _ En diskussion av företagartraditionens och livsformers betydelse. Teoksessa Håkan Bohman, Katarina Pousette (ed.) Konferensdokumentation småföretags-forskning i tiden. IV Nordiska forskningskonferensen om småföretag. 4-6 Juni 1986 Umeå/Vasa.

Pinder Craig C. (1984), Work Motivation, Theory, Issues, and Applications. Glenview, Illinois.

Robbins Stephen P. (1983), Organizational Behavior: Concepts, Controversies and Applications, 2nd ed. Englewood Cliffs N.J. USA.

Scheinberg Sari, MacMillan Ian C. (1988), An 11 Country Study of Motivations to Start A Business. In Kirchhof Bruce A., Long Wayne A., McMullan W. Ed, Vesper Karl H., Wetzel Willian E. Jr. (eds.), Frontiers of Entrepreneurship Research. Wellesley Massachusetts 1988.

Sexton Donald L., Bowman Nancy B. (1983), Comparative Entrepreneurship Characteristics of Students: Preliminary Results. In Hornaday John. A., Timmons Jeffry A., Vesper Karl H. (eds.) Frontiers of Entrepreneurship Research. Wellesley Massachusetts 1983.

Shapero Albert, Sokol Lisa (1982), The Social Dimensions of Entrepreneurship. In Kent C. A., Sexton D. L., Vesper K. H. 1982 Encyclopedia of Entrepreneurship. Prentice-Hall. 72-90.

Stanworth M.J.K. - Curran J. (1977), Management Motivation in the Smaller Business. Farnborough.

Stanworth John, Stanworth Celia, Granger Bill, Blyth Stephanie (1989), Who Becomes an Entrepreneur? International Small Business Journal 1989:Oct-Dec, 11-22.

Staw Barry M. (1985), Intrinsic and Extrinsic Motivation. In Tosi H.L. and Hamner (eds.), Organizational Behavior and Management: A Contingency Approach. Columbus, Ohio.

Vroom Victor H. (1964), Work and Motivation. New York.

Weiner Bernard (1972), Theories of Motivation, From Mechanism to Cognition. Chicago.

4 Venture teams start-ups: An undiscovered field of research

Detlef Müller-Böling

The importance of venture teams

Success or no success - that is the question in economics for managers as well as for entrepreneurs, for single fighters as well as for venture teams. Therefore entrepreneurial success and its requirements are of great importance in scientific research, too. In several research projects scientists analyze it, but they take into account only very factors of influence.

Most stressed of these factors is the new entrepreneur as a *person*. Besides the scientists refer to *economic factors* concerning the enterprise and to *government aid* (Müller-Böling/Klandt 1989: 143 f.). All these single projects lack a connecting *theory of entrepreneurial success* (Picot et al. 1989: 1). Müller-Böling stresses the importance of a *conceptional framework* as a requirement for the development of a scientific theory (Müller-Böling 1984: 17 f.).

Which object is to choose for scientific research - this question is the first problem a scientist has to solve - and it is an important one, because the object might influence the results seriously. In economics *venture teams* are neglected or even ignored in the most cases. And that in spite of the fact that the number of venture teams - especially in technical branches of business - is increasing steadily (Albach/Hunsdiek 1987: 563 f.). But this fact contradicts traditional economic theory, which does not include venture teams. Perhaps they are ignored for that reason.

The entrepreneur as 'single fighter' - described by Schumpeter

Schumpeter founded economic theory of the entrepreneur as it is today. But that was already in 1926. He defined entrepreneurs as 'subjects of economic business, who are the active elements and push through new combinations.' (Schumpeter 1926: 111; translated by Müller-Böling) He excludes teamwork for the real entrepreneur of his definition. For such a person *power* is as important as the will to win and the possibility of being creative himself (Schumpeter 1926: 138). It sounds absurd that someone should share these possibilities. The entrepreneur does not want to share or to work in a team, he fights alone, and he likes it. And Schumpeter is of the opinion that the entrepreneur has to fight, because he has to defend his innovations against legal, political and - last but not least - social sanctions (Schumpeter 1926: 126). Lack of understanding of all the others is the basis of his work, he does not expect and he does not need partners or support of a team. So far Schumpeters theory.

Examples of well-known and successful venture teams in Germany

In reality there are some entrepreneurs of the type described by Schumpeter of course. But there is an equal number of enterprises that was started by two or more founders or was taken over by a team later.

For Schumpeter 'the functions of inventor or engineer and of entrepreneur are separated' (Schumpeter 1926: 129; translated by Müller-Böling). According to his theory only the real entrepreneur is of any importance for national economy. But meanwhile reality proved him wrong, because there are many successful enterprises that were started by teams, in which the partners were able to cooperate and to complement one another.

Some of the examples stem from the American high-tech-market of the last 40 years. Names as Hewlett-Packard, Intel or Apple are well-known all over the world and were started by venture teams. In Germany some well-known brands also were invented by team-start-ups. *Carl Benz* for example went bankrupt twice before he cooperated with marketing-expert *Julius Ganß* and businessman *Friedrich von Fischer* successfully (Simsa 1987: 28 f.).

Engineer *Wilhelm Maybach* and entrepreneur *Gottlieb Daimler* led the *Daimler-Motor-Society* to success (Simsa 1987: 21 f.). And a similar venture team started *Fichtel und Sachs*, one of the most important enterprises in ball-bearing industry (Beck 1987: 280 f.).

Family start-ups also proved successful in Germany. *Kaiser's Kaffeegeschäft*, *Melitta* and *Adidas* were started in such a way. *Melitta* and *Hugo Bentz* were married (Block 1987: 227 f.), and so were the founders of Kaiser's *Wilhelm* and *Louise Schmitz* (Ueffing 1987: 161 f.) as well as *Adi* and *Käthe Dassler* (Kaiser 1987: 82 f.).

Gerhard Dannemann was looking for a partner, who already produced cigars. And he found *Auguste Blase* (Hill 1987: 98 f.). And very well-known German enterprises such as *Haribo* in sugar confectionary industry (Rieck 1987: 201 f.) or tailor *Hugo Boss* (Ingersoll 1987: 55 f.) were started by one traditional entrepreneur, but are now led by a venture team.

These examples are not new. Most of the enterprises mentioned were started in the 19th century. Venture teams are not at all a new phenomenon in connection with business start-ups. And it is an interesting one for scientific research.

Conceptional framework for venture team start-ups

Most of scientists in economics do not see the necessity of research in this field of venture team start-ups. The results published in Germany are few and they are isolated. It is not possible yet to integrate them in a *conceptional framework*, which makes possible a theoretical basis.

During the following chapters the attempt is started to develop such a conceptional framework, which can be discussed afterwards. It is specially developed for venture team start-ups. Another conceptional framework concerning start-ups as a whole has been presented before (Müller-Böling/Klandt 1989).

Entrepreneurial success depends of four factors of influence:

* macro-social environment
* person and partner
* business planning
* start-up firm

Macro-social environment

A new enterprise has to be judged in two different contexts. On the one hand one has to consider the branch, in which it wants to work, the possibilities of training, business cycles, new technologies and public opinion concerning business start-ups as a whole. These factors belong to the general context of the start-up (Müller-Böling/Klandt 1989: 155 f.).

On the other hand the more special infrastructure of the start-up has to be examined. Which persons or institutions help the new entrepreneur starting his enterprise? Are there consultants, banker or venture capitalists to aid him? Does government aid exist, which supports the founder financially? Do scientists deliver results of research, that might prove helpful? The answers to these questions influence success or failure of the new enterprise.

Person and partner

For one single founder a personal theory of business start-ups does already exist. The most important work in this field was published by Klandt in 1984. He describes the influence of character and situation of the new entrepreneur on success or failure of his enterprise. For venture teams a similar theory does not exist yet, but it is possible to deduce it from Klandt's results.

Figure 1
Conceptional framework for venture team start-ups

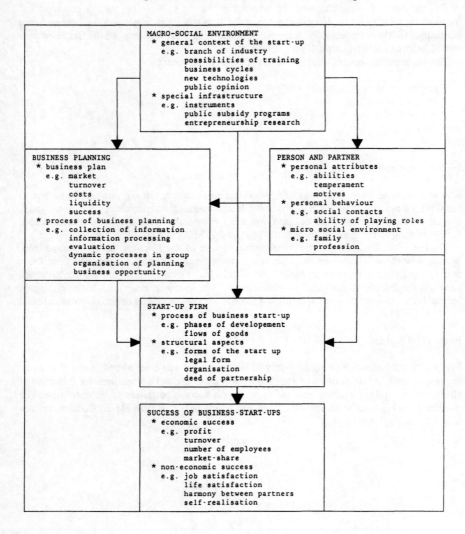

In this context one has to analyze personal attributes such as abilities, temperament and motives as well as personal behaviour for example during social contacts or the ability and necessity of playing roles (Müller-Böling/Klandt 1989: 158 f.).

But the founder does not live as a single or isolated person. Micro-social contacts such as in family, with friends or colleagues play an important role for a person. And so they influence the success of a new enterprise. 'The term 'social' must be applied to all social interaction and in that way refers to the special field of economic integration. 'Micro' means that only a part of the complete social surrounding is sorted out, which is important for one single person or a group in society. (...) Specific situations in family or at work are typical of micro-social surroundings.' (Klandt 1984: 48; translated by Müller-Böling)

Concerning venture teams personal attributes must not be examined isolated for one single individual. Combinations of attributes in the venture team are of even greater importance. Which of these combined attributes have any influence upon economic success? This question is interesting for further research in this part of the conceptional framework presented here.

Business planning

According to consultants as well as financiers and scientists business plans are one of the most important factors of influence upon economic success. But this opinion is not proved yet in economics. Business plans in venture team start-ups afford special chances and problems. On the one hand it is possible that the plan is discussed intensely and is of greater quality therefore. On the other hand discussion might be so intense that no or no good plan can be made at all.

So there are two aspects of business plans that have to be discussed. First research concentrates upon the *business plan as such*. The plans made for venture team start-ups are not different from that made for enterprises with only one entrepreneur (Müller-Böling/Graf 1988: 615 f.). The components are just the same, one can find questions of market structure and costs as well as liquidity and success plans.

Second the *process* of developing a business plan might be extremely different in venture teams. One has to consider dynamic processes in group that influence the collection of information as well as the working on them or their evaluation. Closely connected are the organization and the kind of work necessary for making a plan. The idea, what sort of enterprise the new entrepreneur wants to start, is important in this context, too. Despite it is examined only seldom, even for single entrepreneurs (Picot et al. 1989: 53).

Start-up firm

Even according the enterprise as such one can distinguish processual and structural aspects of research (Müller-Böling/Klandt 1989). Concerning the process of the start-up *steps of development* or *flows of goods and services* have to be examined. In this context one has to distinguish between real goods such as products or services, nominal goods (finances) or information goods (data, accountancy).

Structural aspects are different forms of start-ups, for example a full-time engagement of the entrepreneur in his business start-up versus a part-time engagement, independent enterprises versus dependent foundations or e.g. the form of management-buy outs. Besides one has to consider different legal forms in connection with the start-up in a venture team or the organization of the enterprise, that means division of labour and responsibility between the partners. Picot et al. (1989: 53) stress that one has to judge contracts with others as well as arrangements inside the enterprise.

Success of business start-ups

According to the conceptional framework discussed here success depends on all the other factors mentioned before. On the one hand there is the economic success of an enterprise, to be seen from profit, turnover, number of employees or market-share. On the other hand the phenomenon of non-economic, subjective success of the entrepreneur has to be analyzed. Factors like job or life satisfaction, harmony between the partners or the possibility of self-realization have to be judged in this context (Müller-Böling/Klandt 1989: 160f.)

Some empirical results concerning venture team start-ups

In Germany special empirical analysis of venture team start-ups do not exist. There are only some works that do *partly* refer to venture teams:

Klandt/Kirschbaum (1985): Klandt and Kirschbaum studied start-up and development strategies of young software firms. They questioned 25 business start-ups and addionally used data of 16 cases of an analysis of a market research institute. The managers or partners of the start-ups were interviewed in face-to-face interviews based on an interview guide and after one year additionally by a questionnaire.

Albach/Hunsdiek (1987) and Hunsdiek (1987): Start-ups in technical branches are central in the work of Albach and Hunsdiek, because these branches are of great importance concerning structure and development of national economy. They studied 67 enterprises in West Germany founded at the end of the seventies and in the beginning of the eighties. Albach and Hunsdiek were supported by enterprise centres, consultants and incorporated firms. The scientists used a questionnaire with open questions as well as with closed.

Kulicke (1987): Enterprises in technical branches were analyzed by Kulicke as well. She used a structured questionnaire and questioned 83 entrepreneurs. The start-ups analyzed by Kulicke were settled in industry-branches with high growth founded after 1960.

Picot et al. (1989): Picot et al. questioned 53 founders of innovative enterprises. The scientists were supported by chambers of commerce, ministries of economy, and enterprise centres. The interviews were made in spring and summer of 1987. Picot et al. tried to examine as many branches as possible.

Müller-Böling (1989): Venture teams were theme of a specialized study made by students of business management at the University of Dortmund. On the one hand 31 interviews were made in 16 different enterprises. On the other hand groups of students were observed, which played a management business game simulating a start-up realistically. The groups observed consisted each of a student of information science, of mechanical engineering and of economics.

According to the conceptional framework presented before the results of these four examinations are summarized on the following pages.

Only in the study of Müller-Böling information are given about the infrastructure of start-ups such as finances and consultants:

Finances: In half of the enterprises finances are judged as the most serious problem in context with start-ups (Falkenhagen 1989: 13 f.). Another half knows the need of capital stock correctly even in the beginning. Concerning government aid 66 percent of the interview-partners are of the opinion that venture teams are preferred (Falkenhagen 1989: 17 f.). So they are in contact with their bank.

Consultants: Consultants specialized for start-ups are consulted only in very few cases. Compared with that banker, private friends and wedded partners are judged very helpful (Falkenhagen 1989: 22 f.). On the contrary parents, business partners and consultants in chambers of commerce seem not very helpful to the entrepreneurs questioned. No help is needed in finding the idea, what sort of enterprise to start (0 percent), in conceptioning the enterprise (33 percent), or in finding the ideal team (7 percent) (Falkenhagen 1989: 25 f.).

Person and partner

Personal abilities: Most of the partners in a venture team meet each other at work (97 percent) (Neumann 1989: 35 f.). Teams arranged by agencies play no important role. Only 10 percent of the founders are women, most of them are between 26 and 40 years old (77,4 percent) (Neumann 1989: 27 f.) - the same age as in start-ups of one single entrepreneur. 62,5 percent of the entrepreneurs questioned worked in the branch of their enterprise before. In most of the cases entrepreneurs try a start-up only once, 19 percent tried it twice or even more often.

58 percent went to colleges or universities, only 20 percent of the entrepreneurs left school after 10 years (Neumann 1989: 28). Mostly one member of a venture team has got a degree, the others have not. High and low qualification working together - this constellation is very typical of venture teams. Missing qualification for example in economics is compensated in a team working together (Albach/Hunsdiek 1987: 568).

Picot et al. (1989: 99) also stress the importance of complementing and supporting one another in a venture team. The know-how necessary for entrepreneurial success should be spread between the partners to achieve success. 'Theoretically one founder should fulfil all functions necessary for the enterprise: the function of co-ordinating information (finding and developing of ideas) as well as the functions of co-ordinating resources and markets. In practice the main emphasis often is found in one field, mostly in the technical one. (...) Therefore supplementing of abilities is necessary, most likely in the person of a partner, whose abilities lie in other fields of entrepreneurial necessities.' (Picot et al. 1989: 259; translated by Müller-Böling)

Venture teams consist of specialized partners, single entrepreneurs have a wider range of experience in different functions of the enterprise (Kulicke 1987: 146 f.).

Micro-social surroundings: Most of the new entrepreneurs start their enterprise without concrete help of friends or relatives. But these persons support the founders in another way: they admire their initiative (Neumann 1989: 33 f.). The more other entrepreneurs are known in private contacts the more positive the attitude of friends and relatives is.

Business planning

Ideas for a new enterprise are very stable. 94 percent of the new enterprises follow the first idea (Staude 1989: 52 f.). More time is necessary to make a business plan in a team than by a single entrepreneur. But the partners believe their plan to be of higher quality (Staude 1989: 54 f.).

Looking at the start-ups in the management business game the group found out that during the first period after the start-up all entrepreneurs have to plan most intensely, because each decision is new for the team and many of them are decisions important for all the following periods (Wittram 1989: 129 f.).

Besides the analysis of decisions made in the periods before is important. Most teams discuss objective and functional and avoid emotional quarrels. After a failure longer discussions follow but the number of themes discussed decreases because the teams use their faults made before for learning (Wittram 1989: 126 f.). All the decisions are made in team, none of the partners becomes a specialist for one field or the other.

Start-up firm

Form of new enterprise: Venture team start-up.

In technical branches the trend leads to more venture team start-ups. Hunsdiek proofs a high number of venture teams in this field, and besides he found out that the teams themselves grow in number. 'From 1962 to 1983 the number of partners in one enterprise was 1,7, in 1984/85 it grew up to 2,2.' (Hunsdiek 1987: 55; translated by Müller-Böling)

A similar effect Müller-Böling found out. Only 56 percent of the venture teams consist of two partners. A quarter starts the enterprise with three, 19 percent with four partners (Neumann 1989: 34 f.).The same results Kulicke found out: 'This tendency one can consider since 1974. 64,7 percent of the 34 enterprises founded before 1974 were started by one single entrepreneur. 66,7 percent of the younger enterprises were founded by a venture team.' (Kulicke 1987: 108; translated by Müller-Böling) Picot et al. (1989: 98 f.) found out that more than half of the entrepreneurs questioned by his team started their enterprise with one, two, three or more partners.

Teamwork: Mostly conflicts between partners are solved with the help of discussions, though serious conflicts are quite seldom. Problems between the partners are more probable in teams with great differences of age between the partners (Diegmann 1989: 65).

Success of business start-ups

Economic dimension: Especially in technical branches of industry venture team start-ups are more successful in tendency. Albach/Hunsdiek (1987: 577) found out that 43 percent of the venture teams are successful whereas only 20 percent of the single entrepreneurs have similar success.

In the analysis of Picot et al. (1989: 259) 63 percent of venture teams reach the group of very successful enterprises. On the contrary only 38 percent of the single entrepreneurs reach this group. Klandt/Kirschbaum (1985: 85) also differentiated two extreme groups of success (terciles). Five of 13 venture team start-ups belong to the higher group whereas only two of 11 single entrepreneurs reach this group.

One requirement for such a success are heterogeneous teams, where knowledge is intensed and spread, not multiplied.

According to Kulicke (1987: 269) no interdependency between the pure number of partners and entrepreneurial success does exist. 'The variable number of team-members cannot explain profits in the enterprises examined.' The number of partners cannot positively influence growth. The combination of qualification matters.

Klandt/Kirschbaum (1985: 85,86) find references for a correlation between division of responsibilities and the success of the business start-up. Five of seven successful start-ups divide responsibilities for distribution and production, but only one of seven unsuccessful enterprises has this division.

In the management business game harmony in group is decisive for success (according to profits in the end of all game periods). (Meyer 1989: 146 f.) Recognition of problems and intense discussion influence success positively. Short discussion of the decision concerning the location of the enterprise prevent success as well as stressing such activities as analyzing and predicting in comparison to economic problems. Failing teams need more time to decide and therefore had less time for the many decisions necessary in a successful enterprise (Meyer 1989: 157 f.).

Non-economic dimension: The entrepreneurs questioned told the team of Müller-Böling their own non-economic aims, they planned to achieve with the start-up. Their contentedness with these aims is above-average. Even this contentedness is connected with the combination of different qualifications in the venture team (Staude 1989: 48f.)

Requirements for research and training

This first and only small attempt to present the scientific results in the field of venture team start-ups shows how few these results still are. A more basical research is necessary, and it is necessary soon - not only because of the lack of knowledge, but also because of the serious lack of practical training for entrepreneurs.

Looking at the growing number of venture team start-ups and their increasing importance concerning management-buy outs an intense discussion about their pros and cons would be beneficial - as well as about requirements and obstacles.

References

Albach, Horst and Detlef Hunsdiek, (1987), 'Die Bedeutung von Unternehmensgründungen für die Anpassung der Wirtschaft an veränderte Rahmenbedingungen,' *Zeitschrift für Betriebswirtschaft*, 57. Jahrgang, 5/6, 562-579.

Beck, B., (1987), 'Sachs - Im Vorwärtsgang zu großen Zielen,' in *Die Person hinter dem Produkt. 40 Portraits erfolgreicher Unternehmer*, ed. Barbier, Hans D. and Fides Krause-Brewer, Bad Godesberg: Rentrop, 280-287.

Block, H.-J., (1987), 'Melitta - Eine Hausfrau als Unternehmerin,' in *Die Person hinter dem Produkt. 40 Portraits erfolgreicher Unternehmer*, ed. Barbier, Hans D. and Fides Krause-Brewer, Bad Godesberg: Rentrop, 227-232.

Diegmann, J., (1989), 'Unternehmung,' in *Partnerschaftsgründungen. Entwicklung und Ergebnisse einer empirischen Untersuchung*, ed. Müller-Böling, Detlef, bifego, Dortmund, 61-69.

Falkenhagen, E., (1989), 'Gründungsinfrastruktur,' in *Partnerschaftsgründungen. Entwicklung und Ergebnisse einer empirischen Untersuchung*, ed. Müller-Böling, Detlef, bifego, Dortmund, 13-26.

Hill, S., (1987), 'Dannemann - Ein Konterfei als internationale Marke,' in *Die Person hinter dem Produkt. 40 Portraits erfolgreicher Unternehmer*, ed. Barbier, Hans D. and Fides Krause-Brewer, Bad Godesberg: Rentrop, 98-102.

Hunsdiek, Detlef (1987), *Unternehmensgründung als Folgeinnovation. Struktur, Hemmnisse und Erfolgsbedingungen der Gründung industrieller, innovativer Unternehmen*. Stuttgart: Poeschel.

Ingersoll, R., (1987), ' Boss - Deutschlands Herausforderer der französischen und italienischen Herrenmode,' in *Die Person hinter dem Produkt. 40 Portraits erfolgreicher Unternehmer*, ed. Barbier, Hans D. and Fides Krause-Brewer, Bad Godesberg: Rentrop, 55-61.

Kaiser, U., (1987), 'adidas - Drei Streifen auf Erfolgskurs,' in *Die Person hinter dem Produkt. 40 Portraits erfolgreicher Unternehmer*, ed. Barbier, Hans D. and Fides Krause-Brewer, Bad Godesberg: Rentrop, 81-90.

Klandt, Heinz (1984), *Aktivität und Erfolg des Unternehmensgründers. Eine empirische Analyse unter Einbeziehung des mikrosozialen Umfeldes*. Bergisch-Gladbach: Eul.

Klandt, Heinz and Günther Kirschbaum (1985), *Software- und Systemhäuser: Strategien in der Gründungs- und Frühentwicklungsphase*. St. Augustin, GMD-Studien Nr.105

Kulicke, Marianne (1987), *Technologieorientierte Unternehmen in der Bundesrepublik Deutschland - eine empirische Untersuchung der Strukturbildungs- und Wachstumsphase von Neugründungen*. Frankfurt, Bern, New York: Lang.

Meyer, M., (1989), 'Person als abhängige Variable,' in *Partnerschaftsgründungen. Entwicklung und Ergebnisse einer empirischen Untersuchung*, ed. Müller-Böling, Detlef, bifego, Dortmund, 142-149.

Meyer, M., (1989), 'Entscheidungsobjekte als unabhängige Variable,' in *Partnerschaftsgründungen. Entwicklung und Ergebnisse einer empirischen Untersuchung*, ed. Müller-Böling, Detlef, bifego, Dortmund, 152-164.

Müller-Böling, Detlef (1984), 'Überlegungen zu Strategien der Gründungsforschung.' in *Unternehmungsgründung. Konfrontation von Forschung und Praxis. Festschrift für Norbert Szyperski*, ed. Klaus Nathusius, Heinz Klandt and Günter Kirschbaum, Bergisch Gladbach: Eul, 17-35.

Müller-Böling, Detlef and Helmut Graf, (1988), 'Planungsinstrumente für die Gründung von Unternehmen,' *WiSt - Wirtschaftswissenschaftliches Studium*, 17. Jahrgang, 615-619.

Müller-Böling, Detlef and Heinz Klandt (1989), 'Bezugsrahmen für die Gründungsforschung mit einigen empirischen Ergebnissen,' in *Entrepreneurship: Innovative Unternehmensgründung als Aufgabe*, ed. Norbert Szyperski and Paul Roth, Stuttgart: Poeschel, 143-170.

Neumann, U., (1989), 'Person und Partner,' in *Partnerschaftsgründungen. Entwicklung und Ergebnisse einer empirischen Untersuchung*, ed. Müller-Böling, Detlef, bifego, Dortmund,26-39.

Picot, Arnold, Ulf-Dieter Laub, and Dietram Schneider (1989), *Innovative Unternehmensgründungen. Eine ökonomisch-empirische Analyse*. Berlin et al.: Springer.

Rieck, M., (1987), 'Haribo - Der Weltstar aus Kessenich,' in *Die Person hinter dem Produkt. 40 Portraits erfolgreicher Unternehmer*, ed. Barbier, Hans D. and Fides Krause-Brewer, Bad Godesberg: Rentrop, 201-209.

Schumpeter, Joseph A., *Theorie der wirtschaftlichen Entwicklung. Eine Untersuchung über Unternehmergewinn, Kapital, Kredit, Zins und den Konjunkturzyklus*. 2. Auflage, München, Leipzig 1926: Duncker & Humblot.

Simsa, P., (1987), 'Daimler & Benz - Die Automobil-Pioniere,' in *Die Person hinter dem Produkt. 40 Portraits erfolgreicher Unternehmer*, ed. Barbier, Hans D. and Fides Krause-Brewer, Bad Godesberg: Rentrop, 20-31.

Staude, L., (1989), 'Erfolg,' in *Partnerschaftsgründungen. Entwicklung und Ergebnisse einer empirischen Untersuchung*, ed. Müller-Böling, Detlef, bifego, Dortmund, 40-51.

Staude, L., (1989), 'Gründungsplanung' in *Partnerschaftsgründungen. Entwicklung und Ergebnisse einer empirischen Untersuchung*, ed. Müller-Böling, Detlef, bifego, Dortmund, 52-61.

Trumpp, A., (1989), 'Läßt sich über die Analyse der Führer-Mitglieder-Beziehungen in einer Gruppe eine Aussage über den Erfolg treffen?,'in *Partnerschaftsgründungen. Entwicklung und Ergebnisse einer empirischen Untersuchung*, ed. Müller-Böling, Detlef, bifego, Dortmund, 165-174.

Ueffing, B., (1987), 'Kaiser - Am Anfang war der Kaffee,' in *Die Person hinter dem Produkt. 40 Portraits erfolgreicher Unternehmer*, ed. Barbier, Hans D. and Fides Krause-Brewer, Bad Godesberg: Rentrop, 161-168.

Wittram, A., (1989), 'Allgemeine gruppenunspezifische Auswertungen,' in *Partnerschaftsgründungen. Entwicklung und Ergebnisse einer empirischen Untersuchung*, ed. Müller-Böling, Detlef, bifego, Dortmund, 137-141.

Wittram, A., (1989), 'Entwicklung eines präzisierten Bezugsrahmens für die Beobachtung,' in *Partnerschaftsgründungen. Entwicklung und Ergebnisse einer empirischen Untersuchung*, ed. Müller-Böling, Detlef, bifego, Dortmund, 126-129.

5 Entrepreneurs' competitive definitions: Evidence from computer-software start-ups

Michael Levenhagen and Howard Thomas

Introduction

Entrepreneurship lacks a general theory (Wortman, 1987). Researchers have offered a few plausible explanations for the paucity of theory development. One, entrepreneurs and their ventures seem too diverse to categorize neatly (Gartner, 1985). Two, entrepreneurs and their ventures appear paradoxical when analyzed by traditional, organizational theory (Kao, 1989). Research has suggested that entrepreneurship may, by nature, be contradictory and contentious within traditional management contexts (Smith & Miner, 1983) and even industrially or organizationally destructive (Kets de Vries, 1985; Schumpeter, 1934). Both reasons confound theory development in entrepreneurship. Yet, it is theoretically intriguing that entrepreneurship has escaped categorization attempts (*cf:* Stevenson & Hameling, 1990). Indeed, the failure to typlify entrepreneurial behavior by over 20 years of research may well point to a distinguishing characteristic at a new level of analysis.

This paper argues for a cognitive level of analysis to explain the paradoxes, and it attempts to refocus entrepreneurship theoretically by adopting an unused framework drawn from sociology. It examines start-ups in an emergent, high-technology environment and suggests a set of cognitive and social activities by which entrepreneurs create technological start-ups. After generating a series of research conjectures, this paper reports findings from an exploratory, qualitative investigation. It ends with discussion and recommendations for further research.

A switch in organization-theory assumptions

Traditional, microeconomic assumptions have been seriously questioned by Herbert Simon's (1976) observations of bounded-rationality constraints. This has led Simon and others to investigate cognitive models which address the heuristic processes of individuals' problem-solving, the analyses of problem spaces, and information processes. In extending Simon's views, this article also continues the work of past researchers who have implied that managers of start-ups may adopt higher-order objectives than profit maximization assumed by classical economics. Some researchers have proposed that entrepreneurs have different, work aspirations during the evolution of new ventures (LaFuente & Salas, 1989), and others note that entrepreneurs seek freedom and autonomy and are driven from traditional, managerial settings by discontent (Gartner, Mitchell, & Vesper, 1989; Dubini, 1989; Sexton & Bowman, 1985; Kirp & Rice, 1985). These researchers imply different identification processes for entrepreneurs as they create and manage the conduct of their start-up organizations.

According to traditional, organizational theory, organizations use group-identification processes in important, competitive ways. They communicate values, beliefs, and goals in persuasive manners by identifying with internal and external others (Burke, 1967; Festinger, 1954). Internally, organizations create and then identify with their corporate purposes and cultures through articulations, persuasions, and manipulations of agendas and symbolic activities (Barnard, 1938; Bennis & Nanus, 1985; Conger, 1991; March & Simon, 1958; Pondy, Frost, Morgan, & Dandridge, 1983; Schein, 1985). They also identify with competitors by comparing themselves to other organizations attributionally (Aldrich, McKelvey, & Ulrich, 1984; DiMaggio & Powell, 1983; Hannan & Freeman, 1977). Managerial decision makers compare themselves psychologically with identifiably similar groups when evaluating competitive alternatives in terms of their decisions' consequences

. . . by selecting particular values, particular items of empirical knowledge, and particular behavioral alternatives for consideration, to the exclusion of other values, other knowledge, and other possibilities [Simon, 1976:210].

Yet, strategy theorists stipulate that organizations also need to differentiate themselves (Abell, 1980; Albert & Whetten, 1985) from others in desirable ways to manage their competitive domains and to keep others from imitating their strategies (Aldrich, 1979; McGee & Thomas, 1986; Porter, 1979; Rumelt, 1984).

These external, group-identification dynamics are effective, competitive heuristics when markets are well-defined. Firms may objectively determine their competitors' identities and strategies through competitive analyses (Andrews, 1971; Porter, 1980). They can objectively determine whether their offerings match buyers' demand within product markets advantageously, vis-a-vis their competitors' abilities and offerings. In sum, firms should match distinctive, organizational competencies (Penrose, 1959; Prahalad & Hamel, 1990) to opportunities in product markets beyond those of their competitors for sustainable, competitive advantage (Porter, 1980; Rumelt, 1984).

A question arises, however, as to the accuracy of managerial perceptions about market structures and about one's own firm's and competitors' resources, offerings, and dynamic capabilities. When markets are emergent or rapidly changing, due to technological innovation and revolution (Abernathy & Clark, 1985; Anderson & Tushman, 1990; Foster, 1986; Pavitt, 1986; Tushman & Anderson, 1986; Tushman & Romanelli, 1985), then there may be no obvious, competitive-group standard or reference point with which to identify, compare, or imitate. There may be little consensus about competitive definitions (i.e., a market's structure, the boundaries of a market, the list of competitors, the important stakeholders who establish a competitive environment, or the production functions of firms).

Especially in high-velocity, technological environments (Eisenhardt, 1989), there may be many things managers do not know--the markets' choices of technological designs (Arthur, 1989), the final structures of the markets, or the competitive rules of the games--because, in part, the stakeholders in markets have not made unanimous or clear choices. Emergent, technological markets may appear too unclear and ambiguous for external, objective definition.

From an entrepreneur's perspective, however, quite the opposite may be true. Entrepreneurs' perceptions of competition in emergent, technological environments may not reflect competitive-definition ambiguities apparent to external observers. Given beliefs in their competitive definitions, deep commitments to their ventures, and drives for freedom and autonomy referred to by the entrepreneurship researchers, entrepreneurs' perceptions of markets and competition may seem quite clear and unambiguous. The competitive-definition differences between that of external observers and that of entrepreneurs or between different, market stakeholders may be dependent upon how and what bases competitive definitions are formulated (*cf:* Lyles & Mitroff, 1980).

Anti-organizational theory & entrepreneurship

Theoretically relevant to this study, Burrell and Morgan (1979) present a 2 x 2 classification system of organizational theory dependent upon the epistemological and sociological assumptions economic actors and researchers use. The sociological assumptions range from regulation to radical change, and the epistemological assumptions range from objective to subjective.

According to Burrell & Morgan, most organization studies are oriented to an objective-epistemology / regulatory-sociology perspective. By this perspective, organizations and their environments are objectively measurable phenomena, and status quos are regulated intra- and inter-organizationally through inertia and organizational learning dynamics (*cf:* Nelson & Winter, 1982).

Figure 1
The main schools of organizational analysis (Burrell, G., & Morgan, G., (1979),
Sociological paradigms and organisational analysis, Portsmouth NH:
Heinemann, p. 30.)

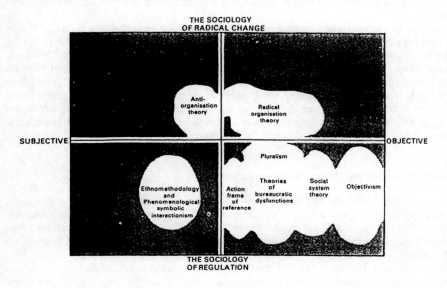

The second perspective (subjective epistemology / regulatory sociology) provides a more interpretive viewpoint (e.g., ethnographies, cognitive investigations). It has been used recently by organization behaviorists (Barley, 1983; Daft & Weick, 1985; Kiesler & Sproull, 1982; Ranson, Hinings, & Greenwood, 1980; Weick, 1979) and strategy researchers (Dutton & Jackson, 1987; Smircich & Stubbart, 1985; Porac & Thomas, 1990; Porac, Thomas, & Baden-Fuller, 1989). Most interpretive studies have applied to more mature or stable environments. Equilibria and organizational status-quos are still organizational objectives, but the environments and organizations are less epistemologically objective and the result of social-construction processes (Berger & Luckman, 1967).

Little research has suggested use of the third perspective (subjective epistemology / radical-change sociology). According to Burrell & Morgan, no organizational theory has been based upon these assumptions, but if there were, then it would have to amount to an 'anti-organizational theory.' Burrell & Morgan deduced that for 'anti-organizationists,' organizations would be perceived as especially cognitive phenomena. Such actors would be oriented to non-incremental/radical-change, social behaviors. Anti-organizationalists would perceive status-quo organizations as psychic prisons which subordinate important essentials of human nature (Burrell & Morgan, 1979)[1].

Anti-organizational theory may be a useful analytical framework to apply to entrepreneurial activity in emergent, technological environments. If autonomy and freedom are indeed important underlying values for entrepreneurs, then anti-organizational theory may suggest that entrepreneurs are attracted to environments which can accomodate multiple or innovative, competitive definitions--where the degrees of freedom are the greatest. Objectively ambiguous environments found in emergent markets may provide suitable settings for successful enactments of innovative, competitive behaviors--viz., for new competitive definitions as entrepreneurial ventures. The degrees of freedom increase still further if emergent markets are based upon competing technologies because market structures would await technical establishment (*cf:* Anderson & Tushman, 1990; Klepper & Graddy, 1990).

Theoretical conjectures about high-technology start-ups

If anti-organizational theory were to describe the formulation of innovative, competitive definitions by start-ups in emergent, high-technology markets, then a number of conjectures can be proposed and empirically explored [2]. The following sections offer conjectures about the objectives of high-technology entrepreneurs, their social-validation processes for innovative, competitive behaviors, the nature of their competitive definitions, and a psychological focus of their activities. A methodology for empirical exploration is later proposed. Exploratory findings are then reported, theoretically explicated, and discussed.

Conjecture 1: Entrepreneurs re-conceptualize competitive definitions

In emergent, technological environments, entrepreneurs are operating cognitively on the edge of what they do not know. Beyond certain technological standards (if they exist), entrepreneurs will believe they have no strong, reference points or reference groups to observe in order to make sense of competitively ambiguous or technologically uncertain environments. For truly innovative concepts, there are none. Or, entrepreneurs ignore 'accepted' competitive definitions because they think they are poorly conceived. Instead of imitation, entrepreneurs will construct competitive and technological solutions exclusive of other interpretations, all the more so because innovative solutions are created by the entrepreneurs themselves (Berger & Luckman, 1967; *cf:* Staw, 1980).

This deep, inward focus on personally constructed, competitive definitions will tend to blind entrepreneurs to more externally oriented functions of marketing and competitive analyses. Yet, this may be a positive factor in start-up activity. Blind adherence to a creative, competitive definition may make entrepreneurs particularly determined and may provide powerful drives and directions for their concepts' enactments. Intense determination in a mission is crucial in initial phases of creativity processes (Simon, 1985; Wallas, 1926).

Thus, the first conjecture states that entrepreneurs in emergent, high-technology markets will create their own competitive and technological definitions, discounting more status-quo, competitive definitions. Entrepreneurial visions transcend traditional, competitive definitions and posit new orders not only for a firm but for the structure of a market in which it will reside.

The most opportunistic and accommodating environment for entrepreneurs would be environments which offer the greatest degree of freedom for cognitive construction and in-

71

terpretation (Weick, 1979), where 'meaning' is most problematic and where rules of competition and technological standards are formative (*cf:* Anderson & Tushman, 1990; Klepper & Graddy, 1990). Competitive environments become more 'objective' as rules and standards of competition and technology evolve (Abernathy & Clark, 1985; Tushman & Romanelli, 1985), are consensually established (Huff, 1982; Spender, 1980), and imitatively followed by market stakeholders throughout value chains (Porac *et. al.*, 1989).

Conjecture 2: Activities initially focus on technology, not competition

Especially ambiguous environments tend to focus actors' attentions to micro-levelled actions. In stable (thus, more consensually established) markets, competitive definitions do not change radically. The markets' structures, the lists of competitors and stakeholders, the production functions, etc. change only incrementally as markets evolve. Thus, competitive responsiveness can be maintained at much higher, strategic levels because micro-levelled tasks are believed solved and organizational routines clearly established. In stable environments, it is easier to keep track of positionings of competitors, their strategies, and stakeholders.

When entrepreneurs are attempting to enact new, technological and competitive definitions, then actors focus on short-term, micro-levelled actions, and they become inflexible to broader, environmental information (Vallacher & Wegner, 1987). New organizations in emergent, technological markets have a tendency to focus exclusively on technological matters. Those tasks are the most basic, immediate, and demanding tasks at hand, and usually technical expertise are the entrepreneurs' strongest skill sets. They are also the most comforting and immediately satisfiable, for they help to alleviate the stress of working in unknown domains (McCaskey, 1982).   Moreover, technological activities contribute most fundamentally to the enactment of high-technology product/service innovations. They are the central elements all other functions support. This leads to the second conjecture: start-up entrepreneurs in emergent, technological environments will tend to emphasize micro-levelled, technological tasks over competitive tasks.

Unlike their technological definitions, however, entrepreneurs' competitive definitions are usually thought safe and defensible because entrepreneurs believe there are no 'similar others.' Competition, it may be believed, need not be considered. High-technology entrepreneurs starting-up may well believe they have conceptualized competitive definitions for new products, services, and markets. (What real competition can there be?) The organization's focus becomes 'getting the technology right.' Surely, success will follow.

Conjecture 3: Profit maximization objectives are not paramount

An anti-organizational perspective on entrepreneurial behavior implies different objectives for actors who start-up high-tech organizations. Profit maximization will not be a paramount motivation for high-technology start-ups. At best, profit maximization will be viewed as a means (rather than an end) to the achievement of more paramount objectives.

As anti-organizationalists, entrepreneurs will be repulsed from previous employers because previous employers will not allow them to exercise or achieve a full realization of their worth, of non-traditional values or of some innovative, competitive definition. Past employers' organizations will be thought of as psychic prisons which constrain their creativity and freedom. Entrepreneurs' reasons for leaving existing employment and starting-up new organizations will emphasize concepts like creativity, idealism, non-conformity, freedom, work aspirations, and novelty. Certainly these are more anti-status-quo objectives in contrast to more traditional, economic assumptions. It is not that profit is not attractive; it is that profit-maximization is *not as attractive* as other intrinsic values. An entrepreneurial organization serves new or different values than more established organizations serve.

Serving other values and objectives may, however, only apply to start-up activities. Later, institutionalization (DiMaggio & Powell, 1983; Hannan & Freeman, 1977) and evolving, standardizing, competitive pressures to conform to more homogeneous demand from stakeholders (buyers, suppliers, competitors--Porter, 1980) become more evident.

Emergent, technological markets eventually stabilize. Closing strategic windows and shakeouts signal markets' choices of technological designs and signal the consensual establishment of value chains, competitive recipes, and stakeholder arrangements (Anderson & Tushman, 1990; Klepper & Graddy, 1990). After those developments, entrepreneurs are no longer in the same position to remain anti-organizationalists. Indeed, they cannot unless they can consensually sell new, competitive or technological innovations (Levenhagen, Porac, & Thomas, 1990). Market-stakeholder arrangements, defined interactively through similar and frequent transactions and cognitive consensus (Porac *et. al.*, 1989), will punish firms using aberrant, competitive definitions by withdrawing available resources (Pfeffer & Salancik, 1978). Profit-maximization objectives will then become more paramount objectives. One of the few externally observable and measureable differences between similarly constructed firms in an established market are profits (Lippman & Rumelt, 1982).

Conjecture 4: Entrepreneurs' validation occurs through personal networking

Status-quo organizations will seem bureaucratic, uninvolved, and uncaring to entrepreneurs, especially in regards to their innovative, technological or competitive definitions (Burgelman, 1985). Since entrepreneurs discount traditional, organizational values in initial stages of start-up, existing status-quo organizations will not be taken seriously as referencepoints because they do not operate upon the same premises. Instead, entrepreneurs will reinforce their own anti-organizational values through personal networking with other entrepreneurs because they, too, need some kind of group-identification validation (Festinger, 1954).

Entrepreneurs will need and tend to validate their values of creativity, idealism, freedom, aspirations, and self-actualization with each other through peer relationships, and these personal networks will transcend market boundaries and competition. Hence, the fourth conjecture proposes that entrepreneurs will tend to recognize other entrepreneurs as legitimate and worthy of their positive regard. Personal networking with other entrepreneurs will be pervasive as means for personal and organizational, external validation.

Moreover, personal networking will assist in technological, knowledge diffusion in dynamic, ill-structured environments. As well, high levels of personal networking may encourage an environmental fluidity marked by inter-changing competitiveness and cooperation (competitor yesterday, supplier today, buyer tomorrow), incestuous inbreeding, and spin-offs of personnel. In these kinds of markets, technological knowledge and expertise are strategically significant assets (Wernerfelt, 1984; Dierickx & Cool, 1989).

Yet personal networking does not necessarily imply that high-technology entrepreneurs will initially imitate one another in product or organizational development. Emergent markets may be consensually ambiguous enough to accommodate a number of different competitive and technological interpretations (Bijker, Hughes, & Pinch, 1987).

Research methodology

In framing research which addresses cognitive orientations towards radical change, an interpretive method is an appropriate vehicle for investigating start-ups' competitive-definition processes. Some current researchers use interpretive methodologies to expose cognitive processes in the context of strategic change. Porac & Thomas (1990) suggest the use of interviews in eliciting cognitive taxonomies of competitive environments in order to identify categorizations of niches, strategic-groups, or industry boundaries. Others (Sandberg, Schweiger, & Hofer, 1988) have used verbal protocols to construct cognitive maps of venture capitalists' business-proposal, evaluation processes.

An interpretive methodology assumes: 1) that activities and organizational structures depend upon micro-momentary actions, 2) that such actions are dependent upon information-processing of cue perception and interpretation--externalized to concrete activities, 3) that interpretation of 'meanings' is problematic and must be constructed by actors, and 4) that actors possess the capabilities to verbalize their interpretations (Porac et. al., 1989). Cognitive methodologies assume that external, task environments are objective, that actors select and construct problem spaces to represent task environments, and that they use elementary information processes to generate solutions (Bromiley, 1981). Emergent, high-technology markets, however, may offer few externally consistent cues for the formation of entrepreneurs' competitive definitions. Nonetheless, cognitive methodologies can elicit actors' perceptions, which can be used in the aggregate to infer the perceptual nature of competitive definitions.

Testing these conjectures entails questioning entrepreneurs retrospectively about their start-up activities and competitive definitions. This method, however, may not be reliable, and great care must be undertaken in research designs. As noted by Ericsson & Simon (1984) and Nisbett & Wilson (1977), human respondents are remarkably adept at providing an infinite number of plausible explanations to almost any set of data or situation. Respondents can recall salient events from long-term memory and thread simpler, more consistent, and favorable representations than they would if protocols were undertaken during task activities (Schwenk, 1985). Yet, a number of triangulation methods may make verbal explanations as data somewhat more reliable and meaningful (Schwenk, 1985)--albeit more complicated. Verbal explanations can be compared within a group of similar actors if all provide evidence of similar behaviors (e.g., starting a business). Even though each member may construct their own story, stories which 'hang together' with one another may be psychologically confirmatory and interesting to researchers operating from interpretive, epistemological assumptions. Verifications can be sought by asking interviewees to summarize in brief lists the major factors which would lead identical actors to similar behaviors. Researchers can also develop a process of negotiating amendments of findings with the interviewees (Harre, 1980; Harre & Secord, 1973) and uninvolved practitioners.

The research reported here followed these guidelines. In semi-structured interviews, an interviewer focused on perceptually important events, recorded key noun and verb phrases, and requested dates and locations of events. The interviews were compared, common eventsaggregated, and theoretical understandings developed. The research as reported here was then drafted. It was verified for reasonableness with an external expert--namely, an ex-Big 12, accounting director with consulting experience particularly in small and mid-sized firms. All entrepreneurs received a copy of the draft of this report and approved it without amendment.

The sample was a local, cross-sectional group of entrepreneurs in the software-development industry. Software is an emergent, technological environment (Ashe, Jowett, McGee, & Thomas, 1986), and software-product development may require extensive cognitive skills and allow high degrees of freedom in its development (AEA, 1990). A snowball, sampling (ethnological) methodology was used to test the networking conjecture. Lists of other software entrepreneurs were supplied by the entrepreneurs after each interview. The research was limited by geography (within 20 miles of a large research university in the Midwest U.S.), time, and support. A total of thirteen software entrepreneurs (about 65% of the local population) were interviewed in this exploratory research. Only one refused to be interviewed.

Findings and discussion

The research propositions are generally supported. The specific findings emerging from the interviews concerning their start-up activities follow. First, the software entrepreneurs reported having an explicit focus and interest in technological, core tasks (programming). Second, they did not emphasize profit-maximization goals. Third, they reported a conflict with previous employers' values. Fourth, they conceptualized risk as existing only in non-start-up conditions (anti-organizational orientations). Fifth, they were and still are involved in high levels of personal networking with other entrepreneurs in software development. Sixth, they initially disregarded external issues such as marketing and competition. These findings are discussed in greater detail below.

Profit-maximization objectives not initially paramount: A core-task orientation

All the software entrepreneurs explicitly made reference to a commitment to the technological, core-tasks of software development. Every entrepreneur mentioned a conviction to be involved in the job of software development in as much as it provided them with an intrinsic sense of worth (Daft & Becker, 1978). Their career, as a sort of calling, was a reward in its own right. Fun (re*creation*), the excitement of being involved in a dynamic industry or work environment, and the satisfaction of technological curiosity were positive, core-task attributes mentioned in the interviews. Consistent with this orientation, almost all of the entrepreneurs explicitly noted that money was not a primary motivator during the inception of the start-up (Block & Ornati, 1987; Collins & Moore, 1964; *cf:* Burgelman, 1985; Kanter, 1983). Although financial performance was not particularly relevant to their initial undertakings, for most it has since become so. It would appear that they have since become constrained by competitive influences in somewhat more mature, competitive and technological enviornments.

Value conflicts leading to anti-organizational beginnings

In many instances, entrepreneurs reported a repulsion from previous employers' competitive definitions, and previous employers were often perceived as incompetent or misdirected. Although unrecordable, their evaluations of previous employers were generally expressed with disdain or ridicule. Their reports express convictions in new values embodied in technological, core tasks rather than decisions made for economic reasons. Relationships with previous employers turned from dissatisfaction (Apter, 1964) to frustration and then finally to exasperation. A sample of recorded statements indicate that previous employers offered little alternative but to leave and start-up: intrinsic motivations were blocked (Brockhaus, 1980) by previous employers:

'there was not much else to do [but start-up]';
'no one was 'doing it right';
'[the previous employer] would not get involved in [a new field of software development]';
'it was dumb; they could've had all this [gesturing to the building and organization] for free.'
'the decision [to start-up] was made by default.'

It could be said that opportunity costs of these software entrepreneurs were measured more in terms of the utilities of self-actualization rather than in terms of specific, financial gain.

These software entrepreneurs looked within themselves for directions dictated by their beliefs in new values. Their values found expression ininternal, competitive definitions not of where technology had developed but (by their way of thinking) to where it ought to be or had to be developed. Innovative, competitive definitions became translated into new products, services, and organizations. This behavior seems opportunistic and may be largely a function of their ambiguous and formative environments at the time of inception (the early 1980s). Ideological values, rather than profit-maximization objectives, were powerful guidelines in the entrepreneurs' search for meaning (*cf:* Kao, 1984). Thus, external group-identification did not occur, and ventures appear to have begun anti-organizationally.

Profit-maximization calculations are impossible to perform when future variables, their relationships, and their market context have yet to be created and established: the consensual frameworks of market structures and technologies are lacking. Motivated by intrinsic values and relying upon strong, technological visions, the entrepreneurs focused their initial efforts within consensually ambiguous environments with themselves as central characters--at the centers of new organizations, new markets, and new social structures. Without an ambiguous, environmental setting--as all emergent, technological, competitive environments are--their visions and intense convictions would not find cognitive spaces open for creative, competitive enactments.

Convictions in underlying values, innovative competitive definitions, and highly ill-structured markets all complement and accomodate one another. It is questionable whether 'rational actors'--with microeconomic assumptions of perfect information, unlimited processing power, and well-defined decision tools--could figure their ways into such empty, cognitive and competitive spaces by means of profit-maximization objectives alone. Assuming the software-development markets were (at the time of these start-ups) consensually ambiguous and uncertain competitively, then profit-maximization objectives *could not be used* as guidelines for strategic actions--if they can ever be successfully [3].

Entrepreneurial perception of start-up risk

There was very little risk perceived by the entrepreneurs during their start-ups. Traditionally, risk is seen as the potential loss of financial and human capital (Baird & Thomas, 1985). It might be argued that these entrepreneurs had little more than their time, intellectual assets, and personal computer to risk. It was, perhaps, perceived as a costless investment. If so, then organizational slack accommodatedentrepreneurial innovation.

Many of these entrepreneurs were approached around the beginning of the 1980s by hardware producers with substantial contracts seeking vertical-integration advantages.

This usually occurred while interviewees were either graduate students at the University, tenured faculty members, or employees at other software/electronics firms. One entrepreneur claimed to be a 'risk shifter,' and others noted a working spouse and/or personal, financial security. Furthermore, many interviewees avoided financial risk because they worked into their own business through part-time contracts for outside vendors or simply because the technological, core tasks interested them. When they saw that they needed to devote more time 'to do it right,' they severed their tethers with previous employers, oftentimes established and secure positions. Then their foreseeable future was measured in weeks. Those experienced in earlier start-ups also expressed a tolerance for failure and high beliefs in their abilities to weather change (*cf*: Kanter, 1983). Should all fail, they thought they could easily pick-up the pieces and move on without harm.

The entrepreneurs interviewed presented a perspective on risk which emphasizes other values than financial risk emphasizes. Instead of a concern for risk involved in *starting up*, there was a kind of risk if an entrepreneur *didn't* start-up (prospect theory--Kahneman & Tversky, 1979), a risk of not achieving an utility ill-measured in monetary terms.

Personal networking: Personal communication and reputation

Many entrepreneurs seemed to be operating in different niches. Yet, they all knew each other well, professionally, personally, and across market boundaries even thought they did not seem to understand one another's markets very well. When requesting sampling referrals from the entrepreneurs, the interviewer would recite the lists received from other entrepreneurs. After the first list was received, it was rare that any more than two additional names were added to the list. The list expanded slightly as other names were added, as though these entrepreneurs' networks were Venn diagrams all slightly off-center from one another. Travel constraints contributed to the limitations of those interviewed in this research, but their networks extend significantly beyond the immediate area. As one entrepreneur noted, advertising one's services was a waste of money because people in software development had personal connections to others in the business; it was a fluid, in-bred industry which knew and cared more about an individual's work than about their companies'. For these kinds of firms in high-technology markets, talent is crucial to success: intellectual resources are inimitable assets leading to competitive advantage (Lippman & Rumelt, 1982; Rumelt, 1984, 1987; Winter, 1987).

Unique competitive definitions

Very rarely was there heard any mention of competition from interviewees concerning the early stage of their start-ups' evolution. At first, this was surprising and contradictory considering the extent of their inter-connecting networks and the apparent fluidity of strategic resources. But *all* entrepreneurs interviewed in this research considered their firm's products unique. There was a lack of external identification or comparison. Perhaps the processing of ambiguous information in ill-defined environments was cognitively discouraged (Dutton & Jackson, 1987). Yet, highly ill-structured or formative environments may be able to accommodate opportunistic, cognitive constructions and multiple, competitive definitions for enactment. (There is no sense from the interviews that the entrepreneurs thought of this.) Concerning attitudes and perspectives leading to and during start-up, there was little or no concern given to market analyses (Stuart & Abetti, 1987). Yet, many entrepreneurs volunteered that their lack of marketing was a woeful oversight. It cannot be ascertained whether their competitive environments have changed or whether the entrepreneurs now consider marketing a preferable activity in all instances.

Summary and suggested further research

The report of this exploratory research is not meant to provide a theoretical explanation of entrepreneurship. Far too much has been left un-investigated. This investigation is merely an attempt to refocus theoretical research to a central element in all entrepreneurial activity: new, competitive conceptualizations as value-creating and innovating, commercial arrangements within economic equilibriums (Schumpeter, 1934). That this exploration uses anti-organizational theory as a point of departure should not be made too much of yet. To test the conjectures fully, a much more systematic research should be undertaken, especially one that would emphasize more validating, quantitative data--for two reasons. One, as note [2] mentions, anti-organizational theory importantly lacks a pedigree and legitimacy. Two, more rigorous, scientific methods are needed than is presently being offered in interpretive studies. It is one thing to investigate entrepreneurs personally and to feel that one has become intimately aware of entrepreneurs' behaviors and their modes of thinking. It is quite another thing to prove a researcher's interpretation is, in fact, the entrepreneur's interpretation to other researchers who are not intimately involved in the study. With these disclaimers made then, a few tentative conclusions and suggestions follow.

Further interpretive investigations into entrepreneurship are warranted by the findings in this research. Indeed, many years of research into entrepreneurs' personality traits may be more descriptive of cognitive processes. Actors who perceive/conceive of innovative, competitive definitions may be very difficult to categorize at superficial or externally observable levels of analysis, especially so if the essence of innovation is a novel conceptualization. Although the dividing line between personality research and cognitive research is arguably thin, the distinction between the two has theoretical and methodological implications for researchers. The warrant opens a large body of cognitive and sociological literature to entrepreneurship scholars.

Secondly, the present research suggests a new analytical focus for entrepreneurship research. Most entrepreneurship research has a supply-side focus to it. The overwhelming body of research in entrepreneurship emphasizes the entrepreneur and the entrepreneur's firm, as though the organizational structures of markets do not matter. But surely the structures (or lack thereof) of markets do matter significantly (Hay & Morris, 1979; Scherer, 1980; Schmalensee & Willig, 1989).

It would be appropriate to research entrepreneurship from a demand-side perspective. What are the natures of markets where entrepreneurship is found in disproportionate quantities? A focus on competitive definitions from all relevant stakeholders might uncover much theoretically about entrepreneurial phenomena--especially so in formative markets. Actors who operate in well-structured environments (with high consensus) will generate predictable solutions because the 'problem domains' are cognitively constrained and well-defined (Bromiley, 1981). A strong consensus among market stakeholders limits the 'possible' to the 'recognized, legitimate, and acceptable.' However, a large number of interpretations and visions can be accommodated in highly ambiguous environments with few recognizable or consensually-agreed-upon cues. Such environments encourage entrepreneurial imaginations as means to bring order, security, and opportunity to chaos, uncertainty, and ambiguity. This exploratory research suggests that ambiguous-environment characteristics define entrepreneurial environments. Interpretive research into the formation of markets simultaneously from a demand-side and a supply-side perspective would perhaps provide new, theoretical and dynamic explanations of entrepreneurial activity and strategic change.

Last, the value and nature of competitive expertise and experience comes into question. Cognitive science has defined the nature of expertise (primarily in physical-science domains) as highly differentiated knowledge representations within strictly defined knowledge domains, with explicit underlying assumptions and clear procedural techniques (Chi, Glaser, & Farr, 1988). But in rapidly changing or new, competitive environments, in what sense can any entrepreneur or strategist be said to be an expert? How can strategists learn and what do they learn in competitive games which are unstable in terms of competitive boundaries and rules of the game? The literature in entrepreneurship and strategy are both replete with recipes for competitive advantage and success. But somehow such prescriptions ignore characteristic novelties of enterpreneurial phenomena and corporate imagination. These issues and questions may only be explicated and answered from a cognitive and social perspective, for entrepreneurial creation--as new, technical and commercial arrangements (Schumpeter, 1934)--is first a socially cognitive task, and secondly an efficient implementation of economic, transactional tasks (Porac *et. al.*, 1989).

Notes

1. The fourth perspective (objective epistemology / radical-change sociology) will not be discussed here for the sake of brevity. Marxism and bother similar theories are found in this perspective (Burrell & Morgan, 1979).
2. The conjectures are based upon an eclectic set of theories and empirical research. A more specific, theoretical foundation than what Burrell & Morgan provided must be woven to apply anti-organizational theory to entrepreneurship. Anti-organizational theory has little notable pedigree; it may appear to be a self-contradictory term; and it is used here to reconcile paradoxical findings according to more traditional, organizational theories. Many academics are repulsed by the term.
3. Hayes & Abernathy (1980) have clearly shown that profit-maximization objectives such as ROI goals alone can result incorporate self-destructions through dis-investments. Corporations need visions, missions, or purposes by which to relate themselves to external constituencies and competitive environments (*cf:* Campbell & Tawadey, 1990). There is no substitute for a competitive definition (Abell, 1980), even if it is anti-organizational in nature. The more ambiguous environments are, the more critical the need for a high-level statements of identity and direction since specific, step-by-step tactics will be largely unknown in advance.

References

Abell, D.F. (1980), Defining the Business: The starting point of strategic planning, Englewood Cliffs, NJ: Prentice Hall.

Abernathy, W., & Clark, K.B. (1985), 'Innovation: mapping the winds of creative destruction', Research Policy, vol. 14, pp. 3-22.

Albert, S., & Whetten, D. (1985), 'Organizational identity', in L.L. Cummings & B.M. Staw (Eds.), Research in Organizational Behavior, Vol. 7, Greenwich: JAI Press.

Aldridge, H.E., McKelvey, B., & Ulrich, D. (1984). 'Design strategy from a population perspective', Journal of Management, vol. 10, pp. 67-86.

Aldridge, H.E. (1985), Organizations and Environments, Englewood Cliffs, NJ: Prentice Hall.

American Electronics Association (AEA) Seminar on Software-Development Management, August, 1990, Stanford University, Stanford, California.

Anderson, P., & Tushman, M.J. (1990), 'Technological discontinuities and dominant designs: a cyclical model of technological change', Administrative Science Quarterly, vol. 31, pp. 439-465.

Andrews, K.R. (1971), The Concept of Corporate Strategy. Homewood, IL: Irwin.

Apter, D.E. (1964), 'Introduction: ideology & discontent' in, Ideology and Discontent, New York: Free Press.

Arthur, B. (1989), 'Competing technologies, increasing returns, and lock-in by historical events', Economic Journal, vol. 99, pp. 116-131.

Ashe, G., Jowett, P., McGee, J., & Thomas, H. (1986), 'The International Software Industry', Alvey Directorate, Department of Trade and Industry, London & London Business School, London.

Baird, I.S., & Thomas, H. (1985), 'Toward a contingency-model of strategic risk-taking', Academy of Management Review, vol. 10, No. 2, pp. 230-243.

Barley, S. (1986), 'Semiotics and the study of occupational and organizational cultures', Administrative Science Quarterly, vol. 28, pp. 393-413.

Barnard, C. (1938), The Functions of the Executive, Cambridge: Harvard University Press.

Bennis, W., & Nanus, B. (1985), Leaders: The strategies for taking charge, New York: Harper & Row.

Berger, P.L, & Luckman, T. (1967), The Social Construction of Reality. New York: Doubleday.

Bijker, W.E., Hughes, T.P., & Pinch, T. (1987), The Social Construction of Technological Systems, Cambridge, MA: MIT Press.

Block, Z., & Ornati, O.A. (1987), 'Compensating corporate venture managers', Journal of Business Venturing, Vol. 2, No. 1, pp. 41-52.

Bromiley, P. (1981), 'Task environments and budgetary decision making', Academy of Management Review, Vol. 6, No. 2, pp. 277-288.

Burgelman, R.A. (1985), 'Managing the new venture division: research findings and implications for strategic management', Strategic Management Journal, Vol. 6, pp. 39-54.

Burke, K. (1967), 'Rhetoric--old and new', in M. Steinmann, Jr., (Ed.), New Rhetorics, New York: Schribner's.

Burrell, G., & Morgan, G. (1979), Sociological Paradigms and Organizational Analysis, Portsmouth, NH: Heineman.

Campbell, A., & Tawadey, K. (1990), Missions and Business Philosophy, Hailey Court, Jordan Hill, Oxford: Heinemann.

Chi, M.T.H., Glaser, R., & Farr, M.J. (1988), The Nature of Expertise, Hillsdale, NJ: Lawrence Erlbaum Associates.

Collins, O., & Moore, D. (1964), The Enterprising Man. East Lansing, MI: MSU Business Studies.

Conger, J.A. (1991), 'Inspiring others: the language of leadership', The Executive, Vol. 5, No. 1, pp. 31-45.

Daft, R.L., & Becker, S.W. (1978), The Innovative Organization, New York: Elsevier.

Daft, R.L., & Weick, K.E. (1984), 'Toward a model of organizations as interpretive systems', Academy of Management Review, Vol. 9, pp. 284-295.

Dierickx, I., & Cool, K. (1989), 'Asset stock accumulation and sustainability of competitive strategy', Management Science, Vol.35, No. 12, pp. 1504-1511.

DiMaggio, P.D., Powell, W.W. (1983), 'The iron cage revisited: institutional isomorphism and collective rationality in organizational fields', American Sociological Review, Vol. 48, pp. 147-160.

Dubin, P. (1989), 'The influence of motivations and environment on business start-ups: some hints for public policies', Journal of Business Venturing, Vol. 4, No. 1, pp. 11-26.

Dutton, J.E., & Jackson, S.E. (1987), 'Categorizing strategic issues: links to organizational action', Academy of Management Review, Vol. 12, pp. 76-90.

Eisenhardt, K.E. (1989), 'Making fast strategic decisions in high-velocity environments', Academy of Management Journal, Vol. 32, No. 3, pp. 543-576.

Ericsson, K.A., & Simon, H.A. (1984), Protocol Analysis: Verbal reports as data. Cambridge: MIT Press.

Festinger, L. (1954), 'A theory of social comparison processes', Human Relations, Vol. 7, pp. 117-140.

Foster, R.N. (1986), Innovation: The attacker's advantage, New York: Summit Books.

Gartner, W.B., Mitchell, T.R., & Vesper, K.H. (1989), 'A taxonomy of new business ventures', Journal of Business Venturing, Vol. 4, No. 3, pp. 169-186.

Gartner, W.B. (1985), 'A conceptual framework for describing the phenomenon of new venture creation', Academy of Management Review, Vol. 10, No. 4, pp. 696-706.

Hannan, M., & Freeman, J. (1977), 'The population ecology of organizations', American Journal of Sociology, Vol. 82, pp. 929-964.

Harre, R. (1980), Social Being: A theory for social psychology, Totowa, NJ: Littlefield, Adams, & Co.

Harre, R., & Secord, P.F. (1973), The Explanation of Social Behavior, Totowa, NJ: Littlefield, Adams, & Co.

Hay, D.A., & Morris, D.J. (1979), Industrial Economics, Oxford: Oxford University Press.

Huff, A. (1982), 'Industry influences on strategy formulation', Strategic Management Journal, Vol. 3, pp. 119-130.

Kahneman, D., & Tversky, A. (1979), 'Prospect theory: an analysis of decision under risk', Econometrica, Vol. 47, No. 2, pp. 263-291.

Kanter, R.M. (1983), The Change Masters, New York: Simon & Schuster.

Kao, J.J. (1983), 'The corporate new wave: entrepreneurship in transition, paper presented at Commemoration of Seventy-Fifth Anniversary of Harvard Business School, HBS Case Services, #9-785-500.

Kao, J.J. (1989), Entrepreneurship, Creativity, & Organization: Texts Cases & Readings, Englewood, NJ: Prentice Hall.

Kets de Vries, M.F.R. (1985), 'The dark side of entrepreneurship', Harvard Business Review, Vol. 63, No. 6.

Kiesler, S., & Sproull, L. (1982), 'Managerial responses to changing environments: perspectives on problem sensing from social cognition', Administrative Science Quarterly, Vol. 27, pp. 548-570.

Kirp, D.L., & Rice, D.S. (1988), 'Fast forward--styles of California management', Harvard Business Review, Vol. 66, No. 1, pp. 74-83.

Klepper, S., & Graddy, E. (1990), 'The evolution of new industries and the determinants of market structure', Rand Journal of Economics, Vol. 21, No. 1, pp. 27-44.

LaFuente, A., & Salas, V. (1989), 'Types of entrepreneurs and firms: the case of new Spanish firms', Strategic Management Journal, Vol. 10, No. 1, pp. 17-30.

Levenhagen, M.J., Porac, J.P., & Thomas, H. (1990), 'Emergent industry leadership and the selling technological visions: a social-constructionist viewpoint', presented at the Cranfield-SMS workshop on Leadership and Management of Strategic Change, Robinson College, Cambridge, England. December, 1990.

Lippman, S.A., & Rumelt, R.P. (1982), 'Uncertain inimitability: an analysis of interfirm differences in efficiency under competition', Bell Journal of Economics, Vol. 13, pp. 418-438.

Lyles, M., & Mitroff, I.I. (1980), 'Organizational problem formulation: an empirical study', Administrative Science Quarterly, Vol. 25, No. 2, pp. 102-119.

March, J.G., & Simon, H.A. (1958), Organizations, New York: Wiley.

McCaskey, M.B. (1982), The Executive Challenge, Marshfield, MA: Pitman.

McGee, J., & Thomas, H. (1986), 'Strategic groups: theory, research, and taxonomy', Strategic Management Journal, Vol. 7, pp. 141-160.

Nelson, R.R., & Winter, S.G. (1982), An Evolutionary Theory of Economic Change, Cambridge, MA: Belknap Press.

Nisbett, R.E., & Wilson, T.D. (1977), 'Telling more than we can know: verbal reports on mental processes', Psychological Review, Vol.84, No. 3, pp. 231-259.

Pavitt, K. (1986), 'Technology, innovation, and strategic management', in J. McGee, & H. Thomas (Eds.), Strategic Management Research. New York: John Wiley.

Pfeffer, J., & Salancik, G.R. (1978), The External Control of Organizations, New York: Harper & Row.

Penrose, E. (1959), The Theory of the Growth of the Firm, Oxford: Oxford University Press.

Pondy, L.R., Frost, P.J., Morgan, G., & Dandridge, T.C. (1983), Organizational Symbolism, Greenwich, CN: JAI.

Porac, J.F., & Thomas, H. (1990), 'Taxonomic mental models in competitor definition', Academy of Management Review, Vol. 15, No. 2, pp. 224-240.

Porac, J.F., Thomas, H., & Baden-Fuller, C. (1989), 'Competitive groups as cognitive communities: the case of Scottish Knitwear Manufacturers, Journal of Management Studies, Vol. 26, No. 4, pp. 397-416.

Porter, M.E. (1979), 'The structure within industries and companies' performance', Review of Economics and Statistics, Vol. 61, pp. 214-227.

Porter, M. (1980), Competitive Strategy, New York: Free Press.

Prahalad, C.K., & Hamel, G. (1990), 'The core competence of the corporation', Harvard Business Review, May-June, pp. 79-91.

Ranson, S., Hinings, B., & Greenwood, R. (1980), 'The structuring of organizational structures', Administrative Science Quarterly, Vol. 25, pp. 1-17.

Rumelt, R.P. (1984), 'Towards a strategic theory of the firm', in R.P. Lamb, (Ed.), Competitive Strategic Management. Englewood Cliffs, NJ: Prentice Hall.

Rumelt, R.P. (1987), 'Theory, strategy, and entrepreneurship', in D.J. Teece (Ed.), The Competitive Challenge. Cambridge, MA: Ballinger.

Sandberg, W.R., Schweiger, D.M., & Hofer, C.W. (1988), 'The use of verbal protocols in determining venture capitalists' decision processes', Entrepreneurship: Theory and Practice, Vol. 13, No. 2, pp. 7-20.

Schein, E.H. (1985), Organizational Culture and Leadership, San Francisco, CA: Jossey-Bass.

Scherer, F.M. (1980), Industrial Market Structure and Economic Performance, Boston, MA: Houghton Mifflin.

Schmalensee, R., & Willig, R.D. (1989), Handbook of Industrial Organization, Vols. I & II, Amsterdam: North-Holland.

Schumpeter, J.A. (1934), The Theory of Economic Development, Cambridge: Harvard University Press.

Schwenk, C. (1985), 'The use of participant recollections in the modeling of organizational decision processes', Academy of Management Review, Vol. 10, No. 3, pp. 496-503.

Sexton, D.L., & Bowman, N. (1985), 'The entrepreneur: a capable executive and more', Journal of Business Venturing, Vol. 1, No. 1, pp. 129-140.

Simon, H.A. (1976), Administrative Behavior (3rd Ed.), New York: Free Press.

Simon, H.A. (1985), 'What we know about the creative process', in R.L. Kuhn, (Ed.), Frontiers in Creative and Innovative Management, Cambridge, MA: Ballinger Publishing.

Smircich, L., & Stubbart, C. (1985), 'Strategic management in an enacted world', Academy of Management Review, Vol. 10, pp. 724-736.

Smith, N.R., & Miner, J.B. (1983), 'Type of entrepreneur, type of firm, and managerial motivation: implications for organizational life cycle theory, Strategic Management Journal, Vol. 4, No. 4, pp. 325-340.

Spender, J.C. (1980), Strategy-making in Business, Doctoral Dissertation, Manchester University.

Staw, B.M. (1980), 'Rationality and justification in organizational life', in

B.M. Staw & L.L. Cummings (Eds.), Research in Organizational Behavior, Vol. 2. Greenwich, CN: JAI.

Stevenson, H., & Hameling, S. (1990), 'The heart of entrepreneurship', Harvard Business Review, Mar-Apr, pp. 85-94.

Stuart, R., & Abetti, P.A. (1987), 'Start-up ventures: towards the prediction of initial success', Journal of Business Venturing, Vol. 2, No. 3, pp. 215-230.

Tushman, M.L., & Anderson, P. (1986), 'Technological discontinuities and organizational environments', Administrative Science Quarterly, Vol. 31, pp. 439-465.

Tushman, M.L, & Romanelli, E. (1985), 'Organizational evolution: a metamorphosis model of convergence and reorganization', in L.L. Cummings & B.M. Staw (Eds.), Research in Organizational Behavior Vol. 7. Greenwich, CN: JAI Press.

Vallacher, R.R., & Wegner, D.M. (1987), 'What do people think they're doing? Action identification and human behavior', PsychologicalReview, Vol. 94, No. 1, pp. 3-15.

Wallas, G. (1926), The Art of Thought. New York: Harcourt Brace Jovanovich.

Weick, K.E. (1979), The Social Psychology of Organizing, Reading, MA: Addison Wesley.

Wernerfelt, B. (1984), 'A resource-based view of the firm', Strategic Management Journal, Vol. 5, pp. 171-180.

Winter, S.G. (1987), 'Knowledge and competence as strategic assets', in D.J. Teece, (Ed.), The Competitive Challenge. Cambridge, MA: Ballinger.

Wortman, M.S. (1987), 'Entrepreneurship: an integrating topology and evaluation of the empirical research in the field', Journal of Management, Vol. 13, No. 2, pp. 259-279.

Part 2
Special methodological approaches in entrepreneurship research

6 Entrepreneurship: Some lessons of social anthropology

Peter Rosa and Alison Bowes

The paper looks at entrepreneurship from the perspective of social anthropology, particularly that of the British School (Kuper 1983). Social anthropology does not possess an exclusive body of theory to explain social phenomena. What distinguishes it as a discipline are three methodological aspects: (a) the tradition of guarding against the dangers of ethnocentrism; (b) its specialisation in participant observation as a method of collecting data which is then used to achieve insights into social phenomena; (c) its holistic approach to explaining social phenomena, particularly apparently irrational behaviour.

Each methodological aspect is outlined illustrated with examples from social anthropology, especially from studies which have incorporated some element of entrepreneurship in their subject matter (for example Barth (1962)'s study of entrepreneurship and social change in Northern Norway. The relevance and implications of each approach to mainstream entrepreneurial studies is also briefly discussed.

The paper moves on to focus on two studies of entrepreneurship recently carried out at the Scottish Enterprise Foundation, and re-examines them from a social anthropological perspective, exposing limitations and drawbacks of non anthropological approaches to anthropological research. These are contrasted to a third study by a social anthropologist (Caulkins 1988), which demonstrates how a social anthropological approach to entrepreneurship can yield fresh and original insights.

The paper concludes by showing that social anthropology has much to contribute to the study of entrepreneurship. The contribution will come not so much from social anthropologists focusing attention to entrepreneurship as an area of study, than from the adoption of social anthropological techniques by non anthropologists already working in mainstream entrepreneurial studies.

Introduction

In a review of economic theories of entrepreneurship Loasby (1988:32) notes the complexity of the subject, and points out that there is no single adequate theory of entrepreneurship - not even a single theory from an economic perspective. Indeed there is not even an agreed definition of the subject.

In this respect social anthropology does not differ from other disciplines. It has no single theory of entrepreneurship, nor does it offer a single better definition. Now does it have an exclusive body of theory to explain social phenomena. Nobody has succeeded, for example, in demarcating social anthropology as a discipline from sociology on theoretical grounds alone. Within social anthropology, moreover, wide consensus is as difficult to observe as it is in any other social science. For instance there are many types of social and cultural anthropology. Here we refer mainly to modern British social anthropology (Kuper 1983).

There are three aspects of social anthropology (particularly the British School) which distinguish it from other disciplines. These are:

-    its tradition of guarding against the dangers of 'ethnocentrism': Social anthropologists argue that socio-cultural observations are constantly subject to biased interpretation as they have to filter through the cultural perspective of the investigator. 'Ethnocentrism' can never be entirely eliminated, but its more blatant distortions can be avoided by awareness of the problem.
-   its specialisation in participant observation as a method of collecting data which is then used to achieve insights into social phenomena: Social anthropologists argue that complex social phenomena cannot be understood without intensive observation over a long period. This is linked with the avoidance of 'ethnocentrism'. Interpretations based on perfunctory observations will usually reflect strongly the 'conventional wisdom' or 'common sense' of the observer.
-   its holistic approach to analysing and explaining social phenomena: The elements of societies and the ways individuals relate to social institutions are subtly interrelated in complex ways. This complexity means that isolating any single element out of context will inevitably lead to biased interpretation.

All three aspects are a legacy of attempts by anthropologists earlier this century to come to terms with the difficulties presented by the analysis of pre-literate societies, both in their indigenous state and in a state of change resulting from colonial and post-colonial experiences. In the last twenty years anthropologists have drawn upon this legacy to study complex societies both in developing and developed countries. It is now argued by many social anthropologists that there are no longer a significant number of isolated indigenous societies. All in some way are integrated into the wider nation state and have to adapt to the impact of world wide economic and social forces. The anthropological approach, however, still retains its basic characteristics and value.

Entrepreneurship has long been considered by some social anthropologists as an important area of study, because it is a manifestation of social change and of integration into world-wide economic and social forces. Only recently, however, have social anthropologists begun to enter the 'mainstream' debates on entrepreneurship in the small business and related areas of study (henceforth called 'mainstream entrepreneurial studies). There is, moreover, a rising demand for fresh insights in the mainstream entrepreneurial literature. Some of these insights, we argue later, could come from drawing on the experience of social anthropology, and by absorbing some of its lessons.

The paper examines the three fundamental aspects of the social anthropological approach just discussed (rejecting ethnocentrism, participant observation and holism), and discusses them in terms of some mainstream entrepreneurial issues. It then moves on to examine the process of applying social anthropology in assessing three research projects that have been carried out in the Institute where one of the authors works.

The dangers of ethnocentrism

'To be enterprising is not uniquely American, but entrepreneurialism seems to be found in the nature of our people more than just about anywhere else.' (Ronald Reagan 1985).

Notions of entrepreneurship are deeply ingrained in the capitalist culture of North America, and are becoming more prominent in Western Europe. What are these notions? For most people they are vague impressions, which make subjective sense. For others who seek to articulate them objectively, however, problems ensue. The literature on entrepreneurship reveals a definitional malaise with no consensus on what entrepreneurship is:

'We ran a research center in entrepreneurial history. For ten years we tried to define the entrepreneur. We never succeeded. Each of us had some notion of it - what he thought was for his purposes a useful definition. I don't think you are going to get further than that.' (Cole, quoted by Gartner 1989).

Gartner illustrates the lack of consensus by listing the diverse definitions of major researchers into entrepreneurship in the last five decades. This diversity in itself is not remarkable. Entrepreneurship, it could be argued, is no different from a large number of other complex concepts that defy a simplistic or universal definition. Social science is littered with such concepts. There is a traditional remedy for conceptual problems like this, which is formulating a working or operational definition, and one aspect of the complex concept is analysed in terms of it. It is left to specialist theorists to integrate the parts. Researchers into entrepreneurship have in practice followed this traditional remedy. The studies listed by Gartner (1989) do not suffer in terms of what they have set out to do merely because their working definition of entrepreneurship is not the same as that in other studies.

Many researchers are concerned that there is no agreed definition, and the implied antipathy of proponents of one definition when faced with that of others. This may reflect a situation where a person's own view of reality is perceived as rational common sense. The interpretations of others naturally then appear distorted. A social anthropologist would tend to view this as a symptom of 'ethnocentrism'. A researcher or scholar is not a rational android. He or she is part of a wider society and culture. The more deeply entrepreneurship is ingrained in the wider society, in terms of the value placed upon it, the more we would expect intolerance towards differing perceptions and definitions of it. 'Ethnocentrism' is usually expressed as an ingrained 'gut feeling', one that is not easy to articulate. It is a feeling, however, that is strong enough to cast doubts on the conceptualisations advanced by others. The type of 'gut feeling' underlying perceptions of entrepreneurship is illustrated by Mitton (1989:9):

'Entrepreneurship and pornography have a lot in common: they are both hard to define. To get consensus on what they mean is virtually impossible. In an obscenity case before the United States supreme court in 1964, Justice Potter Stewart stated that he could not define pornography, 'but', he said 'I know it when I see it'. I look at entrepreneurship in the same way. I can't define it - at least not to everyone's satisfaction - but I know when I see it.'

Ethnocentrism is about applying ones own values and preconceptions unquestioningly to their subjects of study. Mitton's study (unfairly singled out as many other examples abound in the entrepreneurial literature), is full of examples of this process in action, as Mitton describes the qualities of entrepreneurs on the basis of his 'forty years of study' of entrepreneurship. The entrepreneurial qualities he illustrates are things such as 'looking at the usual, seeing the unusual' (p.12); 'a strong sense of mission', 'unrelenting zeal', 'strong sense of urgency and drive that borders on the obsessive' (p.12); 'an ends orientation that makes them impatient to start, anxious to compete, eager to confront, insensitive to failure' (p.12); 'a need to dominate so great that there is seldom room at the top for more than one chief' (p.13). These interpretations of entrepreneurial qualities tell as much about the ideal conception of entrepreneurs in the USA as they do about entrepreneurs.

Social anthropologists, in contrast, constantly guard against the pull of their 'gut feelings', and distrust any fall back on 'common sense' or 'conventional wisdom'. They know that all these types of meaning arise from their own cultural bias. Consequently they do not suffer from the type of definitional malaise just described in the entrepreneurial literature. Because their intuitive feeling of what is 'true' or 'right' is suspect, they are tolerant of different definitions. A good definition thus is not a universal one that reflects 'truth'. Rather it is one that is neutral, and allows data to be collected as free from preconceptions as possible. A good definition leads to comprehensive analysis and makes possible interpretation at several theoretical levels or standpoints.

Barth (1962), for example, in his classic appraisal of the role of the entrepreneur in social change in Northern Norway, is pragmatic in defining entrepreneurship, though acknowledging a need for a definition 'to maintain some clarity and precision in what is meant by the terms 'enterprise' and 'entrepreneur''. Barth states 'Briefly an entrepreneur is someone who takes the initiative in administering resources and pursues an expansive economic policy'. (Barth 1962:1). Barth is not concerned with a comprehensive definition. It is sufficient that it is useful and free from ethnocentric bias. He proceeds to use it to launch a theoretical discussion on the entrepreneurial role and its relation to the wider community. Essentially the definition serves as an 'orientation' by means of which social and economic processes can be meaningfully studied. Using this open-minded approach, Barth was able to illustrate in detail the role that entrepreneurs play in initiating social change, and the social impact of this change. Entrepreneurs were shown to engage in transactions, which over time generated new standards or values, or led to the redefinition of existing ones.

Again Long (1977) in a study of entrepreneurship in the Peruvian Highlands, takes a pragmatic approach:

'Difficult problems arise of course over defining 'entrepreneurship'. Suffice here to say that I am mainly concerned with the management function, and not with such questions as risk-taking or innovation.' (Long 1977:176).

Like Barth, Long is concerned with a non-messianic 'orientation' in which social and economic processes can be meaningfully studied. There is no preoccupation with exciting personal qualities, or with recipes or golden rules for entrepreneurial success.

To some extent the 'open' empirical definition tends to be absent from many mainstream entrepreneurial studies because the study of entrepreneurship is usually from an applied perspective. Quite often it is policy makers that give money for the research, and the paymasters often have great influence on the basic design of a study. Policy makers tend to have a fixed and clear idea of what the problems are, and what the study should find. These ideas are often based on ethnocentric notions, and bind a study in an ethnocentric framework before it even has a chance to get going. These 'top down' approaches pre-determine the results to underpin policy that has already been decided. The ethnocentric bias behind this process can result in the policy having a 'disappointing' impact on the intended beneficiaries, and this is explained away in terms of irrational behaviour.

For example in the UK such ethnocentric 'top down' approaches have been applied to entrepreneurs by government policy makers who assume that managerial training is essential for entrepreneurial success, business growth and wealth creation. The UK government's Training Agency has commissioned studies to assess local training needs to set up support structures to improve managerial training to the business community. The remit of these essentially research studies is set up in a way that allows no deviance from the basic assumption that objective training needs can easily be identified through the simple expedient of asking the entrepreneur what they are. Many research studies have thus been completed, rubber stamping this policy (see Rosa 1989a). Unfortunately the Training Agency has met with a very poor response from many business owners when offering them training based on the researched training needs. The apathy is invariably classed as irrational behaviour by the training providers. Social anthropologists would view this as a typical process in which ethnocentric bias results in a failure to get to grips with the real issues underlying problems of the people whom the policy formulators claim to benefit and help.

Participant observation

The adoption of participant observation as the principal research method of social anthropology is a consequence of seeking to avoid ethnocentrism. Through continued observation over a long period the researcher's preconceptions are eroded, and are replaced (ideally) by understanding of complex social interactions and phenomena whose existence could not have been envisaged before the study began. Agar puts it this way:

'Policy is built on assumptions of what 'people are like'. Yet a little participant observation quickly teaches you that the assumptions, at their very best, are over simplifications. Participant observation, then, offers a social science metaphor within which the richness and variety of group life can be expressed as it is learned from direct involvement within the group itself'. (Agar 1980:11).

The business and economic entrepreneurial literature contains many assumptions, simplifications and reductions. Every study that uses a questionnaire has already reduced complex phenomena to a simplified form. Every model reduces reality into a preconceived scheme. Typologies of entrepreneurs (e.g. Smith 1967; Dunkelberg and Cooper 1982; LaFluente and Salas 1989) reduce often complex and multidimensional data into discrete units which are easier to envisage and manage. Every characteristic entrepreneurial trait, or typical motivation identified, could be construed as a refinement and reduction of complex psychological and social processes.

Participant observation by its multidimensional detail could potentially undermine all these attempts to simplify aspects of entrepreneurial behaviour and the environment in which entrepreneurs operate. There are few assumptions, reduced measures or concepts in the business or economic entrepreneurial literature which could withstand the questions raised by sustained participant observation. The more ethnocentric the basis on which these concepts or measures have been constructed, the more a social anthropologist would expect participant observation to undermine the tenability of the concept or measure.

Social anthropology has built up principally through detailed knowledge gained through participant observation, a tradition of dispelling myths based on simplistic views of what is happening in developing countries. For example Geertz's study of entrepreneurial development in two Indonesian towns (1963) casts doubts on popular views that posited a simple relationship between religious affiliation and entrepreneurial success. For example it is still a popular stereotype that many religious minorities such as Sikhs and Jews naturally produce a high number of entrepreneurs. Geertz contrasted a village where entrepreneurs arose out of a Moslem reformist sect, with a village where entrepreneurs came from a class of Hindu noblemen. In both villages the religions, ethics, values and types of societies differed radically. Nevertheless Geertz was able to demonstrate how in both cases the entrepreneurs were able to capitalise and turn to advantage social resources legitimised through appeals to religious norms, values and beliefs. Therefore he demonstrated that there is no essential connection between entrepreneurial success and one particular religion or marginal status.

Long (1977) in a study of entrepreneurial activity in the Peruvian highlands, showed that small scale entrepreneurship and commerce in developing countries is not a simple process of manipulating in a rudimentary manner small supplies of capital, labour and material assets, as is implied or assumed by many mainstream entrepreneurial studies, particularly those with an economic orientation. Through participant observation he was able to show that kinship and interpersonal networks constituted important social resources to entrepreneurs. He demonstrated that the way entrepreneurs used kinship, affinal and interpersonal ties in the running of their businesses was a highly complex process - much more complex than the simple cultivation of contacts to be used for commercial advantage. The complexity of small scale enterprises in developing countries was also pointed out by Hill (1963) in a study on migrant cocoa farmers in southern Ghana. This again contrasted with assumptions in the economic development literature that the organisation of production by African peasants was essentially a simple process.

Participant observation, however, is not a panacea for all problems. It is a lengthy and costly method of gathering data. It can produce so much detail that sorting the wood from the trees becomes an 'art' rather than a science. It is difficult to evaluate what is collected objectively, and therefore non replicable. There are example of anthropologists studying the same village coming up with quite differing descriptions (e.g. see the Redfield/Lewis debate in Agar (1980:7).

Participant observation, moreover, does not remove the need for abstraction and simplification. All social anthropologists reduce, simplify and make assumptions in their attempts to make sense of their data and in theorising. The value of participant observation lies in improving the basis from which reduction and abstraction takes place.

Holism

Observations on pre-literate peoples have presented social anthropologists with many examples of seemingly irrational actions. For example the originator of modern British Social Anthropology, Bronislaw Malinowski, had to come to terms with a people who did not link procreation with sexual intercourse. Another major figure, Evans-Pritchard, observed that to the Azande of the Southern Sudan witchcraft is as real to them as tangible objects such as air, water and trees. The bizarre New Guinea ritual 'Naven' involving transvestism and actions such as the mother's brother offering his buttocks to his sister's son in a fantastic sex simulation, presented another famous anthropologist, Bateson, with what Kuper calls 'a classic sort of anthropological problem - an apparently absurd ritual which invited the question what sense does in make?' (Kuper 1983:76).

Early explanations based on innate irrationality and psychological maladjustments proved untenable. Anthropologists studying rationality such as Winch (1964); Overing (1985) agree that all apparently irrational actions of the types mentioned are logical once the context in which they occur is understood. Horton (1974) in comparing African traditional thought and Western science, found that differences were more apparent than real:

'those familiar with theoretical thinking in their own culture have failed to recognise African equivalents, simply because they have been blinded by differences of idiom.'(Horton 1977:131).

Social anthropologists, therefore, assume rationality in all contexts. By implication no motivation or behavioural trait can be understood in isolation, separated from its context. A holistic approach to analysing social and behavioural phenomena is thus basic in social anthropology.

The holistic approach does not mean that all aspects of society have to be contained in an explanation. Relevant factors may be few. Finding the relevant factors, however, may require a wide search drawing upon a full holistic study. An example is provided by Dyson-Hudson (1972)'s study of Karimojong pastoralists in Uganda. They seemed to colonial administrators to be acting irrationally, because they had a preference for owning as many cattle as possible without thought to quality and indifferent to environmental degradation through overgrazing. Cattle are highly valued, and Dyson-Hudson sought explanation in terms of social values. The answer, however, was more pragmatic. In times of drought, all cattle yield little milk, irrespective of pedigree. A little milk from twenty cows at such times yields more milk, important for survival, than a fewer number of quality cows. To find this out, a holistic approach was necessary.

A holistic approach is alien to the studies of entrepreneurship in the mainstream business and economic literature. In the common psychodynamic and trait approaches on the nature of the entrepreneurial character (e.g. see Chell's review 1985), entrepreneurial motivations and qualities tend to be abstracted out of context, and are seldom related to the wider society or other potentially relevant areas (Carsrud and Johnson 1989:22). These authors, writing from a social psychological perspective, in essence advocate more holistic approaches to the study of entrepreneurial behaviour which integrate 'micro' and 'macro' levels of analysis, and which relate more systematically to social analyses. They advocate what has been standard practice in social anthropology for decades.

Applying the lessons of social anthropology

We stated in the introduction that social anthropology is a way of approaching the study of social or cultural phenomena. It is not a discipline with unique theories and paradigms. It ought to be possible, therefore, to use the lessons of social anthropology to enrich mainstream approaches to understanding entrepreneurship, and to expose the limitations of more usual approaches. To illustrate this, we have chosen to critically examine from an anthropological perspective three research projects carried out at the Scottish Enterprise Foundation where one of us is research director.

1) A study directed by Tom Cannon and latterly by Peter Rosa of graduate career aspirations towards entrepreneurship and enterprise of Scottish and English University graduates.

The study was concerned with the problem that few graduates pursue an entrepreneurial career on leaving University. It had three elements: firstly to explore why most graduates did not seriously consider a career in entrepreneurship; secondly to ascertain what factors were associated with entrepreneurial activity in the graduate population; thirdly whether certain government initiatives to promote enterprise had had an impact on the attitudes of graduates.

The study was designed around a postal questionnaire of some 80 questions producing close to 300 variables. It was sent to 5,500 graduates from 10 Universities yielding a response from 2,802. Questions drew on the entrepreneurial literature to probe factors which were known to be relevant to career choice in general and on an entrepreneurial career in particular. Factors included actual and preferred career destination, influence of family, friends, education and the careers service; work experience, social class, family role models, attitudes to the world of work, attitudes to entrepreneurs, locus of control and having and pursuing business ideas. The impact of one government initiative, graduate enterprise on graduate attitudes was to be assessed by comparing the attitudes of Scottish graduates, exposed to the initiative, with those of English graduates, not so exposed.

As an example of the survey approach, it was a successful study, and many interesting findings emerged (for example see Rosa 1989; Rosa and McAlpine 1990). From a social anthropological viewpoint, however, it was deficient on several counts.

Firstly measures were all pre-conceived from literature sources or from the questionnaire designer's view of what was an appropriate measure. Graduate's thoughts and attitudes were directed, focused and bounded by the questions. There was an implicit assumption that most of the important and relevant issues were covered in the questionnaire, and that most graduate attitudes fitted the boundaries set by the questions. No direct participant observation with students were taken to assess the extent to which the concepts and measures in the questionnaire were in fact appropriate, covered the full range, or were meaningful to graduates and in what respects.

Secondly the assessment of the impact of the enterprise initiative depended on the ethnocentric view that Scottish and English graduates were fundamentally similar. It particularly failed to take account of distinctive aspects of the Scottish university education, for example the fact that Scottish undergraduate degrees take 4 years and not 3 as in England, and that Scottish Universities contain a much higher proportion of graduates drawn from the local area in which the University is situated than in England. To assume, therefore, that more positive attitudes towards entrepreneurship in the Scottish sample, if found, would thus reflect the impact of the enterprise initiative was clearly problematic. This aspect of the study quickly proved unworkable and had to be abandoned. It was a classic example of the imposition of an unwarranted assumption. Social anthropologists would say that such assumptions are matters for research.

Thirdly the relationship of attitudes and various factors that potentially predispose graduates to entrepreneurship were examined 'out of context' of the wider complex circumstances within which choices are perceived and decisions made. There were no mechanisms in the way the data were collected to permit a more holistic approach to be taken. This lack of a more holistic approach makes the statistical analysis of 'pre-disposing' factors piecemeal and simplistic. Results (still unpublished) did show significant relationships between entrepreneurial activity and various predisposing factors. With an implicit faith in conventional models of entrepreneurial interpretation, these findings could have been used with profit to confirm existing preconceptions (for example the study showed that those who pursued business ideas and entered self employment did have a significantly higher locus of control than those who did not). Critical examination of the findings using multivariate statistical tests, however, proved unsatisfying. The pre-disposing factors proved significant predictors of entrepreneurial outcome, but most of the variation still remained unexplained. The problem of predicting who would emerge as an entrepreneur was thus clearly unsolved. There was a need for more detailed information, and more precise information. For example a social anthropologist would have examined in considerable detail the complex social processes implied by pre-disposing factors, the contexts in which these processes operate in, the implications of resources, the operation of choice within multidimensional constraints and so on (for example see Long 1977's holistic analysis of Peruvian entrepreneurs).

2) A study directed by Sara Carter and Tom Cannon on female entrepreneurs in Britain.

The study was commissioned by a UK Central Government Department to explore in depth, through case studies, the characteristics of female entrepreneurs. Particular interest focused on whether female entrepreneurs face additional problems to those that men face; whether they have different motivations, strategies and tactics to enter and succeed in business; and whether the experience of business ownership differs fundamentally between different categories of women. In exploring these issues sixty on-going businesses were visited and an interview based on a semi-structured questionnaire was conducted with the owner. These were then followed up some weeks later with another unstructured interview.

The study again produced interesting findings and was highly regarded by many (see Cannon, Carter, Rosa, Baddon and McClure 1988; Carter and Cannon 1988 a and b). From an anthropological perspective, however, it still suffered from the reduction of complex concepts into a questionnaire format. Unlike the graduate study, however, the inclusion of open questions and an unstructured follow-up interview enabled some of the disadvantages of the structured questionnaire approach to be overcome. The research team, for example, was able to contrast the reduced and over-simplified concepts in the questionnaire, with the true complexity of the concepts as elicited from the in-depth interviews. It was not surprising, for instance, to find that the desire for independence and 'the challenge' were the most common motivations for business start-up. The in-depth interviews, however, established that 'independence' and 'the challenge' meant quite different things to different women in different circumstances. For example to women managers with bleak promotion prospects in large companies, entry into self employment was a liberation from perceived discrimination. For others whose ideas for expansion were not allowed to be pursued in the large company they worked in, business ownership meant freedom to express their creative ideas to the full. To the mother unable to work because available employment did not allow her to vary her hours to suit her child-care arrangements, self employment meant freedom of choice to accommodate conflicting demands on her life. To the unemployed teenager, self employment was a release from the stigma of unemployment. To the crafts woman, it meant the freedom to pursue her artistic leanings without the frustration of dealing with the constraints of a job.

From a social anthropological perspective, however, in-depth interviews do not go far enough. They only tell you what a person says, not what they actually think or do. The study only scratched the surface of the underlying complexity of issues surrounding female entrepreneurship. The potential complexity was illustrated by the fact that in the follow-up interviews significant changes were detected not only in terms of business performance, but also in terms of attitudes in the style of management. Were these really changes, or were they just the result of an entrepreneur being unable to sustain an image over two interviews? Would this picture of the entrepreneur based on directly interviewing her, be sustained if others in her firm were interviewed about her? How would the picture presented by such interviews change if a researcher had the opportunity to shrink into the background, both in the work and home environment, and just record what was actually being done rather than said? Participant observation in social anthropology is not just un-structured interviewing. It is a thorough series of observations from many perspectives. Clearly the study would have benefited, given more resources, with a much more sustained observation of the female entrepreneurs under study.

Also of concern is the implicit 'feminist' motives for commissioning the study. Discrimination was viewed as a central policy issue, and there was a temptation to interpret many findings as a manifestation of discrimination. From a social anthropological view-point, this would be construed as ethnocentrism. In fact none of the factors which could have been naively interpreted as resulting from discrimination were so cut and dried. Indeed the researchers found it difficult to quantify the extent to which the problems and challenges of female entrepreneurs were exacerbated by gender. Again much more de-tailed information would have been required, especially from a parallel study of men, to establish with authority the presence of discrimination. For example, many of female en-trepreneurs felt that being a woman made it more difficult for them to find clients. With-out a male matched sample this could not be demonstrated. A social anthropologist would not have been satisfied just with interviewing a controlled male sample. He or she would judge it equally important to observe the process in which the female entrepreneur seeks to set up a deal with a male client; and the way a potential male client sets up deals with other male entrepreneurs when the female entrepreneur is not present. Finally the fact that the female entrepreneur feels discriminated against is of considerable interest to the anthro-pologist as a phenomenon in its own right, irrespective of whether it is based on objective fact.

3) Networks and narratives: an anthropological perspective for small business research, a study by Doug Caulkins, a social anthropologist and visiting professor from Grinnell College, Iowa.

Caulkins carried out interviews of Scottish and English entrepreneurs in 1988, to illustrate a method of approaching research on the social structure and culture of small businesses. Taking a more holistic approach, Caulkins (1988) proposed that the unit of analysis should be the entrepreneurial network, not the firm. In saying this, he does not imply that this is the only unit of analysis, or the best way of approaching the study of an entre-preneurial culture within a firm.

The concept of the entrepreneurial network requires for analysis detailed attention to transactions and relationships across corporate boundaries. Caulkins includes in this all individuals involved in the enterprise, whether they are paid members of the firm, unpaid volunteers, families of management or employees, and advisory consultants and helpers (Caulkins 1988:10). The concept does not assume a single entrepreneur at the centre, with all other members of the network subordinate. Caulkins approach thus combines the social anthropological virtues of an open definitional approach, avoidance of ethnocentric pre-conceptions, and a holistic perspective.

Entrepreneurial networks, Caulkins goes on to argue, are variable and change over time. This presents two problems from a social anthropological perspective. How does one capture the variability and reduce it to a form from which meaningful comparisons can be made? Secondly, short of intensive longitudinal participant observation, how can change over time be assessed? What an entrepreneur may say about the history of the firm may bear little relation to what actually happened.

Caulkins approached the first problem of reducing diversity by mapping networks in terms of the social anthropologist Mary Douglas's group/grid analysis (Douglas 1982), which organises social structure into four basic types on the basis of two dimensions, 'group', or the degree to which a person belongs to a group; and 'grid', the degree to which choice is constrained by social rules and obligations. Reducing social structure in this way is controversial in social anthropology. Mary Douglas justifies it on the grounds that:

'the object is not to come up with something original, but gently to push what is known into an explicit typology that captures the wisdom of a hundred years of sociology, anthropology and psychology'. (Douglas 1982:1)

In the favour of group/grid, therefore, is the fact that reduction of complex concepts is done in terms of a theoretical framework, not in terms of ad hoc pre-conceived categories.

The second problem of measuring the history of the firm is approached by treating the statements of entrepreneurs as 'narratives', or 'creation myths' of the founding of the firm. Interest in these narratives is not how close they fit the events that took place, but rather in that they:

'are constructs or interpretations of the nature of the business world, the relationships of the humans who work in it, and, implicitly perhaps, of nature and the supernatural. In the narrative, the teller does not replicate the events of the founding as they might be re-corded by some omniscient observer.' (Caulkins 1988:25).

By integrating narrative plots with the mapped networks on the group/grid model, Caulkins is able to use the model to:

'generate hypotheses and guide empirical research on the culture of the small business manager, including notions of success and failure and the kinds of narrative plots and characters that are used to explain their experiences. These plots and characters are part of a cultural repertory of small business, and illustrate the multiple models of entrepreneur-ship in the culture.' (p.1).

In his study Caulkins has kept closely to the basic principles of traditional social anthro-pology, and has been rewarded with an interpretation of entrepreneurship which is unique in the mainstream entrepreneurship literature. His entrepreneurial network concept is not just an 'interesting' alternative to the traditional notion of a bounded firm. It is a more useful unit of analysis because it includes more of the CONTEXT of entrepreneurial activ-ity. It is thus less apt to lend itself to ethnocentric interpretations. Additionally the entre-preneurial network idea lends itself to holism, another one of the anthropological virtues.

Conclusion

Bronislaw Malinowski developed the basic principles of modern British social anthro-pology outlined in this paper, after four years enforced participant observation of the Tro-briand Islanders when he was interned there during the First World War. Kuper (1963:16) cites the testimony of Father Baldwin, a Catholic missionary who remembered Malinowski at work, and noted that he appeared heroic neither to the 'natives' or to the white settlers and administrators on the Islands. Father Baldwin was cited as saying:

'I preferred not to refer him at all with the white people who had known him. He had made them uneasy, and they had got back at him by referring to him as the anthrofoologist, and his subject as anthrofoology'.

Through its emphasis on participant observation, holism and its distrust of 'common sense' and conventional wisdom, social anthropology is likely to make many engaged in mainstream entrepreneurial studies uneasy too. Some, perhaps, may use stronger terms than 'anthrofoology'.

The sense of unease, however, is minimal at present, as social anthropology has largely ignored mainstream entrepreneurial studies. The best anthropological studies involving entrepreneurship (such as those of Geertz, Barth and Long), have treated entrepreneurship as a means to an end, the understanding of processes of social change. Anthropologists, however, as Caulkins has demonstrated, are beginning to focus primarily on entrepreneurial issues. Though they are not many, it is likely that they will increase in number in the future.

More important than the impact of social anthropologists directly may be the adoption of some of their methods by non anthropologists already researching entrepreneurship from other perspectives. In a subject that is disparate (Carter, Faulkner, Nenadic and Cannon 1989) and 'searching for identity and respectability' (Carsrud and Johnson 1989), new insights are most likely to come through adopting a less ethnocentric, a more empirical and a more holistic approach. In particular conceptions of the entrepreneur as 'hero' exemplified in Mitton (1989) need to be set aside and direct observation made of the murky world of the business owner in the complex environment in which he or she operates. In this complex world the entrepreneur ceases to be a good model of the virtues of the capitalist system, but can display behaviour which to some could appear irrational when contrasted with the 'rational' ideal entrepreneurial virtues thought necessary to make money and create wealth. Making sense of apparent irrationality in business owners is as much a challenge to the modern anthropologist as it was to the previous generation of anthropologist when seeking to make sense of seeming irrational behaviour by pre-literate 'natives' in the colonial era.

From this perspective the potential contribution of social anthropology is large. It is the only discipline that recognises the systematic divergence between what a researcher thinks and does; what the people under study 'say about what they do; what they actually do and what they think' (Kuper 1983:16). The methods of social anthropology can not only lead to better data for 'scientific' analysis, but also to profound subjective insights. 'The ultimate goal', as Kuper states (p16) 'is to grasp a person's point of view, his relation to life, to realise his vision of his world.' No other discipline would attempt to understand the entrepreneur or small business owner from his or her own perspective.

References

Agar, M.H. (1980) The Professional Stranger:An Informal Introduction to Ethnography. Academic Press, New York.

Barth, F. (1962) (ed) The Role of the Entrepreneur in Social Change in Northern Norway. Universitets-Forlaget, Olso.

Cannon, T.; Carter, S.; Rosa, P.; Baddon, L. and McClure, R. (1988 - reprinted 1989) Female Entrepreneurship. Report for the Department of Employment and Shell UK. Ltd. Scottish Enterprise Foundation Report Series (3 Vols) nos 59/60/61/89.

Carter, S. and Cannon, T. (1988) Female Entrepreneurs: A Study of Female Business Owners, their Motivations, Experiences and Strategies for Success. Department of Employment Research Paper No. 65 1-57.

Carter, S.; Faulkner, W. and Nenadic, S. and Cannon, T. (1989) The nature, the role and the impact of small business research. in Rosa, P.; Birley, S.; Cannon, T. and O'Neill, K. (eds) The Role and Contribution of Small Business Research. Gower, Aldershot.

Caulkins, D. (1988) Networks and Narratives, an Anthropological Perspective for Small Business Research. Scottish Enterprise Occasional Paper Series 1/88.

Carsrud, A.L. and Johnson, R.W. (1989) Entrepreneurship: a social psychological perspective. Entrepreneurship and Regional Development, Vol. 1, 21-31.

Chell, E. (1985) The entrepreneurial personality: a few ghosts laid to rest. InternationalSmall Business Journal, vol. 3,3 43-54.

Douglas, M. (1982) Essays in the Sociology of Perception. Routledge and Kegan Paul, London.

Dunkelberg, W.C. and Cooper, A.C. (1982) 'Entrepreneurial typologies', Frontiers of Entrepreneurship Research 1-15.

Dyson-Hudson (1966) Karimojong Politics. Oxford University Press, Oxford.

Gartner, W.B. (1989) 'Who is an entrepreneur?' is the wrong question. Entrepreneurship Theory and Practice. Vol.13,4, 47-68.

Geertz, C. (1963) Peddlars and Princes: Social Development and Economic Change in two Indonesian Towns. University of Chicago Press, Chicago.

Hill, P. (1963) Migrant Cocoa Farmers of Southern Ghana: Study in Rural Capitalism. Cambridge University Press.

Horton, R. (1977) African traditional thought and Western science. In Wilson, R. (ed) Rationaility. Basil Blackwell, Oxford.

Kuper, A. (1983) Anthropology and Anthropologists: The Modern British School. Routledge and Kegan Paul, London.

LaFluente, A. and Salas, V. (1989) 'Types of entrepreneurs and firms: the case of new Spanish firms', Strategic Management Journal, 10(1), 17-30.

Long, N. (1972) Social Change and the Individual. Manchester University Press.

Long, N. (1977) Commerce and kinship in the Peruvian Highlands, in Botton, R. and Mayer, E. (eds) Andean Kinship and Marriage. A special publication of the American Anthropological Association.

Loasby, B. J. (1988) Entrepreneurship: Routines and Networks. University of Stirling, MSc in Entrepreneurial Studies Module 3.5.

Mitton, G.D. (1989) The compleat entrepreneur. Entrepreneurship Theory and Practice. Vol 13,3, 9-19.

Overing, J. (1985) Reason and Morality. Tavistock, London.

Reagan, Ronald (1985) Why this is an entrepreneurial age. J. of Business Venturing, Vol 1,1, 1-4.

Rosa, P. (1989) Family Background and Entrepreneurial Activity in British Graduates. Scottish Enterprise Foundation Conference Paper Series 56/89.

Rosa, P. (1989a) The Nature, Diversity and Complexity of 'Training Needs' and Response to Training in Small Firms. Scottish Enterprise Foundation Conference Paper Series.

Rosa, P. and McAlpine, A. (1989) Career Orientation towards Enterprise in British Graduates. Scottish Enterprise Foundation Conference Paper Series 57/89.

Smith, N.R. (1967) The Entrepreneur and his Firm: the Relationship between Type of Man and Type of Company', Occasional Paper, Bureau of Business and Economic Research, Graduate School of Business Administration, Michigan State University, East Lansing, Michigan.

Winch, R. (1964) Understanding a primitive culture. American Philosophical Quarterly. 1: 307-324.

7 Real and potential entrepreneurs playing a business simulation game

Heinz Klandt

Introduction

In a research project carried out at the University of Cologne, a business simulation game named 'EVa' was developed (Szyperski/Klandt, 1990). It is especially applicable to the world of entrepreneurs. An English translation of the game is being prepared.

Some 290 subjects played the game: business students at the universities of Cologne, Vienna, Berlin and Dortmund, entrepreneurs, managers and other potential entrepreneurs interested in entrepreneurial behaviour.

For each case more than 30,000 data were collected including observations on behaviour related to 4,000 decision possibilities and additional questionnaire data.

It is hypothesised that the simulation game 'EVa' could be considered as a method of observing entrepreneurial behaviour in controlled situations and, that it could therefore be helpful in studying the entrepreneurial processes.

In the long run the game is intended to become a tool for the measurement of entrepreneurial abilities; this research is continuing.

Using the method of computer simulation in entrepreneurship research

When we deal with simulation models we include very different approaches, such as:

* models of closed systems (environment and actors are simulated)

like the world model of Meadows/Club of Rome or - in a simpler way mostly without iterations - like a business plan (spread sheets) for a new venture.

The objective is - after starting the model based on assumption data - to observe what happens after a definite time span; after that the user may change his assumption data (or in some cases the structure of the model too), and take another look at the depending results.

With this kind of simulation one is able to examine, for example, a business concept or carry out experiments on systems one could not have in a controlled laboratory environment:

- to build/prove theories,
- to prove a concept of planned actions.

There exists a second type of simulation model which is intended to be used in a more interactive way; in this case only the environment of a potential subject is represented in the model:

* interactive models (only environment simulated):
  A typical example is a business simulation game which is used normally for training business students or managers:

  - as an educational tool

Besides this, one can use - after an empirical validation corresponding to the psychological theory of tests - such a simulation game instead of personality inventories, intelligence tests or biographical questionnaires:

- as vocational tests

The advantage of this could be a more realistic, better accepted (by subjects) instrument for the diagnosis of entrepreneurial abilities (for example in the venture capital industry).

Last but not least, some remarks should be made about the possibilities of using simulation games as tools for research, especially for entrepreneurship research:

- as a tool for laboratory research:
  -- to study entrepreneurial behavior of single entrepreneur or entrepreneurial teams.

Until today most empirical data in entrepreneurship research were in the worst cases collected by mailed questionnaires or in the better by interviews in a field environment. We are told by methodological research (artifact research) that such an approach has many disadvantages. Especially when direct questions (such as motives to become an entrepreneur) are posed to the entrepreneurs or - what may be even worse - to 'experts', a lot of as yet unrecognised research artifacts may be produced.

A multi-method approach could detect these artifacts. That involves for example, the use of observations besides of questions, the use of standardised situations besides of field study environments, and possible also: experimental situations with the systematic manipulation of independent variables. A computer aided business simulation game like 'EVa' could be used for this.

Simulating the entrepreneurial environment: Firm and markets

Theoretical background for the development of 'EVa'

The construction of the business simulation game 'EVa' is based on the general analysis of vocational tasks by DÖRNER and a special adaptation to the world of young and small firms which is considered to be the typical environment of an entrepreneur.

Professional task fields, especially those of the entrepreneur, can be typically characterised by (mostly along with DÖRNER at al., 1983):

Figure 1
Aspects of professional task fields

* undetermined goals / goals evolution,
* unstructured perception and action fields,
* complexity (many elements),
* meshed shape, connectivity (many relations between elements),
* intransparency: about the existence of and relations between unknown variables,
* feedbacks after gearing in,
* self-dynamic (development even without gearing in caused by active elements of the system),
* often exponential paths of development,
* manipulation only partly possible (partially directly, partially indirectly)
* limited time resources (windows, deadlines),
* limited material resources.
These characteristics demand appropriate behaviour:
* independent, poly-telic goal orientation,
* independent goal modification,
* active search for information,
* restricted search for information (costs vs. benefits of information, economic principle),
* partial analytical diagnosis of problem but
* complemented by intuitive, holistic diagnosis of problem,
* systematic thinking (causal-cybernatical model perceptions),
* considering & digesting system feedbacks,
* repeated (reactive) gearing in,
* decisions in cases of incomplete information/uncertainty,
* appropriate quick decisions.

The use of computer simulation helps you to produce a relevant and complex environment of these characteristics, and to observe subjects and their behaviour when they try to control such a complex system.

Description of the 'EVa' business simulation game

The 'EVa' business simulation game is intended to simulate the start-up and early development of a new venture. The computer reacts to the decisions of the player (or will hopefully!) as the markets and the enterprise would do in reality. Therefore entrepreneurial decisions on the subjects in the business simulation game environment, are intended to have results similar to those in a real enterprise.

Contrary to the traditional business education with its emphasis on big, mature businesses, 'EVa' simulates a young and small firm. The player becomes owner and manager of this enterprise and has to play this role.

Figure 2
Traditional business education versus 'EVa'

Prototype of traditional business education:

  * Mature business
  * Big business
  * Tasks and responsibilities of the board of directors
    or staff of that group of enterprises

EVa's model in contrast:

  * Start-up and early development
    of a new business
  * Small business
  * Task of the entrepreneur:
    Integration of management and ownership (risk)

The following illustration shows the general structure of the 'EVa' simulation game.

Figure 3
The structure of EVa

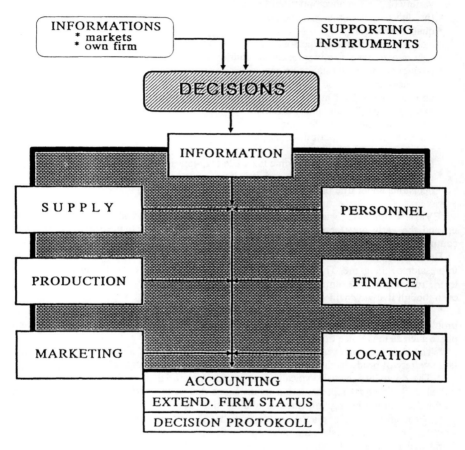

The "EVa" Simulation Game

Figure 4
Important characteristics of 'EVa'

* variety of decision areas
  (procurement/production/sales/personnel/finances/location/information)
* variety of performance opportunities
  (products/services/merchandising)
* qualitative decisions
  (for example in location/personnel)
* necessity to develop entrepreneurial intuition
* strategic and operational decisions
* monthly decisions, not quarterly or
  annual (1 period = 1 month)
* many periods (37) and many different
  possible and necessary decisions
  (more than 100 per period, 4,000 total)
* realistic tax environment
  (turnover tax/corporation income tax/trade tax/wages tax)
* realistic accounting (also managerial)
* decisions under true pressure

'EVa' is a simulation game that allows the player to influence and experience the start-up and the early development phase of a software firm through the use of a personal computer.

Here are some characteristics of the simulation game 'EVa', in order to give an impression of the game. The modelling concept aims to adhere closely the game's contents to the real tasks of the entrepreneur (content validity especially in respect to acceptance), even though it always will be a reduced artifact.

* The simulation game 'EVa', simulating a software firm, is geared especially towards problems of the early development phase. It also comprises typical decisions of the start-up phase such as the choice of the company's location.

* The choice of the exemplary market segment 'software firm' allows for decisions on a large variety of products that comprises trade, services and manufacturing alike.

* The diversity which is typically among entrepreneurial tasks in small businesses, is reflected by an equal representation of decisions due in the personnel, financial, supply, production and marketing, information, and location areas.

* Great importance is placed on the fact that the player is not only confronted with strategic but also with tasks on a more operational level as is typical for the small business world and for young firms. For this reason it is also developed as a two level (micro-analytical) model.

* In respect of this, a large number of possible decisions (normal monthly period with approximately 110 decisions, throughout the game 4,000) exist which demand a conscious choice by the player. This fact reduces the importance of a single decision. The player has the possibility of correcting or improving wrong decisions on the basis of feed-backs.

* Besides measurable, quantitative aspects of financial accounting, qualitative decisions which can be tackled only to a certain degree with an analytical approach must also be made. The player has to develop an entrepreneurial intuition to find the correct solutions here.

* Undemanded feedbacks on the player's company and its market to a degree usual in young, small firms; additional information has to be required and 'honoured' in the game (paid for).

* The time at the players' disposal in order to make their decisions, is short but sufficient; so far, it is intended to create a realistic atmosphere under deadline pressure.

* To be close to reality was an important criterion in the development of 'EVa'. Therefore, even details like the most important taxes (turnover tax [as value added tax], corporation income tax, trade tax and wages tax) were taken into account.

* Modelling as a deterministic model (identical inputs produce identical outputs), subjects play against the computer programme, not against varying competitors, since only this way leads to meaningful results that can be compared between the subjects (players).

* Protocol of all decisions of the player and of important variables describing the system's structure (EVa firm) in each period.

* Final evaluation of the value of the company (such as profitability) to determine the result variable: 'game performance'.

* Additional final analysis of player's activities (e.g. quantity and kind of information demanded) in all periods incorporated in the game is possible.

* The game runs on IBM PC, AT, PS/2. It is written in Pascal with a source code of about 10,000 lines of code.

* The game coordinator (experimenter) gives a standardised introduction and distributes some handouts and the decision sheets.

* The player (subject) makes his decisions based on a game manual and records them in decision sheets. Then he enters his decisions into the computer and receives the reaction by the printer (or optional by screen) such as information about loans granted, profit-and-loss statements, balance sheets, applications for jobs.

Illustration 5 shows the typical course of the management business game.

Figure 5
Course of the management business game

The evening before
    18.00 - 19.30 h:
    - introduction
    - distribution of basic information
    - possibility of ordering additional
      information with costs (start 1st part)
    19.30 - ??.?? h:
    - homework: development of the business plan, strategies

The day of playing the game
    9.00 - 19.00 h
    - Start-up of the enterprise (start 2nd part)
    - playing during 36 months of early development
    - each player acts autonomously
    - breaks are taken when required only (individually)

Table 1
Players of the business-simulation game 'EVa':
vocational groups (dominant vocational activity)

	absolute	in %
Students	175	65,2
Employees		
- business	18	6,7
- R&D	27	10,0
Executives	12	4,5
Entrepreneurs/self-employed	27	10,0
Others	10	3,7
Valid Cases	269	100%
Missing Data	24	

Table 2
Amount of self-employed activities (hours)

	absolute	in %
- not self-employed at all	202	78,0
- less than 40 hours per week	26	10,0
- 40 hours or more per week	31	12,0
Valid Cases	259	100 %
Missing Data	34	

Table 3
Self-employed (also part-time)

	absolute	in %
- never was self-employed, and do not plan to be	81	32,3
- plan to become self-employed	118	47,0
- was self-employed	5	2,0
- presently self-employed	47	18,7
Valid Cases	251	100 %
Missing Data	41	

Table 4
Need of achievement

	val. n	Mean	StdDev.	Median
Groups in this study				
- all players	270	33,2	4,08	33,0
- not self-employed	199	32,9	4,21	-
- all self-employed	49	34,6	3,18	-
- less successful	13	31,9	9,99	-
- more successful	9	36,6	1,88	-
Comparative Groups[1]				
- R&D employees	264	31.7	4.26	31.7
- Business students	95	32.5	5.08	33.0
- Business students	93	29.7	4.64	-
- Middle Management	41	34.1	-	-
- Interested in Entrepr.	59	34.2	4.10	34.5
- Entrepreneurs	77	36.9	5.1	38.0

1) Klandt, 1984, p. 68,148.

Some empirical results

Structure of subjects

Up until now 'EVa' has been played by some 290 players. The following tables show the structure of these subjects.

Table 1 shows that most of the players were students. Additionally, there were office-worker, specialists, executiv managers and entrepreneurs.

Acceptance of the game

It is interesting whether, in the player's opinion, EVa seems to be realistic. The general attidude towards 'EVa' is rather positive. More than 80 % of the players considered the game to be 'realistic' or even 'very realistic'.

Table 5
Do you consider 'EVa' to be realistic? (all cases)

	absolute	in %
very realistic	39	15.2
rather realistic	176	68.8
rather unrealistic	39	15.2
entirely unrealistic	2	0.8
Valid Cases	256	100
Missing Data	36	

Mean = 2.039

So far, more than 80% of the players considered 'EVa' to be very or rather realistic.

It could be criticised that nearly 60 per cent are students and consequently not in a position expert enough to compare 'EVa' with 'reality'. Therefore the subjects were divided into a group of 'self-employed' and a group of 'not self-employed'. The following table provides the results. It shows that even in the group of independent businessmen, more than 80 per cent judged 'EVa' to be 'realistic' or 'very realistic'. Unexpectedly there were more players which thought EVa to be 'very realistic'.

Table 6
Is 'EVa' realistic or artificial ?
(Self-employed cases versus employed cases)

	self-employed (also part time)		employed	
	abs.	%	abs.	%
very realistic	8	17.4	31	14.8
rather realistic	30	65.2	146	69.5
rather unrealistic	7	15.2	32	15.2
entirely unrealistic	1	2.2	1	0.1
Valid Cases	46	100	210	100

Mean = 2.0
Median = 2.0

Figure 6
Measurement of game performance

The following variables are used as measures of game performance:

Variable Name	Variable Meaning
(SPIELE	Number of games started in available time)
PLEITEN	Number of bankruptcies
PLEITE1	First time bankrupt in period # ...
PERIODE	highest period reached in available time
GEWISU	cumulated profits over all periods
GEWI1	profit in the first year
GEWI2	profit in the second year
GEW3	profit in the third year
GESUMSU	cumulated turnover over all periods
GESUM1	turnover in the first year
GESUM2	turnover in the second year
GESUM3	turnover in the third year

Differences in performance between self-employed and not-self-employed subjects

Table 7
Game performance of self-employed vs. not self-employed

	self-employed	not self-employed
SPIELE	2.10 games	1.8 games
PLEITEN	0.63 bankruptcies	0.49 bankruptcies
PLEITE1	24.8 th period	27.5 th period
PERIODE	29.3 periods	29.2 periods
GEWISU	393 Thousand DM	357 Thousand DM
GESUMSU	4.488 Mio. DM	4.158 M. DM
" 1	1.014 Mio.DM	1.036 M. DM
" 2	1.811 Mio. DM	1.680 M. DM
" 3	1.662 Mio. DM	1.442 M. DM

Measures used for entrepreneurial success in real world

In the case of self-employed players, data were collected referring to the first 6 years after start-up:

- number of employees,
- turnover per year and
- profit per year.

A classification of self-employed players into more or less successful (real life) entrepreneurs was made based on turnover and number of employees.

Table 8
More or less than 200,000 DM turnover in 2nd year after start-up (UERF2)

Value Label	absolute	in %
less successful E.	14	58.3
more successful E.	10	41.7
Valid Cases	24	100

Missing Cases   269

Table 9
Less or more than 2 employees in 3rd year after start-up (UERFM)

Value Label	absolute	in %
less successful E.	16	50.0
more successful E.	16	50.0
Valid Cases	32	100

Missing Cases 261

Differences between more and less successful entrepreneurs

Now we refer to relations between game performance (internal) and real life performance (external).

The following table illustrates a lot of notable differences between the two groups; it shows that high entrepreneurial performers in real life also achieve a better game performance.

Table 10
Difference in game performance between more or less successful real life entrepreneurs (means)

	less successful	more successful
SPIELE	1.86 games	1.3 games
PLEITEN	1.29 bankruptcies	0.3 bankruptcies
PLEITE1	19.0 th period	24.3 th period
PERIODE	21.8 periods	28.9 periods
GEWISU	163 Thousand DM	380 Thousand DM
" 1	- 6.5 Thousand DM	48 Thousand DM
" 2	79 Thousand DM	171 Thousand DM
" 3	90 Thousand DM	162 Thousand DM
GESUMSU	2.943 Mio. DM	4.415 M. DM
" 1	887 Thousand DM	1.091 M. DM
" 2	1.150 M. DM	1.708 M. DM
" 3	0.906 M. DM	1.616 M. DM

In summary, the first exploration into the collected empirical data supports strongly the hypothesis that a business simulation game can be developed to represent an environment, which is to a certain degree similar to the real life environment of entrepreneurs. At least a part of the real life entrepreneurial tasks seems to be represented in the EVa game.

References

Dietrich Dörner u.a. (Edit..), *Lohhausen: Vom Umgang mit Unbestimmtheit und Komplexität,(Controlling Uncertainty and Complexity)*, (Hans Huber Verlag, Bern Stuttgart Wien, 1983).

Heinz Klandt, 'Trends in Small Business Start-up in West Germany', in: *Entrepreneurship in Europe, The Social Processes*, ed. by Robert Goffee and Richard Scase (Croom Helm, London - New York - Sydney, 1987).

Heinz Klandt, *Aktivität und Erfolg des Unternehmungsgründers. Eine empirische Analyse unter Einbeziehung des mikrosozialen Umfeldes (The activities and performance of new business owners: an empirical analysis concerning the micro-social context)* (Eul Verlag, Bergisch Gladbach 1984).

Norbert Szyperski, Heinz Klandt, Diagnose und Training der Unternehmerfähigkeit mittels Planspiel (Diagnosis and Training of Entrepreneurial Abilities by Business Simulation Games) in: *Entrepreneurship - Innovative Unternehmensgründung als Aufgabe* ed. by Norbert Szyperski, Paul Roth (C.E. Poeschel Verlag, Stuttgart 1990).

Appendix: Examples of player's information

Appendix 1: Introduction for 'EVa' players
Basic remarks on the simulation game 'EVa'

What is EVa?
- A computer program reacting to your entrepreneurial decisions as a company would do in reality.

What is the purpose of EVa?
- EVa gives you the opportunity to try out the role of an entrepreneur without substantial risks in the form of sand-table manoevring, so to speak.
- to discover your own strengths and weaknesses, to find starting points for your own further development

The simulation game EVa gives you the opportunity to simulate the start-up and early development of a software and system house on a computer. It is your task to make entrepreneurial decisions in every single phase of the game. Your decisions influence your company as well as the markets you are operating in.

For example, you have the possibility to hire and dismiss personnel, to put your employees to work in different work areas in your company, to give them training etc. In the financial area, you can apply for loans or buy capital assets. By making use of marketing instruments you can try to influence the chances   of selling your goods and services. In the production area of your company you can control the scheduling of the software production and other options.

After each game period, which reflects one month of business in reality, you get some basic information on the development of your company. For an additional fee you get more detailed information about your company or the markets.

The simulation game begins with the start-up period that comprises 3 month in reality and is divided into two phases: the first takes 1 month, the second 2 months. This is followed by 36 periods of the early development phase (each of which represents only one month in reality). You find more details about your options in the start-up period and all the following monthly periods of the early development phase of your company in other parts of this handbook.

You have the possibility of offering four different services or products in your company but you are not obliged to be active in all four of them. These four areas are:

1st) doing business with the professional microcomputer called EVa-PC

2nd) doing buisness with the complete word processing microcomputer system, the EVa-system

3rd) production of customized software tailored to individual orders

4th) offering training and consultation services in the data processing sector

You cannot, however, make any sales or turnover during the start-up period of the game.

After you have completed the start-up period, the game lasts for 36 monthly periods and therefore reflects the first 3 years in the life of your software company.

It is crucial for you to avoid illiquidity during the first 3 years, i.e. as in reality, you have to be able to meet all obligations at any given time during the game. The supervision of your current and foreseeable liquidity should therefore be a major task in the game. As far as this knock-out criteria is concerned, EVa treats you as roughly as real life does.

To create equal conditions in the start-up period, your software and system house EVa has to be set up in the legal form of a limited liability company with a capital stock of $50,000. When the game starts those funds are available on your current account.

Since you take over the role of the single executive director, it is your personal duty to file for chapter 11 as soon as you notice heavy indebtedness in your company at the bottom of the balance sheet.

EVa will take care of this duty and you will be provided with a corresponding message.

In the case of bankruptcy - caused either by illiquidity or heavy indebtedness - the game ends for you before the first three years have passed.

Remarks regarding your personal situation are always important when starting up a company, even if it is organised in the form of a corporation. We assume that you already have work experience in the software market in the areas of sales and consultation and that you have also had some experience in programming. Your personal situation - we assume that you are married - requires that you provide your family with at least $ 2,400 a month. Your salary as the executive director of your company is designed to meet these requirements during all 36 periods.

For financial reasons, you continue to work as an employee during the start-up phase, i.e. during the first 3 months of the game, therefore, you have to carry out your start-up activities in after-work hours, on Saturdays, Sundays, holidays and during your remaining vacation time.

From the moment your company is in operation you spend all your working time in your company.

You own a small family home that gives you, apart from the $ 50,000 of capital stock in cash, additional financial reserves to the amount of $ 250,000. You are allowed to take out a personal credit of $30,000 to increase your credit limits (current account, overdraft). Your bank is willing to increase this loan if your company's performance is positive.

When planning the financial side of an enterprise, you have to take into account that government subsidies in the start-up phase as well as bank loans are usually based on collateral securities. The use of these loans is limited to real asset investments. Apart from real estate purchases, which are not allowed in this game, you can only use those loans for buying inventories and fixed assets and the first stock of merchandise (EVa-PC, EVa-Systems). You are, however, you are not allowed to finance salaries, rents or other operating expenses with these funds. Only a line of credit from your bank will allow you to finance such expenses.

You will find that you will need a quite lot of time during the start-up period and the first few game periods, to become acquainted with the numerous options you have to influence the development of the game understand the structure of the game and have made your own plans and decisions for the first few periods of the game. You may use a writing pad and pocket calculator to prepare your decisions. When you have get used to the game you will definitely use much less time because you will mostly be transforming the strategic concepts into operative decisions. You have to remember that every single game period only reflects one month in reality.

It is important that you understand the broad range and large number of different decisions which you can take as a choice of decision opötions but keep in mind that in reality an entrepreneur has a number of options to consider and one of his most important qualities is to distinguish between important and unimportant activities and not to get lost in details.

And once again: watch your liquidity at all times of the game; otherwise chapter eleven is beckoning, and you will not be allowed to finish the game!

If you have problems understanding anything in this text, please refer to the game coordinator at earliest time.

Now we wish you a very successful game and hope you enjoy yourself!

Appendix 2: Conditions and prices for the start-up period and all 36 early development periods

(as far as price changes have to be expected in the course of the game, current prices are explicitly marked as 'current')

(0) START-UP EXPENSES (see also information expenses)

- expenses for notary public	500 $
- Inferior Court registration/public notification	750 $
- corporation tax (1% of capital stock)	500 $
- trade license	10 $

(1) SUPPLY MARKET

	current net price (+14% sales tax)	term of delivery	discount/terms of payment (if applicable) if paid directly	payment payable netto offer:	discount level: n items 10 %	20 %
merchandise:						
* EVa-PC	5,000	1 month	2%	1 month	10	25
* EVa-System	12,000	2 month	2%	after delivery	10	25
capital assets:						
* workstation	30,000	2 month	"		5	10
* equipment	2,000	1 month	"		5	10
* software tools	3,000	1 "	"		5	10

During the start-up phase and during the first 4 months you do not benefit from terms of payment, payments are therefore due on delivery without any discount.

(2) PERSONNEL MARKET/LOAN WORK (average gross wage (40 hrs/week))

	average monthly gross wage curr.	social benefits employer+employee	days of vacation per year	overtime excess pay	wages paid xtime p.a.
* clerical staff	2,400	35 %	21days	25%	13
* DP consultant	4,800	"	"	25%	13
* hardware salesman	3,900	"	"	25%	13
* programmer	4,900	"	"	25%	13

Advertisements for personnel recruiting

	net price (+ 14 % sales tax)	validity	term of publication	reaction applicant
* single publication clerical staff	480 $	immediately	imm.	end of month
* single publication cons./sales/progr.	900 $	"	"	end of month

loan work	current net price (+14 % sales tax) per hour	available	discount	term of payment
* MANPOWER	95 $	immediately	2 %	1 month net
* RANDSTADT	120 $	"	2 %	"
* ROBINSON	85 $	"	2 %	"

* employee training	1. day	400	training + payment	
	additional day	200	immediately	

(3) INFORMATION MARKET

A only for start-up phase	net due price (14% sales tax)	delivery	payment necessary
* start-up consult. (basic)	650 $	immediately	immediately
* " consult. (extend.)	2,600 $	"	"
* location study 1	500 $	immediately	immediately
* " 2	"	"	"
* " 3	"	"	"
* " 4	"	"	"
* " 5	"	"	"

B in all phases	net price (+14% sales tax)	date of delivery	payment due	up-dated
* market analysis, small	80 $	immed.	1 month	every month
* " " , large	320 $	"	"	"
* market forecast, small	500 $	"	"	every 12 months (0,13,25,etc.)
* large	900 $	"	"	
* preliminary monthly statement of income	200 $ +1% inventory supervision	"	"	every month
* yearly balance sheet/statement of income	500 $	"	"	p.a. (14.,26.Per/.)
* financial ratios monthly brief; yearly extended	100 $	"	"	monthly (long: 14.u.26. Per/.)

(4) FINANCIAL MARKET

financial investments	current rate of interesst	minimum amount	commission terms purchase sales		applicable purchase sales/due	
bonds (face value	6 %	100	1 %	1 %	immed.	immed.
deposits 6 month	1.5 %	10,000	0 %	0 %	"	6 m after
" 12 "	2.5 %	10,000	0 %	0 %	"	12 m after

credit/loans:	current interest rate	amortisation starting	monthly annuity per $ 1,000
public subsidies	6 %	25 period	(int.: 5,42 $)(24/120 m)
bank:starting-up loan	7.5 %	immed.	46,42$ (24th month)
bank: long-term	9 %	immed.	47,33 $ (24th month)
bank: medium-term	10.5 %	immed.	92,08 $ (12th month)
bank: line of credit	12.5 %	immed.	(interest:125,00 $)

(5) MARKETING SIDE (current average market price in start-up period)

goods/product/service	price per unit	
merchandise:		
* EVa-PC	6,000 $/item	
* EVa-Systems	14,400 $/item	
services:		
* training/consulting	120 $/hour	
products:		
* software products	800 $/day p. person	
used equipment:		
* used workstation		
1 year old	15,000 $/item	(1/2 of new price)
2 year old	10,000 $/item	(1/3 of new price)

Appendix 3:   Overview of alternative locations

These are taken from the regional daily newspaper 'the Greater Eva Herald' advertising section or compiled from real estate agents' offers.

Due to your previous living and working area you have already decided to locate your planned company in the Groß-EVa town area. Please refer to the enclosed map for the precise location of the alternatives described below.

LOCATION1:

* small store of 50 sq. meter with adjacent office space of 20 sq. meter,
     located in centre of Groß-EVa Stadt
* average passing trade
* located in an apartment/store building erected in 1960
* in good condition, with average heating, electrical and sanitary equipment
* rent $1,350 a month without additional costs
* additional costs (heating, sewage, water, waste disposal, electricity) total $200

LOCATION2:

* only office space
* on 2nd floor
* no lift available
* size including store-rooms 90 sq. meter
* divided into 3 separate rooms and bathroom, kitchenette
* located in a mixed residential and industrial neighbourhood in ADAMSTADT
* the building is in very good condition erected in 1981 and well equipped with all
     installations desirable for offices
* monthly rent without additional costs amounts to $1,080
* additional costs add up to $150
* motorway exit approximately 12 minutes away by car
* sufficient parking space adjacent.

LOCATION3:

* office space located in the Groß-EVa Stadt industrial neighbourhood
* on the 7th floor of a larger office building
* lift available
* accessibility: at centre 20 min. away by car, next motorway exit ten minutes away;
* excellent parking conditions
* modern hotel close by
* public transport stop approximately. a 5 min. walk away
* size: 75 sq. meter divided into 2 rooms, with adjoining store-rooms
* the building was completed 6 years ago
* equipped with excellent electrical facilities, air
     conditioning, very good heating and sanitary installations

* monthly rent without additional costs is $1250
* additional costs add up to $350 a month

LOCATION4:

* store sized 100 sq. meter
* with office space and storage facilities of 50 sq. meter each
* located in the medium-sized, fast-growing town of Oberweiler
  in an area with average trade
* located in an apartment/store building erected in 1958
* in average condition
* separate gas heating for the commercial section
* fair sanitary and electrical facilities
* monthly rent $3500 without additional costs
* additional costs for heating, sewage, water, and waste disposal: $450

LOCATION5:

* office space of 20 sq. meter and separate store-room of 30 sq. meter in the basement
* office located on 3rd floor without lift
* basic sanitary, electrical and heating installations
* located in the Unterweiler country-side , adequate parking conditions
* next motorway exit approximately 25 minutes
* rooms are fully renovated and have to be left behind to the same condition when
  moving out
* rent without additional costs$300
* additional costs $80

Part 3
Survival and exit of enterprises

8 The owner-managers exit route

Sue Birley and Paul Westhead

Introduction

During the 1980s an increasing amount of corporate and political strategic attention was directed towards the revival of an 'enterprise culture' in the United Kingdom. One measure of the success of these strategies was the increasing numbers of new businesses recorded during the decade (Department of Employment, 1989a). However, there is an increasing body of evidence to suggest that a growing small business sector is characterised not only by a positive trend in new firm formation but also by a countervailing trend in firm 'failures'. For example, Beesley and Hamilton (1984,1986) suggest that a high level of business 'turbulence' plays an important seedbed role in the generation of new businesses. Turbulence does not, however, imply simply the contrast between new firms and firms which fail to survive in the market-place but also, for example, those firms which change their ownership through sale to a third party.

The ways in which both founders and investors of new as well as established businesses realise their original investment are commonly known as their 'exit route'. There are five exit routes open to the owners of any business - sale to a third, independent party; sale to another business; sale to the management or employees; public quotation; and liquidation. In an earlier study of the trend in the use of these five exit routes between 1983 and 1987 in the United Kingdom Birley and Westhead (1988) found the private advertised sale to be by far the method most frequently adopted.

Building on the results of this earlier research the aims of this paper are threefold. First, to examine if there have been any significant shifts in national private advertised sales trends and characteristics over the two year period between 1st January 1988 and 31st December 1989 compared to the 1st January 1983 to 31st December 1987 study. Second, to examine the post 'Stock Market Crash' period (1988 to 1989) in detail in order to identify any significant differences between the types of industries most involved, the geographic patterns, the reasons for sale, and the size and price and the professional advisers most frequently involved. Third, to report the results of two surveys of the two main parties in a private advertised sale - the sellers and their advisers.

Methodology

Since businesses for sale are not required by law to register their intent, there is no central listing of the population to be studied. Therefore, in order to estimate the level of activity, the following potential data sources were investigated - the business sections of the national newspapers; local newspapers published daily; the Financial Times published every Tuesday and Saturday; Business and Assets published every two weeks; Daltons Weekly published weekly; Exchange and Mart published weekly; and Stock Exchange Quarterly (now the Quality of Markets Quarterly). Analysis of these potential data sources showed that the national publications were more likely to include larger businesses, from a variety of industries, whilst the local sources tended to concentrate upon local, very small, retail businesses (Birley and Westhead, 1988). However, the Financial Times provided the most comprehensive cover of business sales, both in terms of volume, industry and geographic spread, and so was chosen as the primary source of data for this paper. A subsequent survey of intermediaries and owners advertising business sales between April and May 1988 confirmed this as the 'data source which most business sellers and buyers both advertise in and read'. A list of businesses offered for sale was extracted from every Tuesday edition of the Financial Times (the edition devoted to advertisements for business sales) between 1st January 1983 and 31st December 1989.

Overall trends

Extent of private sales activity

Table 1 compares the overall pattern of business sales during the years 1983 to 1989 for all the available exit routes in the United Kingdom. It is clear from this that the most common method used by owners to realise their investment in their business remains through private advertised sale with management buyouts also providing a frequent mechanism for corporate re-structuring. Moreover, the pattern of activity has increased dramatically over the last two years of the study with, for example, an increase of 25.8% between 1988 and 1989, returning to the very high level of 36.9% recorded between 1983 and 1984. Increased activity in advertised sales is also shown by the fact that between 1983 to 1987 there was on average 1,262 advertised sales per year compared to over 2,020 per year during the last two years.

Seasonal trends

Figure 1 shows an upward trend in private advertised sales over the 1983 to 1989 period. The decline in the second and third quarters of 1983 is mainly due to the fact that advertisements for sales were not published in the Financial Times due to an industrial dispute. Since the Stock Market crash in the third quarter of 1987 the level has consistently risen with a peak of 595 advertised sales being recorded in the second quarter of 1989. Seasonalised trends for private advertised sales were calculated using the centre average method (Harper, 1977). The first quarter was found to be the most active period with an adjusted seasonal variation of 1.08 followed by the second quarter which recorded an average adjusted seasonal variation of 0.98. (Figure 1)

Table 1
Trends in exit routes in the United Kingdom

Year	Private advertised sales	Public listing	USM listing	Third market listing	Mergers listed on the stock exchange	Management buy-outs
1983	868	61	82	0	65	189
1984	1,188	76	95	0	86	209
1985	1,393	70	94	0	97	255
1986	1,338	125	86	0	126	312
1987	1,522	143	68	30	153	335
1988	1,789	118	94	21	102	371
1989	2,250	96	66	19	119	359
Total	10,348	689	585	70	748	2,030

Sources: Financial Times (various issues), Quality of Markets Quarterly (various issues) and the Centre for Management Buy-out Research at the University of Nottingham.

Regional variations

Despite the significant growth in private advertised sales, the *regional pattern* has remained reasonably consistent with the largest number again being recorded in the South East of England (Table 2). Within this overall pattern, however, there has been a marked decrease in the proportion of sales recorded in the West Midlands whilst the South West of England appears to have recorded an increase. The lowest absolute levels of private advertised sales activity over the second period were again recorded in the North of England, Wales and Northern Ireland.

In order to estimate *regional volatility,* sales levels were calculated as a proportion of the *stock* of establishments in the area as represented by the total number of firms registered for Value Added Tax (VAT) at the end of the year prior to the period of study (Department of Employment, 1989b). The 'sales rate' was standardised and divided by 5 for the first period and by 2 for the second period studied in order to allow direct comparison to be made. A marked shift in the regional pattern of standardised private sales rates is shown in Table 2 with a rapid growth in relative sales being recorded over the 1988 to 1989 period in the East Midlands and South West of England compared to a relative slowdown in the West Midlands. The pattern of activity, however, remains relatively low in Northern Ireland, Wales and the North of England.

Spatial trends in advertised sales may also be detailed at the increasingly popular 'north-south' level of analysis (Lewis and Townsend, 1989; Smith, 1989; Birley and Westhead, 1990) which is a much broader and coarser level than the standard region level.

Interestingly, there has been a significant increase in the absolute number of sales in the 'south' (the standard regions of East Anglia, the South East and the South West in England - broadly regarded as the pressurised heart of the 'south~. Moreover, the 'south' also has

125

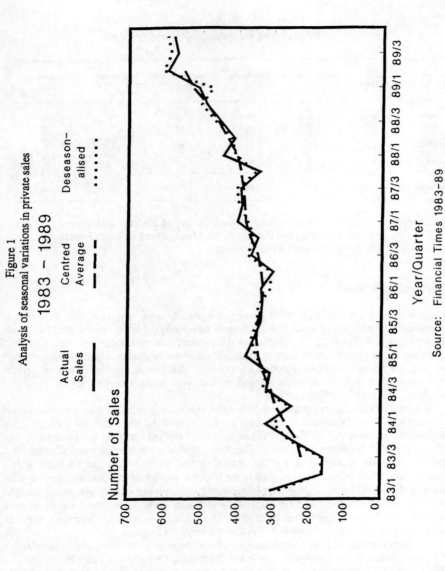

Figure 1
Analysis of seasonal variations in private sales
1983 – 1989

Actual Sales ▬▬▬   Centred Average ▬ ▬ ▬   Deseason- alised ••••••••

Number of Sales

700
600
500
400
300
200
100
0

83/1 83/3 84/1 84/3 85/1 85/3 86/1 86/3 87/1 87/3 88/1 88/3 89/1 89/3

Year/Quarter

Source: Financial Times 1983–89

Table 2

Number of business sales by standard region

Standard region	1983-1987				1988-1989				1983-1989			
	Number of private sales	Rank	Standardised sales rate, (c)	Rank	Number of private sales	Rank	Standardised sales rate, (d)	Rank	Number of private sales	Rank	Standardised sales rate, (e)	Rank
East Anglia (a)	174	8	0.63	5	103	5	0.83	8	277	8	0.83	5
East Midlands (b)	301	5	0.64	4	189	4	0.91	4	490	5	0.88	3
North (b)	116	10	0.43	9	73	9	0.62	10	189	10	0.58	9
Northern Ireland (b)	6	11	0.03	11	12	11	0.12	11	18	11	0.07	11
North West (b)	444	3	0.67	3	244	3	0.88	3	688	2	0.86	4
Scotland (b)	222	7	0.46	8	137	8	0.64	7	359	7	0.62	8
South East (a)	1,806	1	0.81	1	1,339	1	1.28	1	3,145	1	1.17	1
South West (a)	360	4	0.55	6	252	6	0.86	2	612	4	0.78	6
Wales (b)	147	9	0.39	10	86	10	0.55	9	233	9	0.52	10
West Midlands (b)	451	2	0.76	2	179	2	0.69	5	630	3	0.88	2
Yorkshire and Humberside (b)	264	6	0.49	7	170	7	0.75	6	434	6	0.68	7
South (a)	2,340		0.74		1,694		1.16		4,034		1.06	
North (b)	1,951		0.54		1,090		0.74		3,041		0.70	
Total	4,291		0.63		2,784		0.92		7,075		0.87	

Notes: (a) South - standard regions of East Anglia, South East and South West England;
(b) North - remaining standard regions of the United Kingdom;
(c) Number of private sales, 1983-87 per 1,000 total stock of VAT registered businesses at the end of 1982 divided by 5;
(d) Number of private sales, 1988-89 per 1,000 total stock of VAT registered businesses at the end of 1987 divided by 2; and
(e) Number of private sales, 1983-89 per 1,000 total stock of VAT registered businesses at the end of 1982 divided by 7.

the highest standardised sales rates which range from 0.74 to 1.16 compared with a range of only 0.54 to 0.74 in the 'north' (Table 2).

Industrial variations

Table 3 shows the leading industrial sector for advertised sales over the two periods was retail distribution. From this table it can be inferred that there has been a marked shift away from wholesale distribution, manufacture of metal goods, and mechanical engineering towards business services (8.8% and 5.8% between 1983-87 and 1988-89, respectively) and hotels and catering (5.1% and 7.6% between 1983-87 and 1988-89, respectively).

Table 3
Leadin business sales industrial sectors

Standard industrial category	Time period						Total		
	1983-1987			1988-1989					
	No.	%	Rank	No.	%	Rank	No	%	Rank
Retail distribution (6410-6560)	782	12.8	1	419	10.6	1	1,201	11.9	1
Wholesale distribution (6110-6190)	552	9.0	2	273	6.9	4	825	8.2	2
Manufacture of metal goods n.e.s. (3111-3169)	507	8.3	3	259	6.6	5	766	7.6	3
Mechanical engineering (3204-3290)	486	8.0	4	223	5.6	6	709	7.0	4
Business services (8310-8396)	352	5.8	5	349	8.8	2	701	7.0	5
Hotels and catering (6611-6670)	314	5.1	6	300	7.6	3	614	6.1	6

At a seven industrial category level (see Appendix 1) a significant decrease in advertised sales over the two time periods in heavy manufacturing (23.9% and 19.9% between 1983-87 and 1988-89, respectively) and services (28.3% and 25.9% between 1983-87 and 1988-89, respectively) was recorded, whilst there has been a marked increase in advertised sales of light manufacturing (17.5% and 20.5% between 1983-87 and 1988-89, respectively), transport (15.8% and 17.9% between 1983-87 and 1988-89, respectively) and other services (5.8% and 7.3% between 1983-87 and 1988-89, respectively).

Reason for sale

Firms which 'cease to trade' represent over 60% of private advertised sales in both of the periods studied (61.2% and 63.9% between 1983-87 and 1988-89, respectively). Within this, there has been a significant drop in both the percentage and the number of firms in receivership with a more than compensatory increase in firms under 'administration'. Various strategic reasons, such as the need to raise cash for acquisitions, continue to represent around 15% of the firms identified, and approximately 20% of firms are offered for sale due to personal reasons of ill health or retirement.

Size and advertised selling price

Data on both the sales revenue and the advertised selling price was adjusted using a 4% annual inflation rate. The adjusted mean sales turnover of firms rose to a peak of £2,551,608 in 1986, whilst the median sales turnover reached a peak of £1,169,859 in 1985 but has consistently fallen to only £1,000,000 in 1989. However, the adjusted mean advertised selling price rose to a peak of £932,178 in 1989 from an earlier peak of £942,905 in 1987. In contrast, the median advertised selling price has consistently risen since 1986 but the 1989 price (£400,000) still remains the highest on record.

Agencies

Over the 1983 to 1987 period it was possible to identify 624 agencies involved in advising ownermanagers on 3,324 (52.7%) private business sales from the advertisements. The remainder of private sales were advertised through an anonymous Post Office Box Number. Over the last two years 498 agencies were involved in advertising 2,163 sales (53.6%). During the period 1983 to 1987 the twenty most 'active' agencies accounted for only 27.4% of the advertised sales. Similarly, the twenty most 'active' firms over the last two years accounted for only 26.7% of advertised sales.

However, a number of changes in the leading agencies between the two time periods were recorded. Over the first period, the top five agencies were the accountancy firms of Peat Marwick McLintock, Grant Thornton, Cork Gully, Price Waterhouse and Arthur Anderson. The merger in 1989 of Ernst and Whinney and Arthur Young to form Ernst and Young has meant that the firm is now the third leading adviser in the field, along with a new entrant the specialist business brokering firm of Everett, Mason & Furby Ltd (2.5%), and Grant Thornton (2.3%). By contrast, it would appear that Arthur Anderson is less active in the field than previously, having dropped from fifth to fourteenth. Not surprisingly, the real estate firm of Henry Butcher Business Brokerage dropped out of the top twenty during this period, whilst along with Everett, Mason & Furby Ltd the new entries were Leonard Curtis & Partners and Lakey & Co both specialist business brokers.

In the first period of study the majority of businesses offered for sale were advertised by agencies which appeared to have very little experience on which to draw, since 537 firms (86%) had been involved with only one or two firms over the whole period. Indeed, even the 'active' agencies were defined as those intermediaries which had dealt with as few as two or more private sales per year. During 1988 and 1989 there appears to have been a rationalisation of the market. The total number of agencies identified has decreased from 624 to 497 and the number of 'active' agencies has decreased from 87 to 45. Interestingly, the proportion of sales advertised through an 'active' agency has significantly increased over the last two years (29.6% and 33.0% between 1983-87 and 1988-89, respectively). Moreover, there also is increasing evidence of the activity of specialist business brokering firms such as Christies and Henry Butcher.

Trends in advertised sales between 1988 and 1989

The Stock Market Crash of 1987 was a significant deterrent to public quotation for those owner-managers whose firms were large enough or sufficiently successful to consider such an exit route. However, this was not the case for the exit route of private advertised sale which increased significantly over the following two years. This section of the paper analyses the regional and industrial patterns, and the types of advisers used by firms offered for sale during 1988 and 1989 and compares the results with those for the period 1983 -1989.

Analysis of regional variations

Private sales data analysed showed continued evidence of a 'north-south' divide according to industry, size, reason for sale and agency used (the 'north' is defined as all standard regions of the United Kingdom excluding East Anglia, the South East and the South West of England). Whilst a significantly larger proportion of business sales in the 'north' were engaged in manufacturing (43.1% and 35.2% in the 'north' and 'south', respectively), this was a singular reduction from the 68% for the previous five years. However, a larger proportion of sales in the 'south' continued to be engaged in services or other services. The difference in the industrial distribution was also reflected in the mean level of turnover of businesses offered for private sale which was in the 'north' £2,076,855 (median £1m) ranging from £18,000 to £55m whilst in the 'south' it was smaller at £1,613,590 (median £808,000) and ranging from £13,000 to £49m[1].

As for the previous five years, there was no observable difference between the two locations in the selling price advertised. The mean advertised price of businesses offered for sale in the 'north' was £745,158 (median £425,000 and ranging from £15,000 to £5.5m); in the 'south', despite appearances to the contrary, the mean price was not significantly higher at £874,927 (median £375,000 and ranging from £7,500 to £20m)[2] . In both areas over 53% of the businesses were advertised for £350,000 or more (63.2% and 53.9% in the 'north' and 'south', respectively). Furthermore, a clear difference between the two types of location in the reasons for sale was noted. In the 'north' 80.3% of firms had 'ceased to trade', only marginally more than the 76.2% for the previous 5 years, and whilst this reason also predominated in the 'south' (67.0% compared with 61.3% for the previous 5 years), personal (21.1%) and strategic reasons (11.9%) were also of importance. Remarkably, a similar pattern to the previous five years was observed in the agencies advertising private business sales. In the 'north' 50.1% of business sales were advertised by 'active' agencies with 29.7% of businesses having a forwarding address in the Post Office Box of the Financial Times alone. In the 'south' the leading agency negotiating business sales was the Financial Times (41.9%) with only 21.4% of businesses being advertised by 'active' agencies.

Analysis of industrial variations

The businesses offered for private advertised sale by industry also varied according to their location, size, advertised selling price, reason for sale and agency used. Within this, the pattern established in the previous five years was continued in all categories except that of price where a significant difference was observed in the latter two years. Whilst sales of businesses in primary industries were concentrated in the 'north' (63.5% and 36.5% in the

130

'north' and 'south', respectively), over 65% of business sales in transport, services and other services were in the 'south'.

Clear differences between the size of businesses offered for sale in the various industrial categories were recorded. For example, the sales turnover of businesses in both the construction and services sectors (mean levels of turnover of £2,274,404 and £2,128,874, respectively) were significantly larger than those recorded in the other services sector (mean level of turnover of only £791,506)[3] . Moreover, a significantly larger proportion of other service firms offered for sale had values less than £350,000, whilst over 29% of sales in construction, primary and light manufacturing had sales turnover of £2 million or more. At the much coarser level of analysis a significantly larger percentage of businesses engaged in other services (48.5%), services (37.7%) and heavy manufacturing (33.0%) had an advertised price of £700,000 or more. Whilst at the other end of the price spectrum markedly more firms engaged in construction (45.2%), light manufacturing (40.0%) and transport (35.9%) had an advertised price of less than £200,000. Surprisingly, businesses advertised in the 'service' sectors had significantly higher prices than the rest of the group and particularly those engaged in heavy manufacturing (mean advertised selling price £421,133)[4] .

Where a reason for sale was stated, over 62% of all private sales from all industries (excluding transport sales) indicated that they were ceasing to trade, a marginal increase on the 57% of the previous 5 years). There also continued to be a greater tendency for businesses in construction (31.4%), transport (29.5%) and other services (21.9%) to indicate personal reasons such as retirement and ill health. Interestingly, a markedly large proportion of transport (20.9%), heavy manufacturing (18.2%) and services (18.0%) businesses stated that the advertised sale was for strategic reasons. Also, a clear difference between the type of industries in which intermediaries are most actively involved was recorded. More than 35% of businesses from primary, heavy and light manufacturing and other services were advertised by 'active' agencies, whilst 'non-active' agencies advertised more than 22% of business sales from other services and services. Over 63% of private business sales from the transport industry were advertised through a Financial Times PO Box alone.

Analysis of advisers

As for 1983 -1987, clear differences in the characteristics of the business sales advertised by the various agencies were identified. To reiterate, an 'active' agency is an agency which advertised more than four businesses for sale over the 1988 to 1989 period and a 'non-active' agency is one in which advertised four or less businesses. Over 62% of business sales advertised by 'non-active' agencies and the Financial Times PO Boxes were located in the 'south', whilst 46.7% of sales advertised by 'active' agencies were located in the 'north'. Whilst similar in pattern to the previous five years, there is some indication that 'active' agencies are reducing their operations in the 'north'. 'Active' agencies predominantly sold services, light and heavy manufacturing businesses; 'non-active' agencies and the Financial Times PO Boxes dealt in a wider range of industries. Interestingly, a significantly larger percentage of business sales from the transport sector were advertised through Financial Times PO Boxes (24.7%).

As in previous years the sales turnover of businesses advertised by 'active' agencies was significantly larger than those advertised by their counterparts . For example, 'active' agencies had a significantly greater tendency to advertise the sale of businesses with turnovers of £2 million or more whilst over 25% of businesses advertised by 'non-active' agencies had a turnover of less than £350,000. The businesses advertised in the Financial Times PO Boxes had a wider range of sales turnover although 63.9% had a turnover less than £1.3 million. However, no significant difference in the advertised price was recorded between the three types of agencies[6] . Interestingly, a larger percentage of business sales advertised in the Financial Times PO Boxes had been offered for sale for less than £200,000 whilst a larger proportion of businesses offered for sale by 'active' agencies (38.6%) had an advertised price of £700,000 or more.

Ninety-six percent of businesses which had ceased to trade were advertised by 'active' agencies, a proportion remarkably similar to the 95.2% of the previous five years. The majority of 'non-active' agency advertised sales were also due to the ceased to trade reason but a sizeable proportion of sales were the result of personal (29.9%) and strategic (28.1%) reasons. By contrast, the majority of Financial Times PO Box business sales were stated to be due to personal reasons (55.8% compared with 51.6% in the previous 5 years) alone.

Survey of sellers and advisers

The aim of this section of the study was to shed light on the attitudes and procedures adopted by those involved in both buying and selling businesses. More particularly the focus was upon the vast majority of firms in this population - the small, owner-managed firm. Clearly this group was likely to be more difficult to study than the relatively small population of firms which obtained a public quotation and for which information is widely available, particularly regarding the personalities involved. As we very soon discovered this was most certainly not the case for the rest of the firms. Whilst advertisements often give *some* information, this is not always the same. Some give sales and profits but no industry; others identify the industry but not the location; and a few quote the name of the firm, but the majority are advertised either by an intermediary or through a Post Office Box.

Since our aim was to try to learn both about the firms for sale and about the experiences of the sellers themselves it was, clearly, important to try to contact the latter. This proved almost impossible for two reasons: First, two months were selected at random, and attempts were made to contact all 321 firms offered for sale in the Financial Times during the period. Just over half (51%) of those contacted either refused to send details of the firm or simply ignored our request. A further 7% indicated that they would not supply details because they were only selling the company name, the business had already been sold, negotiations were at an advanced stage with prospective purchasers, or the business was no longer for sale. Since it was made clear that we were requesting the information for research purposes this unwillingness to co-operate is regrettable but, perhaps, understandable. Of the rest, details were received from 36% via an intermediary, and 8% direct from the owners. Unfortunately, this part of the study proved relatively fruitless. The details of the firms available for sale added very little to the information which we had already obtained from the advertisements. Whilst most gave details of the industry and products, and what was offered for sale and approximately 50% indicated an asking price, less than 25% stated the level of sales turnover or the number of employees and, hardly any indicated profits or included a balance sheet. In short, the details of firms offered for sale was less than the details usually obtained by a prospective house buyer!

Second, despite the paucity of data on the firms, we were interested to ask the owners offering their firms for sale about their experiences. However, in this situation the intermediaries acted as gatekeepers, almost always, and understandably, refusing either to disclose the name of their clients, or to agree to pass on a questionnaire. Once the firm had been sold, the previous owners were often impossible to find. They did not answer letters to their Post Office Box; the new owners would not or could not disclose their address; and nor would their professional advisers. Consequently, the small number of owners we were able to contact owned firms which were on the market at the time of the interview.

Survey of sellers

When asked why they were selling their firm, or part of their firm, the answers divided into the personal and the strategic with the former dominating. Thus personal reasons included a need to realise cash family money problems, family illness, husband's death, partners death, *'fed up', 'wanted a change, been in the business too long',* or the *'kids not interested'.* Many of these came from owners of first generation firms which were not necessarily in difficulties, a curious result when compared with the general perceptions of adviser's as to the triggers for sale described below. Strategic reasons tended to be concerned with raising money for other parts of the business, with divesting parts of the business which no longer fitted, or with a recognition that it was not possible to grow any further as an independent business.

In order to understand the process adopted in trying to find a buyer for their business, the sellers were asked what methods of sale had they considered. The options which they were offered included:

Advertisement;
Direct approach to another firm;
Sale to the management;
Sale to the employees;
Public Quotation on the Stock Exchange;
Public Listing on the Unlisted Securities Market;
Public Listing on the Third Market; and
Liquidation

The vast majority automatically responded that they had only considered advertisement. Whilst this is not surprising since they were all first generation, small firms, what was surprising, particularly in view of the available advice, only four had considered the other possibilities of sale to either the employees or management, or sale through an estate agent. None of these had, however, come to fruition.

Our initial study of the types of press used for advertising company sales had identified the Financial Times as the preferred medium for nationally advertised sales. This was confirmed in our interviews. Very few had used any other sources. However, the more specialist local newspapers, the Exchange and Mart and trade journals were preferred sources for the owner selling his own business, whilst the Daily Telegraph and the London Evening Standard were preferred by the Intermediaries.

The reluctance to divulge information which we had encountered may well be due to the responses sellers had received from their advertisement. The mean number of enquiries per advertisement was about 40, ranging from 10 to 150, of which, in the seller's view, about 25% were genuine enquiries. From this about one third of sellers received no offers, one third one offer, and one third two offers. In view of this apparently poor performance, we were interested to learn where these sellers sought advice (Table 4).

Table 4
Sources of advice (percentages)

Adviser	Selling method	Negotiating the deal
Accountant	26	5
Banker	5	-
Lawyer	-	-
Estate Agent	5	5
Chartered.Surveyor	-	5
Franchisors	-	5
Business broker	-	5
No-one	64	75

Thus in the majority of cases, the seller explained that they had taken little or no advice. Moreover, in those cases where the firm had been sold, this was also the case in the negotiation of the final deal. It was, therefore, almost impossible to conduct the part of the survey which probed their attitudes to the advice they received. However, a number did volunteer comments which illustrate their overall attitude to the available advice:

* *'Accountants hinder - they don't help'*
* *'We were too small to be of interest to a banker'*
* *'They aren't interested in business'*
* *'Too impersonal'*

Despite their apparent poor experiences, most felt that their decision to sell the business had been correct, though difficult.

Survey of professional advisers

Almost all the professional advisers involved in marketing the firms offered for sale were accountancy firms covering the full range of firms from the largest international firms to the small local partnerships. However, our survey of trends had indicated that even the large firms were dealing with relatively few transactions, particularly since most are serviced from local offices rather than a central, specialist department. Therefore, it was likely that the individual level of experience in private sales was likely to be limited.

The aim of this part of the study was to explore in more detail both the level of activity within the firm, and the general policy adopted towards the sale of private companies. As was the case in most parts of this study, an air of secrecy pervades and it was difficult to obtain agreement to participate. Nevertheless, twenty-five responses were obtained from professionals representing all sizes of organisation, and matching the pattern of deals reflected in Table 4. Those who participated were those designated by their firm as being responsible for private sales. Further, in order to check the validity of the findings, the draft report was circulated amongst a second group of professionals for final comment.

As was expected, the experience of those professionals directly involved in negotiating the sale of businesses would appear to be very limited. The mean number of times that the individual respondent had acted as the principle agent in the sale of a firm over the previous 5 years was 11, or approximately 2 per year. In the case of larger firms, this was more likely to be an average of 3 per year, but in the rapidly changing world of finance, this is still very small.

It is possible, however, that owners may not wish to sell the whole of the equity of the firm, but merely a percentage. Therefore, respondents were asked how many times they had been involved in negotiating the exit of a significant investor of a company. Significant was defined as owning more than 20% of the equity. Unfortunately, this did not appear to add significantly to the base of experience. The mean number of times over the past 5 years was 7.5 or approximately 1.5 per year. In most of the cases, the respondent indicated that his firm acted as the *principle* agent perhaps reflecting the general small size of the firms offered for sale and the fact that syndication was usually un-necessary. Therefore, it was interesting to explore their perception as to why their firm had be selected by their clients. Almost all the professionals indicated that their firms (84%) would take on clients solely for the purpose of selling their business, although most (76%) would prefer to have had some previous relationship with the company. However, rarely did the respondents perceive a long standing relationship to be the primary reason for selecting their firm but rather a combination of professional reputation and quality of service provided.

Table 5
Status of the seller

Seller Status	Percentage Responses
The Founder	46
Second or Third Generation	18
Private Investor	15
Institutional Investor	2
Combination of the Above	13
Receiver	5
Parent Company	1

The profile of their client sellers which the professionals described in this part of the survey supports the conclusion elsewhere that the majority of private sales are likely to be small, independent, ownermanaged firms. Indeed, when asked to state the profile of their client sellers over the past five years, only 1% were parent companies offering subsidiaries for sale, whilst 64% were first, second or third generation owners (Table 5).

Twenty-five percent of the respondents did not wish to indicate any preference for a particular type of exit route but to take each case on its merits - *'Depends upon clients requirements and personality'*. Of the rest, and perhaps reflecting the nature of their client firms, the professionals clearly preferred the exit route of a private sale to a third party over any of the secondary markets (Table 6).

Table 6
Ranking of exit routes

Exit Route	Mean Rank
Private Sale	1
Unlisted Securities Market	2
Full Listing	3
Third Market	4
Over-the-Counter Market	5

The reasons for preferring a trade sale are reflected in the following comments:

'A trade sale for cash is often cleaner and more appropriate for the vendors who do not seek a public profile. Capital markets exist more for growth than for exit. '
'Cash and Bankers Draft - there is no substitute'
'Most appropriate for the type of businesses by which we are consulted '
'Often can secure higher price at less cost'

In those cases where a full listing was preferred *'Maximisation of price and future return is very important'* although interestingly one respondent noted that *'The less risky companies have full listings'.* For the smaller companies - *'There may be a preference not to get involved in the OTC market due to its poor reputation'*

Whatever the preference of the professional adviser, it is clear that the type of exit route chosen must be dictated, in part, by the reasons for the owners wishing to sell. For example, a firm experiencing significant commercial success may well favour a stock market listing in order to gain currency for future expansion. By contrast, a family facing death duties and no succession are likely to want to sell the entire firm to a third party. Therefore, the respondents were asked to rank the three most common types of triggers for the four exit routes of public quotation, private advertised sale, sale to a third party, and management buyout (Table 7).

Table 7
Status of the seller

Trigger for Exit	Public Quotation	Advertised Private Sale	Sale to Third Party	Management Buyout
Outside Investment Decisions	2	2	4	1
Death Duties	3	6	6	5
Commercial Failure / Problems	5	1	2=	2
Commercial Success	1	3=	5	6
Lack of Succession	6	3=	2=	4
Unsolicited Approach from Third Party	4	5	1	3

As expected, the primary triggers for a public quotation are the commercial success of the business combined with external investment conditions whilst commercial failure is seen as the main trigger for an advertised sale. Sales to third parties are, surprisingly, usually initiated by the intending buyer although a lack of succession within the firm, which reflected an inadequate management structure, was also likely to initiate third party sale. Management buyouts are seen as very much reflecting the external environment but it is interesting that the second most frequent trigger remains the commercial failure of corporate subsidiaries or of independent owner-managed firms.

The deal

Around 70% of the firms which are offered for sale are completed, 14% find potential buyers but fail to arrive at a satisfactory deal, and the remaining 16% fail to find potential buyers. In those cases where potential buyers emerged, there was almost always more than one. It is clear, therefore, that even at the very small end of the market, the structure of the proposed deal is an important determinant of success. Therefore, respondents were first asked how they normally valued a firm. No adviser firm appeared to have any rigid methods of valuation, but considered a valuation of the assets combined with an earnings multiple as a starting point, followed by an assessment of *'what the market will bear' 'as an estate agent values a house'*. Indeed, the one firm which did confess to using an algorithm *'based* [it] *on quantitative and qualitative factors'*. Interestingly, approximately 40% of the owners selling the whole or a significant part of their firm continue to manage it after the sale.

The process of arriving at a deal which is satisfactory to all parties can often be protracted. Indeed, most firms were kept on the market for an average of 6 months, although for some this could be as long as 12 months or more. Therefore, the respondents were asked to rank the problems they usually encountered when negotiating a sale (Table 8).

The respondents were almost unanimous. The major problem which they most often faced was greed or lack of realism on the part of the seller, and this was the problem which created the most difficulties for them. Poor information was also frequently encountered but this was not as much of a problem as greed or lack of realism on the part of the potential buyer. Perhaps also because of the often emotional nature of this type of transaction, when asked what types of buyer they preferred, the professionals preferred to deal with trade buyers rather than management or buyers with whom they had not previous contact. Most of all they disliked the process of taking a client to a quotation on the Stock Market (Table 9).

Table 8
Problems encountered when negotiating a sale

Type of Problem	Frequency of Mention (Rank)	Importance (Rank)
Poor Information	2	3=
Poor Management	4=	6
Firm too Small	6	5
Greed / Lack of Realism of Seller	1	1
Greed Lack of Realism of Buyer	4=	2
Finding the 'Right Buyer'	3	3=
Creating a Market	7	7

Table 9
Exit Route Preference

Exit Route	Rank
Trade Buyer	1
Management	2
Cold Contact	3

Conclusion

In our previous study of exit routes for the years 1983 - 1987 we concluded that private advertised sales was the most frequently used exit route but that the evidence which we were able to gather suggested that the market was served poorly by the professional advisers. Whilst in this study of the two subsequent years we find that there continues to be a growing use of all types of exit route but the use of private advertised sales continues to dominate the activity. Over the past two years, the number of private advertised sales has grown dramatically with an increase of 25.8% between 1988 and 1989 alone. The data which we gathered was based upon those firms which were advertised for sale nationally. We are however, confirmed in our view by two further pieces of evidence. First, our previous analysis of local sources had confirmed that this was the primary method of sale, that the activity at the local level was likely to be significantly greater than that at the national level, but that the local pattern mirrored the national pattern. Second, our survey of the advisers confirmed that the majority of the firms which they offered for sale were of independent firms and to third parties.

The level of private advertised sales tends to reflect the general volatility in the local economy. Thus, for example, when standardising sales by reference to the stock of firms in the area, Greater London and the surrounding counties, and the large metropolitan areas continue to dominate; at a regional level, there has been a slow-down in the West Midlands and an increase in the East Midlands and the South East. Moreover, the sale of manufacturing firms from the 'north' has reduced significantly from 68% to 43% of the total activity, whilst the sale of service firms from the south has increased. Nevertheless, the most frequently cited reason for sale (60% of all reasons stated) continues to be 'ceasing to trade', a reason which is still more dominant in the 'northern' regions (80.3% of all reasons stated) than in the 'south'.

Moreover, there is some evidence of a rationalisation in the advisory network and a growth of specialist advisers and market-makers. Overall, there has been a 20% reduction in the number of agencies involved in the market. Whilst there has been some rationalisation of accountancy firms - witness, for example the merger of Ernst and Whinney and Arthur Young - this has had a marginal effect. Clearly, with the apparent increase in business available to them, it is unlikely that this is due to lack of business opportunities but rather that a number of firms have chosen to withdraw from the market. Concurrent with the withdrawal of some of the accountancy firms, the depression in the property market has also prompted the withdrawal of a number of real-estate based firms.

Our previous report recommended that consideration be given to the establishment of a network of local, regulated, financial markets. We are pleased to see that our recommendation has found favour, the market mechanism appears to be working, and that a number of specialist firms, regulated by the voluntary Self Regulating Organisations (SRO) such as FIMBRA, have emerged as active agencies.

For the purposes of both studies, we defined an 'active' agency as one which had dealt with more than two sales per year over the period studied. Whilst this is clearly very small, it does show some evidence of consistent involvement in the field. Between 1983 and 1987, only 14% of the 624 agencies involved qualified as an 'active' agency, and only 30% of all firms identified were offered for sale by an 'active' agency. Over the 1988 to 1989 period, there has been a 48% reduction in the number of 'active' agencies, but an increase in the percentage of firms in which they dealt to 33%. Consequently, experience in negotiating private advertised sales continues to be very limited within the majority of the intermediary organisations.

Despite the apparently significant rationalisation in the market place, the evidence from our data suggests that the number of private advertised sales dealt with by a firm in any year remains very small. As a consequence, the level of individual experience and expertise must be extremely low. It would appear to be the case in both the small, local agencies and the national more 'active' agencies where a regional organisation structure dilutes the apparent build up of organisational strength. This is not surprising for the majority of accounting firms for which it remains relatively small in comparison with the other parts of their business. Indeed, our survey of the intermediary organisations confirmed this conclusion since individuals, as distinct from their firms, stated that they acted as principle agent in the sale of a firm on average only about twice per year. It would seem that buying a company is more difficult than buying a house.

When attempting to gather details of firms apparently offered for sale on the open market we encountered serious difficulties. Although a number of advertisements invited the reader to send for details, we were refused on a number of occasions as soon as we declared that we were researchers, despite indicating that we would present the results in aggregate and that no individual or firm would be named. In some cases, we were asked to sign secrecy agreements. Moreover, those which we did receive often added little to the data already presented in the advertisement. We were left with the overwhelming impression that both the intermediaries and the sellers viewed themselves as gatekeepers rather than salesmen offering less advice and encouragement to the potential purchaser than the professional estate agent selling a house. As a result it appears that secrecy and mystery pervades the whole process. Since our attempts to collect data from the documentation available was notably unsuccessful we decided to survey and to interview both sellers and intermediaries in order to illuminate our conclusions. Obtaining access to the owner of the firm proved almost impossible - we were frequently prevented by either the gatekeeper intermediaries or by total lack of response from our letters to Post Office Box numbers. Moreover, our final survey was confined almost exclusively to those in the process of selling since it also proved impossible to locate successful sellers once the deal had been completed.

Generally, these sellers took little advice and that primarily on the method of sale rather than in negotiating the deal. This is probably a reflection, in part, of the fact that the majority were relatively small in size and so were not necessarily of prime importance in the portfolio of the intermediary agent. Indeed, a number had gained the impression from their advisers that they were viewed as 'small beer'. It is an impression for which we found confirmation in our survey of the intermediaries who considered that their own strengths lay in their professional reputation and the quality of service which they offered. By and large, in their view, greed and lack of realism were the major problems which they encountered in their client sellers, two reasons for the preference on the part of the intermediaries for dealing with trade buyers.

In our previous study, we concluded that there was a need for local financial markets. Despite the reduction in the number of intermediary organisations operating in this field, we still find evidence of a poorly served market which continues to be dominated by the large accounting firms for whom this remains a minute part of their business. We are, however, encouraged by the growth of the more specialist agencies and of professional brokers, but feel that there remains significant room for improvement before the owner-manager can expect the level and quality of advice appropriate to the significance of the strategic step which he is proposing to take.

References

Beesley, M. E. and Hamilton, R. T. (1984), 'Small Firms' Seedbed Role and the Concept of Turbulence'. *Journal of Industrial Economics* vol.23, p.217-23 1.

Beesley, M. E. and Hamilton, R. T. (1986), 'Births and Deaths of Manufacturing Firms in the Scottish Regions'. *Regional Studies* vol.20, no.4, p.281-288.

Birley, S. J. and Westhead, P. (1988), *Exit Routes*. Research Report Published by Cranfield School of Management for Price Waterhouse and Lloyds Bank, Cranfileld, England.

Birley, S. J. and Westhead, P. (1990), 'North-South' Contrasts in the Characteristics and Performance of Small firms'. *Entrepreneurship & Regional Development* vol.2, no.1, p.27-48

Department of Employment. (1989a), *Small Firms in Britain*. HMSO 1V89 Dd8221526 DEMP JO646NJ, London.

Department of Employment. (1989b), *VAT Registrations and Deregistrations Analysis by County 1980 to 1988*. Department of Employment, London.

Harper, W. M. (1977), *Statistics* (third edition). Mac Donald and Evans Ltd, Plymouth.

Lewis, . and Townsend, A. (eds.). (1989), *The North-South Divide: Regional Change in Britain in the 1980s*. Paul Chapman Publishing Ltd, London.

Quality of Markets Quarterly. (various issues), The International Stock Exchange, London.

Smith, D. (1989), *North and South: Britain's Economic and Social Divide*. Pelican Books: London.

Appendix 1: Standard industrial categories (1980)

Primary	Division 0; Division 1 (1113 -1700, 2310 - 2396)
Light manufacturing	Divisions 3 & 4
Heavy manufacturing	Divisions 1 & 2 (except 1113 -1700; 2310 - 2396)
Construction	Division 5
Services	Division 6
Transport	Division 7
Other services	Divisions 8 & 9

9 Survival, entrepreneurship, growth: Which relationship? The Milanese area's case[1]

Guliano Mussati and Andrea Fumagalli

Introduction

This article deals with the process of new firms creation, by taking in account their performance in the economic environment. We think that the birth of a new firm can not be defined only by it inscription in the local Chamber of Commerce, but it should be analysed through the consideration of it first years of activity.

This point highlights the need for a differing approach to the theory of new firms' life cycle, especially for what concerns the exit of the critical period of survival.

If there is a wide literature on the determinants of the process of new firms creation since a lot of years, not the same can be said about the aspect of the survival of new firms. Only recently and only for what concerns empirical aspects at a sectoral level, it is possible to notice an increasing interest of the economists on this topic; more in particular, the literature focuses on determining the critical year for the survival of the new firms. In Italy, Contini and Revelli (1986) pointed out how the most crucial years correspond to the first three years; after this critical period, the probability to survive enormously increases. By using INPS databank, referred to the most medium large size Italian towns, the empirical results show that the third year of life presents the highest number of new firms' failures.

An analogous empirical research is carried on in Mussati (1990a); Fumagalli and Marcora (1990) show that in Milan's Province during the period 1975-86 the most critical year for the survival of new firms is the second one (from a minimum of 20% to maximum of 40% of new firms fail in the first two years of life, according to the type of industry).

These still general results should be thoroughly analysed at a sectoral and spatial level: moreover, as the both articles confirm, they depend on the type of the considered industrial structure and on the existence of more or less binding scale economies and barriers to entry.

Some preliminary theoretical specifications

The conventional and the alternative approaches

An increasing literature on the phenomenon of entry and birth of new enterprises is now available [2]. The still main framework according to orthodox view is the traditional competitive model. In this framework, the equalization of the sector price with the minimum long run average cost is assumed by the free entry of new firms into the sector. If extra profits occur (may be caused by an increase of demand or by the introduction of cost saving innovations or by new products differentiation strategies, etc.), additional agents enter into the market till extra profits disappear through a decrease in the price of the goods (see, for instance, Varian, 1984). This framework assumes perfect and complete information, perfect competition and the entry is 'pulled' by market conditions and no subjective or environmental factor is investigated. The entrepreneurial opportunities are driven by profit conditions and maximization mechanism. Even if other kind of opportunities are considered, the procedure is more or less the same. For instance, localization models (where spatial opportunities are considered) are very similar to the competitive ones in describing the distribution of firms in a linear or circular space (see Salop, 1979). In more articulated models, the maximization procedure takes into account barriers to entry, due to initial cost level or to unfavourable situation about 'finance' and/or 'skill' conditions for new entries [3] (see, among others, Tirole, 1989, chapter 8).

Of course, the basic assumptions of perfect information and complete rationality (that is to say, perfect foresight) bind the results of the considered models, in a less or more thorough way, according to the different point of views. But, as pointed out in Vivarelli (1989), 'the insertion of the hypothesis of uncertainty does not change the substance of the argument . A stochastic framework is introduced and different expectations about future profits and behaviour or rivals modify the form of maximization procedures'.

In conclusion, in these recent neo-classical models, even if entry is not automatic and free as in the traditional competitive framework. profits remain the key variable, eventually corrected by considering uncertainty, barriers to entry, and so on; the *pull factors* are still the only variables which are highlighted to explain the birth of new firms in a given context.

During the Seventies, more and more studies started to give a deeper attention to some subjective variables in explaining the willing to entrepreneurship and analysing the subjective qualities of the founder of a new firm. In a very brief way, starting by the seminal book of Oxenfeldt (see Oxenfeldt, 1943), the present literature recognize three main factors: i) *background factors* (see Storey 1982 and Johnson, 1986), referred to the fact that the founder of a new enterprise is strictly linked to his own background, in term of job experience, level of skills, etc.; ii) *incubator factors*, which underline the importance of environmental factors in facilitating the emergence of new firms: iii) the *self employment choice* (see, after Oxenfeldt, Lucas, 1978, Johnson and Cathcart, 1979, Johnson, 1986, Storey, 1982 and 1987, Blau, 1987), in which pull and push factors are combined with regard to the income choice of the potential founder.

The basic idea, which is implicit in these directions of research, leads to the proposing of a more general framework where the objective conditions of the market are analysed with some *pushfactors* concerning the environment and the subjective conditions of the potential founder. In other words, following the terminology introduced by Kilby (see Kilby, 1971, and the survey in Fumagalli, 1990a), these studies concern both the demand for entrepreneurship (pull factors) and the supply of entrepreneurship (push factors): the former is sufficiently highlighted by the neo-classical models, the last one is analysed through a greater interest in push factors.

The survival aspect

As already pointed out in the introduction, the existence of a wide literature on new firms' entry does not imply as well literature on new firms' exit.

Indeed, even if, it is recognized the fact that an high share of new firms does not succeed in entering permanently into the market, the theoretical literature is quite poor. Only very recently, for what regards Italy, after the seminal paper of Contini Revelli (see Contini Revelli, 1986), some empirical investigation with some theoretical background are available (see, Arrighetti, 1988, Fumagalli 1990b, Fumagalli-Marcora 1990, Marcora 1990, Mussati 1990a e Mussati 1990b).

Moreover, the relationship among the phenomenon of entry and exit is scarcely related to the analysis of industry's dynamics. The available literature deals with the evolutionary approach (see, one among all, Winter 1985) in a schumpeterian perspective.

The joint analysis of entry and exit in a same theoretical context can be very useful in clarifying, from a dynamic point of view, the interrelation between the role played by the above called push factor (supply of entrepreneurship) and pullfactors (demand of entrepreneurship).

Our thesis is that the two kind of factors affect in a different way and in a different time the dynamics of entrepreneurship evolution. In this context, the introduction of the theoretical concept of firms' life cycle can be useful in order to present the dynamic growth of new firms.

The theory of firm's life cycle shows the dynamic of a given variable (usually, the revenue's value of a good) as divided in three stages: a starting one, in which the growth of the new product is quite slow because of the novelty of market, a second one of increasing and strong growth, a third and last one of decreasing and declining dynamics.

If we consider the life of a new firm, two moments seem particularly relevant:
1. the starting point (*start-up*), in which the idea becomes in effect and operative;
2. a second moment, in which the propulsivity of the business idea materializes in an autonomous growth process of the new firm or starts declining.

Start-up (the act of new firm's creation) usually depends on environmental and structural factors, which can not always be described and formalized with the traditional economic tools. In this case, the new entrepreneur's 'willpower' is more important than anything else in determining the act of creation. Of course, this 'will-power' is stimulated by the perception of some economic opportunity (technological, structural, organizing, and so on).

Only after the effective creation of the new firm it is possible to analyse from an 'ex-post' point of view if the starting business idea has been able to seize the right opportunity. According to the 'goodness' of the business idea and to the entrepreneurial ability in adapting it to industry's market and technological conditions, the new firm can survive and then grow . This 'incubation period' lasts moreless two or three years and it represents the crucial moment for the life of the firm. We can call it *survival break-even point*. It varies according to the structural and economic characteristic of the considered industry. Only when it is overcome, we can speak of the *effective birth* of a new firm.

Taking in account these considerations, the first stage of new firms' life cycle can be described by a decreasing curve till the survival break-even point. The decreasing dynamics depends on the fact that each business idea has to face the market selection processes, even if it can be successfully. The selection processes carried out by industry's dynamics tends in any case to put out of the market some starting business idea. The boundaries of this stage lie in the fact that the only business idea is usually not able to face obstacles and operative problems which derive from 'finance', sufficient 'skills', appropriate information set, and so on. We can say that, after the start-up till the survival break-even point, the new firms has to face *exogenous boundaries*, which are independent from new firm's initial behaviour.

In Fig. 1. the point $[p°-t°]$ denotes the minimum expected value of the new firm's probability to survive ($p°$), which allows the new firm to get over the 'survival break-even point'. After this point, there is effective birth of enterprise and the growth of the firm goes on in different way according to success capacity.

As soon as the new firm enters into the market (start-up), the expected value of new firm's survival capacity is measured only by the business idea. The validity of the business idea is already a sort of 'screaming', which determines the failure of some entrepreneurial attempt. The share of surviving firms (n) tends to decrease in the first period. At time 0, it will be equal to one: in the interval between the second and the third year, where the highest share of failures is verified, the n-curve reaches the greatest decrement till the flexus-point ($n°-t°$), after which the share of surviving firms tends to stabilize. In the marshallian language, according to the well-known likeness between firms and trees, we could say that start-up is described by the appearance of a 'steam', after which 'radication' follows. Radication represents the overcoming of the potential survival crises. In this interval, the expected value of survival probability (p) can reach the minimum value under which the new firm is destined to disappear $[p°-t°]$. Before this point the share of surviving firms and the expected probability to survive present the same dynamics, but with a second derivaty with opposite sigh. Beyond the crucial point $[p°-t°]$, whilst the share of surviving new firms stabilizes, the expected value of survival's probability increases according to the life cycle theory (see Fig. 1).

The empirical results

The database we use is based on an elaboration of INFOCENTER of Milan's Chamber of Commerce and it is referred to the period 1975-86 for the whole Province of Milan, divided in three main zones:

* the city of Milan;
* Hinterland (that is the first ring of towns around the city);
* the rest of the Province.

The industrial disaggregation regards manufacturing industries plus production services, which have been classified according to ISTAT (National Bureau of Italian Statistic) methodology.

The data give information about the number of inscriptions of new firms to the Milan's Chamber of Commerce, which covers the whole territory of the Province, and the cancellations, so that it is possible to build the historic series of stocks and flows of entrepreneurial demographic evolution by year, by zone and by second digit Istat classification.

The main problem of database lies in the fact that cancellation flows need to be partially extimated because not each firm which ceases the activity communicates it to the Chamber of Commerce [4]. Because of the presence since 1982 of a new corrected series, we divided the analysis in

two different periods 1975-81 and 1982-86.

Nevertheless, on the other hand, the databank contains information on the history of each inscribed firm, so that it is possible to take in account the survival period of each cancelled firm, even in the past.

In this context, we first analysed the natality and mortality rates, defined as the ratio between new inscriptions (or cancellations) in a given period and the corrispective stock of existing firms at the beginning of the period (usually one year), and, secondly, the survival rates, defined as the ratio of the living firms at 1988 on the new firms born at a given year and as the ratio of the cancelled firms in the first two years on the same new firms born in a given year ('infantile mortality rate').

The extended and complete results are presented in Mussati (1990b). Here, we summarize the main ones.

By the analysis of natality and mortality rates at a general level it follows that the variability of the former does not imply the variability of the latter. Looking at Tab. 1 and 2, the natality rate of period 1975-81 is higher than that related to the following period 1982-86 (from 10.92% to 8.90%), while the mortality rate present more or less constant values (respectively, 8.61% and 8.62%). If only manufacturing industries are considered, the divergence between the two rates are more significant. Even a disaggregation at industry level present high differences in the dynamics of natality and mortality rates. An opposite dynamics in the two rates can be pointed out for all the industries except two high-tech sectors (Col. 33, computers and Col. 37, precision instruments) and for two 'matured' industries, like foods (Col. 41) and paper, printing and publishing (Col. 47) (see Table 1 and 2). The first two are characterized by high entry and exit turnover, so that high natality rates correspond to high mortality rates, whilst the second ones have not been touched in a relevant way by the recession of the first '80s (Col. 41) or play an important role in the local economic structure (Col. 47).

For what concerns manufacturing industries, these short observations show that there is no usual positive correspondence in the dynamics of natality and mortality. They seems to be dependent on different factors. The situation is difference if producer services are considered; in this case, in fact, the data shows a similar evolution of the two considered rates in both the periods.

Moreover, the disaggregation in two periods highlights that natality rates tend to decreasing in time, while mortality presents a more constant dynamics. This interesting fact shows that the 70s presented more entrepreneurial activity than the '80s and that, in any case, a physiological mortality level can be accounted, independently from conjunctural, technological and economic evolution.

The analysis of correlation index, presented in Tab. 3, confirms this kind of consideration, showing that the demographic evolution of firms' number defined as difference between natality and mortality (growth rate) depends more on natality rate dynamics than on mortality rate dynamics.

* * * * *

The dynamics of survival rates are shown in Tab. 4, 5, 6 and 7.

In a general view, the most important observations concern the following point:
a. producer services survival rates present higher values than those of manufacturing industries in both the considered periods;
b. producer services survival rates increase from centre to periphery: the opposite dynamics is verified for what regards manufacturing industries. This is valid for the first period 1975-81. In the '80s, also the producer services survival rates of Milan are higher than those of the boundary and of the rest of the Province. This fact confirms that i) tertiarization process is more relevant in the '80s than in the '70s; ii) the municipality of Milan goes on playing an incubator role with respect to the whole area and to the whole considered period.

From a sectoral point of view, it is interesting to notice that in both periods the industries with higher survival rates are the ones which represent more than 70% of industrial activity of the city: metal transformation and production, vehicles, printing and publishing, machine tools production and chemistry. Secondly, it is possible to highlight a decreasing order Milan --> Hinterland --> rest of the Province for what regards the traditional production like foods and beverages (Col. 41 and 42), wood (Col. 46) and metal productions (Col. 31).

For what concerns the analysis of the critical year for new firms survival, Tab. 6 and 7 show that the year with the highest number of cancellations is the second one. About the manufacturing industries, this result is quite confirmed for both the considered periods and independently from the spatial disaggregation. About producer services, instead, the results are more or less analogous, with the difference that survival absolute values are lower.

In spite of the high data aggregation of Tab. 6, some spatial characteristics seem to be relevant:

1. the second year maximum value of cancellation increases by moving from centre to periphery and interspatial values' spectrum tends to widen from 1975-81 to 1982-86;

146

2. at a temporal level, the second year maximum value increases from the '70s to the '80s.
3. It follows, as already noticed, that the new firms of the Eighties present an higher survival capacity than those of the Seventies.

* * * * *

Nevertheless, why it seems more important in the analysis of the interrelation of survival and growth are the data shown in Tab. 8, where the correlation indexes are presented.

Previous tables have shown an high turn-over in the natality of new firms. This phenomenon can explain the existence of high natality rates faced to a not as much higher mortality rates. From this point of view, only a minority of new firms is able to go over the first two crucial years and to enter the consolidated core of the existing industry's firms.

In Tab. 8, the data highlight that there is scarce correlation between natality dynamics and survival dynamics, that is to say that explanations of natality is different from that of survival. Even if the correlation is calculated by taking account a lag of two years in determining the rate of infantile mortality (since after two years, there is the highest number of deaths of new firms), the results are not very different from the previous ones (see Tab. 8).

If mortality and natality of new firms and, therefore, the demographic growth of the manufacturing firms in Milan's Province cannot be explained through the dynamics of infantile mortality, it follows that creation of new firms implies the consideration of different factors with respect to the ones which explain survival dynamics.

Some conclusive remarks

Some points need to be underlined:

1. The dynamics of demographic growth of the firms in Milan's Province depends more on natality evolution than on morality.
2. The dynamics of mortality rates presents a more or less constant evolution which contrasts with the greater variability of natality evolution.
3. Whilst it seems that natality rate is more related to structural and environmental factors, mortality rates show a physiological level, which is independent from economic and technological conjuncture. Even if the considered period has been theatre of deep modifications in energical, technological and organizing structure, these facts has not affected in a relevant way the dynamics of mortality rates. in the other side, economic, technological and conjunctural factors have structurally influenced the dynamics of manufacturing composition in the '70s and in the '80s by encouraging high-tech industries' growth and decreasing the weight of restructuring sectors.
4. It follows that in high-tech industries high growth rates often correspond high natality and mortality rates: in other words, their demographic increment is accompanied by greater level of firms' change and by industry's turbulence.

5. Nothing denotes the existence of a positive correlation between high mortality and low survival; the dynamics of mortality rates is almost complete independent from survival and infantile mortality rates.

6. Therefore, it follows that the new firm's penetration in an industry's growth pattern occurs by three non correlated stages, whose analysis needs three different theoretical models:

   a. the new firm's creation (defined by the inscription in the local Chambers of Commerce and measured by the corrispective natality rate), that is the 'act of conceiving'; in this stages, we think that subjective, environmental and traditionally familiar factors (push variables) are predominant on the economic and conjunctural variables (market or pull factors);

   b. new firms' survival till the break-even point of second year of live (that is to say the period of potential radication of the new entrepreneurial activity) more depends on the existing nature of market selection process in term of the entrepreneurial ability to seize the economic, technological and conjunctural opportunities;

   c. hence, it is only after the overcome of the survival break-even point that it is possible to talk about the effective birth of a new firm, which is able to enter into industry's growth patterns with an active role.

7. In conclusion, it seems that entrepreneurial dynamics and new firms survival capacity should be analysed by using different methodological tools in the structural and environmental context of the territory which they are referred to. Thus, entrepreneurial demographic evolution is the result of a complex dialectic process between human action, it adaptation capacity, from one side, and the characteristics of the economic and environmental structure, from the other. From this point of view, the entrepreneurial subject and it survival capacity become dynamics factors of the existing productive structure's change.

Figure 1
The theory of new firm's life cycle

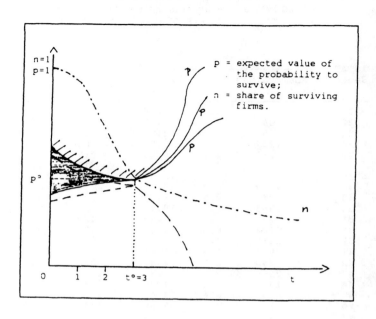

Table 1
New Firms inscriptions in the Milan's province:
1975-81 and 1982-86; natality rates and manufacturing composition
by ISTAT classes

ISTAT Sectors	1975-1981			1982-1986		
	Abs. values	%	birth rates	abs.values	%	birth rates
21	8	0.01	3.36	5	0.31	4.00
22	345	0.4	8.60	166	0.3	5.21
23	32	0.04	2.56	22	0.04	3.89
24	1107	1.5	8.95	684	1.4	7.67
25	1139	1.6	6.51	819	1.7	7.82
26	5	0.06	2.10	10	0.02	7.69
31	9844	13.6	12.55	5655	11.8	8.17
32	4169	5.8	12.72	2778	5.7	9.16
33	270	0.4	19.88	323	0.7	20.63
34	6985	9.7	18.14	4065	8.4	7.50
35	239	0.3	12.28	120	0.2	7.50
36	204	0.3	13.87	125	0.2	9.43
37	1238	1.7	11.83	905	1.9	9.78
41	901	1.2	8.44	667	1.4	8.50
42	255	0.3	4.87	236	0.5	8.69
43	2064	2.9	9.77	1112	2.3	7.59
44	1307	1.8	11.72	737	1.5	8.30
45	6048	8.4	9.41	3479	7.2	7.99
46	5286	7.3	8.05	2540	5.2	5.13
47	3406	4.7	9.65	2035	4.2	7.95
48	2204	3.1	12.24	1402	2.9	9.55
49	3025	4.2	15.01	1892	3.9	9.96
Tot. mon.	50081	69.42	11.07	29777	61.46	8.19
83	22069	30.58	10.60	18672	38.54	10.32
Total	72150	100.00	10.92	48449	100.00	8.90

Source: our elaborations on Infocenter-Cicogna databank.

Table 2
Firms' cancellation in the Milan's province:
1975-81 and 1982-86; mortality rates and manufacturing composition
by ISTAT classes

ISTAT Sectors	1975-1981			1982-1986		
	Abs. values	%	death rater	abs. values	%	death rater
21	17	0.03	7.14	7	0.01	5.60
22	274	0.5	6.83	189	0.4	5.93
23	96	0.1	7.70	22	0.04	3.89
24	1082	1.9	8.75	849	1.8	9.52
25	1525	2.7	8.72	740	1.6	7.06
26	13	0.02	5.46	12	0.02	9.23
31	7208	12.7	9.18	6710	14.29	9.69
32	2774	4.8	8.46	2549	5.4	8.41
33	148	0.3	10.89	199	0.4	12.71
34	4389	7.7	11.4	4101	8.7	10.16
35	193	0.3	9.91	151	0.3	9.43
36	147	0.3	10.00	123	0.3	9.28
37	878	1.5	8.39	760	1.6	8.22
41	856	1.5	8.02	666	1.4	8.49
42	458	0.8	8.75	215	0.5	7.91
43	2122	3.7	10.04	1418	3.0	9.68
44	1121	2.0	10.05	1029	2.2	11.59
45	6500	11.4	10.12	4498	9.6	10.33
46	4782	8.4	7.28	4107	8.75	8.30
47	3277	5.8	9.28	2014	4.3	7.87
48	1832	3.2	10.17	1491	3.2	10.16
49	2095	3.7	10.39	2014	4.3	10.60
Tot. man.	41787	73.51	9.24	33864	72.16	9.32
83	15058	26.49	7.23	13070	27.84	7.22
Total	56845	100.00	8.61	46934	100.00	8.62

Source: our elaborations on Infocenter-Cicogna databank.

Table 3

Correlation indexes (r2) among natality, mortality and growth rates by classes, by years and by areas in Milan's province: 1975-86

CL	TN --> TS	TM --> TS	TN --> TM	TN --> TM2
21	0.88	0.21	0.021	0.006
22	0.72	0.42	0.023	0.022
23	0.43	0.60	0.001	0.013
24	0.68	0.71	0.156	0.040
25	0.57	0.25	0.031	0.012
26	0.50	0.46	0.001	0.020
31	0.82	0.73	0.319	0.238
32	0.88	0.68	0.349	0.156
33	0.85	0.00	0.097	0.000
34	0.91	0.58	0.286	0.097
35	0.84	0.25	0.014	0.285
36	0.78	0.06	0.050	0.018
37	0.94	0.12	0.016	0.146
41	0.35	0.25	0.160	0.001
42	0.48	0.72	0.044	0.002
43	0.74	0.05	0.081	0.000
44	0.69	0.49	0.039	0.001
45	0.64	0.42	0.004	0.000
46	0.72	0.74	0.216	0.032
47	0.84	0.51	0.144	0.040
48	0.75	0.41	0.034	0.099
49	0.81	0.26	0.010	0.148
83	0.95	0.20	0.060	0.310
AREA				
MI	0.52	0.35	0.016	0.000
IC	0.79	0.17	0.001	0.018
RP	0.73	0.13	0.027	0.012
YEAR				
1975	0.94	0.06	0.000	=
1976	0.67	0.41	0.008	=
1977	0.59	0.20	0.047	=
1978	0.79	0.27	0.006	=
1979	0.78	0.00	0.182	=
1980	0.68	0.22	0.012	=
1981	0.91	0.28	0.076	=
1982	0.60	0.04	0.208	=
1983	0.53	0.34	0.014	=
1984	0.77	0.15	0.009	=
1985	0.62	0.01	0.261	=
1986	0.73	0.20	0.006	=
TOT.	0.735	0.185	0.005	=

Notes: TN = natality rate;
       TM = mortality rate;
       TS = growth rate;
       TM2= two years lagged mortality rate;
Source: our elaborations on Infocenter-Cicogna databank.

Table 4
Share % of surviving firms in the manufacturing industry at 1988
by year and by area

YEAR	% living Milan	% living hinterland	% living re. prov.
1975	42.6	43.9	39.3
1976	44.8	44.0	42.9
1977	48.7	44.4	47.2
1978	48.4	49.3	47.8
1979	52.7	48.5	43.8
1980	57.2	52.4	53.4
1981	60.1	53.9	56.1
1982	65.4	59.6	54.9
1983	71.0	62.3	65.5
1984	74.8	65.9	69.5
1985	83.3	78.2	79.4
1986	87.9	85.9	80.9

Source: our elaborations on Infocenter-Cicogna databank.

Table 5
Share % of surviving firms on the total amount of inscribed firms year by year by ISTAT class: 1975-81 and 1982-86

	1975 - 81				1982 - 86		
CL	MILAN	HINTER.	RES.PR.	CL	MILAN	HINTER.	RES.PR.
22	64.7	59.3	76.4	22	84.1	83.0	88.2
24	50.5	47.8	55.8	24	71.4	65.3	72.0
25	61.0	56.6	49.3	25	79.1	76.1	70.4
26	0.2	0.7	33.3	26	66.7	50.0	0.0
31	45.9	46.2	46.3	31	73.8	68.4	68.3
32	55.2	53.7	58.2	32	77.1	74.2	74.3
33	46.8	43.0	35.2	33	80.5	72.3	78.2
34	48.0	45.6	44.6	34	75.0	68.4	60.9
35	61.4	44.4	44.0	35	82.0	67.7	66.7
36	63.6	58.5	57.1	36	81.6	67.2	90.9
37	49.9	50.5	50.6	37	80.8	79.5	80.3
41	50.5	58.4	64.3	41	79.8	80.1	77.4
42	61.2	53.0	69.5	42	82.1	75.0	85.0
43	46.4	45.9	35.1	43	68.6	66.9	62.9
44	39.3	41.4	33.3	44	69.5	63.7	65.0
45	47.2	44.0	39.8	45	72.6	65.0	58.0
46	48.5	53.0	53.2	46	74.1	72.5	76.6
47	59.5	47.1	39.2	47	82.0	80.2	66.9
48	48.8	47.1	39.2	48	74.0	67.6	64.9
49	50.6	42.6	36.6	49	74.2	66.2	61.8
T.MAN.	50.4	48.3	45.6	T.MAN.	75.8	70.1	67.1
83	65.3	65.9	73.5	83	83.5	81.3	82.8

Source: our elaborations on Infocenter-Cicogna databank.

Table 6

Yearly share % of cancelled firms on the total amount of inscribed firms year by year:
weight averages 1975-81 --> 1982-86: manufacturing industry by area

AREAS	1975 - 81														
	1°	2°	3°	4°	5°	6°	7°	8°	9°	10°	11°	12°	13°	14°	%LIV.
MILAN	5.3	6.8	6.4	5.4	5.5	5.2	4.8	3.3	2.4	1.9	1.4	0.7	0.3	0.1	50.3
HINTER	6.2	8.8	7.1	5.7	5.1	4.7	4.1	3.2	2.5	1.7	1.4	0.7	0.3	0.1	48.3
R.PROV	6.7	9.6	6.5	6.2	5.7	5.3	4.3	3.5	2.3	2.0	1.1	0.7	0.4	0.1	45.6
TOTAL	5.9	8.1	6.8	5.7	5.3	5.0	4.4	3.3	2.4	1.8	1.4	0.7	0.3	0.1	48.9

AREAS	1982 - 86							
	1°	2°	3°	4°	5°	6°	7°	%LIV.
MILAN	4.8	7.5	5.3	3.7	2.0	0.9	0.1	76.8
HINTER	6.4	9.3	6.5	4.3	2.2	1.1	0.1	70.1
R.PROV	7.4	11.	6.7	4.5	2.3	1.1	0.1	67.1
TOTAL	5.9	8.8	6.1	4.1	2.1	1.0	0.1	71.9

Source: our elaborations on Infocenter-Cicogna databank.

Table 7
New firms mortality in the first two years of life and in the following years:
1975-81 and 1982-86

AREAS	PERIOD: 1975-81								
	0 - 2 years			3 - 5 years			next years		
	a	b		a	b		a	b	
		MAN.	TOT		MAN.	TOT		MAN.	TOT
MILAN	36.0	18.5	15.5	33.4	16.1	14.4	30.6	15.1	13.2
HINTERLAND	41.5	22.7	20.1	30.4	15.5	14.7	26.4	13.5	12.8
REST PROVINCE	41.3	22.8	20.9	31.9	17.2	16.1	26.8	14.4	13.5

AREAS	PERIOD: 1982-86					
	0 - 2 years			next years		
	a	b		a	b	
		MAN.	TOT		MAN.	TOT
MILAN	68.4	17.6	13.8	31.6	6.6	6.4
HINTERLAND	74.2	22.2	20.0	25.8	7.7	7.0
REST PROVINCE	75.3	=	22.6	24.7	=	7.4

NOTA: a = % on the total amount of cancellations
b = % on the total amount of inscribtions.

Source: our elaborations on Infocenter-Cicogna databank.

Table 8
Correlation indexes (r2) among natality, mortality, growth and infantility mortality rates,
by classes, by areas and by year in Milan's province: 1975-86

CL	TMP --> TN	TMP --> TM2	TMP --> TS2
21	0.005	0.000	0.000
22	0.105	0.004	0.033
23	0.304	0.046	0.001
24	0.002	0.040	0.066
25	0.297	0.050	0.028
26	0.014	0.763	0.018
31	0.024	0.160	0.072
32	0.112	0.030	0.000
33	0.103	0.068	0.071
34	0.010	0.330	0.099
35	0.039	0.017	0.098
36	0.031	0.071	0.115
37	0.144	0.291	0.006
41	0.001	0.000	0.044
42	0.001	0.002	0.004
43	0.223	0.032	0.029
44	0.029	0.143	0.074
45	0.063	0.059	0.008
46	0.378	0.379	0.435
47	0.217	0.007	0.158
48	0.070	0.040	0.004
49	0.015	0.296	0.000
83	0.035	0.000	0.028
AREA			
MI	0.000	0.018	0.010
IC	0.136	0.040	0.063
RP	0.001	0.014	0.001
YEAR			
1975	0.051	0.080	0.000
1976	0.003	0.000	0.128
1977	0.033	0.056	0.002
1978	0.326	0.004	0.018
1979	0.426	0.373	0.003
1980	0.003	0.026	0.041
1981	0.148	0.001	0.025
1982	0.159	0.043	0.064
1983	0.132	0.042	0.023
TOT.	0.017	0.002	0.009

Notes: TMP = infantile mortality rate;
TN = natality rate;
TM2 = two years lagged mortality rate;
TS2 = two years lagged growth rate;

Source: our elaborations on Infocenter-Cicogna databank.

157

Notes

1. Giuliano Mussati has written paragraph 3, while Andrea Fumagalli paragraph 2. The introduction and the conclusion are the result of both authors' considerations. Moreover, this work is part of a wider research project carried on with the helpful participation of Luca Marcora. The authors are also grateful to Marco Vivarelli for suggestions and comments. Usual caveats apply.
2. After the first contribution of Mansfield (1962), see Gorecki (1975), Orr (1974). Empirical results are available in Storey (1982), Johnson (1986) for what concerns Great Britain, Contini-Revelli (1986), Terrasi (1986), Mussati (1990a) for what concerns Italy. A complete survey on these topics is in Mariti (1987), Fumagalli (1990a) and Vivarelli (1990).
3. For an analysis of barriers to entry in a more formalised neo-classical context, see Orr (1974).
4. Since 1982 it is compulsory for each inscribed firm to Milan's Chamber of Commerce to pay an yearly amount for segretary expenditures. Thus, it is possible to recognize the firms' effective cancellations. For a discussion of these problems on English, see Corridori Fumagalli-Rovida-Vinciguerra-Vivarelli (1989).

References

Arrighetti A. (1988): 'La mortalita delle imprese industriali: evidenze empiriche e implicazioni sulla politica del lavoro', IRES, *Quaderni di Ricerca*, Milano.

Blau D.M. (1987): 'A Time Series Analysis of Self-employment in the United States', in *Journal of Political Economicy*, vol. XCV.

Contini B.-Revelli R. (1986): 'Natalita e mortalita delle imprese italiane: risultati preliminari e nuove prospettive di ricerca' in *L'Industria*, n. 2.

Corridori A.-Fumagalli A.-Rovida F.-Vinciguerra L.-Vivarelli M. (1989): 'New Firms Dynamics: Statistical and Methodological Problems' in P. Dubini (ed.) (1989): *The Evaluation of Entrepreneurial Prolects and Profiles*, EGEA, Milan.

Fumagalli A. (1990a): 'L'imprenditore nella storia dell'analisi economica', cap. II, in *Mussati G. (ed.)* (1990a).

Fumagalli A. (1990b): 'L'analisi dei tassi di sopraw ivenza nella provincia di Milano nel periodo 1975-86', in *Mussati G. (ed.)* (1990b) .

Fumagalli A.-Marcora L. (1990): 'Nuove imprese in Provincia di Milano', in *Mussati G. (ed.)* (1990a).

Gorecki P.K. (1975): 'The Determinants of Entry by New and Diversifying Enterprises in the U.K. Manufacturing Sector 1958-1963: some tentative results', in *Applied Economics*, vol. VII.

Johnson P.S. (1986): 'New Firms: an Economic Perspective', Allen and Unwin, London.

Johnson P.S.-Catchcart D.G. (1979): 'The Founders of New Manufacturing Firms: a Note on the Size of their Incubators Plants' in *Journal of Industrial Economics*, vol. XXVIII, n. 2.

Kilby P. (ed.) (1971): *Entrepreneurship and Economic Development*, Freeprint, London.

Lucas R.E. (1978): 'On the size Distribution of Business Firms', in *Bell Journal of Economics*, vol. IX.

Mansfield E. (1962): 'Entry Gibrat's Law Innovation and the Growth of Firms' in *American Economic Review*, vol. 52.

Marcora L. (1990): 'L'analisi della natalita e della mortalita imprenditoriale', in *Mussati G. (ed.)* (1990b).

Mariti P. (1987): 'Una nota sulle determinanti della formazione di nuove imprese nel settore manifatturiero' in *Note Economiche*, n. 2.

Mussati G. (ed.) (1990a): *Alle oriqini dell imPrenditoria- lita*, Etas Libri, Milano .

Mussati G. (ed.) (1990b): *Nuovi imprenditori a Milano neqli anni '80*, vol. I, Formaper, Camera di Commercio di Milano, Milano.

Orr D. (1974): 'The Determinants of Entry: a Study of the Canadian Manufacturing Industries', in *Review of Economics and Statistics*, vol. LVI.

Oxenfeldt A.R. (1943): 'New Firms and Free Enterprises: PreWar and PostWar Aspects', American Council of Public Affairs, Washington, D. C.

Salop S. (1979): 'Strategic Entry Deterrence' in *American Economic Review*, n. 69.

Storey D. J. (1982): 'Entrepreneurhip and the New Firm' Croom Helm, London.

Storey D. J. (1987): 'Regional Variations in Entrepreneurship in the U. K.' in *Scottish Journal of Political Economy*, n. 2.

Storey D. J.-Johnson S. (1987): 'Regional Variations in Entrepreneurship in the U. K.' in *Scottish Journal of Political Economy*, n. 2.

Storey D.J.-Jones A.M. (1987): 'New Firm Formation. A Labor Market Approach to Industrial Entry' in *Scottish Journal of Political Economy*, n. 1.

Terrasi Balestrieri M. (1986): 'Nuove imprese e sviluppo regionale' in *Camaqni R.-Malfi L. (ta cura di)* (1986).

Tirole J. (1989): *The Theory of Industrial Orqanization*, MIT Press, Cambridge (mass.) .

Varia H.R. (1984): *Microeconomic Analysis*, Norton, New York.

Vivarelli M. (1989): 'Determinants in the Causes of the Birth of New enterprises', mimeo, SPRU, University of Sussex, Brighton.

Vivarelli M. (1990): 'Le determinanti economiche della nascita di nuove imprese: analisi della letteratura anglosassone, risultati statistici, problemi di stima' in *Mussati G. (ed.)*, (1990a).

10 New firm and plant survival in United States manufacturing

David D. Audretsch

Introduction

The entry of new firms into has generally been assumed to be greatly deterred in the presence of scale economies and capital intensity. However, a rather startling result has emerged in a recent series of studies - new-firm start-ups are apparently not substantially deterred in capital-intensive industries where scale economies play an important role. For example, Acs and Audretsch (1989a and 1989b) found that even small firms are not significantly deterred from entering industries which are relatively capital intensive. This raises a fundamental question at the core of market dynamics: What happens to new firms subsequent to entry? And how are they able to survive?

In fact, little is known about the ability of firms to survive subsequent to entry. In trying to test the validity of Gibrat's Law, Hall (1990), Evans (1987a and 1987b), and Contini and Revelli (1989) found that not only do smaller firms have significantly higher growth rates, but they also have a substantially greater propensity to exit the industry than do their larger counterparts. Evans (1987a), for example, identified the existence of a strong positive relationship between the likelihood of survival and firm size in 81 of 100 American industries he examined.

Phillips and Kirchhoff (1989) also found that firm survival tends to increase with enterprise age. Similarly, based on 200,000 plants that were classified by the United States Census of Manufactures as being established between 1966 and 1977, Dunne et al. (1989) found that failure rates tend to decrease as plant size increases and decrease along with an increase in the age of the plant. Similar results have been found for the Federal Republic of Germany by Preisendörfer, Rudolf, and Ziegler (1989).

However, none of these studies provide any insight as to whether the ability of firms to survive varies across industries, and if so, to which factors such variation in firm survival can be attributed. The purpose of this paper is to fill this gap in the literature by identifying the extent to which the survival of new firms and plants varies across a broad spectrum of manufacturing industries in the United States. Because of the importance of measurement issues, the primary source of data is introduced, explained, and qualified in the following section. In the third section the ability of new-firm start-ups in 1976 to survive throughout the subsequent decade is analyzed. In the fourth section the survival pattern exhibited by new plants is examined. The relationships between the presence of scale economies in the industry, start-up size, technology, and the ability of new firms and plants to survive are explored in the fifth section. Finally, a summary and conclusion are presented in the final section. While a strikingly low rate of survival for new manufacturing firms and plants in the United States can be attributed to the presence of scale economies, a low start-up size, and technological risk, it is beyond the scope of this paper to judge whether this is a virtue or liability.

Data sources and measurement issues

The greatest constraint on measuring the ability of new firms and plants to survive over time on any basis other than a relatively small sample (see for example Dunkelberg and Cooper (1990)) has been the lack of comprehensive longitudinal data sets comprised of individual plants and firms that identify the actual start-up and closure dates. While Dunne, Roberts, and Samuelson (1988 and 1989), Evans (1987a and 1987b), Hall (1987), Ivernizzi and Revelli (forthcoming), Revelli and Tenga (1989), and Contini and Revelli (1990) all had access to such a longitudinal data set, none of these studies explicitly examined new firm and plant survival. One reason why the U.S. Bureau of Census data employed by Dunne, Roberts, and Samuelson do not lend themselves to estimation of precise survival rates, is that while observations over time are available, they are only identified at five-year internals.

Thus, I employ a data set which provides bi-annual observations on firms and plants -- the United States Small Business Administration's Small Business Data Base (SBDB). The data base is derived from the Dun and Bradstreet (DUNS) market identifier file (DMI) which provides a virtual census on about 4.5 million U.S. business establishments every other year between 1976 and 1986.

Prior to 1976, there was no United States Government agency responsible for collecting and disseminating statistics on the dynamic aspects of all enterprises and establishments. Various agencies of the United States Government, such as the Census Bureau of the United States Department of Commerce, did and do publish statistics on business enterprises and establishments, but only at five-year intervals, and the observations not only are not linked over time, but they are also aggregated to the industry level to avoid conflicts in confidentiality.

In response to its dissatisfaction with the lack of knowledge about the dynamic nature of American business, the United States Congress established the Office of Advocacy of the Small Business Administration in 1976. Four years later, the Congress passed the Economic Policy Act of 1980, which mandated the President to submit to the Congress an annual report on the state of small business, and authorized the creation of the Small Business Data Base (SBDB).

In order to fulfil its congressional mandate of disseminating statistics on the state of small business and its relationship to the entire size-distribution of enterprises and establishments, the Office of Advocacy turned to the Dun and Bradstreet corporation. The SBDB is derived from the Dun and Bradstreet (DUNS) market identifier (DMI). The essential building block and unit of observation in the SBDB is the establishment, which is defined as a particular economic entity operating at a specific and single geographic location. While some establishments are legally tied to parent firms through either a branch or subsidiary relationship, other establishments are independent and therefore are, in fact, firms (enterprises) in their own right. In cases of multiproduct firms, or where the establishments operate in different industries or even sectors, each establishment is classified according to its appropriate four-digit standard industrial classification (SIC) industry. By linking the establishments by ownership to their parent firms, each establishment is then classified by the size of the entire firm, and not just by its own size.

The SBDB covers a changing business population of nearly twenty million establishments. Each record includes the establishment location in terms of state and county, employment, the primary and secondary industry, the starting year, sales, organizational status and legal connection to other establishments, and the employment of the entire firm if the establishment belongs to a multi-establishment enterprise.

Establishments are generally referred to as plants in manufacturing, but not in nonmanufacturing. The distinction between the firm and its constituent establishments is particularly crucial in manufacturing. Although over 96 percent of manufacturing firms in 1984 were comprised of establishments within a single industry, about 72 percent of employment in manufacturing was in firms with establishments in at least two different industries (Starr, 1987).

The SBDB makes it possible to identify if each record, or establishment, is (1) a single-establishment firm, in which case the establishment is an independent legal entity, as explained above, (2) a branch or subsidiary belonging to a multi-establishment firm, or (3) the headquarters of a multi-establishment firm. Besides a detailed identification of the ownership structure of each establishment, the USELM file of the SBDB links the performance of each establishment within two-year intervals beginning in 1976 and ending (under the current version) in 1986, thereby tracking each establishment over what constitutes a ten-year longitudinal data base.

Storey and Johnson (1987) argue that because the underlying data have been assembled by a commercial organization whose principal purpose is to provide credit rating information, the reliability of the data is probably enhanced. They point out that the data are not based upon confidentiality but rather on publicly available information (for a fee). In addition, Dun and Bradstreet has a commercial incentive to provide data that are both current and accurate. Similarly, the reporting establishments themselves have an incentive to provide accurate information to a credit rating company.

Nonetheless, the Dun and Bradstreet data have been subjected to serious criticism. Perhaps one of the most significant weaknesses in the DUNS data is missing branch records. Because the Dun and Bradstreet files are compiled on the basis of credit rating, branches and subsidiaries of multi-establishment firms that are unlikely to require credit independently from the parent firm are often not recorded. In one of the first applications of these data, Birch (1981) dealt with this discrepancy by recalculating the total enterprise employment from the aggregation of the employment recorded in each affiliated establishment. By contrast, Armington and Odle (1982) recalculated the employment level of each affiliated establishment from the reported enterprise employment level. As Storey and Johnson (1987) note, the effect resulting from attempts to reconcile this discrepancy between the aggregation of establishment data and the enterprise data was that Birch tended to understate the extent of employment in multi-establishment firms, while Armington and Odle tended to overstate it.

A second problem with the Dun and Bradstreet data is their chronic under representation in industries where there is a propensity for the establishments not to apply for credit. There are still certain other dynamic weaknesses with respect to non updated records in the data base. As Jacobson (1985) found, in a few cases firms and establishments are not included in the data base until several years after they have been established. This leads to a slight understatement of the number of new business units, particularly in rapidly expanding industries, such as certain types of services, and in new industries, such as microcomputers and software-related industries.

In order to correct for at least some of these deficiencies in the DUNS data, the Brookings Institution in conjunction with the Small Business Administration and the National Science Foundation restructured, edited, and supplemented the DUNS data with data from other sources in creating the SBDB. These procedures, along with the development and editing of the SBDB are explained in considerable detail in Brown and Phillips (1989), Harris (1983), Acs and Audretsch (1990, chapter two), and the United States Small Business Administration (1986 and 1987). In particular, a 'family tree' is constructed for each firm, identifying each branch and subsidiary. These family trees are then used to reconcile the organizational status and employment figures between member establishments of multi-establishment enterprises. The employment figures for the entire enterprise are compared to those reported by the individual establishments. Any discrepancy arising between the employment reported for the entire firm and the aggregation of all the individual establishments is then corrected either by increasing the total amount of employment attributed to the entire enterprise to be consistent with that reported by the individual establishments, or else by imputing proxy branch establishments to represent affiliates implied by the employment reported by the enterprise (Armington and Odle, 1983).

Thus, it should be emphasized that the SBDB data have been adjusted by the United States Small Business Administration to clean up the raw data contained in the original DMI files. Several important studies have compared the SBDB data with analogous measures from the establishment data of the U.S. Census of Manufactures (Boden and Phillips, 1985; and Acs and Audretsch, 1990, chapter two), and from the establishment and employment recors of the Bureau of Labor's BLS data (Brown and Phillips, 1989). Such comparisons have generally concluded that the SBDB data are remarkably consistent with three other major data bases providing observations on establishments and enterprises.

The survival of new firms

To measure new-firm survival, all establishments that were classified by the SBDB as being founded in 1976 were identified. Those new establishments belonging to an established firm or identified as a branch or subsidiary of a new firm were then discarded. The remaining establishments thus represent newly created firms. Most of these are single-plant firms, although some are multi-plant firms.

Table 1 shows that the number of new firms established in 1976 varied considerably across two-digit SIC manufacturing sectors. For example, 16.18 percent of the new firms in manufacturing were in the printing sector, 13.62 percent were in the non-electrical machinery sector, and 7.75 percent were in the textile sector. Thus, nearly forty percent of all new firms were established within these three industrial sectors. Other industrial sectors, such as tobacco, chemicals, and paper all experienced a relatively low number of new-firm start-ups.

The dynamic evolution of these new-firm start-ups is tracked over the ensuing decade and is also shown in Table 1. The survival rate in each year is defined as the number of firms from the 1976 cohort of new-firm start-ups, as a percentage of the total number of new firms that were established in that sector in 1976. There are four important points that emerge from the survival patterns over time.

First, and least surprising, the probability of a firm surviving over any given time period is negatively related to the length of that time period. That is, for the entire cohort of firms established in 1976, slightly more than three-quarters were still in existence after two years, slightly fewer than one-half were still operating after six years, and about one-third had survived ten years.

Second, as Phillips and Kirchhoff (1989) and Evans (1987a and 1987b) found, the probability of survival generally increases with the age of the firm. That is, firms which were two years old in 1978 had an 81.45 percent chance of surviving until 1980; those firms that were four years old in 1980 had a 71.94 percent chance of surviving until 1982; six-year old firms in 1982 had an 82.10 percent chance of surviving another two years; and eight-year old firms in 1984 had a 95.04 percent chance of surviving until 1986.

Of course, these aggregate survival rates in no way control for the business cycle - a qualification which needs to be explored more explicitly in subsequent research. Still, the overall trend generally confirms the stylized fact identified by Phillips and Kirchhoff (1989) that the probability of a firm surviving an additional increment of time increases with the amount of time that the firm has already survived.

Third, the survival rate apparently varies considerably across manufacturing sectors. For example, the ten-year survival rate is relatively high in paper, non-electrical machinery, primary metals, and fabricated metal products, all of which had survival rates in 1986 exceeding forty percent. By contrast, over the same time interval the survival rate is relatively low in the petroleum, apparel, furniture, transportation equipment, and leather sectors. None of these sectors experienced a ten-year survival rate in excess of 27 percent.

Table 1
New-firm (1976) survival rates over time by manufacturing sector*

Sector	Year					
	1976	1978	1980	1982	1984	1986
Food	474	340 (71.7)	277 (58.4)	203 (42.8)	152 (32.1)	144 (30.4)
Tobacco	2	2 (100)	2 (100)	1 (50)	1 (50)	1 (50)
Textiles	308	225 (73.1)	165 (53.6)	111 (36.0)	88 (28.6)	84 (27.3)
Apparel	864	622 (72.0)	477 (55.2)	332 (38.4)	256 (29.6)	236 (27.3)
Lumber	794	601 (75.7)	514 (64.7)	349 (44.0)	267 (33.6)	256 (32.2)
Furniture	531	393 (74.0)	310 (58.4)	196 (36.9)	161 (30.3)	141 (28.4)
Paper	126	99 (78.6)	80 (63.5)	67 (53.2)	58 (46.0)	57 (45.2)
Printing	1,805	1,482 (82.1)	1,255 (69.5)	931 (51.6)	799 (46.0)	768 (45.2)
Chemicals	322	248 (77.0)	197 (61.2)	146 (45.3)	119 (37.0)	114 (35.4)
Petroleum	41	27 (69.5)	18 (43.9)	14 (34.1)	11 (26.8)	11 (26.8)
Rubber	430	341 (79.3)	280 (65.1)	207 (48.1)	181 (42.1)	176 (40.9)

Year

Sector	1976	1978	1980	1982	1984	1986
Leather	124	89 (71.8)	75 (60.5)	41 (33.1)	33 (26.6)	30 (24.2)
Stone, Clay, Glass	545	429 (78.7)	341 (62.6)	246 (45.1)	197 (36.1)	182 (33.4)
Primary Metals	168	135 (80.4)	108 (64.3)	82 (48.8)	74 (44.0)	71 (42.9)
Fabricated Metal Products	962	758 (78.8)	638 (66.3)	493 (51.2)	414 (43.0)	394 (41.0)
Machinery (non-electrical)	1,519	1,243 (81.8)	1,054 (69.4)	820 (54.0)	708 (46.6)	675 (44.4)
Electrical Equipment	635	489 (77.0)	378 (59.5)	259 (40.8)	220 (33.1)	196 (30.9)
Transportation Equipment	420	304 (72.4)	229 (54.5)	144 (34.3)	103 (24.5)	97 (23.1)
Instruments	312	251 (80.4)	205 (65.7)	147 (47.1)	123 (39.4)	120 (38.5)
Miscellaneous	772	559 (72.4)	432 (56.0)	272 (35.2)	200 (25.9)	185 (24.0)
Total	11,154	8,637 (77.4)	7,035 (63.1)	5,061 (45.4)	4,155 (37.3)	3,949 (35.4)

* The survival rate is defined as the number of firms surviving in an industry in a given year, as a percentage of the total number of new firms established in 1976.

167

Finally, there is no apparent relationship between the number of new-firm start-ups and the probability of surviving. Both the paper and non-electrical machinery sectors had ten-year survival rates of about 45 percent. However, the non-electrical machinery sector experienced the greatest number of newly established firms, while there were only 126 new firms established in the paper sector. Similarly, in both the chemical and textile sectors there were slightly more than three hundred new firms established in 1976. However, the ten-year survival rate in the chemical sector was nearly one-third greater than the survival rate in the textile sector.

New-plant survival

As Table 2 shows, the SBDB identifies 12,251 new manufacturing establishments, or plants, which were opened in the United States in 1976. The dynamic evolution of those new plants over the subsequent decade is also identified. In addition, the new plants are classified as being either 'large' during their first year of existence if they employed at least fifty workers, or else 'small', if they employed fewer than fifty people. One of the most striking features of Table 2 is the skewed size distribution of new plants. While 11,662 (95.19 percent) had fewer than fifty employees during their first year of existence, only 589 (4.81 percent) had at least fifty employees.

Table 2 also shows that new plants to be opened at a somewhat larger scale in the primary metals, textile, apparel, food, and petroleum sectors, where the number of larger plants opened was at least one-tenth as great as the number of smaller plants opened. By contrast, new plants in the printing, non-electrical machinery, instruments, and leather sectors consisted predominately of establishments with fewer than fifty employees.

It should be noted that these comparisons of initial establishment size are in terms of the number of workers employed by the plant. A comparison based on sales could yield somewhat different results due to variations in capital intensity and therefore sales-employee ratios across manufacturing sectors. However, it should be emphasized that the employment criterion is the most common measure used to distinguish both establishment and enterprise size (Armington and Odle, 1982; Storey and Johnson, 1987; and Storey, 1989).

The ability of a plant to survive over time is apparently related to establishment size. Of the large plants opened in 1976, 45.7 percent had closed by 1986. By contrast, 69.0 percent of the small plants opened were forced out of business during this same ten-year period. However, the survival rate of the larger plants did not exceed that of their smaller counterparts in every manufacturing sector. For example, the ten-year survival rate of the smaller plants which were opened in 1976 actually exceeded that of larger plants in the lumber, petroleum, and rubber sectors.

As proved to be the case for new firms, the probability of a plant exiting an industry increases with the time period considered, but decreases with the age of the plant. That is, the survival rate tends to decrease as the time interval considered also increases, but the conditional probability of a plant surviving increases with the amount of time it has already survived. These two tendencies hold regardless of the initial size of the plant.

Table 2
Plants start-up size and survival rates by manufacturing sector,
1976-1986

Sector	Start-up Size	1976	1978	YEAR 1980	1982	1984	1986
Food	Large	57	47 (82.5)	41 (71.9)	35 (61.4)	29 (50.9)	26 (45.6)
	Small	504	367 (72.8)	293 (58.1)	208 (41.3)	157 (31.2)	129 (25.6)
Textiles	Large	38	30 (79.9)	24 (63.2)	16 (42.1)	13 (34.2)	12 (31.6)
	Small	303	221 (72.9)	161 (53.1)	108 (35.6)	86 (28.4)	72 (23.8)
Apparel	Large	96	80 (83.3)	69 (71.9)	55 (57.3)	46 (47.9)	38 (39.6)
	Small	851	603 (70.9)	459 (53.9)	313 (36.8)	236 (27.7)	179 (21.0)
Lumber	Large	31	24 (77.4)	19 (61.3)	17 (54.8)	11 (35.5)	7 (22.6)
	Small	821	619 (75.4)	525 (64.0)	356 (43.4)	276 (33.6)	230 (28.0)
Furniture	Large	21	14 (66.7)	13 (61.9)	13 (61.9)	11 (52.4)	10 (47.6)
	Small	559	409 (73.2)	317 (56.7)	197 (35.2)	162 (29.0)	135 (24.2)

Table 2 (Cont.)

Sector	Start-up Size	1976	1978	YEAR 1980	1982	1984	1986
Paper	Large	11	6 (54.6)	5 (45.5)	5 (45.5)	5 (45.5)	5 (45.5)
	Small	145	111	88	72	63	59
Printing	Large	25	21 84.0	15 60.0	13 52.0	12 48.0	11 44.0
	Small	1,877	1,541 (82.1) (76.6)	1,307 (69.6) (60.7)	975 (51.9) (49.7)	832 (44.3) (43.5)	736 (39.2) (40.7)
Chemicals	Large	16	14 (88.9)	11 (68.8)	10 (62.5)	9 (56.3)	9 (56.3)
	Small	360	265 (73.6)	210 (58.3)	155 (43.1)	127 (35.3)	110 (30.6)
Petroleum	Large	5	3 (60.0)	3 (60.0)	2 (40.0)	1 (20.0)	1 (20.0)
	Small	51	34 (66.7)	24 (47.1)	20 (39.2)	14 (27.5)	12 (23.5)
Rubber	Large	27	32 (85.2)	17 (63.0)	13 (48.2)	12 (44.4)	8 (29.6)
	Small	450	352 (78.2)	293 (65.1)	216 (48.0)	187 (41.6)	162 (36.0)

Table 2 (Cont.)

Sector	Start-up Size	1976	1978	YEAR 1980	1982	1984	1986
Leather	Large	7	7 (100.0)	6 (85.7)	6 (85.7)	4 (57.1)	4 (57.1)
	Small	122	87 (71.3)	74 (60.7)	39 (32.0)	30 (24.6)	27 (22.1)
Stone, Clay, Glass	Large	20	17 (85.0)	16 (80.0)	12 (60.0)	10 (50.0)	10 (50.0)
	Small	595	472 (79.3)	371 (62.4)	272 (45.7)	276 (36.3)	173 (29.1)
Primary Metals	Large	24	22 (91.7)	20 (83.3)	19 (79.2)	19 (79.2)	19 (79.2)
	Small	180	144 (80.0)	116 (64.4)	83 (46.1)	73 (40.6)	63 (35.0)
Fabricated Metal Products	Large	59	51 (86.4)	39 (66.1)	34 (57.6)	28 (47.5)	24 (40.7)
	Small	1,009	789 (78.2)	659 (65.3)	508 (50.4)	427 (42.3)	360 (35.7)
Machinery (non-electrical)	Large	54	50 (92.6)	41 (75.9)	37 (68.5)	33 (61.1)	32 (59.3)
	Small	1,595	1,296 (81.3)	1,094 (68.6)	848 (53.2)	734 (46.0)	621 (38.9)

171

Table 2 (Cont.)

Sector	Start-up Size	1976	1978	YEAR 1980	1982	1984	1986
Electrical Equipment	Large	39	31 (79.5)	26 (66.7)	2 (56.4)	20 (51.3)	18 (46.2)
	Small	674	519 (77.0)	400 (59.4)	273 (40.5)	221 (32.8)	184 (27.3)
Transportation Equipment	Large	21	16 (76.2)	12 (57.1)	11 (52.4)	9 (42.9)	9 (42.9)
	Small	440	318 (72.3)	243 (55.2)	154 (35.0)	111 (25.2)	93 (21.1)
Instruments	Large	11	10 (90.0)	9 (81.8)	9 (81.8)	8 (72.7)	8 (72.7)
	Small	328	260 (80.0)	210 (64.6)	151 (46.5)	126 (38.8)	115 (35.4)
Miscelleneous	Large	27	19 (70.4)	16 (59.3)	13 (48.2)	10 (37.0)	10 (37.0)
	Small	799	578 (72.3)	440 (55.1)	272 (34.0)	201 (25.2)	158 (19.8)
Total	Large	589	485 (82.3)	401 (68.1)	343 (58.2)	290 (49.2)	261 (44.3)
	Small	11,622	8,987 (77.1)	7,286 (62.5)	5,221 (44.8)	4,280 (36.7)	3,681 (31.0)

* The survival rate is defined as the number of firms surviving in an industry in a given year, as a percentage of the total number of firms established in 1976.

Although not included in Table 2, plant size in the initial year is apparently strongly influenced by ownership status. There is a distinct tendency for the start-up size of independent plants to be smaller than that of subsidiaries and branches of existing firms. The mean initial size of independent plants opened in 1976 was 9.55 employees. By contrast, the mean initial size of branch and subsidiary plants opened in 1976 was 58.9 employees. This disparity in start-up size exists across individual manufacturing sectors as well as for manufacturing as a whole.

Survival, scale economies and technology

Why does the ability of new-firm start-ups and new plants vary so much across industrial sectors? As Table 2 suggests, one answer may be the initial start-up size. To some extent, the size of a start-up will reflect the ability of the establishment to attract financial resources, which will subsequently determine its ability to survive. Furthermore, the greater the size of the initial start-up, the less it will need to grow in order to attain the minimum efficient scale (MES) level of output, or the level of output which is required to attain the minimum average cost and exhaust scale economies. The smallest start-ups will presumably need to experience substantial growth in order to attain the MES, whereas only a more modest growth rate, if any at all, is required of the largest start-ups.

The ownership status of an establishment may also influence the decision to exit an industry. As Evans and Leighton (1989 and 1990) show, and De Wit and Van Winden (1989 and 1991), the opportunity costs of the self-employed tends to be lower than that for other workers, even after controlling for individual and industry characteristics. The owners of independent establishments may tend to have a lower opportunity cost and therefore be willing to accept a lower rate of return than is set for subsidiaries of a multiplant firm. Not inconsistent with this is the finding of Hall and Weiss (1967), among others, that profitability tends to be positively related to firm size. Caves and Porter (1976, p. 43) argue that '...diversification can remove or combat managerial sources of exit barriers. Multi-industry firms may be controlled by their top managements, but the evaluation and removal of managers of the firm's individual business units is the responsibility of top management. Top management may maintain an effective internal capital market, reviewing divisional performance internally and facilitating managerial changes or exit from the business when necessary. The possibility of internal placement of employees displaced from an extinguished business makes it easier for top management to wield the axe. And the greater the breadth and extent of the firm's diversification, the less threat does exit from one industry represent to its continuity, the more dispassionate can be the decision to exit.'

The probability of a new firm or plant making an innovation also presumably affects its ability to remain in, or exit from an industry. This is because innovative activity is a vehicle by which a firm or plant can grow and ultimately attain the MES level of output. An implication of the Jovanovic (1982), and Pakes and Ericson (1987) learning-by-doing models is that firms begin at a small scale of output and then, if merited by subsequent performance, expand. While entrepreneurs may be unsure about their ability to innovate upon establishing a new firm, this becomes clearer with the passage of time. Those firms which successfully innovate can expect future sales growth, while those that face only dim prospects of innovating are more likely to be forced to leave the industry.

In my 1990 and 1991 papers the ability of new firms and plant to survive was found to be clearly reduced in the presence of scale economies and capital intensity. Similarly, the likelihood of survival was identified as being positively influenced by the start-up size. Both of these results support the notion that most new-firm start-ups and new plants open at a scale of output that is sub-optimal. Only by entering industries where scale economies do not play an important role, or by expanding the start-up size, can the inherent size disadvantage of new start-ups be offset.

In addition, the empirical results suggest that the ability of plants which are subsidiaries or branches of existing enterprises to survive is substantially greater than that for independent plants, that is for new-firm start-ups. This may be because new subsidiaries and branches have both the resources and experience of the parent enterprise to fall back on.

New-firm survival is apparently promoted in industries where the small firms have the innovative advantage over their larger counterparts. This suggests that a strategy of innovation and the introduction of new products to develop niches is one viable mechanism by which new firms and plants can, at least to some extent, offset their inherent scale disadvantage.

Conclusion

A remarkable finding of this paper is that most new firms and plants in United States manufacturing do not survive for even one decade. One of the apparent reasons for the low rate of survival is the strikingly small scale at which the bulk of new firms and plants operate. This points to the importance of deploying a strategy of innovation as a mechanism to offset the inherent scale disadvantages.

Why do so many firms and plants enter, knowing that the prospects for survival are so dismal? One answer is that they incur a risk. If they are able to innovate, or in some other way successfully adapt, a new firm or plant will grow and ultimately attain the MES level of output. If not, they will be forced to exit from the industry.

Should something be done about the relatively low propensity of new manufacturing firms to survive? As Scherer (1991) and Cohen and Klepper (1991) emphasize, many new-firm start-ups represent an experiment, in that they are introducing a new product, procedure, or way of managing the firm. Only those successful experiments ultimately survive, while the others are doomed to fail. The empirical evidence suggests that this high rate of turbulence is inextricably intertwined with the process by which technological change takes place. The nations of Eastern Europe provide a historical counter-example of economies where firms were neither allowed to enter nor allowed to fail (Bannash, 1990). Therefore, whether or not the strikingly high propensity of new firms and plants in United States manufacturing to fail is a virtue or a liability needs to be explicitly examined in future research.

References:

Acs, Z. J. and Audretsch, D. B. (1987), 'Innovation, Market Structure and Firm Size', *Review of Economics and Statistics*, November, pp. 567-575.
Acs, Z. J. and Audretsch, D. B. (1988), 'Innovation in Large and Small Firms: An Empirical Analysis', *American Economic Review*, September, pp. 678-690.
Acs, Z. J. and Audretsch, D. B. (1989), 'Births and Firm Size', *Southern Economic Journal*, 56(2), October 1989, pp. 467-475.
Acs, Z. J. and Audretsch, D. B. (1989), 'Small-Firm Entry in U.S. Manufacturing', *Economica*, 56(2), May 1989, pp. 255-65.
Acs, Z. J. and Audretsch, D. B. (1990), *Innovation and Small Firms*, Cambridge, MIT Press.

Armington, C. and Odle, M. (1982), 'Small Business - How Many Jobs?', *The Brookings Review*, 1, pp. 14-17.

Armington, C. and Odle, M. (1983), 'Weigthing the USEEM Files for Longitudinal Analysis of Employment Growth', Working Paper No. 12, Business Microdata Project, The Brookings Institution, April 1983.

Audretsch, D. B. (1990), 'Start-Up Size and Establishment Exit', Discussion Paper FSIV 90-8, Wissenschaftszentrum Berlin für Sozialforschung.

Audretsch, D. B. (1991), 'New Firm Survival and the Technological Regime', *Review of Economics and Statistics*, August.

Bannasch, H.-G. (1990), 'The Role of Small Firms in East Germany', *Small Business Economics*, 2(4), pp. 307-312.

Birch, D. L. (1981), 'Who Creates Jobs?', *The Public Interest*, 65, pp. 3-14.

Boden, R. and Phillips, B. D. (1985), 'Uses and Limitations of USEEM/USELM Data', Office of Advocacy, U.S. Small Business Administration, Washington, DC.

Brown, H. S. and Phillips, B. D. (1989), 'Comparison Between Small Business Data Base (USEEM) and Bureau of Labor Statistics (BLS) Employment Data: 1978-1986', *Small Business Economics*, 1(4), pp. 273-284.

Caves, R. E. and Porter, M. E. (1976), 'Barriers to Exit', in P. D. Qualls (ed.), *Essays on Industrial Organization in Honor of Joe S. Bain*, Cambridge, Ballinger.

Cohen, W. and Klepper, S. (1991), 'Firm Size versus Diversity in the Achievement of Technological Advance', in Z. J. Acs and D. B. Audretsch (eds), *Innovation and Technological Change: An International Comparison*, Ann Arbor, University of Michigan Press, pp. 183-203.

Contini, B. and Revelli, R. (1990), 'The Relationship between Firm Growth and Labor Demand', in Z. J. Acs and D. B. Audretsch (eds), *The Economics of Small Firms: A European Challenge*, Boston, Kluwer Academic Publishers, pp. 53-60.

De Wit, G. and van Winden, F. (1991), 'An M-Sector, N-Group Behavioral Model of Self-Employment', *Small Business Economics*, March, pp. 49-66.

De Wit, G. and van Winden, F., 'An Empirical Study of Self-Employment in the Netherlands', *Small Business Economics*, 1(4), pp. 263-272.

Dunkelberg, W. C. and Cooper, A. C. (1990), 'Investment and Capital Diversity in the Small Enterprise', in Z. J. Acs and D. B. Audretsch (eds), *The Economics of Small Firms*, Boston, Kluwer Academic Publishers, pp. 119-134.

Dunne, T., Roberts, M. J. and Samuelson, L. (1988), 'Patterns of Firm Entry and Exit in U.S. Manufacturing Industries', *Rand Journal of Economics*, 19(4), pp. 495-515.

Dunne, T., Roberts, M. J. and Samuelson, L. (1989), 'The Growth and Failure of U.S. Manufacturing Plants', *Quarterly Journal of Economics*, 104(4), pp. 671-698.

Evans, D. S. (1987a), 'The Relationship Between Firm Growth, Size and Age: Estimates for 100 Manufacturing Industries', *Journal of Industrial Economics*, 35, June 1987, pp. 567-581.

Evans, D. S. (1987b), 'Tests of Alternative Theories of Firm Growth', *Journal of Political Economy*, 95, August 1987, pp. 657-674.

Evans, D. S. and Leighton, L. S. (1989), 'The Determinants of Changes in U.S. Self-Employment, 1968-1987', *Small Business Economics*, 1(2), pp. 111-120.

Evans, D. S. and Leighton, L. S. (1990), 'Some Empirical Aspects of Entrepreneurship', in Z. J. Acs and D. B. Audretsch (eds), *The Economics of Small Firms: A European Challenge*, Boston, Kluwer Academic Publishers, pp. 79-97.

Hall, B. H. (1987), 'The Relationship Between Firm Size and Firm Growth in the U.S. Manufacturing Sector', *Journal of Industrial Economics*, 35, pp. 583-605.

Hall, M. and Weiss, L. W. (1967), 'Firm Size and Profitability', *Review of Economics and Statistics*, August, pp. 319-331.

Harris, C. S. (1983), *U.S. Establishment and Enterpride Microdata (USEEEM): A Data Base Desciption*, Business Microdata Project, The Brookings Institution, June 1983.

Invernizzi, B. and Revelli, R. (forthcoming), 'Small Firms in the Italian Economy: Structural Changes and Evidence of Turbulence', in Z. J. Acs and D. B. Audretsch (eds), *Small Firms and Entrepreneurship in West and East Countries*, Cambridge, Cambridge University Press, forthcoming.

Jovanovic, B. (1982), 'Selection and Evolution of Industry', *Econometrica*, May, pp. 649-670.

Pakes, A. and Ericson, R. (1987), 'Empirical Implications of Alternative Models on Firm Dynamics', manuscript, Department of Economics, University of Wisconsin-Madison.

Phillips, B. D. and Kirchhoff, B. A. (1989), 'Formation, Growth and Survival: Small Firm Dynamics in the U.S. Economy', *Small Business Economics*, 1(1), pp. 65-74.

Preissendörfer, P., Schüssler, R. and Ziegler, R. (1989), 'Bestandschancen neugegründeter Kleinbetriebe', *Internationales Gewerbearchiv*, 37(4), pp. 237-248.

Revelli, R. and Tenga, S. (1989), 'The Determinants of New Firm Formation in Italian Manufacturing', *Small Business Economics*, 1(3), pp. 181-192.

Scherer,. F. M. (1991), 'Changing Perspectives on the Firm Size Problem', in Z. J. Acs and D. B. Audretsch (eds), *Innovation and Technological Change*, Ann Arbor, University of Michigan Press, pp. 24-38.

Starr, E. (1987), 'Small Business in Manufacturing', prepared for the U.S. Small Business Administration, July 1987.

Storey, D. J. (1989), 'Firm Performance and Size: Explanations from the Small Firm Sectors', *Small Business Economics*, 1(3), pp. 175-180.

Storey, D. J. and Johnson, S. (1987), *Job Generation and Labour Market Changes*, London, Macmillan.

U.S. Small Business Administration (1986), *The Small Business Data Base: A User's Guide*, Washington, DC, July 1986.

U.S. Small Business Administration, Office of Advocacy, *Linked 1976-1984 USEEEM User's Guide*, Washington, DC, July 1987.

Part 4
Factors influencing entrepreneurial intentions and activities

11 Entrepreneurial interest among business students: Results of an international study

Hermann J. Weihe and Frank-Rainer Reich

As part of the Entrepreneurship Research project in the Business school of the Fachhochschule Nordostniedersachsen, a total of 507 first-year students and graduates of business schools both in Germany and abroad were questioned during the winter semester 1989 and the summer semester 1990.

The objects of this international comparative study are:
- a study of the image of self-employed business people
- an investigation of the willingness of business students to go into business for themselves
- an investigation of the motives and reservations concerning starting up a business
- a stock-taking of students already self-employed
- an investigation of the role of the university as an incubator organization for entrepreneurs.

In addition to the international comparison the study allowed a comparison between German first-year students and graduates.
The study comprised the following subgroups:
- all 114 first-year students in the winter semester 1989 at the Fachhochschule Nordostniedersachsen, School of Business, who were studying either Business Administration (66 cases) or Business Information Studies (45 cases), or both, as well as 101 graduates with a similar distribution of degrees
- 60 first-year students at the Manchester Polytechnic (Business Studies major) in England
- 60 first-year students at the Ecole Supérieur de Commerce de Compiègne, in Compiègne, France

179

- 88 first-year students at the University of Economics in Vienna, Austria
- 51 first-year students in the MBA program at Appalachian State University, Boone (North Carolina) as well as 33 first-year students at the University of Tampa, Tampa (Florida). Both subgroups were combined into a USA group.

The study was carried out with the use of written questionnaires. Those returned by the graduates and foreign students represent random samples.

The standard version of the questionnaire (for first-year students) includes 38 detailed questions with 194 variables, while the graduates were confronted with an expanded version with 42 questions and a total of 207 variables.

The great quantity of data generated by this study was evaluated with the help of the program SPSS (Statistical Package for the Social Sciences) in the mainframe version.

Unreserved interest in self-employment

The key question of the study was: 'In principle are you interested in going into business for yourself?'

The possible answers were: yes, certainly; maybe; no; yes, am already self-employed. With the help of this question it was possible to divide each sample into the groups: 'interested' and 'indifferent', as well as to determine the percentage of students already self-employed.

Those who were already self-employed or who answered the key question with 'yes, certainly' were categorized as 'interested'. Those whose interest was conditional (maybe) were put in the 'indifferent' group, along with those who answered in the negative. The following table shows the interest in entrepreneurship both according to country as well as according to the categories 'interested' and 'indifferent'.

Internationally, an average of 34.3 % of those questioned had an unreserved interest in self-employment. This figure includes a percentage of 3.2 % of those who are already self-employed. Subtract the seven graduates already self-employed and there is 1.8 % of those questioned (9 cases) who combine university and self-employment.

The percentage of those who were undecided ('maybe') was 50.5 %. An unqualified refusal, 'no', was given by 15.0 % of those questioned.

A comparison among the different national groups revealed the greatest interest in self-employment in the American group (57.1 %), and the least in the group of German graduates (21.8 %). Of the German first-year students 34.2 % were unreservedly interested. The percentage of unreservedly interested differs significantly between the two

Table 1
Interested in entrepreneurship

item	G 1st year No. (%)	Int. (%)	Ind. (%)	G grads No. (%)	Int. (%)	Ind. (%)	GB No. (%)	Int. (%)	Ind. (%)	A No. (%)	Int. (%)	Ind. (%)	F No. (%)	Int. (%)	Ind. (%)	USA No. (%)	Int. (%)	Ind. (%)	total No. (%)	Int. (%)	Ind. (%)
yes, certainly	37 (32,5)	39 (34,2)		5 (14,9)	22 (21,8)		21 (35,0)	21 (35,0)		25 (28,4)	27 (30,7)		17 (28,3)	17 (28,3)		43 (51,2)	48 (57,1)		158 (31,2)	174 (34,3)	
already self-employed	2 (1,8)			7 (6,9)			–			2 (2,3)			0 (0,0)			5 (6,0)			16 (3,2)		
maybe	62 (54,4)		75 (65,8)	53 (52,5)		79 (78,2)	30 (50,0)		39 (65,0)	51 (58,0)		61 (69,3)	35 (58,3)		43 (71,7)	25 (29,8)		36 (42,9)	256 (50,5)		333 (65,7)
no	13 (11,4)			26 (25,7)			9 (15,0)			10 (11,4)			8 (13,3)			10 (11,9)			76 (15,0)		
no response																1 (1,2)			1 (0,2)		
total (%)	114 (100,1)	39	75	101 (100,0)	22	79	60 (100,0)	21	39	88 (100,1)	27	61	60 (99,9)	17	43	84 (100,1)	48	36	507 (100,1)	174	333

German groups. Hypotheses explaining this phenomenon could include:

- 'The good chances in the labor market in salaried employment creates reservations about taking on a greater risk by being self-employed.'
- 'The university socializes students for salaried work.'

Further explanations are given in the analysis of reservations about entrepreneurship.

Low interest in self-employment was shown by the French group (28.3 %), as well as by the Austrian group (30.7 %). We found the highest number of students already self-employed (6.0 %) in America. The greatest number of unqualified refusals was given by the West German graduates (25.7 %). All the other groups ranged between 11 and 15 %.

Entrepreneurial motivation

We asked the interested as well as the indifferent about the motives that would be important in making a decision to go into business. Along with other motivation theory authors we assume that a developing or existing entrepreneurial interest is the expression of the specific needs structure of an individual. Five needs groups will be examined here more closely.

As can be seen from the numbering of the variables the statements were in a mixed order. The question was formulated, 'What would be important motives for you to go into business for yourself?' The degree of an individual's agreement to these statements was set on the five-stage Likert scale.

Need for social recognition

attractive appearance	*V147
lead others	V141
more contact to others	V159
set up a successful organization	V160
gain power and influence	V152
work in a small organization	V155
positive example	V162
work together with spouse/family	V156
family tradition	V142

Need for development of personality

prove own ability	V158
realize own ideas	V139
make something important for myself	V150
make something lasting	V153
desire for adventure	V157

Need for independence

financial independence	V140
freedom of action and decision-making	V138
set my own income	V154
do the work I want to do	V161

* V = Variable of the standardized questionnaire

Need for prosperity

desire for a higher income	V143
income commensurate with performance	V145
financial investment and wealth creation	V144
tax benefits	V149
labor market and state of the economy	V146

Need for escape

trouble in salaried employment	V148
not to work for others	V151

The following table expresses arithmetic mean values, which eliminates extreme answers. Means lower than 3.0 were interpreted as tending toward agreement to a statement.

In the final analysis the needs for independence (2.1) and personality development (2.2) were ahead of the needs for prosperity (2.7), prestige (2.9) and escape (2.9). These findings at an international level show the initial motivation for an interest in going into business for oneself. All needs tend to be acknowledged (mean value less than 3.0).

The need for prestige plays a greater role in France (2.5), while in Germany it has the least important role (3.1 and 3.3). The German subgroups put less emphasis on the need for personality development (2.3 and 2.5) than the French (1.8). The USA group shows the highest need for independence (1.8), while the German graduates were at the end of the scale with a value of 2.4. The need for prosperity is roughly similar for all groups. The need for escape plays a greater role for the Austrians and the German first-year students than for the German graduates.

Table 2
Entrepreneurial motivation

country variable	G 1st year	G grads	GB	F	A	USA	total	need
V147	3,3	3,5	2,6	2,8	3,2	2,5	3,0	social status
V141	2,8	2,8	2,5	2,3	2,7	2,6	2,7	
V159	2,7	3,0	2,4	1,9	2,4	2,5	2,5	
V160	2,4	2,6	2,1	1,7	2,2	1,8	2,2	
V152	3,3	3,5	2,5	2,5	2,8	2,6	2,9	
V155	2,7	3,0	3,0	2,2	2,7	2,8	2,7	
V162	2,7	3,0	2,6	2,8	2,7	2,5	2,7	
V156	3,2	3,5	3,8	-	3,4	3,3	3,4	
V142	4,5	4,4	4,2	4,1	4,3	4,0	4,3	
average	**3,1**	**3,3**	**2,9**	**2,5**	**2,9**	**2,7**	**2,9**	
V158	2,4	2,5	1,9	2,2	2,2	2,0	2,2	development of personality
V139	1,5	1,8	1,8	1,5	1,5	1,6	1,6	
V150	2,2	2,3	2,2	1,4	2,2	2,0	2,1	
V153	2,6	2,8	2,4	1,9	2,6	2,3	2,5	
V157	3,0	3,0	2,1	2,2	2,3	2,3	2,6	
average	**2,3**	**2,5**	**2,1**	**1,8**	**2,2**	**2,0**	**2,2**	
V140	2,2	2,3	2,2	2,4	2,0	2,0	2,2	independence
V138	1,5	1,7	1,8	1,3	1,4	1,6	1,6	
V154	2,5	2,8	2,3	3,0	2,3	2,1	2,5	
V161	2,2	2,6	1,8	2,3	2,0	1,5	2,1	
average	**2,1**	**2,4**	**2,0**	**2,3**	**1,9**	**1,8**	**2,1**	
V143	2,4	2,6	2,0	2,5	2,4	2,0	2,3	prosperity
V145	2,3	2,7	2,5	2,3	2,2	2,1	2,4	
V144	2,6	3,0	3,0	2,9	2,5	3,0	2,8	
V149	3,1	3,1	3,1	3,6	3,4	3,1	3,2	
V146	2,9	3,1	3,2	2,8	3,0	3,1	3,0	
average	**2,7**	**2,7**	**2,8**	**2,8**	**2,7**	**2,7**	**2,7**	
V148	3,3	3,7	3,3	3,3	2,9	3,8	3,4	escape
V151	2,2	2,5	2,4	2,4	2,6	2,1	2,4	
average	**2,8**	**3,1**	**2,9**	**2,9**	**2,8**	**3,0**	**2,9**	

184

Within the individual groups the following motivation structures were determined:

For the German first-year students, graduates and the Austrian group:
1. independence
2. development of personality
3. prosperity
4. escape
5. prestige.

There was also a high degree of agreement to the statements:
- 'realize own ideas' (V139)
- 'freedom of action and decision-making' (V138).

For the English group:
1. independence
2. development of personality
3. prosperity
4. escape and prestige.

There was also a high degree of agreement to the statements:
- 'prove one's ability' (V158)
- 'realize own ideas' (V139)
- 'freedom of action and decision-making' (V138)
- 'do the work I want to do' (V161).

For the French group:
1. development of personality
2. independence
3. prestige
4. prosperity
5. escape.

There was also a high degree of agreement to the statements:
- 'more contact to others' (159)
- 'build up a successful organization' (V160)
- 'realize own ideas' (V139)
- 'make something important for myself' (V150)
- 'make something lasting' (V153)
- 'freedom of action and decision-making' (V138).

For the American group:
1. independence
2. development of personality
3. prestige and prosperity
4. escape.

There was also a high degree of agreement to the statements:
- 'build up a successful organization' (V160)

- 'realize own ideas' (V139)
- 'freedom of action and decision-making' (V138)
- 'do the work I want to do' (V161)

The key motives among all national groups are 'realize own ideas' (V139) and 'freedom of action and decision-making' (V138). 'Family tradition' (V142) is - against a background of a low proportion of self-employed in the population - a motive that received little agreement throughout (average greater than 4.0).

Reservations about entrepreneurship

In order to obtain information about undecided or rejecting behavior by the roughly two thirds of respondents in regard to interest in self-employment we put the following question to the groups: 'What would be serious reservations for you about going into business for yourself?'

A total of 24 statements were given, which were evaluated with the aid of the five-stage Likert scale. The statements can be divided into the following groups: stress expectation, risk expectation, negative image held by self or others, unfavourable conditions.

Stress expectation

higher stress and pressure to perform	V131
little separation possible between work and private life	V130
self-employment creates a lot of trouble in life	V135
no settled working hours	V116
more work compared with salaried position	V115
irregular salary	V126
an independent businessperson has to do a lot of uninteresting things	V132
problems with employees	V120

Risk expectation

too high a risk	V114
good career opportunities in salaried position	V119
good salary in present position	V122
unsatisfactory provision for retirement	V121

186

Image held by self and by others

not the entrepreneurial type	V128
have only a particular skill, lack general commercial or management experience	V125
poor experience when I was self-employed	V136
could already be too old	V134
lack of understanding from spouse/family	V129
public has a negative image of entrepreneurs	V127
negative examples from relatives/acquaintances	V137

General conditions

political developments	V117
low growth in prospective branch	V133
no start-up capital	V123
clause in employment contract restricting competition	V124
tax burden	V118

The final analysis shows that internationally merely the statements 'too high a risk' (V114), 'good career opportunities in salaried position' (V119), 'no start-up capital' (V123) tended to receive agreement (mean value low 3.0). When aggregated to clusters the findings show that stress expectation, risk, negative image held by self or by others, and unfavourable conditions were by and large not agreed to (mean value high 3.0).

Apparently the group of potential entrepreneurs extends to those who answered the question about an unreserved interest in going into business with 'maybe' (50.5%) and were at first classified as 'indifferent' by us.

The findings of aggregated average values right of 3.0 (more a rejecting attitude) contrast with the results of the questions about entrepreneurial motivation given above and which on average shows acceptance.

The following table shows the mean values according to variables and reservation groups:

Table 3
Reservation about entrepreneurship

country variable	G 1st year	G grads	GB	F	A	USA	total	Reservation about going into business
V131	3,0	3,3	2,8	2,7	3,1	3,0	3,0	stress
V130	3,1	3,4	3,1	3,0	3,1	3,4	3,2	expecta-
V135	3,3	3,4	3,4	3,2	3,5	4,0	3,5	tion
V116	3,6	3,7	3,0	2,7	3,9	3,4	3,4	
V115	3,4	3,6	3,1	2,7	3,6	3,4	3,3	
V126	3,6	3,5	2,9	3,4	3,6	2,8	3,3	
V132	3,6	3,8	3,5	3,3	3,4	4,1	3,7	
V120	3,8	4,1	3,3	3,8	3,6	3,3	3,7	
average	3,4	3,6	3,1	3,1	3,5	3,4	3,4	
V114	2,5	2,5	2,7	2,8	2,8	2,3	2,6	risk
V119	2,7	2,8	2,4	3,4	3,1	2,7	2,8	expecta-
V122	3,3	2,7	3,1	3,1	3,2	3,0	3,0	tion
V121	3,5	3,8	3,5	3,8	3,3	3,4	3,5	
average	3,0	3,0	2,9	3,3	3,1	2,9	3,0	
V128	3,9	3,7	3,6	3,6	3,8	4,0	3,8	negative
V125	3,5	3,8	3,3	2,9	3,6	4,0	3,6	image held
V136	4,6	4,7	4,2	4,3	4,6	4,5	4,5	by self or
V134	4,5	4,5	4,2	4,7	4,5	4,6	4,5	others
V129	4,1	4,2	3,9	3,9	4,2	4,2	4,1	
V127	4,2	4,4	3,9	4,2	4,0	4,4	4,2	
V137	4,4	4,4	4,0	4,3	4,2	4,4	4,3	
average	4,2	4,2	3,9	4,0	4,1	4,3	4,1	
V117	3,5	3,9	3,1	3,7	3,6	3,7	3,6	unfavor-
V133	3,3	3,6	3,3	3,0	3,4	3,7	3,4	able con-
V123	3,3	2,7	2,9	2,5	2,5	2,3	2,5	ditions
V124	3,6	4,3	3,2	3,3	3,3	4,5	3,7	
V118	3,4	3,9	2,8	3,0	2,9	3,4	3,3	
average	3,4	3,7	3,1	3,1	3,1	3,5	3,3	

A comparative look at the international reservation portfolio shows:

The German first-year students agree to the statements: 'too high a risk' (V114: 2.5) and 'good career opportunities in a salaried position' (V119: 2.7), while the German graduates also agreed to the statement: 'good salary in present position' (V122: 2.7).

The English group agreed to the following statements: 'higher stress and pressure to perform' (V131: 2.8), 'irregular income' (V126: 2.9), 'too high a risk' (V114: 2.7), 'good career opportunities in salaried position' (V119: 2.4), 'no start-up capital' (V123: 2.9, and 'tax burden' (V118: 2.8) and showed on the whole agreement to the aggregated risk statements (2.9).

The French group agreed to the following statements: 'higher stress and pressure to perform' (V131: 2.7), 'no settled working hours' (V116: 2.7), 'more work compared with salaried employment' (V115: 2.7), 'too high a risk' (V114: 2.8), 'have only a particular skill, lack general commercial and management experience' (V125: 2.9) and 'no start-up capital' (V123: 2.5).

The portfolio of reservations of the Austrian group looks like this: 'too high a risk' (V114: 2.8), 'no start-up capital' (V123: 2.5) and 'tax burden' (V118: 2.9).

And finally the USA: 'irregular income' (V126: 2.8), 'too high a risk' (V114: 2.3), 'good career opportunities in salaried position' (V119: 2.7) and 'no start-up capital' (V123: 2.3) are the important reservations. Like the English, the Americans tend to agree to the aggregated risk statements more than other national groups.

Image of the entrepreneur

Within the scope of our image study, we were furthermore interested in the image of the entrepreneur in the various countries. The students and graduates were asked to give the degree of their agreement to the following statements:

Business people are mainly responsible for mass unemployment	V64
Business people are committed to the public good	V65
Environmental protection only works if there are laws	V66
The wealth of our society is primarily the result of efforts made by business people	V67
Business people develop only new technologies which they can later make good economic use of	V68
Entrepreneurial initiative provides new jobs	V69
Business people should be able to count on the support of the consumer	V70
Business people expend large amounts of resources in the battle against environmental pollution	V71
Our high standard of living is based on the efforts of business people	V72
Business people strive only for maximum profit	V73
Technological advances in our society are the result of commercial initiative	V74
In their advertisements business people promise more than their products deliver	V75

To obtain unambiguous statements about the image profile, a hidden control question was used. There were pairs of statements, one representing a positive judgement, the other a negative one. The Likert scale was used here too. If a subgroup agreed to both the positive and the negative judgements (mean value low 3.0), or rejected both (value high 3.0), we assume a neutral judgement (entry '0' in the image profile).

Table 4

Image of entrepreneurs among German first-year students

item	positive judgement		negative judgement		image profile
employment	V69	2,5	V64	3,6	+
common good	V65	3,7	V73	2,1	−
environment	V71	4,0	V66	1,8	−
prosperity	V67	2,8	V72	2,4	0
technology	V74	2,3	V68	2,5	0
consumer protection	V70	2,9	V75	2,3	0

The image of entrepreneurs held by German first-year students is (as an example) to be interpreted as follows:

German first-year students are of the opinion that business people:

- primarily create jobs
- are more likely not to be oriented to the common good
- are more likely to take part in environmental protection if forced to by the law
- are *together* with employees responsible for social prosperity
- out of interest in profit create innovative technology, which triggers a positive general dynamic
- try to gain the trust of the consumer, but are untrustworthy in their communication policy.

Table 5
Image of entrepreneurs among German graduates

item	positive judgement		negative judgement		image profile
employment	V69	2,2	V64	3,9	+
common good	V65	3,5	V73	2,7	−
environment	V71	3,7	V66	2,0	−
prosperity	V67	3,0	V72	2,8	−
technology	V74	2,4	V68	2,4	0
consumer protection	V70	3,0	V75	2,7	−

Table 6
Image of entrepreneurs among English first-year students

item	positive judgement		negative judgement		image profile
employment	V69	2,4	V64	4,0	+
common good	V65	3,5	V73	3,1	0
environment	V71	3,9	V66	2,5	−
prosperity	V67	2,9	V72	3,3	+
technology	V74	2,9	V68	2,9	0
consumer protection	V70	3,2	V75	2,8	−

Table 7
Image of entrepreneurs among French first-year student

item	positive judgement		negative judgement		image profile
employment	V69	3,0	V64	4,4	0
common good	V65	3,5	V73	2,0	−
environment	V71	3,9	V66	2,6	−
prosperity	V67	2,8	V72	2,7	0
technology	V74	2,4	V68	3,2	+
consumer protection	V70	2,9	V75	2,8	0

Table 8
Image of entrepreneurs among Austrian first-year students

item	positive judgement		negative judgement		image profile
employment	V69	1,9	V64	3,9	+
common good	V65	3,7	V73	2,1	−
environment	V71	3,8	V66	1,8	−
prosperity	V67	2,5	V72	2,9	0
technology	V74	2,3	V68	2,5	0
consumer protection	V70	2,5	V75	2,2	0

Table 9
Image of entrepreneurs among American first-year students

item	positive judgement		negative judgement		image profile
employment	V69	1,7	V64	3,9	+
common good	V65	3,4	V73	2,5	−
environment	V71	3,3	V66	2,3	−
prosperity	V67	2,3	V72	2,5	0
technology	V74	2,4	V68	−	0
consumer protection	V70	3,1	V75	2,8	−

Table 10
General image of entrepreneurs

item	positive judgement		negative judgement		image profile
employment	V69	2,2	V64	3,9	+
common good	V65	3,6	V73	2,4	−
environment	V71	3,8	V66	2,1	−
prosperity	V67	2,7	V72	2,8	0
technology	V74	2,4	V68	2,6	0
consumer protection	V70	3,0	V75	2,5	−

The entrepreneur's image is a positive one in just one area, employment. Other positive judgements concerning prosperity and technology cannot be considered positive since the corresponding negative judgements were also agreed to. In the areas common good, environment and consumer protection the businessperson has a poor image. This finding of a poor image of entrepreneurs contrasts with the higher agreement to entrepreneurial motivation as well as a lower agreement to reservations about entrepreneurship.

The influence of the national media

We also asked how the media (TV, radio and newspapers) influenced an individual's willingness to go into business for himself.

Comment on percentages: Under the rubric 'Number' (No.) the calculation is in the column while the rubrics 'Interested' and 'Indifferent' the calculation is in the row. For example, 31 German first-year students (equals 27,7%) consider the influence of the media to be more positive. Of those students 35.5% are interested and 64.5% are indifferent.

In the final analysis the view predominates that the media have no influence on personal interest in entrepreneurship (57.9%). The

view that the media have more of positive influence (30.6%) is double the opposite opinion (11.5%). About two thirds (63%) of those who attribute a positive influence to the media are however according to our yardstick indifferent (personal reservations about entrepreneurship?).

A comparative analysis shows that the influence of the media in England is considered the strongest (54.9%). Surprisingly - considering the low interest in entrepreneurship - France follows with 42.6%. Also a surprise was the finding that in the USA the positive influence of the media was considered the lowest (18.8%). Austria follows with 23.0%.

The highest agreement to the assessment 'more negative' was in France (14.8%). Altogether however the French group revealed a non-uniform picture with higher agreement to both the negative as well as the positive influence of the media.

In the English group we found a uniform picture of high agreement to the positive role of the media and comparatively lower agreement to the negative role (9.8%). In the USA there is the greatest proportion of those (68.8%) who do not at all feel influenced by the media. In addition there was a high number of refusals to this question.

In the German subgroups there was the same assessment of the positive influence of the media (27.7% and 27.3%), though the German first-year students in comparison to the graduates had double so high a level of agreement to the negative judgement (12.5% : 6.1%).

Influence of the primary social surroundings

Alongside the media, the people and individual relates must be regarded as a potential influence of interest in entrepreneurship. We asked, 'How have relatives, friends and acquaintances influenced you in your interest in entrepreneurship ?'

Table 11
Influence on the media

item	G 1st year No. (%)	G 1st year Int. (%)	G 1st year Ind. (%)	G grads No. (%)	G grads Int. (%)	G grads Ind. (%)	GB No. (%)	GB Int. (%)	GB Ind. (%)	F No. (%)	F Int. (%)	F Ind. (%)	A No. (%)	A Int. (%)	A Ind. (%)	USA No. (%)	USA Int. (%)	USA Ind. (%)	total No. (%)	total Int. (%)	total Ind. (%)
more positive	31 (27,7)	11 (35,5)	20 (64,5)	27 (27,3)	8 (29,6)	19 (70,4)	28 (54,9)	12 (42,9)	16 (57,1)	23 (42,6)	8 (34,8)	15 (65,2)	20 (23,0)	7 (35,0)	13 (65,0)	9 (18,8)	5 (55,6)	4 (44,4)	138 (30,6)	51 (37,0)	87 (63,0)
more negative	14 (12,5)	3 (21,4)	11 (78,6)	6 (6,1)	1 (16,7)	5 (83,3)	5 (9,8)	1 (20,0)	4 (80,0)	8 (14,8)	3 (37,5)	5 (62,5)	13 (14,9)	3 (23,1)	10 (76,9)	6 (12,5)	3 (50,0)	3 (50,0)	52 (11,5)	14 (26,9)	38 (73,1)
not at all	67 (59,8)	25 (37,3)	42 (62,7)	66 (66,7)	13 (19,7)	53 (80,3)	18 (35,3)	3 (16,7)	15 (83,3)	23 (42,6)	5 (21,7)	18 (78,3)	54 (62,1)	17 (31,5)	37 (68,5)	33 (68,8)	22 (66,7)	11 (33,3)	261 (57,9)	85 (32,6)	176 (67,4)
no answer	2		2	2		2	9		9	6		6	1		1	36		36	56		56
total (%)	114 (100,1)	39	75	101 (100,1)	22	79	60 (100,0)	16	44	60 (100,0)	16	44	88 (100,1)	27	61	84 (100,1)	30	54	507 (100,0)	150	357

Table 12

Influence of the primary social surroundings

item	G 1st year						G grads						GB						F						A						USA						total					
	No. (%)		Int. (%)		Ind. (%)		No. (%)		Int. (%)		Ind. (%)		No. (%)		Int. (%)		Ind. (%)		No. (%)		Int. (%)		Ind. (%)		No. (%)		Int. (%)		Ind. (%)		No. (%)		Int. (%)		Ind. (%)		No. (%)		Int. (%)		Ind. (%)	
more positive	56	49,6	22	39,3	34	60,7	33	33,3	14	42,4	19	57,6	26	51,0	12	46,2	14	53,8	27	48,2	9	33,3	18	66,7	41	47,1	15	36,6	26	63,4	23	47,9	17	74,0	6	26,0	206	45,4	89	43,2	117	56,8
more negative	5	4,4	2	40,0	3	60,0	11	11,1	1	9,1	10	90,9	3	5,9	0	0,0	3	100,0	5	8,9	1	20,0	4	80,0	6	6,9	2	33,3	4	66,7	3	6,3	2	66,7	1	33,3	33	7,3	8	24,2	25	75,8
not at all	52	46,0	15	28,8	37	71,2	55	55,6	7	12,7	48	87,3	22	43,1	4	18,2	18	81,8	24	42,9	7	29,2	17	70,8	40	46,0	10	25,0	30	75,0	22	45,8	11	50,0	11	50,0	215	47,4	54	25,1	161	74,9
no answer	1				1		2				2		9				9		4				4		1				1		36				36		53				53	
total (%)	114	100,1	39		75		101	100,0	22		79		60	100,0	16		44		60	100,0	17		43		88	100,0	27		61		84	100,0	30		54		507	100,1	151		356	

195

Internationally 45.4% of the respondents said that their immediate social surroundings had more of a positive influence on a possible business start-up, while a similarly high proportion agreed to the statement that their immediate surroundings had no influence ad all. The remainder - just 7.3% - felt their surroundings had a negative influence.

A comparative analysis among national groups shows:
- About 50% of the members of each subgroup regarded the influence of their social surroundings as positive, expect for the German graduates (33.3%) who had a significantly different judgement.
- The German graduates had the highest level of agreement to the assessment 'more negative influence' (11.1%), followed by the French with 8.9%.
- The German first-year students feel less 'not influenced' (46.0%) by their social surroundings than the German graduates (55.6%), that is all in all more strongly influenced than the graduates.
- The American, the English and the Austrian groups have the following profile:
- slightly above average agreement to an acceptance of positive influence
- slightly under average agreement to an acceptance of negative influence
- slightly under average agreement to a rejection of influence.

The French group shows above average agreement to an acceptance of negative influence (8.9%), while the German first-year students show a below average agreement to the statement 'more negative' influence.
We can summarize our findings regarding the influence of the media (extended social surroundings) and immediate social surroundings as follows:

1. Slightly more than half of the 507 respondents (an average of 52.7%) feel uninfluenced by media and social surroundings (57.9% and 47.4%).
2. Inasmuch as however an influence can be seen, the following table is valid:

Table 13
Influence in comparison

influence effect	media	immediate social surroundings
more positive	30,6	45,4
more positive	11,5	7,3

This means that the immediate social surroundings have a significantly higher positive influence than the media, or extended social surroundings, and the media have a higher negative influence than the immediate social surroundings.

Assessment of the entrepreneurial climate

We confronted the national groups with the question: 'Would you say that the conditions for starting up a business in your country are favourable or unfavourable ?'
The final analysis shows that internationally 44.1% of the respondents consider the conditions to be more favourable, 33.4% are undecided and just 22.5% consider them to be more unfavourable.

Table 14
Assessment of the conditions of entrepreneurs

item	G 1st year						G grads						GB						F						A						USA						total					
	No.	(%)	Int.	(%)	Ind.	(%)	No.	(%)	Int.	(%)	Ind.	(%)	No.	(%)	Int.	(%)	Ind.	(%)	No.	(%)	Int.	(%)	Ind.	(%)	No.	(%)	Int.	(%)	Ind.	(%)	No.	(%)	Int.	(%)	Ind.	(%)	No.	(%)	Int.	(%)	Ind.	(%)
more positive	52	45,6	24	46,2	28	53,8	54	53,5	14	25,9	40	74,1	33	55,0	13	39,4	20	60,6	17	28,8	3	17,7	14	82,4	17	19,8	5	29,4	12	70,6	49	59,0	33	67,3	16	32,7	222	44,1	92	41,4	130	58,6
more negative	24	21,1	6	25,0	18	75,0	13	12,9	2	15,4	11	84,6	4	6,7	2	50,0	2	50,0	18	30,5	8	44,4	10	55,6	43	50,0	16	37,2	27	62,8	11	13,3	4	36,4	7	63,6	113	22,5	38	33,6	75	66,4
undecided	38	33,3	9	23,7	29	76,3	34	33,7	6	17,6	28	82,4	23	38,3	6	26,1	17	73,9	24	40,7	6	25,0	18	75,0	26	30,2	5	19,2	21	80,8	23	27,7	11	47,8	12	52,2	168	33,4	43	25,6	125	74,4
no response																			1		1				2		2				1		1				4				4	
total (%)	114	100,1	39	100,1	75	100,1	101	100,1	22		79		60	100,0	21		39		60	100,0	17		43		88	100,0	26		62		84	100,0	48		36		507	100,0	173		334	

197

A comparative analysis reveals:

- The proportion of favourable assessments is highest in the American group (59.0%) and lowest in the Austrian group with 19.8%, followed by the French (28.8%).
- The proportion of unfavourable assessments is, as to be expected, highest in the Austrian group with 50.0% and the lowest in the English group (6.7%), ahead of the German graduates with 12.9%.
- A final picture appears in which the following classification of entrepreneurial climate is possible:
  1. USA and England: a high value regarding favourableness and a low one regarding unfavourableness
  2. Germany: a middle value regarding favourableness and a middle or low one regarding unfavourableness
  3. Austria and France: a low value regarding favourableness and a high one regarding unfavourableness.

Expectations concerning studies

Of a total of 507 respondents, 377 (with 6 missing responses) expressed the expectation that their studies would have a positive effect if they chose to start-up a business, and in the case of the graduates actually had had a positive effect.

An average of 75.2% of the responding business students connected higher education with entrepreneurship training.

The corresponding rate among German first-year students was 78.8%, among graduates 69.7%.

Is higher education ready to take up this challenge ?

12 'Ecological' basis for the analysis of gender differences in the predisposition to self-employment

Daphne Hamilton

Gender is an issue all too frequently ignored by researchers in the small business/self-employed sector. It is a complex issue which impacts on all stages of the social and economic existence of the individual. This paper sets out to illustrate how an 'ecological' approach to research can strengthen the level of understanding of apparent gender differences in the predisposition to self-employment. Bronfenbrenner (1977 & 1979) outlines an ecological topology describing the systems which together form the ecological environment in which the individual is a participant. 'In ecological research' he argues, 'the investigator seeks to 'control in' as many theoretically relevant ecological contrasts as possible...' (1977:518). There is an experimental element built into his research propositions, an element which could indeed prove to be of interest in a small business action research project but will not be included in this paper. The purpose of this paper is to explore how aspects of his concept of the 'ecology of human development' can be adapted to provide a potentially useful model for the analysis of gender differences in the predisposition to self-employment.

'The ecology of human development:-

is the scientific study of the progressive, mutual accommodation, throughout the life span, between a [growing][1] human organism and the changing immediate environments in which it lives, as this process is affected by relations obtaining within and between these immediate settings, as well as the larger social contexts, both formal and informal, in which the settings are embedded' (1977:514).

Bronfenbrenner's ecological environment is presented as 'anested arrangement of structures each contained within the next' (1977:514). The basic system is the microsystem which is constituted by the individual, the complexity of relations between that individual and those people and artifacts of the environment in which the person is located at any one moment in time. In such a location the individual will play a particular role, e.g. mother, or a number of roles, e.g. mother, wife, daughter-in-law; and will carry out particular activities in relation to these roles. The next level of the topology is the mesosystem. The mesosystem is constituted by the interrelations between the microsystems in which the individual is a participant. Clearly the interrelations change as the individual changes. Containing the mesosystem is the exosystem which embraces other social structures, formal and informal which affect the social and physical environment of the individual in the mesosystem. 'These structures include major institutions of the society, both deliberately structured and spontaneously evolving, as they operate at a concrete level. They encompass among other structures, the world of work, the neighbourhood, the mass media, agencies of government..., the distribution of goods and services, communication and transportation facilities, and informal social networks'(1977:515). At the outer most reaches of the topology is the macrosystem. The macrosystem provides the main institutionalised cultural and sub-cultural influences on the nested systems. 'Macrosystems are conceived and examined not only in structural terms but as carriers of information and ideology that, both explicitly and implicitly, endow meaning and motivation to particular agencies, social networks, roles, activities, and their interrelations'(1977:515).

Bronfenbrenner uses the example of child care and the effect its order of priority within the macrosystem has on the lower order systems. This macro to micro effect in terms of self-employment is illustrated in an example from the continent. In 1982 the French government benefited the 'family-run' business by introducing legislation which recognised the work of women in such business and enabled them to claim state maternity benefit. This benefit was designed to enable the business to finance replacement labour for the limited period of one month (Clutterbuck and Devine 1987:132).

Bronfenbrenner's topology is useful because it provides researchers with a systematic ecological approach. The nested system provides particular foci which serve to remind us of the importance of taking an holistic approach in researching predispositions to self-employment. This allows for an analysis of those not proceeding to self-employment and those interrelating with the ones that move into self-employment. It provides a check system against which to determine whether or not elements or variants which have been 'controlled out' have been fully explained. Clearly the complexity of carrying out research which attempts to take into account each and every level of an individual's ecological environment would be beyond the means of most research projects and would require a team of researchers and a number of different methodological approaches. However attempting to account for gender differences at microsystem level without exploring how these differences are likely to effect and be affected by the higher order systems would be to misrepresent the respondent's subjective and objective reality in identifying their predispositions to self-employment [see Figure 1 overleaf].

In order to see how this model might be implemented we will take an example from the research literature on female entrepreneurs[2]. We will focus on a brief randomly selected extract from a paper by Goffee and Scase[3] in which we will assume that the husbands are hoping to shift to a position of self-employment.

'...married women are often forced to give up their jobs and to abandon their careers in order to underwrite the efforts of their husbands.'

We will attempt an ecological analysis of the type of hypothetical situations which many women face under similar circumstances. In this analysis we will explore some of the many different factors which lie behind the decisions taken by women to underwrite the efforts of their husbands.

Figure 1
Adaption of Bronfenbrenner's topology

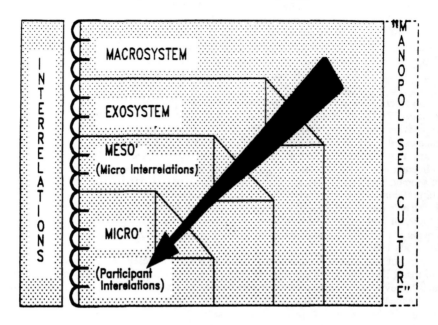

Gender influences within any microsystem are likely to have major consequences on the types of relationships and subsequent actions that any individual is likely to take. Therefore gender affects the nature of interrelations within the individual's mesosystem and affects their predisposition to self-employment. Before proceeding we will briefly examine the concept of gender and its implications within the wider society.

Gender has been described in a number of ways:

'gender...is...what a culture makes of sex - it is the cultural transformation of male and female infants into adult men and women. Invariably, how they do it - how they organize the spectrum of human attributes around sex - has a significant impact on their structuring of the world beyond sex as well - indeed it permeates all aspects of their existence' (Evelyn Fox Keller 1986:172).

'The division of sex is a genetic one, clearly inscribed in our chromosomes.... Everything that is not attributable to the workings of our genes is a difference not of sex, but of gender.... The opposing of gender to sex is very definitely something progressive... this is one instance of a wider distinction between nature and culture, between the raw material and what human society constructs...' (Fernbach 1981:15)

Gender differences then are socially constructed. Crucial to this concept of social construction and gender are the concepts of male domination and power relations. Weedon (1987) argues that power relations are fundamental to life's structures and that the dominant power is patriarchal. A power which 'rests on the social meanings given to biological sexual difference'...where the...'nature and social role of women are defined in relation to a norm which is male' (Weedon 1987:1-3).

The cultural transformation of male and female infants is directed within the social context of the dominant power relations founded on male heterosexuality. 'Our society constructs a situation of ascribed rather than achieved gender... The actor is forced to slot into patterns of behaviour, or is relegated to the categories of sick, dangerous, or pathological'(Brake 1976:178, see Hearn and Parkin 1987:82[4]). In theoretical terms it shares much in common with Weber's concept of social closure. The purpose of social closure being 'the closure of social and economic opportunities to outsiders' (Weber in Parkin 1974:3). In terms of gender the concept of closure can be realised in the subjective oppression and subordination of the objective outsiders, in gender terms 'women', at the hands of the 'superordinate group' men[5]. The interest in women and small business has come about because a degree of 'solidarism' has taken place through the actions and deliberations of mainly women who, through a feminist analysis of the social construction of women's position in society, have been able to expose the subjective nature of male cultural domination. 'Because they generally lack legal or state support, solidaristic efforts are heavily dependent upon the capacity of social mobilization on the part of the excluded' (Weber in Parkin 1974:3-9). Therefore even where there is legal or state support, as in 'equality' legislation, the balance of power is only marginally shifted (England and Swoboda 1988).

It is not uncommon for gender effects to be left out of research. It would probably be fair to say that historically women were left off the small business research agenda or made invisible by research practices or in some other way written out of the analysis of self-employment. This historical tradition is still in evidence. Despite a rise in the number of studies of female entrepreneurs (Carter 1989; Donckels and Meijer 1986; Surti and Sarupria 1983; Nelson 1989; Sexton and Bowman-Upton 1990, Hisrich and Brush 1986, 1988) very few entrepreneurial studies have comprehensively adopted a gender perspective. Rees and Shah (1986) provide a blatant example of how women are written out of the analysis of self-employment. In their paper 'An Empirical Analysis of Self-employment in the U.K.' they exclude a number of categories of people and then a whole gender ' ...in order to obtain sharper results'(1986:101). Among the excluded are:

- those who were not heads of their households   [mainly women][6]
- those who worked for less than thirty hours a week   [mainly women]
- females [i.e. all women!] (on the basis that 'self-employment is predominantly a male preserve')

This single example serves as a clear statement of androcentricism. Androcentricism allows for the 'elevation of the masculine to the level of the universal and the ideal; it is the honouring of men and the male principal above women and the female. This perception creates a belief in male superiority and a value system in which female values, experiences, and behaviours are viewed as inferior' (Shakeshaft and Nowell 1984:187-188). This is illustrated in a number of ways, e.g. in the subordinate nature of female definitions in relation to men (Spender 1985). Elevating the masculine to this level is to create a blind spot on the researchers lens.

Rees and Shah in this piece of research appear to have absorbed and reproduced the androcentricism of the macrosystem in ignoring the value of 'unpaid' work at home and its contribution to male human capital development. 'The practice has been to define work as 'something that men do', ...with the result that women's work is made 'invisible' while the superiority of the male life style is artificially strengthened'(Spender 1985:69). This approach is illustrated at the macrosystem level in the estimations of total production of goods and services. Quah points to the estimates of the Gross National Product failing to take account of 'the production which occurs at home' (Quah 1989:1632; Whatmore 1988; Folbre and Abel 1989).

To return to the scenario of the Goffee and Scase extract where the potential business owner wants his wife to give up one working situation as a consequence of his anticipated shift in employment. This demand is indicative of a wife being able to offer something of particular value which assists in his predisposition to self-employment. It is important that the nature of this value is identified, qualified and quantified to begin to understand:

a) why this change is being demanded by the woman's marital partner and
b) why the marital partner is of greater value to the potential business than some other person

In addition, identification of the rationale behind the business proposition, will help to provide the researcher with an indication of the exosystem in which it is to be located and an indication of the nature and level of interrelations the intended business will have within the existing mesosystem.

This kind of approach will assist in teasing outpredisposing factors by identifying what the intending entrepreneur sees as the conditions considered to be necessary in order to attempt a shift to self-employment. Gartner (1989) argues that the 'researchers must observe entrepreneurs in the process of creating organizations. This process must be described in total and the activities systematised and classified'(1989:63). However he also argues that the focus should be on the actions of the entrepreneur and 'not on who the entrepreneur is' (1989:57). Clearly this approach would not facilitate an ecological analysis as it would ignore a key element, the role definitions of the individual and their impact on the interrelations within the topology. In our own example we have married women: 'wives' and married men: 'husbands' and 'who' they are may well be of significance.

In the hypothetical situation of the married women who are forced to give up their jobs and abandon their careers to underwrite the efforts of their husbands, we must first recognise the existence of a power relationship. Unless one believes that power is vested in men in terms of it being the natural order (Goldberg 1989), then we need to proceed by looking at how the power relations within this example may have been constructed. Starting at the level of the macrosystem we can look for indications of how power relations have become institutionalised within marriage by looking at some of the reporting of attitudes towards marital relations and employment.

Delphy and Leonard add weight to the generally accepted premise that the marital sphere is socially constructed. It 'is a particular form of social relationship...it is a hierarchical system. Marriage and parenthood and kinship are no more natural, no less social institutions than, say, parliament or factories, and women do housework and child care not because of natural abilities, or for love, or as a hobby, or from choice, but because that is how they earn their living and secure protection for themselves (from other men) and gain rights to have children (their major, if two-edged resource as society is currently constituted) in a particular form of society - Western, industrial, patriarchal'(1986:61-62). Women generally appear to do all these things or take responsibility for the doing of them whether they are court judges (Martin and Keyes 1988:144) or themselves self-employed within a marital relationship (Longstreth, Stafford and Maudlin 1987). There are some contradictory findings reported in a study of working couples in small business which suggests that there was agreement that 'In a two income family, housekeeping and child-rearing responsibility should be evenly divided between parents' (Cox, Moore and Van Auken 1984:25). However the reality is often very different (Equal Opportunities Commission 1987) and as Frable points out '...new norms pertaining to gender have emerged, and social approval concerns mask individual differences...' just as '..explicit avowals of racism have gone underground, but racist behaviours certainly have not'(1989:106).

The focal point of the marital relationship may be posited in the 'family' home. The institution of the family, the microsystem in which gendered relations are clearly enacted, is described by Bradley as being 'androcentric', that is 'the arrangements within ...[the family]...are still moulded to the requirements of men'(Bradley 1989:227). However men like women are not a homogeneous group and nor is the family a single type (Gittins 1985). The ecology of the familial environment is crucial to its formation and its internal relations because, as Phoenix (1990) reminds us, the family is not isolated nor monocultural. Its level of exposure to and its ability to resist or conform to the androcentric domination of external power relations must therefore affect the immediate actions of the incumbents.

Where the expectation is clearly one of the male being the family breadwinner, the expectation is that the male will earn sufficient money to allow for family dependents. This expectation is not fixed and is dependent on cultural and sub-cultural expectations and conditions. Phoenix for example, reported that black West Indian women in a white society may expect to be the main breadwinner because of structural discriminatory practices which make it difficult for black males to find employment. One outcome of this is that the women teach their daughters to be economically independent (Phoenix 1990:125). Even within a single ethnic context Gerson reminds us that:-

'...women's [and men's][7] needs and desires are rooted in social-historical contexts that are variable and present different groups of women [and men] with different dilemmas and constraints' (1986:620).

Therefore in purely financial terms women who, for example, have been earning a 'component-wage' (see Siltanen 1986:107-118) would be likely to have different options from women who have been earning a 'full-wage' in terms of choices of response to their husband's demands. Equally the options to the household in making the change between being a household with perhaps a full-wage head of household to one with an unknown-wage head of household will necessarily be affected by different resource and expenditure components. In order to identify why a woman may not want to give up her job it is important to tease out the motivation for entering and continuing to participate in particular kinds of work and for working outside the home at all. For example women who take up self-employment from a previous position of unpaid houseworker frequently do so not primarily as a means of income but as a means of interest and personal development.

In researching why a woman may not want to give up her job and abandon her career, it is important to identify the predisposing factors which affected her original entry into paid employment and those which affect her desire to continue. The attributes of her work microsystem and its interrelations with her wider mesosystem need to be explored. It may be that in giving up an external work situation 'women working with their husbands in small businesses where they do not receive wages,..[will be]..in a position which reproduces dependency very similar to that of domestic labour' (Westwood and Bhachu 1988:6). It may also be the converse of this where involvement in the family firm may 'empower' women (Bhachu 1988). However if the former is closer to the image for the women being forced to abandon their careers their reluctance becomes even more understandable. At European Community level research indicates a number of problems specific to women in family businesses:

- lack of an official occupational status
- lack of an independent income
- lack of regulations on working hours
- poor social security provision
- lack of replacements
- problems with regard to occupational training
- few opportunities to voice their concerns through professional organisations

'Only a few Member States have specific forms of legal protection for such women; notably West Germany [Germany][8] and France' (Maij-Weggen 1986:11; see also Meijer, Braaksma and van Uxem 1986). Therefore research into motivations for changing work and home situations must take these negative and positive factors into account. If such factors were taken into account it may be possible to build into the proposed home working/self-employed environment those elements which were particularly valued by the women who chose to work as employees outwith the home.

More general research into stress levels adds to the ecological picture. Pascall reports findings by the Department of Employment indicating high stress levels of unpaid homeworkers/housewives. The levels of stress for these women exceeded the level of those married women that were in paid employment outside the home. In research by Hunt a higher level of oppression in terms of interpersonal relations was identified among women who were unpaid homeworkers compared with those who were economically active (Pascall 1986:56).

'..structural variation produces deep divisions among women in terms of what they want and define as their interests in heterosexual relationships' (Gerson 1986:620).

The choices open to women may be considerable depending on the power relations within their mesosystem (e.g. the support or pressure from their or their husbands extended family or friends) and its exosystemic context (e.g. the availability of alternative work, housing, transport, social networks). In other words factors of power interrelations need to be explored throughout the ecological topology in order to understand the power relations within the microsystem of the home which will contribute to the husbands having a predisposition to self-employment. The structure of these power relations, whether subjective or objective, needs to be explored to understand how they affect the relations within the institution of marriage. The implications of structural changes which impact on the institution of marriage at the micro and meso levels, e.g. moving from employee status into self-employment, from unpaid housewife status (arguably a job and life-time career), or from paid employee status to unpaid family worker in a 'family business' would need to be considered.

The degree of influence of the macro cultural and sub-cultural ideologies and institutions will limit the options available to the women being forced to withdraw from their work situation to underwrite the work of their husbands. Divorce may be an option available within their culture. Married women may or may not be aware of the financial consequences of choosing to divorce rather than comply with their husbands demands. However research has shown that previously married women differ in their remarriage behaviour dependent on their income and therefore domestic security (Ambert 1983). Women are structurally discriminated against in the divorce situation. Recent research in the United States and Scotland, indicates that in the outcome of divorce settlements the economic position of women generally deteriorates while the economic position of the men generally improves. Whatever the class differences or 'the exact percentages, it is clear that divorce economically disadvantages women' (Risman 1990:106; see also Dobash and Wasoff 1986). This area requires further investigation in relation to small businesses where there are also indications of gender differences in the income of divorced women. Honig-Haftel and Martin found that 'Marital status of the females made a significant difference on gross revenue of the business, Never married women, divorced and widowed women made less revenue than their male counterparts' (1986:52).

The primacy of the heterosexual relationship results in the primacy of male power. Male power in the marital sphere leads to a process whereby the majority of women entering adulthood with 'non-domestic aspirations' find themselves caught up in a gendered career process that is generally weighted towards the male partner. There is evidence of a progression in this process:

1. a commitment to a traditional heterosexual partnership means a commitment to the male career
2. a commitment to the male career means that the male career takes precedence
3. the male career taking precedence means that the female career opportunities will take second place and may be relinquished (Gerson 1986:621)

It would appear that in the women abandoning their careers for their husbands a number of influences will be coming into play: considerations of relations within the domestic sphere; the possibility of the loss of the domestic sphere and the actors within it, e.g. children; the alternatives open to women in order to maintain the domestic sphere or leave and create a new domestic sphere. Ramu points to the emergence of entrepreneurship in an Indian study, depending not only on the pooling of money but also on the restructuring of arrangements in the household. He identifies that in a number of cases this was essential to the continuation in business. Businessmen who were 'copartners' were 'forced' to become individual proprietors because they had failed 'to maintain family solidarity' which within the particular mesosystem was 'crucial for continuing partnerships' (Ramu 1973-251).

In her research Gerson found there were a number of structural reasons for accepting an androcentric base to marital decisions:

- the man's job constantly paid more
- failure to comply with male demands might damage the marital relationship and 'undermine security' at home'
- there was sufficient to live off from their husband's income without working
- personal blocked mobility for women at work lead to a retreat into the home, autonomy and self-fulfilment[9]
- pressure from within and outwith home to bear and rear children

The women's perception of their position in these often countermanding situations will be influenced by the exosystem in which her mesosystem operates. The women's perception of this as being action taken within an androcentric marital/sphere will be coloured by her perception of the macrosystem's gendered ideologies and the options open to her within such an environment. Clearly the level of resources available to a woman and the level of power over these resources will be contributory factors in the nature and type of relationships she has within her mesosystem. A study by Granrose and Hochner (1985) is a useful exemplar of this kind of analysis.

The ideological gendering of roles within the domesticsphere continues with the traditional situation where women are basically economically dependent on their partners even in dual earning households, with the dependent partner remaining the less powerful partner (Risman 1990:107).

The significance of gendered ideology at the macrosystemlevel particularly affects women to their disadvantage in the economic and public spheres. 'The concept of the occupational career has, for the most part, been conceived in the context of the male experience'(Symons 1988:41). The support of the development of the male human capital is paramount in the marital relations sphere. Even where wives are running their own businesses, full-time or part-time, husbands have high expectations of the wife's contribution to the work in the household while their own contribution to this kind of work is minimal (Longstreth, Stafford and Maudling 1987:36; Equal Opportunities Commission 1987; England and Swoboda 1988). Likewise Simon and Landis report that:

'the large majority of both women and men believe that it is the wife who should quit her job and relocate with her husband if the husband is offered a more attractive position in another city. There is no quid pro quo of that issue. If it is the wife who is offered the better job the majority of both women and men believe that she should turn it down and stay where she is so that her husband can continue working at his job.' (1989:269)

The relative strength of such an ideological background, upheld and promoted by the actions of 'manopolised' institutions[10], eaves researchers examining the predispositions to self-employment with an holistic task. Bronfenbrenner's concept of the ecology of human development helps to contextualise entrepreneurs within their immediate microsystem and provides an analytical approach which can be used for any unit of analysis within the confines of the area of research. In using the single example from Goffe and Scase, to illustrate how this approach can be utilised, this paper has been able to emphasise the importance of taking gender differences into account when examining predispositions to self-employment. While the suggested scenarios were hypothetical and took their focus from a female point of view, this was deliberate within the limitations of this presentation and served to illustrate the importance to researchers of avoiding 'a gender blind research lens'.

Notes

[1.] My bracket.

[2.] Entrepreneur, self-employed and small business owner are used interchangeably.

[3.] 'Women, business start-up and economic recession' in Donckels (1986).

[4.] 'Most mundane of all is the control of school children's dress, through uniform, banning trousers for girls, and of make-up - the reproduction of genders in action...' (Parkin and Hearn 1987:82)

[5.] Fernbach (1981) points to the particular position of men and women who do not conform to gender definitions of femininity and masculinity. He points out that there are certain rewards for women who conform. However ...'While women are oppressed by being what the gender system requires them to be, offering them a certain reward for legitimacy for being a 'proper' woman and accepting oppression, gay people are oppressed by..[their] inability - or refusal - to be 'proper' women or men' (1981:18). Thus creating another category of objective outsiders.

[6.] My addition.

[7.] My addition.

[8.] My addition: as from 3 October 1990.

9. It was reported by Sally Westwood that women factory workers '...in the home, ...felt they organized for real needs and their labour went to support and sustain children and men - real people, not factory owners and profits...' in Pascall (1986:58).

10. See McInnes M (1990); '...most social institutions are shaped around male definitions, priorities, requirements, preferences; men run most of them, if not all; the political and social ideals that rule our epoch come from men, in sum society revolves round men, is literally 'androcentric' (Simon and Landis 1989:231).

References

Ambert, A.M. (1983) 'Separated women and remarriage behavior: A comparison of financially secure women and financially insecure women', Journal of Divorce 6,3:43-54

Bhachu, P. (1988) 'Apni Marzi Kardhi: Home and work: Sikh women in Britain' in S. Westwood and P. Bhachu Enterprising Women: ethnicity, economy and gender relations, Routledge: London

Bradley, H. (1989) Men's work, Women's work, Polity Press: Cambridge

Brake, M. (1976) 'I may be Queer, But at least I am a Man: Male Hegemony and ascribed versus achieved gender' in D. Leonard Barker and S. Allen [eds.] Sexual division and Society: Process and Change, Tavistock: London

Bronfenbrenner, U. (1977) 'Toward an experimental ecology of human development', American Paychologist July: 513-531

Bronfenbrenner, U. (1979) The Ecology of Human Development, Harvard University Press: London

Carter, S. (1989) 'Female business ownership : current research and possibilities for the future', University of Bradford Conference : Women Entrepreneurs

Clutterbuck, D. and Devine, M. (1987) Business Woman : Present and Future, MacMillan Press: Basingstoke

Cox, J.A. et al (1984) 'Working Couples in Small Business', Journal of Small Business Management Oct:24-30

Delphy, C. and Leonard, D. (1986) 'Class analysis, gender analysis and the family' in R. Crompton and M. Mann [eds.] Gender and Stratification, Polity Press: Cambridge

Dobash, R.E. and Wasoff, F. (1986) Financial Aspects of Divorce, Economic and Social Research Council: London

Donckels, R. and Meijer, J.N.[eds.] (1986) Women in Small Business : Focus on Europe, Van Gorcum: Assen/Maastricht

England, P. and Swoboda, D. (1988) 'The Asymmetry of Contemporary Gender Role Change', Free Inquiry in Creative Sociology, 16,2:157-161

Equal Opportunities Commission (1987) Women and Men in Profile, H.M.S.O.: London

Fernbach, D. (1981) The Spiral Path, Gay Mens Press: London

Folbre, N. and Abel, M. (1989) 'Women's work and women's households: Gender bias in the U.S. Census', Social Research, 56,3

Frable, D.E. (1989) 'Sex typing and gender ideology: two facets of the individual's gender psychology that go together', Journal of Personality and Social Psychology 56,1:95-108

Gartner, W.B. (1989) 'Who is an entrepreneur?' Is the wrong question', Entrepreneurship Theory and Practice 13,4:47-68

Gerson, K. (1986) 'What do women want from men? Men's influence on women's work and family choices', American Behavioral Scientist 29,5:619-634

Gittins, D. (1985) The Family in Question, Macmillan: London

Goffee, R. and Scase, R. (1986) 'Women Business Start Up and Economic Recession' in R. Donckels and J.N. Meijer [eds.] Women in Small Business : Focus on Europe, Van Gorcum: Assen/Maastricht

Goldberg, S. (1989) 'The theory of patriarchy : a final summation, including responses to fifteen years of criticism', International Journal of Sociology and Social Policy 9,1:15-62

Granrose, C.S. and Hochner, A. (1985) 'Are women interested in saving their jobs through employee-ownership', Economic and Industrial Democracy 6,3:299-324

Hearn, J. and Parkin, W. (1987) 'Sex' at 'Work': The power and paradox of organisation sexuality, Wheatsheaf: Brighton

Hisrich, R. and Brush, C. (1986) The Woman Entrepreneur, Lexington Books: Massachusetts

Hisrich, R. and Brush, C. (1988) 'Women entrepreneurs: strategicorigins impact on growth', Frontiers of Entrepreneurship (Babson College Report),612-625

Honig-Haftel, S. and Martin, L.K. (1986) 'Is the female entrepreneur at a disadvantage?', Thrust Journal for Employment and Training 1,2:49-64

Keller, E.F. (1986) 'How gender matters, or, why it's so hard for us to count past two' in J.Harding [ed.] Perspectives on Gender and Science, Falmer Press: London

Longstreth, M. (1987) 'Self-employed women and their families: time use and socioeconomic characteristics', Journal of Small Business Management 25,3:30-37

Martin, E. and Keyes, B. (1988) 'Professional women: Role-innovation and sex role conflict', Michigan Academician 20,2:139-152

Meijer, J.N. et al (1986) 'Contributing Wife: partner in business', in R. Donckels and J.N.Meijer Women in small business: Focus on Europe, Van Gorcum: Assen/Mastricht

Nelson, G.W. (1989) 'Factors of friendship : relevance of significant others to female business owners', Entrepreneurship Theory and Practce Summer:7-18

Parkin, F. (1974) 'Weber's concept of social closure' in F.Parkin [ed.] The Social Analysis of Class Structure, Tavistock: London

Phoenix, A. (1990) 'Theories of Gender and Black Families' in T.Lovell [ed.] British Feminist Thought, Basil Blackwell: Oxford

Pascall, G. (1986) Social Policy : a Feminist Análysis, Tavistock: London

Quah, E. (1989) 'Country studies and the value of household production', Applied Economics 21,12:1631-1646

Ramu, G.N. (1973) 'Family Structure and Entrepreneurship: an Indian Case', Journal of Comparative Family Studies

Rees, H. and Shah, A. (1986) 'An empirical analysis of self-employment in the U.K.', Journal of Applied Econometrics 1:95-108

Risman, B. (1990) Critique of 'The divorce revolution : the unexpected social and economic consequences for women and children in America' L.J. Weitzman (1985) New York : Free Press, Gender and Society March:105-107

Sexton, D. and Bowman-Upton, N. (1990) 'Female and male entrepreneurs : psychological characteristics and their role in gender discrimination', Journal of Business Venturing 5,1:29-36

Shakeshaft, C. and Nowell, I. (1984) 'Research on theories, concepts and models of organizational behavior : the influence of gender', Issues in Education II,3:186-203

Simon, R.J. and Landis, J.M. (1989) 'Women's and men's attitudes about a woman's place and role', Public Opinion Quarterly 53,2:265-276

Siltanen, J. (1986) 'Domestic responsibilities and the structuring of Employment' in Crompton, R. and Mann, M. Gender and Stratification, Polity Press: Cambridge

Spender, D. (1985) Man Made Language, Routledge and Kegan Paul: London

Surti, K. and Sarupria, D. (1983) 'Psychological factors affecting women entrepreneurs: some findings', Indian Journal of Social Work 44,3:287-295

Symons, G.L. (1989) 'Women's occupational careers in business :managers and entrepreneurs in France and in Canada' in N.J. Adler and D.N. Izraeli [eds.] Women in Management Worldwide, M.E. Sharpe: New York

Weedon, C. (1987) Feminist Practice and Postructuralist Theory, Basil Blackwell: Oxford

Westwood, S. and Bhachu, P. (1988) [eds] Enterprising Women :Ethnicity, Economy and Gender Relations, Routledge: London

Whatmore, S. (1988) 'From women's roles to gender relations', Sociologia Ruralis XXVIII-4:239-247

13 Social continuity and change: The contextual environment of self-employment

Dieter Bögenhold and Udo Staber

Introduction

Self-employment, as a form of entrepreneurship, has generally not received much academic attention, although it has always played a critical role in the reproduction of industrial economies. Marxist scholars considered the self-employed (small shopkeepers, street peddlers, artisans, etc.) an anachronistic social class, industrial sociologists focused on large corporations as the building blocks of modern societies, and organization scientists built their theories of bureaucracy, business policy, and management strategy mainly on their observations in large-scale organizations. In recent years, however, interest in self-employment as a social and labor market phenomenon has been growing. There are many reasons for this growing interest, chief among which is the argument that small businesses can be important sources of job creation and industrial dynamism. In organization theory, and population ecology in particular, increasing attention has been paid to small organizations (most of the small organizations are operated by self-employed workers, and most of the self-employed employ no one or only a small number of workers) as an important source of innovation and variation in strategies and structures. Measures to promote self-employment have been introduced by many national governments in recent years and further measures are being considered to broaden the choice facing potential entrants to the labor market as well as unemployed or displaced workers.

Most of the recent literature on self-employment has been micro-oriented and focused on individuals' personality traits, demographic characteristics, and social background to explain the choice between self-employment and paid employment. Some attempt has also been made to locate changes in the level of self-employed activity in a broader context of the labor market and institutional arrangements. These studies, however, have tended to focus on individual countries (mainly the United States and Britain) and/or have generally followed cross-sectional research designs. Cross-sectional studies estimate static models of self-employment and implicitly assume that relationships between relevant variables are in equilibrium. Self-employment, however, is a dynamic phenomenon, and the level of self-employment has varied dramatically in the course of industrial development (Bechhofer and Elliott, 1985). Cross-sectional relationships cannot be assumed to hold for over-time data. A few time-series studies of self-employment and new business foundings exist, but they are typically individual country based and thus are unable to account for cross-country differences in relationships.

In the present study, we use pooled time-series data on aggregate self-employment rates for seven major OECD countries to examine some of the determinants of year-to-year changes in aggregate self-employment rates for men and women since the early 1960s. The results of our analysis are broadly consistent with the disadvantage theory which views entrepreneurs as misfits cast off from wage work (Evans and Leighton, 1989) who move into self-employment in times of slack labor markets. Thus, the fact that self-employment rates tend to rise in times of economic stress should not be interpreted as prima facie evidence that self-employed workers make a significant contribution to the economy.

Theoretical background

The traditional literature focused on self-employment as a personal choice driven mainly by cultural and social motives. Personality-based theories of entrepreneurship posit that self-employed workers possess particular traits (such as creativity, risk aversion, need for achievement) which set them apart from other people. Culture-based models posit that the values and traditions of particular social groupings (defined by religion, ethnicity, etc.) predispose their members to set up their own business. A currently popular argument is also that the recent resurgence of self-employment is associated with a growing disaffection in the broader population with employment in bureaucratic large-scale organizational settings.

The problems with traditional explanations of entrepreneurship and self-employment have been reviewed elsewhere (Aldrich and Zimmer, 1986; Wiedenmayer, Aldrich, and Staber, 1991), and we will not repeat the critique here. Instead, we focus on the explanatory role of structural changes in the economy, especially in the labor market, as well as institutional developments to partially account for the revival of self-employment since the 1970s. We view these developments as evolving structures of opportunities and constraints affecting the decision of motivated entrepreneurs to set up their own business. Human capital and group characteristics matter, but they are not a complete explanation of people's decision to enter or leave self-employment. General economic and institutional factors set the conditions under which new businesses are founded, and prosper or fail. Our objective in this study is not to explain *who* becomes self-employed, but to examine some of the contextual conditions under which some people start their own business.

Self-employment has steadily eroded since the beginnings of large-scale industry, but it has not disappeared. In countries such as the United States and Germany self-employment declined from over 40 percent of the labor force around the middle of last century to between 10 and 15 percent of the labor force today. Not all of this decline is accounted for by the shrinking labor force in agricultural production (as the nonfarm self-employment rate has declined as well), but recent indications are that the historical decline of self-employment has come to a halt and in some countries has even been reversed. The revival of self-employment cries out for an explanation, for it contradicts the predictions of classic economic and sociological theory.

Labor market and economic change

The fact that the resurgence of self-employment in most OECD countries (OECD, 1986) roughly coincided with a period of economic stress beginning in the early 1970s, characterized by slow economic growth, rising levels of unemployment, and the spread of various forms of contingent employment, indicates the importance of labor market developments as an explanatory factor in the reversal of self-employment trends. Boissevain (1981, p. 12) concluded that the rise of self-employment in Western Europe during the 1970s was 'related to the current economic recession', and officials of several national governments argued that the rising inclination among many people to become self-employed was less the result of reduced risks and improved oportunities than a reaction to worsening conditions in the labor market (Bögenhold, 1987).

Unemployment and economic growth. Several empirical studies report an inverse relationship between self-employment rates and the general business climate. Bregger (1963) found that the self-employment rate in the United States between 1948 and 1962 declined slightly or remained constant during economic upturns, while wage and salary employment grew substantially. The reverse relationships held during downturns in the business cycle. Ray's (1975) time-series regression analysis showed a positive and significant effect of the aggregate rate of unemployment on the U.S. nonfarm self-employment rate for the period of 1948 to 1973. Also Steinmetz and Wright (1989) found evidence supporting the argument that aggregate self-employment moves countercyclically with unemployment, but their regression estimates for the period from 1948 to 1984 suggest that this relationship has declined over time. Unfortunately, their analysis extends only to 1984, and so it is unclear whether 'there appears to be a significant and *sustained* (emphasis ours) reversal in the decline of the 'petty bourgeoisie' in the past decade or so in the United States' (Steinmetz and Wright, 1989, p. 998).

Bögenhold and Staber (1990; 1991) studied the effects of unemployment and GNP growth rates on self-employment rates in ten OECD countries for the period from the early 1950s to 1987. They found significant positive effects of unemployment in most of the countries and significant negative effects of GNP growth in half of the countries they examined. That is, self-employment rates rose in times of high levels of unemployment and slow growth. The only other study of cyclicality in self-employment rates in countries other than the United States produced a rather mixed bag of results (OECD, 1986). In some countries, self-employment behaved countercyclically (as measured by the ratio of actual to trend GNP), in other countries the estimated self-employment rate was insensitive to the business cycle. Unfortunately, the time series examined in this study began for some countries as late as 1975 and ended in 1984, and so the estimated coefficients must be interpreted with some caution.

Highfield and Smiley (1987) studied changes in the rate of new business incorporations in the United States for the period from 1947 to 1984 and found that incorporations tended to increase in times of rising unemployment and declining real growth. Hudson (1989) also found a positive effect of unemployment rates on the number of company births in the United States from 1951 to 1983. This finding is consistent with the results from a time-series analysis of company births in Britain for the period from 1952 to 1984 which showed that new company registrations tended to increase in times of slack labor markets, as measured by levels of unemployment and job vacancies (Hudson, 1987). Hudson (1987, p. 57) interpreted this finding as evidence that 'new firms are not being born in response to a healthy climate for enterprise but because a slack labour market encourages the unemployed to try their hand at entrepreneurial activity'.

Cross-sectional research in the United States has shown that unemployed workers are more likely to enter self-employment and the probability of self-employment is higher for individuals with relatively more unemployment experience (Evans and Leighton, 1989a). A British labor force survey indicated that about a third of the self-employed had involuntarily, or at least reluctantly, entered self-employment between 1983 and 1987 (Hakim, 1988). Some of them had been unable to get a wage job, while about ten percent cited redundancy from their last job as the reason for becoming self-employed. Storey and Johnson (1987) report research showing that between one quarter and one half of all new businesses in Britain are started by individuals who are unemployed or likely to lose their job immediately prior to founding a business.

Clearly, not all unemployed workers (attempt to) set up on their own or start any kind of self-employed activity. Börsch-Supan and Pfeiffer (1990) found in a panel study of 185 self-employed workers in West Germany that regional unemployment rates in the previous period lowered the probability of being self-employed in professional activities, but raised the probability of self-employment in other (non-agricultural) activities. This finding is particularly interesting, for it suggests the necessity to disaggregate the class of self-employed into subcategories whose members may be differentially affected by forces in their economic and institutional environments.

Hamilton (1989) argued in favor of a curvilinear relationship between unemployment and business formation rates. Using data on new firm registrations in Scotland for the period from 1950 to 1984, he found that business foundings increased with higher rates of unemployment up to some level beyond which foundings declined. Hamilton interpreted this finding in terms of a 'push-pull' model. At low levels of unemployment, when the local economy is depressed, increased unemployment raises the perceived net benefits of self-employment relative to paid employment and some workers are 'pushed' into starting their own business. At very high levels of unemployment, however, depressed market conditions send a signal to potential founders that few opportunities (the 'pull' factor) are left for new and successful business formations, and so the rate at which new firms are founded declines.

Thus, there is some cross-sectional and longitudinal evidence supporting the hypothesis that depressed market conditions, as measured by high unemployment and slow growth, 'push' individuals into self-employment, ceteris paribus. Nevertheless, the evidence from previous research must be interpreted with some caution. Because in most studies measures of aggregate self-employment rates and unemployment rates share a common denominator (total employment), definitional dependence may partly account for the estimated relationship (OECD, 1986). The argument that rising rates of self-employment show the reaction of wage workers to job loss or document the response of school-leavers, retirees, women, etc. to the absence of (good) employment opportunities would be strengthened if it could be shown that other indicators of labor market conditions -- which are not mathematically related to self-employment rates -- have similar effects. Below we test the effect of changes in rates of job vacancies and real wages.

Job vacancies and wage rates. Evans and Leighton (1989a), in a study of young white men in the United States, found that low income earners are more likely to switch to self-employment, net of other labor market characteristics. The interpretation of this finding is straightforward if one assumes that individuals switch from wage-employment to self-employment if the expected utility (which depends partly on the earnings differential) of self-employment exceeds the expected utility of wage work. In our empirical models below, we use year-to-year changes in real wage rates as a measure of changes in the 'quality' of employment opportunities in the wage sector. The fact that in many OECD countries the earnings distribution widened since the late 1970s, while real wages stagnated, is usually interpreted as an indication that the proportion of low-paying jobs increased (Loveman and Tilly, 1988; OECD, 1989; Costrell, 1990), encouraging more individuals to start their own business. Accordingly, we test the hypothesis that self-employment rates tend to increase in times of stagnating or declining wages. Similarly, following the argument by Hudson (1989), we expect that self-employment rates tend to rise in times of declining job vacancies.

Service sector growth. The rise of self-employment has also been associated in previous studies with changes in industrial structure. Because most of the growth in self-employment has occurred in the service sector, the expansion of this sector alone is said to account for part of the rise in self-employment rates. This argument is appealing for its simplicity, but it does not explain why self-employment rates continued to decline during the 1950s and 1960s, when service industries were already expanding. Nor does this argument consider the fact that self-employment has not grown uniformly throughout the service sector, and has even declined in some service industries. For example, in the United States during the 1970s, the rate of self-employment increased in business services and real estate but declined in entertainment and retail services (Steinmetz and Wright, 1989). Nevertheless, we include service sector growth in our model to control for long term and general structural change in national economies. We expect service sector growth to have a positive effect on self-employment rates.

Female labor force participation. One of the more pronounced, but poorly understood, recent developments in the self-employment sector is the increase in female self-employment. Although women entrepreneurs are generally under-represented compared with all women employed in the nonagricultural sector, they have been entering self-employment at disproportionately high rates. In the United States, for example, the relative increase in self-employed women from 1970 to 1983 was five times greater than that of self-employed men, and exceeded three times the rate of entry of women into wage and salary employment (Becker, 1984). Steinmetz and Wright (1989, p. 1009) speculated that the revival of self-employment 'could be partially an indirect effect of the increasing participation of women in the labor force' to the extent that the increased prevalence of two-earner households implies declining risks for people who attempt self-employment. One might also expect that women with higher rates of labor-force participation are more likely to become self-employed, on the assumption that individuals discover self-employment opportunities through their experience in the labor market (Evans and Leighton, 1989b). Other explanations of the rising rate of self-employed women include technological innovations which permit women to combine gainful economic activity with domestic activities, the general increase in womens' human capital, and certain attitudinal changes which have been reported in a number of surveys of women entrepreneurs (White, 1984). These explanatory factors are difficult to operationalize, especially in longitudinal and cross-country comparative studies. In this preliminary analysis, we use the female labor force participation rate as a crude proxy variable to measure the involvement of women in gainful economic activities. We expect a positive effect of the female labor force participation rate on the female self-employment rate, and no effect on the male self-employment rate.

The institutional environment

Many time-dependent processes which affect business foundings and self-employment rates are taking place in the institutional environment (Wiedenmayer, Aldrich, and Staber, 1991). Some are dramatic, one-of-a-kind historical events with far-reaching implications for new business opportunities, such as German unification and the restructuring of East European economies. Others are more mundane and repetitive events which no one may notice but whose cumulative effects can be substantial. Institutional factors include: governmental policies, spatial complexes, capital sources, and other events specific to particular historical periods. For example, deregulation of the U.S. airline industry substantially raised the founding rate of airlines at the end of the 1970s (Kelly, 1988). Staber (1989) found that favorable government tax policies stimulated the foundings of three different types of cooperatives in Canada. In West Germany, government suport for high technology businesses through special loans and research grants has encouraged foundings, beginning in the 1980s (Bögenhold, 1987).

Institutional factors may have explanatory power in comparative research on the revival of self-employment for at least two reasons. First, in many countries a number of policy changes have been introduced in the 1970s which may have contributed to the resurgence of self-employment. Some policy initiatives are directly aimed at assisting the self-employed, such as the Enterprise Allowance Scheme in Britain and the Unemployed Entrepreneurs Program in France (Bendick and Egan, 1987). Other policy changes may have had indirect effects, such as changes in the rate of corporation tax in Britain or the deregulation of financial markets in the United States which altered the contextual environment of the self-employed. Thus, it seems important to include time-variant measures of institutional environments in models of self-employment.

A second reason for modeling institutional factors in comparative research is to control for cross-country differences in public policy and ideology, independent of long-term changes in institutional environments. In Britain and the United States, for example, small business owners have received far more ideological support than has been the case in Scandinavian countries at any time in the post-WW II era. Also the level of public ownership and privatization efforts have varied across countries and created different opportunities for people interested in self-employment.

Several previous studies have introduced strictly political factors to explain the recent rise of self-employment (e.g., Hudson, 1987), but generally have not included such variables in their empirical models. One notable exception is a study by Blau (1987) which examined the effects of changes in tax rates, minimum wages, and social security retirement benefits on male self-employment rates in the U.S. for the period 1948-82. Blau found that increases in the real minimum wage had a strong negative effect on the self-employment rate, and increases in the marginal tax rate at high income levels had a strong positive effect on the self-employment rate. Blau interpreted these findings as suggesting that higher tax rates and lower minimum wages raise the expected utility of self-employment relative to that of wage-employment and thus induce shifts toward self-employment. Also Evans and Leighton (1989b) found some evidence of a positive relationship between federal tax rates and aggregate self-employment rates. Hudson (1987) found a positive but weak relationship between real interest rates and new company registrations in Britain for the period from 1952 to 1984. Unfortunately, these studies are limited to the United States and Britain, and so the generalizability of the findings to other countries is not clear. We are not aware of cross-country comparative empirical studies which have included institutional variables in models of self-employment rates.

It is difficult, if not impossible, to obtain quantifiable and reliable measures of institutional variables appropriate for longitudinal and comparative analyses which capture some of the developments indicated above. We thus employ two crude proxy variables: unemployment insurance replacement ratio and an index of corporatism.

Unemployment insurance. In an effort to enhance the flexibility of labor markets, the governments of many OECD countries have introduced policies in recent years which had the effect of halting or reversing the post-WW II trend towards increased labor or social protection (Lee et al., 1987). In some countries minimum wages were frozen or reduced, in other countries unemployment benefits became taxable, and the right to strike has been restricted. Consistent with these policy changes have been fluctuations in the unemployment insurance replacement ratio, which is used by the OECD as a broad indicator of the relative 'generosity' of unemployment insurance schemes. For most countries (the exception are Italy, Norway, and Sweden) replacement ratios have been rising in the late 1960s and early 1970s, and stable or falling in the 1980s. Replacement ratios may be interpreted as indicators of changes in economic opportunities and work incentives facing the self-employed relative to wage and salary employees. On the assumption that more restrictive unemployment insurance schemes raise the relative attractiveness of self-employment (by lowering the relative expected utility of wage-employment), we hypothesize that falling replacement ratios have a positive effect on self-employment rates.

Corporatism. We use an index of corporatism as a qualitative and, admittedly, rather crude indicator of cross-country differences in ideology and central government and labor union strength. Corporatism reflects the ability of elites in central governments and interest associations to implement public policies. Corporatist countries also tend to have active labor market programs and protective labor regulations which lower the relative attractiveness of self-employment. While the relationship between corporatism and labor market policies is by no means simple, there is a tendency of corporatist-oriented governments to pursue structural policies which are aimed at achieving production flexibility *and* maintaining a high level of employment (Schmid, 1990). Accordingly, we hypothesize that countries with corporatist regimes have lower rates of self-employment.

Methods

Our objective is to include in the analysis as many countries over as long a period as possible, given the availability of data. The sample of countries includes Australia, Canada, Federal Republic of Germany, Italy, Sweden, United Kingdom, and United States, and for individual countries the period of observation ranges from 1962-87 to 1966-87.

The dependent variable, self-employment rate, is defined in the present analysis as the number of employers and persons working on own account (including unpaid family workers) as a proportion of all persons active in non-agricultural activities (OECD Labour Force Statistics, various years). We include unpaid family workers among the self-employed to maximize the time-series data available (for some countries and some periods data are not available on self-employed workers alone) and to recognize the importance of family labor in many small business settings.

We estimate separate models for male and female self-employment rates. Previous time-series studies have not made this distinction (for an exception, see Evans and Leighton, 1989b), despite the general recognition of gender differences in self-employment rates. The growing role of women in the self-employment sector raises a number of interesting research questions, principal among which is the question of why the self-employment rate among women has grown relative to that of men in recent years. Our data do not permit a direct examination of this issue, but we can test the extent to which male and female self-employment rates are similarly affected by the variables included in our model.

Variables and measures. The independent variables used in the analysis are as follows (data sources are shown in parentheses): (1) annual male and female unemployment rate (OECD Labour Force Statistics); (2) year-to-year percentage change in real GNP (IMF International Financial Statistics); (3) year-to-year percentage change in real hourly earnings (ILO Yearbook; OECD Historical Statistics); (4) year-to-year percentage change in the job vacancy rate, defined as the number of listed vacancies divided by total employment (OECD Main Economic Indicators); (5) service sector rate, defined as the proportion of males and females active in the service sector (OECD Labour Force Statistics); (6) female labor force participation rate, defined as the proportion of women in the labor force (OECD Labour Force Statistics); (7) unemployment insurance replacement ratio, defined as (standard national accounts unemployment compensation payments/number of unemployed) divided by (compensation in manufacturing/number of production workers in manufacturing) (Lee et al., 1987); and (8) corporatism, defined on a three-point scale as weak (=1) for the U.S., Canada, Italy, and U.K., medium (=2) for Germany and Australia, and strong (=3) for Sweden (Schmidt, 1982). The corporatism index is assumed to be time-invariant for each country, and it serves as a variable to account for between-country differences in our pooled time-series analysis.

Model estimation. We argued above for the need of cross-country comparative and longitudinal analyses to improve our understanding of the revival of self-employment. Because cross-sectional research designs truncate the variation and degrees of freedom needed for multivariate analyses (given the small number of countries available for analysis), and time-series data introduce a dynamic component to the study of self-employment rates, we pool cross-sectional (country) and time-series data. A pooled model allows testing both of country-specific (e.g., corporatism) and country-common hypotheses (e.g., unemployment). The pooling procedure generates a sample size of 87 to 172 observations, depending upon which variables with missing values are included in the model. This time-dominant sample is sufficiently large for multivariate analysis and contains adequate variation in the variables.

Pooling time-series with cross-sectional data means that the sample units (countries) are no longer independent, and the model errors may be correlated over time. For a variety of reasons (e.g., different measurement techniques, population sizes, time frames), the countries may not have constant error variances. Therefore, generalized least squares (GLS) models with adjustments for serial correlation and with controls for between-country differences are preferable to ordinary least squares (OLS) models (Stimson, 1985).

Results and discussion

We proceed in three steps. First, we estimate a GLS model which includes all independent variables. Next, we estimate a GLS model with each variable entered one at a time, to test for the influence of multicollinearity among the regressors. Finally, we estimate seven GLS models, each with one country deleted, to test for the disproportional influence of a single country. To remove the underlying time trend in self-employment rates, we first regress self-employment on time (measured in years) and then regress the residuals from this estimation on the independent variables. The estimated coefficients are reported in Table 1.

The results are generally consistent with our expectations. Equations (1) and (2) show the parameter coefficients estimated in models that include all variables. The estimated coefficients are generally in the expected direction, but only unemployment and vacancy rate show statistically significant effects. Equations (3) and (4) report the coefficients of variables that were entered one at a time, without controls. This procedure does not alter the direction of the estimated coefficients (the exceptions are male earnings growth and male services) , but raises the standard error of some of the coefficients, indicating the possibility of collinearity among the regressors. Re-estimating all models with one country omitted at a time does not significantly alter the results, suggesting that none of the countries has disproportionate effects on the estimated coefficients.

Our strongest finding concerns the relationship between labor market conditions (as measured by unemployment rate and year-to-year changes in the job vacancy rate) and self-employment. In times of slack labor markets, when unemployment is high and job vacancies are declining (the simple correlation between unemployment rates and changes in job vacancy rates is close to zero) , both male and female self-employment rates show a tendency to rise, suggesting that self-employment plays a countercyclical role. The estimated coefficients are robust, regardless of the inclusion of other controls in the models. This finding is thus consistent with previous research on the effects of unemployment and job vacancies on self-employment rates and new firm registrations.

The instability of the coefficients of other structural variables (GNP growth, earnings growth, service sector, and female labor force participation) in models which include all controls suggests that the estimated effects must be interpreted with caution. Some of these variables are collinear, possibly because they follow a common upward trend (e.g., female labor force participation rate and service sector growth). Nonetheless, the estimated coefficients are in the expected direction, suggesting that the revival of self-employment has occurred at a time of slow economic growth, declining real earnings, and expanding services. As expected, the male self-employment rate is not associated with the female labor force participation rate.

The estimated effects of institutional variables are in the expected direction, although the statistical significance of coefficients drops in models that include control variables. Thus, the results permit only a tentative conclusion. Corporatist-oriented countries tend to have lower self-employment rates, and self-employment rates have risen in countries whose unemployment insurance schemes have become more restrictive, but these relationships are not strong when structural developments in the economy are controlled for.

The recent revival of self-employment has occurred at a time of economic stress, characterized by persistently high levels of unemployment (by post-WW II standards), slow economic growth, and stagnant real wages. This observation raises questions about the potential contribution of self-employment to job creation. Many govenments have developed self-employment assistance programs in the hope that such programs would promote entrepreneurship among the unemployed and would generate job opportunities where they are needed most (Department of Employment, 1985).

Table 1
Pooled cross-section time-series unstandardized regression coefficients for male and
female non-farm self-employment rates (incl. unpaid family workers) in seven countries[a],
1962-1987 (standard errors in parentheses)

Independent Variables	(1) male	(2) female	(3)[b] male	(4)[b] female
Intercept	.405	- .498	---	---
Unemployment	.050*** (.014)	.044*** (.018)	.054*** (.019)	.019*** (.009)
GNP growth	- .006 (.016)	- .015 (.011)	- .023* (.014)	- .034*** (.012)
Earnings growth	.002 (.013)	- .002 (.009)	- .007* (.004)	- .001 (.004)
Job vacancies	- .003** (.001)	- .003** (.001)	- .003** (.001)	- .002** (.001)
Service sector	- .002 (.006)	.001 (.007)	.011** (.005)	.008*** (.002)
Female labor force	- .013 (.014)	.007 (.020)	- .008 (.008)	.015** (.007)
Replacement ratio	- .002 (.002)	- .001 (.003)	- .005** (.002)	- .005** (.002)
Corporatism	- .022 (.069)	- .014 (.084)	- .136*** (.055)	- .053 (.050)
adj. R^2	.22	.19	---	---
Durbin-Watson	1.77	1.75	---	---
N observations	87	87	87-172	87-172

```
  * p < .10  two-tailed
 ** p < .05  two-tailed
*** p < .01  two-tailed
```

[a] Australia, Canada, Italy, Sweden, United Kingdom, United States,
West Germany.

[b] Single-variable equations, with each variable entered one at a
time.

The available evidence, however, suggests that employment growth in the small business sector is concentrated in a small minority of businesses (Teitz, Glasmeier, and Svensson, 1981; Storey and Johnson, 1987) and that self-employment assistance programs are generally ineffective in promoting long-term job creation without at the same time displacing existing small businesses. The results of a study of small business development schemes in Britain and France, aimed at assisting unemployed workers in starting on their own, were not particularly encouraging (Bendick and Egan, 1987). Two-thirds of the entrepreneurs surveyed said they would have set up their business even without government assistance. Most of the program participants founded firms in industries (mostly services, construction, and retailing) where competition was already intense, so that the net employment contribution at the level of the local economy was reduced by significant displacement effects. Almost half of the British businesses were closed before the end of their third year of operation, and two thirds of the survivors provided employment only for their owner. The few additional jobs that were created included employment for part-timers and family members who may or may not have been paid.

The evidence from the effects of self-employment assistance programs in other countries is similarly discouraging. For example, a study of 61 participants in self-employment training programs in Ohio in the United States found that fewer than ten percent of the newly founded businesses had created any additional jobs within a year (Mangum and Tansky, 1987). A study of the employment effects of government assistance to help unemployed workers in West Germany create their own jobs found that of the 28,000 workers who had received financial assistance in 1987 and 1988 about 14 percent (this represents an underestimate for methodological reasons) were registered as unemployed within two years (Kaiser and Otto, 1990). The proportion of business 'failures' is probably even higher and depends on the number of people (unknown) who returned to paid employment or withdrew from the labor force altogether.

The picture of a vibrant and expanding small business is atypical. The large majority of self-employed do not employ workers, and surveys in a variety of countries have shown that the proportion of one-person businesses has been increasing in recent years. 'So it cannot be assumed that the self-employed are invariably entrepreneurs who are building businesses that will eventually employ more people than themselves' (Hakim, 1988, p. 430).

Summary and conclusion

To our knowledge, this is the only empirical study of determinants of self-employment using time-series *and* cross-country data. Apart from likely measurement errors, this study is limited in a number of ways, the most serious of which is that we use aggregate data. Aggregate statistics of self-employment mask the heterogeneity of the 'petty bourgeoisie' class which includes persons who, given their social origin and material circumstances, are better described as 'grand bourgeois' (e.g., certain self-employed professionals), but it also includes self-employed workers (e.g., many street peddlers and home-workers) who operate at the fringes of the economy. Not all self-employed persons own their means of production and not all enjoy autonomy in the labor process. Some of the self-employed operate no real firms; they are 'independent' only in a formal and statistical sense and they experience many of the disadvantages of wage-dependent employment, without enjoying the rights associated with wage-employment. Self-employment includes different positions in the social and economic structure, and one would expect that the occupants of these positions are differentially affected by labor market and institutional developments. Aggregate data, however, do not permit an analysis of these effects.

Aggregate statistics also shed little light on the determinants of the *choice* between unemployment, self-employment, and paid employment. Aggregate data cannot explain movements into and out of self-employment at the micro-level. Our findings provide no direct evidence that in times of slack labor markets unemployed or displaced persons themselves start their own businesses, although this interpretation of estimated effects of unemployment at the aggregate level is not uncommon (e.g., Bregger, 1963; Hudson, 1987). Self-employment rates may have risen because high levels of unemployment discourage potential entrants to the labor market from seeking wage jobs or because an increased number of early retirees start their own business, although they would prefer to continue in wage-employment.

Finally, lacking micro-level data on the characteristics of entrepreneurs themselves, we cannot address many of the traditional psychological and sociological questions of entrepreneurship (biography, social mobility, etc.). Our intention in this study was not to test several (alternative) theories of entrepreneurship, but to focus on some of the macro-contextual developments that may explain, in part, the recent resurgence of self-employment. In this vein, our findings challenge the currently popular assumption that higher rates of self-employment reflect and/or contribute to macro-economic vitality.

For lack of systematic and comparative data we have not considered in this study other contextual variables which might contribute to an explanation of the revival of self-employment. Consistent with our interpretation of the evidence we presented in this chapter are arguments about the implications of an increased tendency among large employers to adjust production to intensified market competition through various forms of decentralization. While product markets have become more turbulent and uncertain since the 1970s, relatively slack labor markets have afforded many employers the opportunity to realize their need for greater manpower flexibility by expanding their use of 'peripheral' workers, including short-duration hires, homeworkers, and self-employed freelances. Many large companies have been experimenting with strategies of fragmentation to delegate production activities to supplier firms and subcontractors. In an attempt to rationalize operations, they contracted out specific services and cut back on peripheral activities. Such strategies have the effect of shifting many of the risks of flexible adjustment to small firms, but they also create opportunities for new businesses by opening new market niches to which small specialists are often better adapted than large diversified corporations (Staber and Aldrich, 1989).

Another development providing opportunities for self-employment are changes in technology (particularly information technology) which have lowered the minimum efficient scale for many operations. The effect of such technological change is probably most pronounced in activities in which microprocessors find ready application, and in these industries (real estate, accounting, etc.) self-employment has in fact grown considerably.

To conclude, our findings raise some doubt that 'the way to reduce unemployment is through more businesses, more self-employment and greater wealth creation, all leading to more jobs' (policy statement by the British Department of Employment, quoted in Storey and Johnson, 1987, p. 3). Rising rates of self-employment may be a reflection of labor market deficiencies rather than a development contributing to their solution. This is not to say that higher self-employment rates are without any benefits. At the individual level, self-employment may be a useful stepping stone back into wage-employment and an opportunity to develop human capital. For others, it may offer certain non-material benefits, such as a sense of autonomy and self-control at the workplace. From the perspective of the economy at large, self-employment may play an important role as a seedbed of innovation, while encouraging individuals to develop their own solutions to unemployment using resources that otherwise would have to be spent on income maintenance.

References

Aldrich, Howard and Catherine Zimmer (1986) 'Entrepreneurship through social networks.' In D. Sexton and R. Smilor (eds.) *The Art and Science of Entrepreneurship.* New York: Ballinger.

Bechhofer, Frank and Brian Elliott (1985) 'The petite bourgeoisie in late capitalism' *Annual Review of Sociology*, 11.

Becker, Eugene (1984) 'Self-employed workers: An update to 1983' *Monthly Labor Review*, 107.

Bendick, Marc and Mary Egan (1987) 'Transfer payment diversion for small business development: British and French experience,' *Industrial and Labor Relations Review*, 40.

Blau, David (1987) 'A time-series analysis of self-employment in the United States,' *Journal of Political Economy*, 95.

Bögenhold, Dieter (1987) *Der Gründerboom: Realität und Mythos der neuen Selbständigkeit.* Frankfurt and New York: Campus.

Bögenhold, Dieter and Udo Staber (1990) 'Selbständigkeit als ein Reflex auf Arbeitslosigkeit? Makrosoziologische Befunde einer international-komparativen Studie' *Kölner Zeitschrift für Soziologie und Sozialpsychologie*, 42.

Bögenhold, Dieter and Udo Staber (1991) 'The Decline and rise of self-employment' *Work, Employment and Society*, 5.

Börsch-Supan, Axel and Friedhelm Pfeiffer (1990), 'Determinanten der Selbständigkeit in der Bundesrepublik Deutschland' Paper presented at the SFB3 Conference on 'Person und Haushalt in Wirtschaft und Gesellschaft, Frankfurt, Germany.

Boissevain, Jeremy 'Small Entrepreneurs in Changing Europe: Towards a Research Agenda,' Unpublished manuscript, Maastricht: European Centre for Work and Society, 1981.

Bregger, John (1963) 'Self-employment in the United States, 1948-62' *Monthly Labor Review*, 86.

Costrell, Robert (1990) 'Methodology in the 'job quality' debate' *Industrial Relations*, 29.

Department of Employment (Britain) (1985) *Employment: The Challenge for the Nation*, London.

Evans, David and Linda Leighton (1989a) 'Some empirical aspects of entrepreneurship' *American Economic Review*, 79.

Evans, David and Linda Leighton (1989b) 'The determinants of changes in U.S. self-employment, 1968-1987' *Small Business Economics*, 1.

Hakim, Catherine (1988) 'Self-employment in Britain: Recent trends and current issues' *Work, Employment and Society*, 2.

Hamilton, R.T. (1989) 'Unemployment and business formation rates: Reconciling time-series and cross-section evidence' *Environment and Planning A*, 21.

Highfield, Richard and Robert Smiley (1987) 'New business starts and economic activity: An empirical investigation' *International Journal of Industrial Organization*, 5.

Hudson, John (1987) 'Company births in Great Britain and the institutional environment' *International Small Business Journal*, 6.

Hudson, John (1989) 'The birth and death of firms' *Quarterly Review of Economics and Business*, 29.

Kaiser, Manfred and Manfred Otto (1990) 'Übergang von Arbeitslosigkeit in berufliche Selbständigkeit' *Mitteilungen der Arbeitsmarkt und Berufsforschung*, 2.

Kelly, Dawn (1988) 'Organizational transformation and failure in the U.S. airline industry, 1962-1985' Doctoral dissertation, Northwestern University.

Lee, James, David Coe, and Menahem Prywes (1987) 'Microeconomic changes and macroeconomic wage disinflation in the 1980s' *OECD Economic Studies*, 8.

Loveman, Gary and Chris Tilley (1988) 'Good jobs or bad jobs?' *International Labour Review*, 127.

Mangum, Stephen and Judy Tansky (1987) 'Self-employment training as an intervention strategy for displaced or disadvantaged workers' *IRRA 40th Annual Proceedings*, Madison, Wisconsin.

Organization of Economic Cooperation and Development (OECD) (1986) *OECD Employment Outlook*. Paris: OECD (Sept.).

OECD (1989) *OECD Employment Outlook*. Paris: OECD.

Ray, Robert (1975) 'A report on self-employed Americans in 1973' *Monthly Labor Review*, 98.

Schmid, Günther (1990) 'Vollbeschäftigung in der sozialen Marktwirtschaft' Discussion paper FS I 90-1, Wissenschaftszentrum Berlin, Germany.

Schmidt, Manfred (1982) 'Does corporatism matter?' In Gerhard Lehmbruch and Philippe Schmitter (eds.) *Patterns of Corporatist Policy-Making*, Beverly Hills: Sage.

Staber, Udo (1989) 'Organizational foundings in the cooperative sector in Atlantic Canada: An ecological perspective' *Organization Studies*, 10.

Staber, Udo and Howard Aldrich (1989), 'Human resource strategies: Some ecological cracks?' *Industrial Relations Journal*, 20.

Steinmetz, George and Eric Wright (1989) 'The fall and rise of the petty bourgeoisie: Changing patterns of self-employment in the United States' *American Journal of Sociology*, 94.

Stimson, James (1985) 'Regression in space and time: A statistical essay' *American Journal of Political Science*, 29.

Storey, David and Steven Johnson (1987) *Are Small Firms the Answer to Unemployment?* London: Employment Institute.

Teitz, Michael, Amy Glasmeier, and Douglas Svensson (1981) 'Small business and employment growth in California,' Working paper no. 348, Berkeley: University of California, Institute of Urban and Regional Development.

White, Jerry (1984) 'The rise of female capitalism - women as entrepreneurs' *Business Quarterly*, 49.

Wedenmayer, Gabriele, Howard Aldrich, and Udo Staber (1991) 'Von Merkmalen zu Quoten: Organisationsgründungen aus ökologischer Sicht', Unpublished paper, University of Munich, Department of Sociology.

Part 5
Factors influencing entrepreneurial performance

14 Factors associated with relative performance amongst small firms in the British instrumentation sector

Graham Hall and Sally Fulshaw

Background

Remarkably little is known about the reasons underlying relative performance amongst small firms facing similar market conditions. Within journals focusing on individual disciplines there may be surveys of the methods employed by practitioners within companies but the results are rarely correlated with the performance of these companies, and, in any case, the surveys are almost invariably conducted with managers of large companies.

One approach might lie in consulting the literature on failure amongst small firms. Unfortunately, the source of data for such studies (the exception being Hall and Young, 1991), most notably those Storey et al (1987) and Keasey and Watson (1987), are published accounts so that, at best, they provide clues to sound management on only a narrow range of areas and, at worst, simply present a set of symptoms rather than causes, though it should be emphasised that, for the purpose of prediction, the distinction between causes and symptoms is largely irrelevant. Whatever the range of factors that these studies have included, however, it still need not follow that the lessons to be drawn about avoiding failure will serve as pointers to how high rates of growth or profitability may be achieved.

The purpose of this study is to provide such pointers. Specifically, our objectives are to gain insights into:-

a) whether the education levels of owners, management or the workforce are associated with the success of their companies.
b) within each of the areas of management, which particular policies would appear to be pursued by successful firms, in order to identify 'best practices'.

c) the relative importance of the various disciplines in achieving success, to establish whether it is in the interests of a chief executive to concentrate on, for instance, marketing, at the expense of some other discipline.

Methodology

Between January and April, 1990, interviews were conducted with the chief executives of forty companies, operating in instrumentation, that, in 1983, might have fairly been described as small. The interviews covered a wide range of topics. The information they supplied was employed as explanatory variables in regressions which had, as alternative dependant variables, various measures of performance relating either to 1988 or to change between 1983 and 1988. The latter represented the most recent year on which, at the beginning of the project, data were available.

For the purposes of this study a causal relationship was assumed between the explanatory variables and levels of performance, though it would readily be agreed that it can be spurious to draw conclusions about policy from statistical relationships[1]. Apart from the danger, endemic to all econometric research, that results are specific to the sample on which the estimation is based and, if different, the sample on which it is subsequently tested, the interpretation of causation may not be unambiguous. In this case, however, it is, perhaps, more difficult to argue reverse causality than in other studies of performance; there would seem only very special circumstances under which high performing firms would commonly adopt a particular mode of behaviour and yet that mode had no influence on their performance. The most likely of such circumstances would be where conditions external to firms both induce a particular mode of behaviour and lead to a high level of performance, though by focusing on a single sector such differences in conditions are limited to those arising between segments.

Separate regressions have been carried out on seven groups of variables intended to represent aspects of

- the educational levels of decision-makers and the workforce
- strategy
- marketing
- financial control
- the management of innovation
- operations management
- market conditions

As the majority of variables are introduced as constant dummies their values are directly comparable. The R2 has been used as a measure of the relative importance of each set of variables. The low degree of first-order multi-collinearity, as revealed by the correlation matrices, enables a sanguinity that running a series of separate regressions has not lead to any significant risk of omitted variable bias.

Regressions have been run with the dependant variables:

-    return on sales, 1988
-    change in return on sales, 1983-88
-    percentage change in real sales, 1983-88
-    sales in 1988

Sample

The sample of forty firms was drawn from the population of firms that

- in 1983, were independent, operated solely in instrumentation and had a labour force of two hundred or less
- in 1988, had remained independent and in instrumentation. No con straints were imposed on their size in the later period.

Hence the interviewees were the chief executives of firms that had, a few years earlier, been small but which could have exhibited any rate of growth in the intervening period.

The sample was drawn from the FAME data base, from which the data on performance were extracted.

Choice of variables

Dependants

The most obvious measures of success are profitability and growth. The former should be measured by the internal rate of return but, as this is based on expectations of revenue and cost flows, and of the cost of capital, we have adopted the proxy of return on sales i.e. the ratio of earnings before interest and tax to revenue. This has slightly less theoretical underpinning than return on assets but is less susceptible to the idiosyncrasies of accounting measurement.

Additionally change in the level of profitability, 1983-88 was employed. In so doing the assumption was that the data from the interviews were on average a representation of the situation during the intervening period.

Growth has been measured as the percentage change in real sales, 1983-88, with the appropriate price series for each segment of the market adopted as a deflator. The absolute level of sales at the time of interview has also been introduced as a dependant variable. Size is commonly viewed within the business community as a measure of success but it may not have resulted from growth during the period considered.

Explanatory Variables

(A) Personal

From the myriad of personal factors relating to founders, owners, managing directors, or their employees, which could affect the performance of their companies, the focus in this study was on their education levels which can, at least, be defined unambiguously. The specification of the variables was:

a) whether the founder, owner or managing director (MD) had ever attended a short management course.
b), c) and d)
whether the MD has a PhD, BSc or HND[2].
e) and f) the proportion of employees with any level of higher education or with HNDs.

(B) Strategic

a) the percentage of sales from the most important product (designed to reflect the breadth of the product portfolio).
b),c),d),e) and f)
whether the marketing strategy was targeted by
- the sector in which the instrument would be employed (e.g. chemicals).
- the joint product to which the instrument would be attached (e.g. mass-spectrometer).
- the application of the instrument (e.g. temperature control).
- the features of the instrument, irrespective of the above.
- geographical region.
g) and h) whether the underlying strategy was of low cost or of high quality.

(C) Marketing

a) and b) whether the company carried out surveys amongst
- customers
- distributors
c),d) and e)
whether the interviewee believed his products were purchased because of the quality of
- the product
- the service
- the delivery times
f) the number employed in the marketing function.
g) the advertising to sales ratio
h) the proportion of sales in 1989 to current customers (to establish the importance of repeat purchasing).

(D) Financial control

a) percentage shortfall on intended volume of borrowing at the inception of the company (to establish the founder's effectiveness at negotiating with the Capital Market).
b) and c) whether cashflows were forecast
- yearly
- quarterly
d) and e) whether records of cashflow were updated monthly or quarterly.
f) the number of days before a bill was typically paid.

230

g) the number of days before an invoice was typically dispatched.

h) whether procedures were typically formalised in writing (as an indication of the degree of bureaucratisation of the company).

(E) Innovation

It would be expected a priori that the management of the innovation process would be important for success in the instrumentation sector. This would appear to be confirmed by previous studies (Rothwell et al, 1974, Von Hippel, 1976 and 1977, Maidique and Zirger, 1985) which have also provided some pointers to the specification of the model:

a) whether products were typically launched as a result of advances from a programme of R and D which is carried out autonomously of signals from the market as to what form the outcome of the process should take.

b) whether the design of products was typically specified by customers.

c) whether they would typically work closely with customers in the development of their products.

d) whether they would regard themselves as essentially sub-contractors.

e) percentage of sales from products launched since 1983.

f) percentage of sales spent on R & D

g) number employed in R & D.

h) number of patents taken since 1983.

(F) Operations management

a) average throughput time of the major product.

b) average stock turn i.e. the ratio of stock to sales.

c) whether using computer aided design.

d) whether using materials requirement planning.

e) whether using Just in Time.

(G) Market conditions

a) the percentage change in total sales within the market segment at mini mum list heading level (to establish how far performance mirrors conditions within the total market).

b) number of competitors in the market served by the major product as perceived by interviewees.

c) number of new products launched since 1983 (to reflect 'dynamism' of the served markets, though with an obvious overlap with some of the variables specified in E e) above.

d) number of customers in total (to reflect the concentration of the custo merbase).

e) percentage of sales from servicing (as a measure of the degree to which the company's market might be described as 'captive').

f) volume of major product sold in 1989 (as a surrogate for economies of sale).

g) whether competitors in the segment served by major product were typi cally bigger.

Results

Throughout the following discussion 'importance' will be measured by the size of the R^2, relative importance by comparison of the coefficients on the variables (the majority of which were measured by 0/1 and , are, therefore, directly comparable) and the likelihood of the existence of a relationship by reference to the value of the relevant 't' statistic. In the interests of parsimony the econometrics have been omitted.

Education levels

Profitability would not appear to be affected by the education levels within companies, with just a hint that the proportion of employees with Higher National Diplomas, and the possession of a degree by the managing director, might make a difference.

Education would appear, however, to have affected the change in profitability experienced by companies. The proportion of employees with a degree was positively correlated with the change and the proportion of employees whose qualifications were limited to a Higher National Diploma was negatively correlated. When the model is reduced to these variables alone the R^2 rises from 0.1 to 0.17 and the 'F' statistic from 1.6 to 5.0.

This relationship is reversed with respect to the size of the companies. Bigger companies employed lower proportions of people with degrees, but higher proportions with HNDs. Their managing director was also more likely to possess a degree.

The growth in sales of companies would not appear to be influenced by education levels. Nor would any of the measures of performance appear to be affected by the attendance by the founder, owner or managing director on short management courses, or their possession of a doctorate.

Strategy

The results suggest fairly strongly that the highest returns were earned by firms concentrating on particular sectors. None of the other candidates for focus generated 't' statistics that were statistically significant at the normally accepted levels, nor indeed were their coefficients of the same order of magnitudes. Similarly, their low 't' statistics did not initially suggest that strategies of concentrating on either the low cost or high quality ends of the cost-quality spectrum would increase the probability of achieving higher levels of profitability. However, whilst the coefficient on the dummy for companies specialising by sector remains unchanged, regardless of the composition of the model, there is some suggestion that multicollinearity is masking the importance of 'underlying strategy of quality'. A model limited to these variables produces a R^2 of 0.25 and 'F' statistic of 7.4. They would appear equally important in contributing to growth. The pursuance of such a strategy of high quality would appear, furthermore, as reflected by the size of coefficients and 't' statistics, to be positively related with both size and change in return on sales.

Marketing

Marketing variables would appear to be quite strongly associated with profitability. Firms enjoying high profitability were more likely to carry out market research, whether amongst distributors or customers, and less likely to rely on repeat purchases for their sales, or have been chosen, in the opinion of respondents, because of their reliability or speed of delivery.

The high correlation of size with the variables in our model is to a large extent driven by the number employed in the marketing function. It would not appear that this is a fixed factor of production. Respondents in the sample were also more likely to identify higher quality as the reason for their products being chosen by customers. It would not appear that size is associated with the other variables in the model. In particular it should be noted that, whilst market research was associated with profitability, it was not limited to the larger companies.

None of the variables in the model would appear to have influenced the changes in either profitability or sales experienced by the companies in the sample.

Financial management

Financial management would appear important to the profitability of companies but not necessarily in the direction expected. Interviewees reporting the largest shortfalls, over the last five years, between their intended and actual borrowing, on average managed the most profitable firms, confirming the common criticism that the capital market is inefficient at identifying the potential winners.

The most profitable would also appear to be the most prompt at paying bills, suggesting, perhaps, that efficiency is perceived in terms of quick responses rather than exploiting the opportunities to earn interest on late payments. There is some suggestion that profitability is associated with maintaining records of cashflows on a quarterly basis, rather than monthly or yearly (the latter not introduced as a variable because of the possibility of a dummy trap).

The importance of updating records of cashflow on a quarterly basis is confirmed with respect to changes in both profitability and in sales. Other relationships were also similar. Companies quick to dispatch their invoices were more likely to have experienced increases in both profitability and sales, but, again, there is some suggestion that they were also the more prompt at settling bills.

The importance of forecasting cashflow varies between measures. Quarterly forecasts would appear to be important for achieving high rates of growth in sales, irrelevant to change in profitability and to be weakly related, albeit with a high coefficient, to differences in profitability considered cross-sectionally.

Size was apparently not associated with any of the aspects of financial management considered.

Management innovation

There would seem little doubt that the instrumentation sector is characterised by a high rate of innovation. What is less clear is how firms, including small, should manage the process of innovation in order to fully exploit its potential benefits. The results of the seminal SAPPHO project (Rothwell et al, op cit.) would strongly suggest that innovations are more likely to be commercially successful if they are developed in close conjunction with their likely users. This approach should be contrasted with that in which a product is developed as a result of research initiatives which are, to some extent, autonomous of market signals, and potential users are then persuaded of its benefits. Clearly the difference is only one of degree. The amount of truly pure research will be slight in any instrument producer, but especially one that is small, nor, once the initial research has been undertaken, would it seem prudent to develop a new instrument without some minimal involvement from its possible users.

Our results do not indicate either approach to have had any impact on the performance of firms within our sample. There was not a statistically significant difference between those which interviewees claimed worked closely with customers in their R and D and those claiming more autonomy.

The notion that manufacturers are the initiators of innovation has been challenged by Von Hippell (op cit.) who persuasively argues that in the majority of cases the initiative will come from the user, who will delegate the production to the manufacturer. Von Hippell did not explicitly state this was against the interests of manufacturers but it might be expected a priori that working to the specification of a user, or even worse, acting as a sub-contractor to another instrument manufacturer, would lead, on average, to a lower level of performance. However, neither companies that worked to the specification of customers or which described themselves as sub-contractors suffered in terms of the performance measures employed.

There was, however, a mild suggestion that both profitability, and change in profitability, was affected by the R & D intensity of the companies. Companies apparently slightly benefited from devoting more of their resources to this activity. On the other hand, the number of patents taken out was not correlated with performance.

Operations management

None of the variables in the model had any significant impact on any of the measures of performance. Hence, firms employing Computer Aided Design , Materials Requirement Planning or Just In Time, or firms enjoying short throughput times or high rates of stock turnover, did not, on average, experience any benefit in terms of improvements in the most obvious measures of performance.

Market conditions

Perhaps the most surprising of the results is the apparent lack of any relationships between the performance of the companies in our sample and the characteristics of the sectors in which they operated. Given the commonly accepted importance of market conditions to performance it is worthwhile to spell out the implications of the results.

The change in sales within the segment served by the company's principle product would not appear to have affected its performance. Indeed, whilst in the regression to explain growth in sales, this was the only variable with a coefficient statistically significant at the 5% level, its sign was negative. This would seem clear evidence of the fragmentation of the instrumentation sector, with sales reflecting very specific conditions unrelated to aggregate trends.

Ceteris Paribus, one would expect performance measures, with the possible exception of absolute size, to be negatively correlated with the degree of competition. In the survey this was surrogated by the number of competitors that was faced in the market served by their major product. This becomes increasingly less appropriate with the degree of diversification, which provides one explanation for its apparent irrelevance to performance. Alternatively, interviewees may have had inaccurate perceptions of the number of firms with which they were actually in competition.

Such ignorance may have led to other variables being similarly poorly measured but it should be noted that at a 0.25% level of significance, companies apparently earned lower returns if, in the market served by their major product, they faced generally bigger competitors, if they relied on servicing for a high proportion of their sales, or if they had a large customer base. The first two results would confirm intuition, whilst the third would weakly point to the dangers of spreading one's marketing, and general customer care, too broadly. The number of new products launched between 1983 and 1988 was also negatively related to profitability, perhaps reflecting the importance of selectively in R & D. The only variable in the model explaining profitability, which was statistically significant at the 5% level, was the percentage of sales from products launched since 1983, demonstrating, perhaps, the dynamism of the instrumentation sector.

Relative importance of factors (table 1)

Comparison of the R2 would suggest:

a) The model employing marketing variables explained about a quarter of the variation in profitability within our sample with that based on variables reflecting aspects of financial management a close runner-up. Strategic variables were collectively of some importance, otherwise nothing else.

b) The model employing financial management variables explained about a quarter of the variation in change in profitability experienced by the companies in our sample, education, ten per cent and innovation nine percent.

c) Variations in growth of sales could be predominantly explained by dif ferences in financial management and strategy, though the education levels within the companies would also appear to have played a part.

d) When differences in size are considered cross-sectionally the only si gnificant correlation would appear to be with marketing variables. Within the range of sizes encompassed by the sample, scale was not apparently strongly related to any of the other sets of variables considered.

Table 1
Summary of R2 of the models employed

Dependents	Education Management	Strategic Management	Marketing Conditions	Innovation	Financial	Operations	Market
Profitability	0.001	0.14	0.24	0.02	0.21	0	0.04
Change in Profitability	0.1	0.04	0	0.09	0.23	0	0
Sales	0.008	0.09	0.37	0	0	0.08	0.05
Change in Sales	0.19	0.28	0	0	0.39	0	0.02

Notes

[1] See Hall and Howell (1985) and Hall (1986) for critiques of two of the most popular statistically based approaches to strategy formulation.

[2] The lowest level of qualification obtainable full time in UK higher education.

References

HALL G. (1987). 'When Should Market-Share Matter?' Journal of Economic Studies Vol. 14, No. 4

HALL G. AND HOWELL S. (1985). 'The Experience Curve from the Economist's Perspective' Strategic Management Journal July/September Vol. 16, No. 3

HALL G. AND YOUNG B. 'Factors Associated with Small Firm Insolvency in the London Area' 1991 International Journal of Small Businesses Vol. 9 No. 2.

KEASEY K. AND WATSON R. (1987). 'Non-Financial Symptoms and the Prediction of Small Company Failure: A Test of Argenti's Hypotheses' Journal of Business Finance and Accounting Vol. 14,

MAIDIQUE M.A. AND ZIRGER B.J. (1985) 'The New Product Learning Cycle' Research Policy No. 14

ROTHWELL R., FREEMAN C., HORSLEY A., JERVIS V.T.P. ,

ROBERTSON A.B. AND TOWNSEND J. (1974) 'Project Sappho Updated Project Phase II' Research Policy No. 3

STOREY D., KEASEY K., WATSON R. AND WYNARCZYE P. (1987) 'The Performance of Small Firms' London, Croom Helm.

VON HEPPEL E.A. (1976) 'The Dominant role of Users in the Scientific Instrument Innovation Process' Research Policy No. 5.

15 Intensity of planning conviction among entrepreneurs: Differences between zealots and non-believers

Harold P. Welsch and Gerhard R. Plaschka

Introduction

Generally, the entrepreneurial mystique is characterized by instinct, shooting from the hip, pulling oneself up by their own bootstrap, risk, special talent, charisma and something mysterious in one's genes. Despite calls from advisors, consultants, financiers and scholars for formal planning, not all entrepreneurs are convinced of the importance and the value of formal planning [1]. The stereotypic entrepreneur has often been labelled as an action-oriented, nonthinker who follows a 'shoot, ready, aim' sequence of activities. Business planning is thought to be inappropriate, even insulting, to entrepreneurs who like to be flexible, fast on their feet, and ready to change direction overnight. Those who value intuition and drive more are not predisposed to formal planning.

Contrary to this popular mystique is the modern successful entrepreneur who relies on training, discipline and a predisposition for planning. Planning allows the entrepreneur to work in a proactive mode to accomplish his/her goals. This belief is based upon anticipation of the future by avoidance of unreasonable risk and adoption of a logical and systematic mode of behavior. Planning therefore allows one to avoid crisis management by utilizing a more fluid, rational and well-thought out contingency approach which is followed by an action plan. This approach allows entrepreneurs to take advantage of opportunities they have identified through their research and investigation.

Impediments that hinder planning

In a review of studies where planning was conspicuously absent, Robinson and Pearce (1983) described the planning attempts as 'unstructured, irregular and uncomprehensive.'

Attempts were seldom formalized, rarely communicated, and followed a reactive or passive approach which is characterized by the acceptance of the first attractive option.

In many cases, entrepreneurs have their business plan only in their mind. It is often felt that this conceptual plan or vision is enough to see the organization through its difficult periods to its ultimate success. Often the entrepreneur does not have a 'handle' on all the variables and uncertainties which should be incorporated into the plan. Robinson and Pearce (1984) believe that entrepreneurs

'have minimal exposure to and knowledge of the planning process. They are uncertain as to components of the process and their sequence. They are unfamiliar with many planning information sources and with how they should be utilized.'

Hence it is not unusual for entrepreneurs to consider planning relatively worthless and unimportant. In addition to the difficulty of writing a business plan, several obstacles make it troublesome for entrepreneurs to use this tool in the manner proposed in the literature. The business founder can be considered the crucial factor influencing and determining the planning activities. His or her intensity of conviction or attitude toward the importance of planning is one of the decisive determinants of planning behavior. It is a well known fact that many entrepreneurs prefer to manage their enterprises on the basis of instinct, intuition and 'gut feel', or, as Stoner and Fry (1987) state that some entrepreneurs feel that 'intuitive, unwritten plans are sufficient' (p. 7).

An additional reason why entrepreneurs do not plan is the lack of time available for planning (Golde, 1984). Most of them are involved in the day-to-day business and do not find time to structure their future systematically. They believe it is important for managers of large businesses to plan but 'unnecessary for owners of small businesses' (Stoner and Fry, 1987). The time commitment needed to work out a formal business plan for a new venture is rather high and has been empirically verified as a planning barrier (Sautner, 1985). Entrepreneurs report that their time is scarce and have difficulty concentrating on planning given their persistent and continual operating problems. A comparatively simple business plan can take up to six months of concerted effort (Timmons et al., 1985). For a more complex venture, developing a formal plan can take nine months to a year (Kuriloff and Hemphill, 1988).

The time required could provide one reason why Siropolis (1986, p. 137) suggested that only 5% of entrepreneurs prepare formal business plans. Frank et al. (1989), in their comprehensive review of new venture studies, concluded that the frequency of formal planning by entrepreneurs ranged between 20% and 50 %. Bamberger (1986) reported that only 15 % of his sample of small business owners developed written business plans for more than three years in advance.

The costs are often judged to be higher than the benefits of planning. Because of the extensive time commitments required to complete a comprehensive business plan, considerable financial outlays may be necessary. This is especially true when an external consultant is called in to assist or write the plan. Some entrepreneurs fear that systematic plans will reduce their firms' flexibility to adapt quickly to environmental changes. Locking in on one particular plan may constrain the search for creative solutions (Osborne, 1987). Other entrepreneurs are concerned with their perceived loss of control. Robinson and Pearce (1984) report that entrepreneurs 'are highly sensitive and guarded about their businesses and decisions that affect them. Consequently, they are hesitant to share their strategic planning with employees or outside consultants.'

Once their formal plan has been written, they may feel a sense of loss because they shared their idea(s) with others. Their underlying assumptions can be examined and questioned and held under scrutiny (Posner, 1988). They have invited 'outsiders' into their own 'private' world, thus losing some of their entrepreneurial ego (Osborne, 1987).

A further barrier to planning may be the perception by some entrepreneurs that planning is not related to performance, profit or other measures of success. Bracker and Pearson (1986) cite seven studies which concluded that there was no significant positive relationship between planning and financial performance. Kallman (1977), Kallman and Shapiro (1980) and Shuman (1975, 1985) also found no relationship between them.

Also, the entrepreneurial firm may not have access to the experience, expertise or trained employees needed to perform the formal planning function. In some cases entrepreneurs must wear many hats as generalists and often lack certain specialized skills that are necessary in the planning process. In other cases, Golde (1984) found that entrepreneurs may tend to focus on technical aspects rather than on ill-defined managerial problems. Others consider financial problems and legislation/regulation more important than planning. Entrepreneurs are in a constant struggle with critical issues that demand their attention because they may have affect the firm's survival. The factors discussed above provide some reasons and justifications for why the intensity of planning conviction may be low.

Factors that foster (stimulate) planning

In the counter-argument, both researchers and practitioners attest to the importance of planning. Steiner (1967) was one of the first scholars to recognize the benefits of long-range planning in entrepreneurial firms: 'long range planning today is looking ahead in a methodical, organized and conscious fashion. Managers have found that formalization of the long range planning process produces better results' (p.3). Since Steiner, numerous scholars also have indicated that benefits accrue to new ventures which engage in formal planning (Hisrich and Peters, 1989; Kuratko and Hogdetts, 1989; Kuriloff and Hemphill, 1988; Ackelsberg and Arlow, 1985; Thurston, 1983; Welsh and White, 1983). The entrepreneur needs to systematically consider the opportunities and threats and determine the strengths and weaknesses of the venture (Hisrich and Peters, 1989; Timmons et al., 1985; Cohen, 1983; Thune and House, 1970). This analysis provides the entrepreneur with an evaluation of the risks and pitfalls involved in the undertaking (Kuratko and Hodgetts, 1989). Ramanujam and Venkatraman (1987) stress the importance of planning roles that not only determine the system's effectiveness but also enhance its creativity and innovation.

Entrepreneurs also need the ability to activate their concept and to install it in others, to have the discipline to sit down and plan (Timmons et al., 1985) what they aim to do, and to put the entrepreneur's enthusiasm and vision on paper in the form of a business plan, enabling one to think through all facets of the new venture. This vision of the future is what pulls the entrepreneur through the day-to-day details and problems that must be dealt with in coping with the future.

However, to be effective, every long-range planning system must achieve a 'workable compromise' between vision and realism (Shank et al., 1973). Such a compromise can be readily implemented by varying those design features of planning which relate to the plan's interface with budgeting and financing. This component of planning is concerned with gathering financial (and non-financial) resources to operate the new venture. This planning process can take the form of receiving assistance from external sources, seeking venture capital, convincing investors to inject money into the enterprise and persuading suppliers to grant the new venture credit. This process of assembling and obtaining resources is a major aspect of entrepreneurial effort as described in the prescriptive literature (Rich and Gumpert, 1985; Hisrich and Peters, 1989; Kuratko and Hodgetts, 1989; Timmons et al.,

1985; Schilit, 1987; Block and MacMillian, 1985; Henderson, 1988). Robinson and Pearce (1984) suggested that 'systematic incorporation' of both internal and external resources 'should enhance creativity and ultimately the firm's performance' (p. 30). Rich and Gumpert, (1985) see the business plan as the 'ticket to the investment process' geared toward bankers, lenders, venture capitalists, investors, creditors and promoting or subsidizing institutions. Thus the plan is viewed as the instrument to increase the probability of gaining financial or other resources.

The plan is also a guide and a blueprint for decision making (Burch, 1986; Church, 1984; Baumback, 1981). As the firm's direction becomes clearer, employees can be 'allowed to make more crucial decisions and to utilize their skills more fully' (Stoner and Fry, 1987, p. 9). Also, the business plan can be used as an orientation device for new employees and outsiders as well as a training tool for employee development (Kao, 1981; Longenecker and Moore, 1987). In the long run, the business plan should be used to control and manage the new venture.

The empirical evidence also shows that there is a link between business planning and performance (Frank et al., 1989). In their comprehensive review of studies of long-range planning for small firms between 1958 and 1983 Robinson and Pearce (1984) concluded that, in general 'strategic planning is of value to the small firm' (p. 129). Sexton and Van Auken (1985) as well as Bracker and Pearson (1986) concluded that 'planning processes that are well-developed, soundly implemented, and properly controlled contribute to a firm's success' (p. 503).

A critical lesson was learned by unsuccessful entrepreneurs studied by Frank et al. (1989), who concluded that risk reduction as a planning purpose is more important for unsuccessful than for successful entrepreneurs. Going through the formal planning process increases the odds of survival because the plan serves as a roadmap for success.

If the entrepreneur is made aware of the links between planning and success, it is assumed that his/her conviction to planning should be fairly high. The arguments above suggest a high level of planning conviction among those 'zealots.' The research question is, 'What other variables are associated with this planning conviction?'

Research design

On the basis of the above discussion the research question further evolved to: What are the factors that differentiate between those entrepreneurs with intense planning value conviction and those with low planning value conviction?

Planning value conviction

Some entrepreneurs are convinced of the value and benefits of planning and have a strong conviction that it is absolutely necessary. The intensity of their belief has been established and reinforced by successful outcomes of previous planning efforts through achievement of performance objectives and financial rewards. This group can be considered staunch believers in the value of planning. For this study this group will be called 'planning zealots.'

Other entrepreneurs are less convinced of the value and benefits of planning and do not have strong belief it is absolutely necessary. They are indifferent or believe that planning may reduce the firm's flexibility and may have little impact on performance and profitability. This group can be considered sceptics that doubt or scoff at the perceived benefits of planning. This group will be called 'indifferent/non-believers.'

242

Predictions

Managerial approaches. Managerial approaches were composed of planning behavior, decision making styles and tools utilized by the management of the venture. Committed entrepreneurs tend to have a strong belief in the successful outcome of his/her ability, idea, market niche and career choice that they are convinced that planning should take place to improve the chances of success. Entrepreneurs are often called upon to solve complex and ill-structured problems. Multiple skills are needed to reduce those problems into solvable units. Problem solving thus requires the planning process.

It was expected that planning zealots have a different planning behavior than indifferent/non-believers. In this study a concept developed by Frank et al. (1990) was used to measure planning behavior. The two factors, *strategic vision* (seven item list) and *resource assembling* (five item list), represented the important and distinguishing elements of the planning process. Strategic vision was described as the ability to conceptualize the essentials of the enterprise in terms of its comprehensiveness, its strengths, the evaluation of opportunities, goal specification and control mechanism. Resource assembling represented the ability to convince investors and acquire capital, to receive assistance and to persuade suppliers to grant credit.

It was also expected that planning zealots would engage in *proactive* and *rational* decision making as a managerial style, incorporate an *emphasis on growth*, and identify a *time horizon*. Similarly, planning zealots would apply analytical *management tools*, such as an internal analysis of strength and weaknesses of functional management areas more intensely than indifferent/non-believers. These analytical activities are almost inherent in the planning process, and a higher utilization of such tools is expected for planning zealots.

Industry structure. Industry structure included *intensity of competition, ease of entry* and *stabilization of the industry*. It was expected that *intensity of competition* and *ease of entry* would be positively related to planning connection. More competition and higher barriers of entry force the entrepreneur to invest extra effort in generating a more comprehensive set of alternatives as he/she seeks to make more optimum decisions in order to compete more effectively.

In terms of *stabilization of the industry*, it was expected that planning zealots would operate in more stable environments. In more unstable environments many of the critical factors are ill-defined, thus making planning less valuable and convictions would wane. As the industry becomes more stable, more factors would be predictable allowing the firm to anticipate and design its planning path and place greater weight on planning.

New venture demographics. New venture demographics are composed of size and performance oriented measures. It was expected that planning zealots would have larger sized ventures than indifferent believers since larger sized ventures will be more complex and require greater coordination as well as a rational plan for managing and controlling a myriad of activities. Size of the venture was operationalized with *sales, number of employees* and *initial capital invested*.

It was further expected that the performance-related demographic variables *profitability, net profit* and *employee growth* would distinguish between the two groups. Successful growth calls for planning activities to take place so that additional growth is channelled in a continuous, rational manner and not in an uncontrolled or random fashion.

Method

A questionnaire was created which included a series of questions on formality of planning, as well as demographic, managerial and industry information. The entrepreneurs in the sample were asked to respond to their convictions about the value of planning activities in the firm. The questionnaire contained a four item list of planning conviction characteristics. The answering pattern were analyzed and cases with internal inconsistencies were eliminated The range of the responses was on a five point scale from (1) Strongly Agree to (5) Strongly Disagree. By separating subjects at the mean, they were grouped into subsamples of 'indifferent/non-believers' and 'zealots.'

The questions were based on a comprehensive review of the theoretical and empirical literature; also original items were generated specifically for this study. The instrument was pretested and revised two times over a period of three months.

To test the impact of the different identified groups an ANOVA [SAS, 1988] and Duncan's multiple range test [Duncan, 1955] were performed. All data were analyzed using SAS package (SAS Institute, 1988).

Sample

Four thousand seven hundred thirty-five (4735) questionnaires were mailed to a randomly selected sample of a Dun and Bradstreet list of northeastern Illinois entrepreneurs. The target population included manufacturers, service companies and retail/wholesale companies. Six hundred nineteen (619) (13.1 % response rate) were returned. Twenty questionnaires were not usable, reducing the usable response rate to 12.7 %.

Results and discussion

The research question was whether there were any differences between planning zealots with a high level of conviction regarding the value of planning and the indifferent/non-believer group. Differences were expected in the categories of planning behavior, decision-making style, analytical tools, industry structure and business demographics. Significant differences between the two groups appeared in planning behavior variables of *strategic vision* and *resource assembling* (Table 1).

Entrepreneurs with intense planning convictions had higher levels of *strategic vision* which is characterized as an intellectual concept which drives the business. It is also seen as a long-term challenge of sustaining an entrepreneurial culture and keen awareness of the burden of instilling a sense of future directional balance. It is often the process of putting the entrepreneur's enthusiasm and vision on paper in the form of a business plan. Entrepreneurs with intense planning convictions also engaged in higher levels of *resource assembling*, which often takes the form of acquiring assistance from external sources, seeking venture capital, convincing investors to inject money into the enterprise and persuading suppliers to grant the new venture credit. Entrepreneurs not engaging in resource assembling behavior had less intense planning convictions.

Significant differences between the two groups were also found in the decision-making style of the entrepreneurs. Those entrepreneurs with intense planning convictions had a more *proactive* and *rational* decision-making process and had identified a *time horizon* in their plans. Their convictions must have been strong enough to begin implementing their plans through the decision-making process. Convinced of the value of planning, they proceeded to take their concept(s) to the next stage and carry out their plan by bringing it to fruition. They further operationalized their plan by identifying a time horizon or deadline wherein these goals should be met.

Further implementation of their goals was seen in the analytical tools which planning zealots utilized. *Assessments of strengths and weaknesses* in the areas of *finance, marketing, personnel, products* and *management* as well as the *identification of target markets* and *changing customer requirements* were all associated with stronger planning conviction. Indifferent/non-believers utilized significantly fewer analytical tools, perhaps because they did not see the connection between the goals and the means to accomplish them.

No differences were found in the industry structure variables of *ease of entry, intensity of competition* and *stability of the environment*. This is surprising since one of the ways of coping with or responding to hostile elements and external threats would be with a business plan based on strong planning conviction. However, other variables appear to be more strongly related to planning conviction than industry and environmental ones.

Several business demographic variables showed significant differences between planning zealots and indifferent/non-believers. Entrepreneurs with a higher level of total *initial in vested capital* had more intense planning conviction ($75,000 to $100,000) than those with lower planning conviction ($50,000 to $75,000). Planning zealots also placed a higher emphasis on the goal of *growth* when they started their business. This intention of 'growing the firm' rather than sitting back enjoying the status quo may have been a factor in generating a strong planning conviction. These entrepreneurs believed that they would be able to accomplish and carry out the growth objective they had established. Entrepreneurs with strong planning conviction also had a higher *net profit* as a percentage of sales than those with less planning conviction. It is difficult to specify a causality relationship with these statistics, but there appears to be some evidence that planning zealots are more successful.

Conclusion

Planning zealots were characterized by a higher profit, greater initial investment and placed greater emphasis on growth. The question is whether these successful attributes are the result of their following through with implementation behaviors based on their intense planning conviction. The relationships found to be significant appear to follow a normative pattern of beneficial outcomes accruing to those who believe in the value of planning.

Of course, intensity of belief in planning is not enough to bring about successful growth. Statistical evidence reported here indicates that planning zealots followed through in their conviction by utilizing analytical managerial tools, engaged in formal planning processes and were proactive and rational in their decision behavior and established targets and time horizons to accomplish their goals.

Table 1
Descriptive statistics and ANOVA tests

	SS	F	Planning Zealots Mean	Indifferent/ Non-Believers Mean
Planning Behavior				
Strategic Vision	1343.76	52.30***	21.79 A	18.83 B
Resource Assembling	273.67	13.58***	14.02 A	12.65 B
Decision-Making Style				
Pro Active Decision Behavior	22.87	24.93***	2.12 A	2.53 B
Rational Decision Behavior	10.47	9.33**	2.18 A	2.45 B
Planning Time Horizon	6.74	8.54**	2.39 A	2.18 B
Analytical Tools				
Financial Strengths	13.82	13.58***	3.32 A	3.02 B
Customer Change	6.03	6.73**	3.31 A	3.12 B
Marketing Strengths	11.39	12.26***	3.12 A	2.86 B
Personnel Strengths	2.62	3.09 a	3.22 A	3.09 A
Identifying Markets	14.81	14.97***	3.21 A	2.91 B
Product Strengths	10.48	8.75**	3.17 A	2.92 B
Management Strengths	7.96	7.76**	3.15 A	2.93 B
Industry Structure				
Ease of Entry	0.16	0.20	2.56 A	2.60 A
Intensity of Competition	0.30	0.60	1.63 A	1.67 A
Business Environment	0.02	0.04	1.98 A	1.97 A
Business Demographics				
Sales	11.08	1.24	9.93 A	9.67 A
Current Employees	1182.36	2.65	19.86 A	16.98 A
Initial Capital Invested	186.17	17.80***	4.29 A	3.20 B
Emphasis on Growth	11.02	11.02**	3.01 A	2.74 B
Employee Growth	90.62	0.30	10.03 A	10.83 A
Net Profit in % of Sales	9.68	5.09*	4.25 A	4.00 B

Means with the same letter are not significantly different.
a = $p \leq .10$, * = $p \leq .05$, ** = $p \leq .01$, *** = $p \leq .001$.

Notes

[1] In this research 'formal planning' and 'business planning' are used synonymously.

References

Ackelsberg, R., and Arlow, P. (1985), 'Small Businesses Do Plan and It Pays Off', *Long Range Planning*, vol. 18, no. 5, 61-67.

Bamberger, I. (1986), 'Values and Strategic Behaviour', *Management International Review*, vol. 26, no. 4, 57-69.

Baumback, C.M. (1981), *Baumback's Guide to Entrepreneurship: What It Takes and How To Do It*, Englewood Cliffs.

Block, Z., and MacMillian, I.C. (1985), 'Milestones for successful venture planning', *Harvard Business Review*, vol. 63, Sept/Oct, 184-196.

Bracker, J.S., and Pearson, J.N. (1986), 'Planning and Financial Performance of Small, Mature Firms', *Strategic Management Journal*, vol. 7, no. 4, 503-522.

Burch, J.G. (1986), *Entrepreneurship*, New York: Wiley.

Church, O.D. (1984), *Small Business Management and Entrepreneurship*, Chicago: South-Western Publishing.

Cohen, W.A.,(1983), *The Entrepreneur & Small Business Problem Solver: An Encyclopedic Reference and Guide*, New York.

Duncan, D.B. (1955), 'Multiple Range and Multiple F-Tests', *Biometrics*, vol. 11, 1-42.

Frank, H., Plaschka, G.R., Roessl, D., and Welsch, H.P. (1990), 'Planning Behavior in New Ventures: A Comparison Between Chicago and Vienna Entrepreneurs', *Frontiers of Entrepreneurship Research*, Wellesley: Babson College.

Frank, H., Plaschka, G.R., and Roessl, D. (1989), 'Planning Behavior of Successful and Non-Successful Founders of New Ventures', *Journal of Entrepreneurship and Economic Development*, vol. 1, no. 2, 191-206.

Gilmore, F.F. (1971), 'Formulating strategy in smaller companies', *Harvard Business Review*, vol. 49, May/June, 71-81.

Golde, R.A. (1984), 'Practical Planning for Small Business' in Gumpert D.E. (ed.), *Growing Concerns:Building and Managing the Smaller Business*, New York: Wiley, 343-359.

Grant, J.L. and King, W.R., *The Logic of Strategic Planning*, Boston: Little, Brown, 1982.

Henderson, J.W. (1988), *Obtaining Venture Financing: Principles and Practices*, Lexington: Lexington Books.

Hisrich, R.D., and Peters, M.P. (1989), *Entrepreneurship: Starting, Developing, and Managing a New Enterprise*, Homewood: Irwin.

Kallman, E.A., and Shapiro, H.J. (1980), 'The Motor Freight Industry-A Case Against Planning', *Long Range Planning*, vol. 11, no.1, 81-86.

Kallmann, E. (1977), *An Empirical Study of Long-Range Planning in the Motor Freight Industry*, Unpublished doctoral dissertation, City University of New York.

Kao, R.W. (1981), *Small Business Management:A Strategic Emphasis*, Toronto.

Kuriloff, A.H., and Hemphill, J.M. (1988), *Starting and Managing the Small Business*, 2nd ed., New York: Harper Row.

Kuratko D.F., and Hogdetts R.M. (1989), *Entrepreneurship: A Contemporary Approach*, Chicago: Dryden Press.

Longenecker, J.G., and Moore, C.W., (1987), *Small-Business Management*, 7th ed., Cincinnati: South-Western Publishing.

Osborne, L.B. (1987), 'Planning: The Entrepreneurial Ego at Work', *Business Horizons*, January/February, 20-24.

Pearce, J.A., Robbins, D.K., Robinson, R.B. (1987), 'The Impact of Grand Strategy and Planning Formality on Financial Performance', *Strategic Management Journal*, vol. 8, 125-134.

Posner, B.G. (1988), 'Real Entrepreneurs Don't Plan', *Inc.*, November, 128-130.

Ramanujam, V., and Venkatraman, N. (1987) 'Planning and Performance: New Look at an Old Question', *Business Horizons*, May-June, 19-25.

Rich, R.S., and Gumpert, D.E. (1985), *Business Plans That Win $$$*, New York: Harper Row.

Robinson, R.B., and Pearce, J.A. (1984), 'Research Thrusts in Small Firm Strategic Planning', *Academy of Management Review*, vol. 9, no.1, 128-137.

Robinson, R.B., Jr., and Pearce, J.A. (1983), 'The Impact of Formalized Strategic Planning on Financial Performance in Small Organizations', *Strategic Management Journal*, vol. 4, 197-207.

SAS Institute Inc. (1988), *SAS/STAT User's Guide, Release 6.03 Edition*, Cary, NC:SAS Institute Inc.

Sautner, M (1985), *Motive und Probleme der Unternehmensgruendung*, Wien: Service Publishing.

Schilit, W.K. (1987), 'How to Write a Winning Business Plan', *Business Horizons*, Sept/Oct., 13-24.

Sexton, D.L, and Van Auken, P. (1985), 'A Longitudinal Study of Small Business Strategic Planning', *Journal of Small Business Management*, vol. 23, no. 1, 7-15.

Shank, J.K., Niblock, E.G., and Sandalls, W.T. (1973), 'Balance `Creativity' and `Practically' in Formal Planning', *Harvard Business Review*, vol. 51, Jan/Feb, 87-96.

Shuman, J.C. (1975), 'Corporate Planning in Small Companies: A Survey', *Long Range Planning*, vol. 8, 81-90.

Shuman, J.C., Shaw, J.J., and Sussman, G. (1985), 'Strategic Planning in Smaller Rapid Growth Companies', *Long Range Planning*, vol. 18, no. 5, 48-53.

Siropolis, N.C. (1986), *Small Business Management: A Guide to Entrepreneurship*, 3rd ed.,Boston: Houghton Mifflin.

Steinhoff, D., and Burgess, J.F. (1986), *Small Business Management Fundamentals*, 4th ed., New York.

Steiner, G.A. (1967), 'Approaches to Long-Range Planning for Small Business', *California Management Review*, vol. 10, 3-16.

Stoner C.R., and Fry, F.L. (1987), *Strategic Planning in the Small Business*, Cincinnati: South-Western Publishing.

Thune, S.S., and House, R.J., (1970), 'Where Long-range Planning Pays Off-Findings of a Survey of Formal and Informal Planners', *Business Horizons*, vol. 13, no. 4, 81-87.

Thurston, P.H. (1983), Should Smaller Companies Make Formal Plans?, *Harvard Business Review*, vol. 61, Sept/Oct, 162-188.

Timmons, J.A., Smollen, L.E., and Dingee, A.L. (1985), *New Venture Creation. A Guide to Entrepreneurship*, 2nd ed., Homewood: Irwin.

Welsh, J.A., and White, J.F. (1983), *The Entrepreneur's Master Planning Guide: How to Launch A Successful Business*, Englewood Cliffs.

Part 6
Entrepreneurial versus administrative behaviour

16 Profiling entrepreneurs: Multiple perspectives and consequent methodological considerations

Elizabeth Chell and Jean M. Haworth

Problems of identification of entrepreneurs

Research, the purpose of which has been to identify the personality attributes of entrepreneurs, has been severely criticised (Chell, 1985; Ginsberg and Buchholz, 1989; Sexton 1987; Stevenson and Sahlman, 1989; Wortman, 1986). A critical problem which has bedevilled attempts to explore the attributes of entrepreneurs is the lack of an agreed definition amongst scholars and lay personnel. This has resulted in some empirical studies in which business owner, or business founder have been used as equivalent to 'entrepreneur' and hence the results of such studies have often yielded conflicting findings. Furthermore, various researchers have focused upon different traits as being definitive and have paid scant attention to the identification of sets of attributes. The upshot is a dearth of studies which attempt to differentiate or single out the truly entrepreneurial individual from amongst other business owners.

Lack of an agreed definition

In 1971, Kilby (quoting from A.A. Milne) intrigued his readers by comparing the search for entrepreneurial traits with 'the hunt for the Heffalump'. A key point being made was that we all feel we know an entrepreneur when we see and meet one but we are unable to describe the definitive set of characteristics which distinguish them. Other researchers have put forward definitions which have emphasised different characteristics (Carland et al., 1984; Ginsberg and Buchholz, 1989; Harwood, 1982; Hull et al., 1980; Meredith et al., 1982; Stevenson, 1983; Timmons et al., 1985), whilst still others have investigated the presence of single, distinguishing traits (Boyd, 1984; Brockhaus, 1982; Hoy and Carland, 1983; Kets de Vries, 1977; McClelland, 1961, 1965; Schere, 1982).

Equivocal research findings A number of traits have been put forward as attributes which distinguish an entrepreneur from the general populace or more usually from a manager or non-founder. Examples which have been more extensively researched are: need for achievement (McClelland, 1961, 1965; Hull et al., 1980; Begley and Boyd, 1986), locus of control (Brockhaus and Nord, 1979; Brockhaus, 1982) and risk taking behaviour (Palmer, 1971; Kilby, 1971; Brockhaus, 1980; Timmons et al., 1985).

In all three cases the evidence is conflicting and open to interpretation, largely as a consequence of the differing use of the term 'entrepreneur'. For example, Hull et al. (1980) found potential entrepreneurs to have a greater propensity to take risks. Their definition of 'entrepreneur' included anyone who owned a business, assumed risk for the sake of profit *and* had the explicit intention of expanding the business. Whereas Brockhaus (1980) defined 'entrepreneur' as an owner-manager of a business venture not employed elsewhere and confined his sample to people who had very recently decided to become owner-managers. He could not distinguish the risk-taking propensity of new entrepreneurs from managers or from the general population.

In the case of risk-taking, a key issue appears to be: from whose perspective is the decision or action considered to be risky? A multiple perspectives approach facilitates clearer thinking. Thus, from an observer's perspective the business person or entrepreneur may be viewed as a risk-taker. From the business person's perspective, he or she may see themselves as 'hedging their bets' and attempting to minimise risk.

A set of entrepreneurial attributes There has been little attention given to the identification of a set of attributes which distinguish the entrepreneur. However, the research evidence suggests that we do not know precisely what personality attribute or set of attributes distinguish entrepreneurs from other business owners, managers or the population generally. Some researchers have put forward a set of such characteristics, but whilst there may be some commonality they are not identical and quite often the population sampled is different. For example, they may be based upon a sample of business start-ups, successful versus average or unsuccessful business owners, ideal types of entrepreneur, etc. (McClelland, 1987; Meredith et al., 1982; Timmons et al., 1985).

Methodology adopted

A further problem is the actual methodology adopted. For example, the use of psychometric measures holds in its wake a number of problems. It assumes that the individuating traits are known, whereas the psychometric approach does not indicate what attribute should be measured, that is, the determination of an appropriate set of attributes is logically a prior exercise. Second, most, if not all, psychometric measures have been developed for purposes other than the measurement of traits in the entrepreneurial setting. A third assumption made is that the trait concept assumed by the psychometrician is appropriate in the context of this type of research. This is particularly questionable given that psychometric tests do not allow for an assessment of important contextual influences on the respondent's behaviour. Furthermore, there are practical difficulties with the use of a battery of psychometric tests in the field, in that they are neither sympathetically received nor taken seriously by most business owners. Given such difficulties, it is contended that an alternative method must be adopted.

Recent work of the authors in the field of entrepreneurship

Chell et al. (1991) put forward a research paradigm for the differentiation of types of business owner and their businesses. The main aspects of the method adopted are that: (i) it is holistic; (ii) it assumes a particular social psychological theory of personality; (iii) it assumes further that it is possible to differentiate amongst a heterogeneous set of business owners by identifying critical contextual dimensions which, along with the personality dimension, form the basis of a three fold typology; (iv) it adopts neural networks as a means of modelling the expert judgement underpinning the categorisation so that it can be used for prediction purposes (that is, to reduce the reliance on the 'expert' in the future).

The holistic method

Entrepreneurial and other business behaviours are explored using an holistic method. This comprises a biographical approach and the adoption of a critical incident technique. A drawback of this method is that it is time consuming; the ability to refine this technique such that key entrepreneurial behaviours are reliably distinguished is highly desirable.

The constructivist theory of personality

Hampson (1982, 1988) has propounded a social psychological theory of personality which assumes that personality traits do not reside *within* individuals but *between* actors in varying social contexts. In order to assess an individual's personality it is important to take into account *multiple perspectives*. Further, Hampson assumes that traits are categorising concepts which classify observed behaviours. This theory has aroused considerable controversy yet it has a number of attractions with respect to the research being proposed. The presence or absence of a particular trait is based upon observed behaviours. Evidence is gleaned from a number of perspectives not simply from that of the expert (the researcher) or from self reports, etc. It assumes behavioural consistency, as does trait theory, and it poses a problem for the researchers as to how to reconcile contradictory evidence.

Hampson advocates the adoption of Rosch's concept of 'prototypicality' as the criterion of category membership (Rosch, 1978). This raises the issue of the breadth or narrowness of a particular trait term: for example 'restless' is rather more inclusive than the somewhat narrower concept of 'fidgety'. It is clear that an important advantage of using the Hampson approach is that it enables the researcher to relate personality traits to business behaviours. This affords the method considerable face validity. One criticism is that constructivism is about person perception and not the measurement of personality *per se*. This criticism appears to assume that perceived personality is a gross distortion of actual personality and

Table 1

Attributes used for the categorisation of business owners and their firms

```
Alert to business opportunities      Yes = 1    No = 0
Pursues opportunities regardless
         of current resources        Yes = 1    No = 0
Adventurous                          Yes = 1    No = 0
Ideas person                         Yes = 1    No = 0
Restless/easily bored                Yes = 1    No = 0
High profile image-maker             Yes = 1    No = 0
Proactive                            Yes = 1    No = 0

Innovative                           High   = 3
                                     Medium = 2
                                     Low    = 1

Financial strategy                   Broad  = 3
                                     Medium = 2
                                     Narrow = 1

Has formal minuted meetings          Yes = 1    No = 0
Roles are clearly defined            Yes = 1    No = 0

Has structured strategic plans       Yes = 1    No = 0
Planning is informal                 Yes = 1    No = 0

Employment               Number employed in 1989

Age group of owner                   55+yr.  = 4
                                     45-54yr.= 3
                                     35-44yr.= 2
                                     25-34yr.= 1

Age of business          Number of years

Has previous business experience/
                   training          Yes = 1    No = 0
Founded                              Yes = 1    No = 0
Bought                               Yes = 1    No = 0
Inherited                            Yes = 1    No = 0
Has a professional management team   Yes = 1    No = 0
Sons/daughters in the business       Yes = 1    No = 0
Has shown reluctance to change       Yes = 1    No = 0
Wants to grow in numbers employed    Yes = 1    No = 0

Change in employment                 Increased = 1
                                     Stable    = 0
                                     Decreased =-1

Change in floorspace                 Increased = 1
                                     Stable    = 0
                                     Decreased =-1
```

Source: Chell et al. (1991)

that only personality psychologists can assess the latter (Hampson, 1984,1988). Hampson presents two arguments. Firstly, she points out that there is no truly objective study of personality; test-designers rely on their beliefs about trait-behaviour relations as do lay people. Secondly, the assessment of personality relies on an inference from the observed behaviour or behaviour ratings; personality cannot be observed directly only behavioural acts. The assessment of personality ultimately relies upon perception and inference.

Typology of business owners and their businesses

Using the concept of prototypicality, a three-fold typology was put forward which includes: (a) a set of entrepreneurial person attributes which Chell et al. (1991) suggest distinguish the entrepreneur from other types of business owners; and, (b) a further set of contextual factors which enabled the stage of development of the business and growth orientation to be identified (see Table 1).

Description of attributes associated with different types A set of key ingredients was identified such that the blend of these ingredients determines the categorisation of the business owner into four basic level categories. These are defined as entrepreneur, quasi-entrepreneur, administrator and caretaker. Further, the nature of the firm was defined in terms of its stage of development and its growth orientation. Stage of development comprised three stages: post start-up, established and professionally-managed. Start-up firms were deliberately excluded. Growth orientation included four categories of growth: declining, plateauing, rejuvenating and expanding.

Subsets of attributes were considered to be associated primarily with a particular typology. However, it is important to be aware of the interactions of all the attributes in determining the categorisations on the three dimensions and that the attributes are not necessarily exclusively associated with a particular dimension. Questions arise as to the completeness of this set, whether other dimensions should also be identified, and/or whether a parsimonious set of characteristics might be arrived at after further refinements of the method.

Type of business owner Nine defining characteristics of the business owner were identified such that the prototypical 'entrepreneur' and the prototypical 'caretaker' fell at the opposite ends of a spectrum.

The prototypical entrepreneur is alert to business opportunities which will be pursued if thought to have a moderate to high probability of success, regardless of resources currently controlled. That is, they will pursue the opportunity in the confidence that the necessary resources will follow. In essence this means that entrepreneurs are proactive that is, they take the initiative, attempting to control events rather than simply reacting to them. Entrepreneurs are also highly innovative. This may be manifested by innovation in product or service, markets served, means of production and/or fixed asset investment. In addition to using available resources, entrepreneurs utilise a variety of sources of finance such as bank loans, overdrafts, hire purchase, leasing and various government or local authority grants (cf. Smith, 1967, pp.46-7).

In developing the business, the entrepreneur strives to be the best, seeking opportunities to enhance the visibility of the company through the development of an image or product concept. In so doing they promote themselves by developing elaborate business networks, thus establishing the reputation of the company and creating a high profile. In this regard the entrepreneur is a high profile image-maker.

Entrepreneurs appear to become bored easily. This results in visible restlessness and a need to constantly modify their environment in order to create stimulation. One other coping behaviour which sustains their interest is the pursuit of a challenge as is demonstrated in many of their business activities. In this regard the entrepreneur may be viewed as both adventurous and an ideas-person. The intuitive way in which the entrepreneur sees an opportunity, and is able to develop ideas for exploiting it, results in a highly dynamic situation. Entrepreneurs thus create situations which result in change.

In all these nine attributes, the entrepreneur contrasts with the prototypical 'caretaker' who possesses none of these.

Between these two extremes we have defined two other categories, the prototypes for which are less clearly defined. The quasi-entrepreneur has many, but not all, of the characteristics in common with the entrepreneur. The prototype is that of someone who is adventurous, an ideas-person, a high profile image-maker, moderately innovative and proactive plus a mixture of other entrepreneurial characteristics. The prototypical administrator is reactive rather than proactive; they are moderately innovative and they may take opportunities but not regardless of current resources. As in the case of the entrepreneur they utilise a wide variety of sources of finance.

Stage of development of the business The prototypical professionally-managed business is relatively formal, of a size sufficient to support a professional management team and an owner-manager who has had previous business experience and/or training. The prototypical established business is semi-formal in its management procedures and insufficiently resourced to have a professional management team. The prototypical post start-up firm has an under-developed infrastructure, low employment levels and has been trading for a relatively short period of time.

Level of formality is defined by whether or not the company has: (i) formal minuted meetings, (ii) clearly defined roles, (iii) structured strategic plans, (iv) implicit or explicit operational plans.

It is also suggested that there is an association between the age and experience of the person and the stage of development of the business. For example, the younger person with no previous business experience or training is unlikely to be leading a professionally-managed business.

Growth orientation In the prototypical expanding business the owner is not reluctant to change, intends to grow in terms of people employed, and has demonstrated growth over the past three years by increasing employment and floor space. In contrast, the declining business displays none of these attributes. In the rejuvenating business the owner has shown some reluctance to change but changing circumstances, often brought about by sons or daughters joining them in the business, result in some actual or desired growth. In the prototypical plateauing business, the owner is reluctant to change and consequently the business has experienced a period of arrested growth, whilst in the short term some contraction may have occurred. However, there is a particularly fuzzy boundary between the rejuvenating and the expanding firm. Rejuvenation suggests expansion after a period of stagnation or decline which begs the question: After how long a period of expansion does a rejuvenating become an expanding firm?

Adoption of neural networks

Using the research tools described, the heterogeneity of business owners has been captured in a systematic way. We may now pose the question, how might this qualitative technique of categorisation based on judgmental methods be modelled? Recent developments in the cognitive modelling of thought processes present a way forward. The unique ability of the human brain to perform categorisations, etc. has inspired researchers to develop systems that are thought to be used by the brain. Artificial neural networks is the result. We were able to train a network using twenty-six of the respondents' profiles and to predict the categorisations of the remaining five with a high degree of success (Chell et al., 1991). This aspect of the research will be the subject of a further paper.

Summary and discussion

The ability to develop a research paradigm for distinguishing between types of owners and their business has been clearly demonstrated. Several assumptions were made at the outset. They were that:
  (1) several types of business owner can be identified, of which one may be labelled 'entrepreneur';
  (2) entrepreneurs cannot be distinguished from non-entrepreneurs on the basis of one characteristic or trait; there is a set of interacting characteristics which require simultaneous investigation;
  (3) traits are categorising concepts which organise and make sense of actual behaviour observed from multiple perspectives (Hampson, 1988);
  (4) behaviours are prototypical of a particular trait but not exclusively so;
  (5) success of an enterprise may be distinguished from type of business owner;
  (6) stage of development of the business and growth orientation are critical dimensions of the business situation which need to be taken into account in order to understand the behaviour of the owner.

The size of the sample of business owners has inevitably been a constraint, although the research has never claimed to be anything other than exploratory.

The typology of business owners incorporates labels which are not universally accepted terms rendering the categorisation process difficult. Terms like 'entrepreneur' feature in our everyday language; for the lay person it is part of common parlance. But the definition assumed is largely *implicit*. An objective of the research being reported was to make *explicit* the defining attributes associated with such labels. The next question to be posed is to what extent the defining attributes of each type coincide with an 'expert' categorisation. Beyond this, a further angle which has not been explored is that of the impact of different cultural perspectives on the proposed typology of business owners.

Using terms like 'opportunistic', 'innovative', 'adventurous' to label aspects of entrepreneurial behaviour suggests that the latter is a multi-faceted construct. In terms of current thinking, the term 'entrepreneurial' is a relatively broad categorising concept. Our prototypical entrepreneur is *opportunistic, innovative, imaginative,* an *ideas-person,* an *agent of change, restless, adventurous, proactive* and *adopts a broad financial strategy.* There is some overlap between these trait terms which means that care is needed in the interpretation and categorisation of their behavioural manifestations. For instance, the pursuit of a particular business strategy might suggest both imagination and vision, so too might the development of a particular innovation or the pursuit of a particular opportunity. Further, the entrepreneur's ability to generate ideas might be managed by adopting the role of catalyst. A combination of imagination, awareness of an opportunity and adventurousness ensures that the entrepreneur takes the idea further. The interaction between such traits demonstrates the need to think of the entrepreneurial personality as a complex set of traits.

Is the quasi-entrepreneur, perhaps, a non-prototypical entrepreneur? Would such an assumption not simplify our categorisation of business owners? Clearly it would. The quasi-entrepreneur is at the fuzzy boundary between the entrepreneur and the administrator. However, whilst entrepreneurs are alive to opportunities with an eye to the main chance, quasi-entrepreneurs do not follow this through with the same conviction. They thus have a tendency to let opportunities go. This seems to 'dilute' other aspects of their otherwise entrepreneurial behaviour. It means, for example, that they are adventurous to a point; that they may be imaginative, but not in all areas of business activity, and so on. The quasi-entrepreneur nevertheless warrants separate categorisation.

The three fold categorisation and the holistic method which has been propounded in this paper raises other issues regarding the movement between categories. Social learning theories of development, for example, suggest that personal development occurs throughout life (Levinson, 1978). How might such an assumption articulate with the proposed typology of business owners? The empirical part of our investigation suggested strongly that it was highly unlikely that a caretaker would become an entrepreneur. On the other hand, it was possible for an entrepreneur to become a caretaker (Chell et al., 1991). We would add that the likelihood of a quasi-entrepreneur becoming an entrepreneur is quite high through the normal process of experiential learning. For the administrator such a transition was less likely; effectively, they did not feel comfortable with the entrepreneurial mode of management.

Categorisation of the business situation in terms of growth orientation and stage of development of the business was, of course, a reflection of the business owner's actions and decisions. Progression from one stage to another was not inevitable and there was the problem of transition to be addressed. Fieldwork showed quite clearly that the progression of the business could become arrested even in entrepreneurially-led firms, largely due to the inadequate people/communications skills of the owner. The problem was compounded by the reluctance of the owner to delegate those responsibilities which impacted upon the management of the human resource.

A final comment takes us back to criticisms of the methodology and the subject of this workshop. We have defined the characteristics of the entrepreneur in positive terms and the caretaker negatively. One way forward would be to attempt to achieve a balance by investigating the attributes which the entrepreneur and caretaker have most **and least** of.

Acknowledgements

We would like to thank the University of Salford Research Committee 1989 for their support in making available research monies to enable this research to be carried out. We are also grateful to the E.S.R.C. and the Nuffield Foundation for research grants which have enabled us to accumulate a body of knowledge and experience which has born fruit in the current project. Thanks are also due to the thirty one anonymous business owners who gave of their time freely and cheerfully.

References

BEGLEY, T.M. and BOYD, D.P. (1986) 'Psychological characteristics associated with entrepreneurial performance', in R. Ronstadt, J.A. Hornaday, R. Peterson and K.H. Vesper, (eds.) *Frontiers of Entrepreneurship Research*, Wellesley, Mass.: Babson College, Center for Entrepreneurial Studies: 146-165.

BOYD, D.P. (1984) 'Type A behaviour, financial performance and organizational growth in small business firms', *Journal of Occupational Psychology*, 57: 137-140.

BROCKHAUS, R.H. (1980) 'Risk taking propensity of entrepreneurs', *Academy of Management Journal*, 23, 3: 509-520.

BROCKHAUS, R.H. (1982) 'The psychology of the entrepreneur', in C.A. Kent, D.L. Sexton and K.H. Vesper, (eds.) *Encyclopedia of Entrepreneurship*, Englewood-Cliffs, N.J.: Prentice-Hall.

BROCKHAUS, R.H. and NORD, W.R. (1979) 'An exploration of factors affecting the entrepreneurial decision: personal characteristics vs. environmental conditions', *Proceedings of the National Academy of Management*.

CARLAND, J.W., HOY, F., BOULTON, W.R. and CARLAND, J.A.C. (1984) 'Differentiating entrepreneurs from small business owners: a conceptualization', *Academy of Management Review*, 9, 2: 354-359.

CHELL, E. (1985) 'The entrepreneurial personality: a few ghosts laid to rest?', *International Small Business Journal*, 3, 3: 43-54.

CHELL, E., HAWORTH, J.M. and BREARLEY, S.A. (1991) *The Entrepreneurial Personality: Concepts, Cases and Categories*, London: Routledge (forthcoming).

GINSBERG, A. and BUCHHOLTZ, A. (1989) 'Are entrepreneurs a breed apart? a look at the evidence. *Journal of General Management*, 15, 2: 32-40.

HAMPSON, S.E. (1982) *The Construction of Personality*, London: Routledge & Kegan Paul.

HAMPSON, S.E. (1984) 'Personality traits: in the eye of the beholder or the personality of the perceived?' in M.Cook (ed.) *Psychology in Progress: Issues in Person Perception*, London: Methuen

HAMPSON, S.E. (1988) *The Construction of Personality*, 2nd Ed. London: Routledge.

HARWOOD, E. (1982) 'The sociology of entrepreneurship', in C.A. Kent, et al. (eds.) *Encyclopedia of Entrepreneurship*, Englewood-Cliffs, N.J.: Prentice-Hall.

HOY, F. & CARLAND, J.W. (1983) 'Differentiating between entrepreneurs and small business owners in new venture formation', in J.A. Hornaday, J.A. Timmons and K.H. Vesper, (eds.) *Frontiers of Entrepreneurship Research*, Wellesley, Mass.: Babson Center for Entrepreneurial Studies: 157-166.

HULL, D.L. BOSLEY, J.J. and UDELL, G.G. (1980) 'Renewing the hunt for the heffalump: identifying potential entrepreneurs by personality characteristics', *Journal of Small Business*, 18, 1: 11-18.

KETS DE VRIES, M.F.R. (1977) 'The entrepreneurial personality: a person at the crossroads', *Journal of Management Studies*, (Feb.): 34-57.

KILBY, P.M. (ed) (1971) *Entrepreneurship and Economic Development*, New York: Macmillan.

LEVINSON, D.J. (1978) *The Seasons of a Man's Life*, New York: Knopf.

McCLELLAND, D.C. (1961) *The Achieving Society*, Princeton, N.J.: Van Nostrand.

McCLELLAND, D.C. (1965) 'Achievement motivation can be developed', *Harvard Business Review*, 43: 6-24, 178.

McCLELLAND, D.C. (1987) 'Characteristics of successful entrepreneurs', *Journal of Creative Behavior*, 21, 3: 219-233.

MEREDITH, G.G. NELSON, R.E. and NECK, P.A. (1982) *The practice of entrepreneurship*, Geneva: International Labour Office.

PALMER, M. (1971) 'The application of psychological testing to entrepreneurial potential', *California Management Review*, XIII, 3: 32-38.

ROSCH, E. (1978) 'Principles of categorization', in E. Rosch, and B.B. Lloyd (eds.) *Cognition and Categorization*, Hillsdale, N.J.: Eribaum.

SCHERE, J.C. (1982) 'Tolerance of ambiguity as a discriminating variable between entrepreneurs and managers', *Academy of Management Proceedings*: 404-408.

SEXTON, D.L. (1987) 'Advancing small business research: utilizing research from other areas', *American Journal of Small Business*, 11, 3: 25-30.

SMITH, N.R. (1967) *The Entrepreneur and His Firm: The Relationship Between Type of Man and Type of Company*, East Lansing, Michigan: Michigan State University Press.

STEVENSON, H.E. (1983) 'Entrepreneurship: hunting the heffalump', *Harvard Business School Bulletin*, (June): 50-51.

STEVENSON, H.H. and SAHLMAN, W.A. (1989) 'The entrepreneurial process', in P. Burns and J. Dewhurst (eds.) *Small Business and Entrepreneurship*, ch.5: 94- 157.

TIMMONS, J.A., SMOLLEN, L.E. and DINGEE, A.L.M. (1985) *New Venture Creation*, 2nd ed. Homewood, Ill.: Irwin.

WORTMAN, M.S. (1986) 'A unified framework, research typologies, and research prospectuses for the interface between entrepreneurship and small business', in D.L. Sexton and R.W. Smilor (eds), *The Art and Science of Entrepreneurship*, Cambridge, Mass.: Ballinger, 273-331.

17 A new perspective of entrepreneurship: A dialectic process of transformation within the entrepreneurial mode, types of flexibility and organizational form

Henk W. Volberda and Hock-Beng Cheah

Introduction

Most entrepreneurial activity is undertaken within organizations. However, the analysis of the organizational context of entrepreneurial activity is still a relatively new field of study. More fundamentally, ambiguity and controversy exists over the meaning and the nature of entrepreneurship. This paper provides a new perspective of entrepreneurship, and of the changes in the appropriate flexibility types and organizational forms in the entrepreneurial process.

Analysis of entrepreneurial activities within an organizational context

In recent years, several scholars have begun to explore in greater depth the various factors which seem to contribute to successful innovation (see Burgelman, 1983; Tushman and Anderson, 1986; Tushman and Moore, 1982; Van de Ven, 1986, and others). However, almost all the writers in this field have assumed the existence of only one mode of entrepreneurship. In contrast, drawing upon the works of Schumpeter (1934) and the Austrian school, Cheah (1990) has postulated the existence of two distinct modes of entrepreneurship, associated with the Schumpeterian (S) entrepreneur and the Austrian (A) entrepreneur. The entrepreneurial process is then conceived to consist of the dynamic alternation between these two modes over time.

We suggest that this entrepreneurial process creates significantly different situations, in response to which innovative organizations have to alter their strategies, structures and operational activities. This implies that organizations must possess a capacity for flexibility in these respects, so as to influence their environment or to adapt to changes in their environment. However, the existing ideas relating to the notion of organizational flexibility have tended to be rather ambiguous and superficial. Volberda (1990) developed a conceptual model of organizational flexibility which has been operationalized in terms of a flexibility audit [1]. This paper applies that model to an analysis of the dynamics of organizational flexibility in the entrepreneurial process.

In undertaking this analysis we bring together two subjects which have previously been treated as separate disciplines. The first subject relates to the ideas about entrepreneurship and entrepreneurial activities stemming from the works of Joseph Schumpeter and the Austrian School. These ideas have remained largely within the domain of economic theory, and have often been cited or treated in a peripheral manner in the field of entrepreneurial studies [2].

The second subject relates to organizational behavior theory which has largely been the domain of sociologists, psychologists and some unorthodox economists as Herbert Simon and Harvey Leibenstein. In economic theory, the entrepreneur has been perceived only as an individual, not as a member of a group, team, department or organization. As a result, the analyses of management and organization tasks within the firm is neglected or underestimated, under the assumption of 'ceteris paribus.' Organizational processes are presented in simplistic terms, based upon the layman's ('common sense') notion of rationality (see Minkes and Foxall, 1980). In contrast to this, organizational behavior theory explores in greater detail the complexities of management tasks and organizational conditions, but takes a simplistic approach to the substantive complexities of different technologies, markets and product life cycles (Dougherty, 1989).

To develop a better analysis of entrepreneurial activities in an organizational context, it is necessary to integrate these two different bodies of theory. This enables us to explore the impact and the implications of the entrepreneurial process on organizations.

The entrepreneurial process

From the ideas of Schumpeter and his Austrian critics, it is possible to distinguish two principal modes of entrepreneurship. Schumpeterian entrepreneurship (1934) promotes disequilibrium. It results in change *of* an existing situation. Schumpeterian entrepreneurial activities result in major innovations and even systemic change that increase or create uncertainty and promote new development processes which serve to create and/or widen the (e.g. technological) gap between leaders and followers.

In contrast, Austrian entrepreneurship promotes equilibrium. This results in change *within* an existing situation. Austrian entrepreneurship stems from the discovery of the existence of profitable discrepancies, gaps, mismatches of knowledge and information which others have not yet perceived and exploited, and the entrepreneur acts to capitalize upon the opportunity for gain or advantage which that discovery presents. Austrian entrepreneurial activities increase knowledge about the situation, reduce the general level of uncertainty over time and promote market processes which help to reduce or to eliminate the gap between leaders and followers.

However, these need not be contradictory processes. Instead, Schumpeterian and Austrian entrepreneurship (and their associated opportunities, activities and processes) may be perceived as opposites and yet complements to each other (Kirzner, 1985, p. 162). Furthermore, we postulate that this complementarity is manifested also in a systemic alternation in dominance between the two entrepreneurial modes. This is illustrated in Figure 1 where the point S represents an ideal-type equilibrium situation. That is, it is a situation characterized by complete certainty. In this situation there are no longer any 'scraps of existing information that are present in scattered form throughout society' which remain to be exploited by an alert (Austrian) entrepreneur. This situation presents the greatest scope for the disequilibrium-generating activities of the 'long-run' Schumpeterian entrepreneur.

These innovative activities lead to 'the discovery of an inter temporal opportunity that cannot, even in principle, be said to actually exist before the innovation has been created' (Kirzner, 1985, p. 85), and this causes disruption and transformation of the pre-existing equilibrium situation. The result is 'a continual series of steps that together propel the engine of long-run economic growth and development' (Kirzner 1985, p. 68).

As the level of uncertainty rises, as a consequence of Schumpeterian activities and processes, the scope for 'short-run' Austrian entrepreneurs grows. The short-run processes, which Kirzner (1985, pp. 84-85) perceives to be comprised of arbitrage and speculative activities, are based on the fact that 'at a given date a market economy is likely to be less than fully coordinated *with respect to information currently. possessed....What* the entrepreneur does, in this case, is discover the existence and/or the value of *available* knowledge' (Kirzner 1985, pp. 157-158).

Figure 1 depicts that at almost every point between **S** and **A**, both Schumpeterian and Austrian opportunities, activities and processes can occur. However, from the viewpoint of the overall entrepreneurial process, their respective periods of hegemony revolve in an alternating fashion. At points to the right of **S**, the scope for Schumpeterian opportunities, activities and processes diminishes progressively. Conversely, at points to the left of **A**, the scope for Austrian opportunities, activities and processes diminishes progressively. Indeed, on the basis of the analysis postulated so far, we could go even further and argue that Schumpeterian and Austrian entrepreneurship are *interdependent* in the overall evolutionary development process. Specifically, it is the activities and processes generated by Schumpeterian entrepreneurs which, over time, increase the scope for Austrian entrepreneurs, and vice versa. This may be viewed as follows.

The launching of a Schumpeterian innovation produces systemic change(s) which destroys the existing equilibrium and re-creates uncertainties, mismatches of information, and a proliferation of new unexploited opportunities within a particular situation. Through the exploitation of those opportunities, the specific function of Austrian entrepreneurs is to help to define the full potential and approximate limits of a Schumpeterian innovation. Indeed, from an Austrian perspective, those limits could not otherwise be determined. With the creation of an equilibrium situation, after Austrian entrepreneurs have (more or less clearly) established the limits of the previous Schumpeterian innovation, the foundation has been prepared for subsequent Schumpeterian entrepreneurs to use that knowledge as the new foundation from which to launch the next Schumpeterian innovation.

Figure 1

The relationship between Schumpeterian (S) and Austrian (A) entrepreneurial opportunities, activities and processes

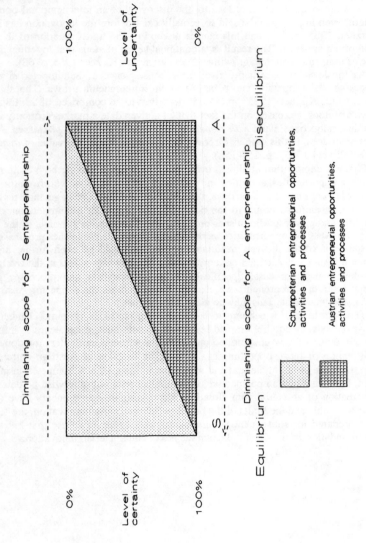

In the subsequent sections, we suggest that this entrepreneurial process has a significant bearing upon the appropriate forms of organization and the corresponding types of flexibility for the promotion of innovation at different points in time. This conception serves to relate innovation and the evolution of organizational forms directly to the activities of entrepreneurs (and entrepreneurial organizations).

Organizational flexibility

The issue of organization flexibility has recently received much attention from researchers, management consultants and practitioners. Nevertheless, fifteen years ago, Steers (1975) demonstrated in an ASQ article based on seventeen organizational effectiveness studies that flexibility was the evaluative criterion mentioned most frequently. However, its meaning in relation to the functioning of an organization is still ambiguous. Indeed, the multiple interpretations of the term organizational flexibility highlights this ambiguity (Volberda & Van der Stelt, 1988). The basic assumptions of many 'theories in use' of researchers as well as practitioners is that flexibility stimulates entrepreneurial processes and that entrepreneurial processes require organizational flexibility. However, this proposition is rather simplistic. Although entrepreneurship and innovation cannot be accomplished without some potential for change, not every change results in the same kind of entrepreneurship and innovation. In the following sections, therefore, we will examine more closely the relationship between organizational flexibility and the two modes of entrepreneurship introduced above. It will be argued that significantly different types of flexibility and their corresponding organizational conditions are related to each of the two modes of entrepreneurship.

Definition of flexibility

A clear formulation of the concept of flexibility can be derived based on some insights drawn from systems theory and cybernetic principles [3]. In this approach flexibility is treated as a two-dimensional concept (see Figure 2). First, flexibility is perceived to be a management or entrepreneurial task. In this connection, the concern is with the quality of the 'steering capacity' or the competence of the management or entrepreneur. Second, flexibility is perceived as an organizational task. The concern here is with the 'steerability' of the organization under different conditions: is it possible to implement different types of flexibility within the organizational context [4]. These two dimensions result in the following definition:

Flexibility is the degree to which an organization possesses a variety of actual and potential procedures, and the rapidity by which it can implement these procedures, in order to increase the steering capacity of the management and improve the steerability of the organization.

This definition will be explained below.

Figure 2
Flexibility and the associated management and organization task

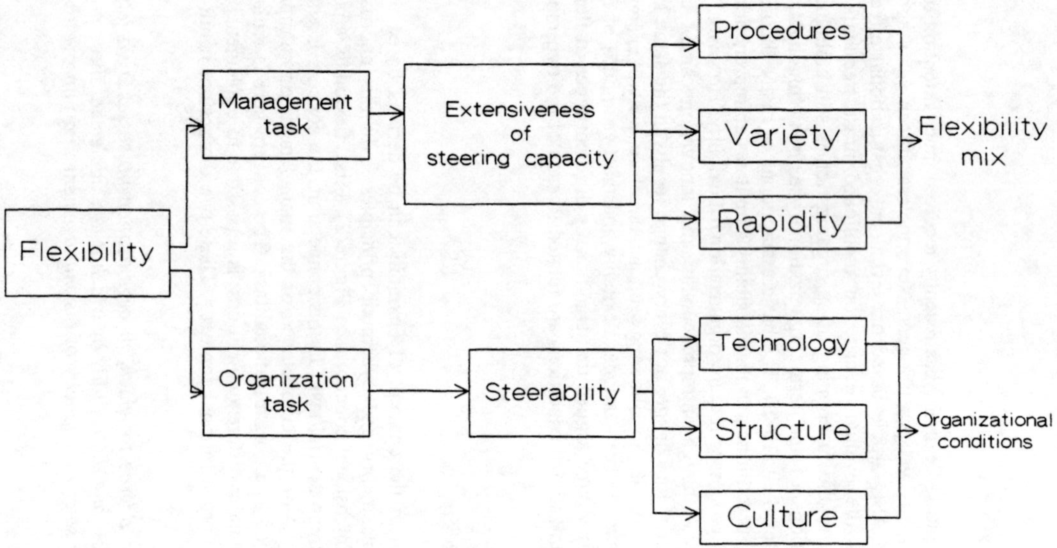

The management task

As a management task, flexibility is concerned with the creation or promotion of the organization's steering capacity, especially in situations of unexpected disturbance. Core components of this management task are:

(a) the existence of actual and potential procedures --- not only the actual arsenal of procedures is important, but also the collection of potential flexibility-increasing procedures. The possible emergence of opportunities or threats require management to have some potential procedures to rely upon as an insurance against risk (see Scott, 1965);

(b) the variety of procedures in the organization --- Ashby (1964) demonstrated that the required variety of procedures within the organization must, at a minimum, be equal to the variety of disturbances in the environment. This is the 'Law of Requisite Variety', or variety in the environment can only be absorbed by variety in the organization. The variety of procedures within the organization can be in terms of either the quantity, that is the number of procedures, or the quality of the procedures (such as one-off versus durable flexibility-increasing procedures). For instance, the training of multi-skilled personnel results in a more durable mode of flexibility, while the contracting out of certain peripheral activities or 'hire and fire' employment practices, tend to result in a one-off improvement in flexibility;

and (c) the rapidity by which an organization can implement its procedures --- an organization may possess the right procedures, but this does not necessarily mean that the management can implement these measures in time. Flexibility is not a static condition, but it is a dynamic process. Time is a very essential factor of organizational flexibility (see Figure 3).

The management task is manifested in the organization's *'flexibility mix'*. This refers to the collection of flexibility increasing procedures that an organization possesses, and the rapidity by which an organization can implement these procedures. The flexibility-mix consists of three types of flexibility [5] (see Figure 4): operational flexibility, structural flexibility and strategic flexibility (Ansoff & Brandenburg, 1971; Eppink, 1978).

Operational flexibility or routine manoeuvring capacity consists of routines based upon existing structures or goals of the organization. This most occurring type of flexibility relates to the volume of activities rather than the kinds of activities undertaken within the organization. These routines are primarily directed at the operational activities and are largely reactive in nature. The time horizon involved is often short term. An example of internal operational flexibility is the variation of production volume in the organization. Examples of external operational flexibility are the contracting out of certain peripheral activities or the obtaining of resources from more than one supplier.

Structural flexibility or adaptive manoeuvring capacity refers to the capacity of the management to adapt the organization structure, and its decision and communication processes, to suit changing conditions, as well as the rapidity by which this can be accomplished (Krijnen, 1979). Examples of this are the application of horizontal or vertical job enlargement, the creation of small production-units or work cells within a production line, or the transformation from a functional grouping to a market oriented grouping, with personnel and equipment that is interchangeable.

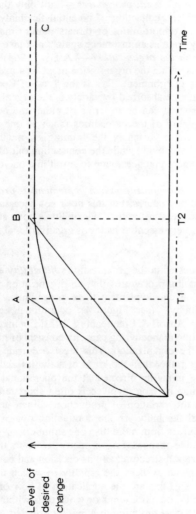

Figure 3
Flexibility and response time

The management of organizations A, B and C possess the same collection of procedures. Nevertheless, in the figure, organizations A is able to implement these procedures faster than organizations B and C. Their respective times of attainment of the desired level of performance are t1, t2 and indefinite. That is, organization C is not able to accomplish the desired change within the time span depicted.

Figure 4
Types of flexibility

	internal flexibility (I)	external flexibility (E)
Operational (R) flexibility	internal routine steering (IR)	external routine steering (ER)
structural (A) flexibility	internal adaptive steering (IA)	external adaptive steering (EA)
strategic (G) flexibility	internal goal steering (IG)	external goal steering (EG)

Strategic flexibility or non-routine steering capacity refers to procedures related to the goals of the organization or the environment (Aaker & Mascarenhas, 1984). This radical type of flexibility is much more qualitative and goes together with changes in the kind of organizational activities, such as the creation of new product market combinations (external strategic flexibility) or the application of a new technology (internal strategic flexibility). The creation of new activities in new situations has great importance.

Besides these three different forms of flexibility, we can distinguish the *metaflexibility* of an organization, that is, the supporting monitoring or learning system of the organization. Of particular importance in this connection is the sensor function of the organization. Meta-flexibility involves the processing of information to facilitate the continual adjustment of the composition of the organization's flexibility-mix in line with changes in the environment. This requires the creation, integration and application of flexibility increasing procedures in a flexible way.

The organization task

The ability to initiate these flexibility increasing procedures is dependent upon the organizational conditions, namely the organization's technology, structure and culture. These determine the volume and composition (operational, structural, strategic) of the flexibility-mix, and its limitations. The creation of specific organizational conditions constitutes the organization task.

This is in line with De Leeuw's (1984) 'Law of Managerial Busyness', demonstrating that there are limitations to the steering capacity of an organization. An organization that has a surplus of flexibility-increasing procedures, will experience chaos. This leads to the consideration of the second dimension of flexibility, namely the 'steerability' of the system. This is an organizational task which involves creating the appropriate organizational conditions necessary to effectively realize certain types of flexibility. Core aspects of this organization task are 'stability' and 'preservation.' These frequently neglected conditions are indispensable elements for the realization of flexibility (Van Ham, Pauw & Williams, 1987). Just as there cannot be differentiation without integration (Lawrence & Lorsch, 1967), similarly, there cannot be flexibility without some stability or preservation. Stability provides certainty for organizational members and preservation facilitates steerability or controllability of the organization.

Thus, this two-dimensional conception of flexibility creates a paradox: an organization must possess some procedures which enhance its potential flexibility to avoid becoming rigid, but it must also be anchored in some way in order to avoid chaos. There has to be a constructive tension (Kanter, 1983) between that which must be changed and that which is necessary to preserve. This anchoring can be a result of the identity or mission stemming from the organizational culture, the organizational structure, or the operational technology.

The *operational technology* refers to the hardware (means of transformation, like machinery and equipment) and the software (knowledge) by which and the configuration in which the organization transfers materials and/or information. The characteristics of the technology can range from routine to non-routine [6].

By the *organizational structure is* meant not only the actual distribution of responsibilities and authority among the organization's personnel, but also the planning and control systems and the processes of decision-making, coordination and execution. The former is related to the construction of the organization in functions and divisions/units (organizational form or 'Aufbau' [Kieser & Kubicek, 1978]). The latter is related to the organizational regulations of processes ('Ablauf'). The structure of the organization can range from mechanistic to organic (Burns & Stalker, 1961), corresponding to the opportunities for adaptive procedures [7].

The *organizational culture* can be defined as the shared interpretations about the kind and usefulness of work and cooperation. It is the idea system of the organization, which is contained in the minds of the organization members (Hofstede, 1980). This means that culture is in our conception something different from the explicit behavior, which is an effect of the organizational structure. Culture cannot be observed directly, it can only be felt. This culture can range from conservative to innovative, depending upon the slack within the existing norms and value systems [8].

These aspects of organization flexibility can be portrayed in the following conceptual model (see Figure 5).

In this conceptual scheme the flexibility-mix represents the actual flexibility of the organization (extensiveness of steering capacity). Because of changes in the environment, the management must continuously change the composition of the flexibility-mix in line with the environment. The preservation of this dynamic fit is called the meta-flexibility. The possibilities to implement these flexibility increasing procedures depend on the organizational conditions; they create the design limitations of the flexibility-mix.

Schumpeterian and Austrian entrepreneurial modes and their related flexibility types and organizational conditions

In this section, the model of organizational flexibility presented above will be applied to the two modes of entrepreneurship. First, we will examine the differences in the management tasks in terms of types of flexibility with respect to the Austrian and Schumpeterian entrepreneurial organizations. After that, the corresponding organizational conditions as part of the organization task will be considered.

Differences in the management task

Austrian entrepreneurial organizations seek to exploit presently available knowledge and existing opportunities. The domain of the organization ('what business are we in') is relatively clear, and there is little or no ambiguity concerning the boundaries of the organization and its environment (Thompson, 1967). As the external environment is relatively well defined, the organization's principal concerns become more internally focused. Consequently, the flexibility-mix of the A-organization is dominated by *operational flexibility*. This means that the organization tends to develop an increasingly large variety of routines to reduce uncertainty to a minimum, and to enable it to operate as efficiently as possible. The organization becomes very concerned with 'doing things right.' By developing a greater number and variety of routines, the organization tries to adapt to different demands

Figure 5
Conceptual model of organizational flexibility

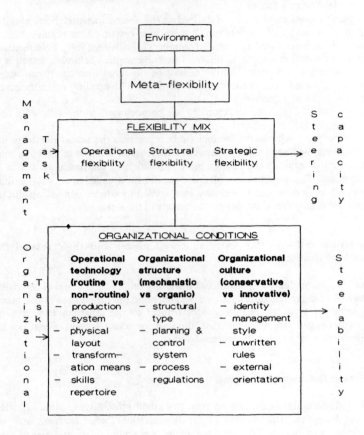

in the environment. Its growing concern is to achieve stability and equilibrium. This deterministic process assumes that there is only one optimal organizational configuration (Hannan & Freeman, 1984).

Within the organization, innovations tend to be *incremental* rather than radical (Tushman & Anderson, 1986), based upon refinements or extensions of existing concepts or approaches. According to Clark (1985, p.249), 'Innovation of this kind strengthens and reinforces existing commitments. The organization becomes more conservative in nature: it strengthens and improves the fit between organization and environment and thus entrenches the established approach.' The operational difficulties also tend to become of a routine nature, capable of being solved on the basis of acquired experience. In this context, the management task tends to become a matter of optimization (Simon, 1960).

Besides experience, incremental innovations occur through imitation and extrapolation. These are all forms of 'single-loop learning' which do not involve changes in the existing criteria of evaluation or in fundamental values and norms (Argyris & Schon, 1978). The risk of the preponderant emphasis in the Austrian organization on achieving operational flexibility is that it can lead to organizational inertia. Those routines first have to be unlearned before an organization can change (Starbuck, 1983).

In contrast, the flexibility-mix of the S-entrepreneurial organization is dominated by an emphasis on *strategic and structural flexibility*. Strategic flexibility is externally oriented, and requires the existence of organizational slack for making 'strategic choices' (Child, 1972). The organization has to reduce or abandon past routines to become more receptive to new possibilities. The domain of the organization is not yet well-defined and the boundary between the organization and its environment is still fuzzy. The signals and the feedback received from the environment tend to be indirect and open to multiple interpretations. Extrapolation or other conventional management tools are not useful in this context. The organization has to conduct searches based on heuristics and nonroutines.

The issues and difficulties relating to strategic flexibility are by definition very unstructured and non-routine. Totally new values and norms are required and, thus, past experience may not provide any advantage. In this context, 'double-loop learning' by 'trial and error' is essential; it involves a change in the criteria of evaluation (Argyris & Schon, 1978). Indeed, past practices would need to be called into question, new assumptions about the organization have to be raised and significant changes in strategy are considered (Van de Ven, 1986).

These changes assist the S-organization to promote *radical innovations,* instead of incremental or adaptive innovations (Tushman & Anderson, 1985). These innovations are associated with departures from existing approaches, destroying the value of established commitments and competence, and requiring new resources and skills. These revolutionary changes also require a great deal of structural flexibility, that is, procedures directed at the renewal or transformation of existing structures and processes as an essential part of the overall change process. Restructuring of the organization often occurs during the radical innovation process (Schroeder et al., 1986). This restructuring can take many forms including the formation of joint ventures, changes in organizational responsibilities, use of project teams, and alterations in control systems.

While strategic and structural flexibility can lead to radical change, it can also produce low trust, defensive behavior, encounter unmentionable or sensitive issues, and lead to avoidance or bypass tactics. Management has to be alert to these possibilities and endeavor to channel actions or changes towards constructive ends (Van de Ven, 1986). If not, strategic and structural flexibility could result only in chaos.

Differences in organizational conditions

The A-entrepreneur is focused on operational flexibility, resulting in incremental and evolutionary changes, but leaving the nature of the firm intact; the basic task is developing the right routines for reducing uncertainty. By developing a larger number and variety of these routines, the firm tends to move towards an equilibrium - or static fit - with the environment. Ideally, the A-entrepreneur seeks to eliminate slack completely, so as to achieve an 'optimal' organizational form.

In this situation, structural contingency theory (Thompson, 1967) suggests that such an organization would have a routine technology, a mechanistic structure and a conservative culture (see Figure 6).

The production system of the *routine technology* of the A-entrepreneur is focused on volume in order to create 'learning by doing' or 'economies of scale'. Mass or process production and a typical line lay-out is most appropriate here. The means of production are very specialized and the production repertoire (variety of production techniques) is limited. In Thompson's typology (1967) we could speak of a 'long-linked technology' with sequential interdependence.

Characteristics of the *mechanistic structure* (Burns & Stalker, 1961) are a functional type of organization, based on process grouping (Gulick, 1937), many hierarchical levels, and high functionalization of management tasks. Processes are highly regulated through planning and control systems, specialization of tasks (small and simple tasks), a high degree of standardization, formalization and centralization. As a result, the levels of participation and delegation are low. This organizational type is very similar to Mintzberg's 'machine bureaucracy' (Mintzberg, 1979). It is consistent with the findings of Cohn & Turyn (1984), who concluded that evolutionary innovations (modest, incremental changes) are more likely in formalized and centralized organizations.

Finally, the *conservative culture* consists of a very dominant and more important homogeneous identity, a directive management style based on authority and reliance on routines. There are large repositories of unwritten rules as a result of a strong socialization processes, an emphasis on discipline, and a low tolerance for ambiguity. Organizational members do not accept a difference between the formal and actual structure. There is a strong internal orientation, which is mainly short-term and reactive.

The *weaknesses* of the organizational conditions of the A-entrepreneur are associated with a tendency towards conservatism, delay in decision-making and implementation, and ossification.

As explained above, the S-entrepreneur promotes structural and strategic flexibility to facilitate radical or discontinuous changes. It is not a 'slack destruction' process, but a

Figure 6
Model of the A-organization

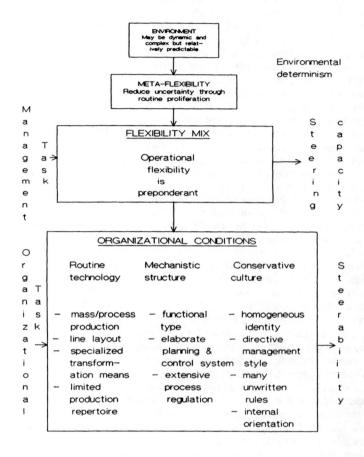

Environmental determinism

ENVIRONMENT
May be dynamic and complex but relatively predictable

META–FLEXIBILITY
Reduce uncertainty through routine proliferation

FLEXIBILITY MIX

Operational flexibility is preponderant

Management Task

Steering capacity

ORGANIZATIONAL CONDITIONS

Organizational Task

Steerability

Routine technology	Mechanistic structure	Conservative culture
– mass/process production	– functional type	– homogeneous identity
– line layout	– elaborate planning & control system	– directive management style
– specialized transformation means	– extensive process regulation	– many unwritten rules
– limited production repertoire		– internal orientation

275

'slack creation' process, which means that resources can be combined in many different ways. We would expect here a non-routine technology, because for radical changes the organization has to violate rules (Dougherty, 1989), an organic structure in order to allow the organization to restructure itself during the transformation process and a innovative culture oriented at renewal (see Figure 7).

The *non-routine technology* gives leeway for difficult search processes based on satisfying criteria. Increasing efficiency in the form of 'economies of scale' is less important than increasing the possibilities for search processes based on bounded rationality (Simon, 1960). Unit or small batch production systems together with an autonomous group lay-out (Van Donk, De Vries & Van de Water, 1991) or functional lay-out meet those requirements. The means of transformation are not very specialized, but multi-purpose and the operational production repertoire is extensive. It fits with Thompson's (1967) 'intensive technology' type based on reciprocal interdependence.

The type of structure of the *organic structure* can range from the divisionalized form, based on purpose grouping with few hierarchical levels and limited functionalization to the project or matrix form, based on process and purpose grouping. According to Hrebiniak & Joyce (1984) the project form is preferred to the divisional form, when there is a need for a dual focus, there is a need to share resources and there is a high need for information processing and decision making. On the basis of these conditions we would postulate that radical innovations start in project form and are further developed in the divisionalized form. Essential for both the divisional and project form is the creation of autonomous self-organizing units, which possess all relevant elements of the whole (Van de Ven, 1986). Galbraith (1982) views innovations as iterations of inseparable and simultaneously-coupled stages linked by a major ongoing transition process. This need for simultaneous coupling instead of sequential coupling requires an integration of essential functions and resources. Purpose grouping stimulates direct client contact and boundary spanning activities, thereby reducing the threshold for innovation activities. A flat structure, that is limited hierarchical levels shortens the reaction time of organizations (Quinn, 1985). Also restricted functionalization integrates management tasks, thereby reducing coordination problems and resulting in fast decision-making.

The planning and control systems leave some space for ambiguous information and necessary experimentation and intuition. This in contrast with rigid planning systems that only stimulate repetitive actions, which may have little to do with previous success and nothing with future success. Those systems only create superstitious learning, discouraging every kind of innovation. (Starbuck, 1983). Therefore, the S-entrepreneurial organization prefers a rough planning in the form of mile stone planning (Block, 1985).

The process regulation is very limited. Revolutionary changes require little standardization and formalization, and high decentralization (Cohn & Turyn, 1984). This is because standardization and formalization reduce the perceptible variety of innovation stimuli (Beer, 1985) Also, specialization is restricted. A high degree of specialization violates the synergy process, which is necessary for innovation. Redundancies in functions (Trist, 1981), that is broad and complex tasks (Kanter, 1988), create an understanding of the essential considerations and constraints of all aspects of the innovation in addition to those immediately needed to perform the individual task. It means 'think globally, while acting locally' (Van de Ven, 1986). Lateral relations between units (divisions or projects) are minimized, but intensified within the autonomous units. It creates a form of multistability;

Figure 7
Model of the S-organization

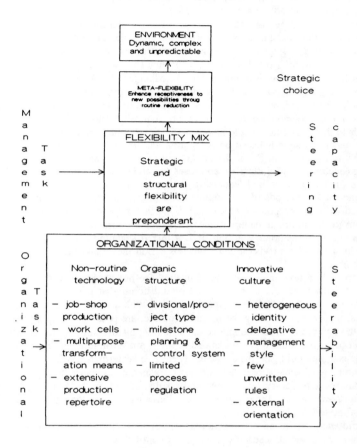

ENVIRONMENT
Dynamic, complex
and unpredictable

META-FLEXIBILITY
Enhance receptiveness to
new possibilities throug
routine reduction

Strategic
choice

FLEXIBILITY MIX

Strategic
and
structural
flexibility
are
preponderant

Management Task

Steering capacity

ORGANIZATIONAL CONDITIONS

Organizational Task

Steerability

Non-routine technology	Organic structure	Innovative culture
– job-shop production	– divisional/project type	– heterogeneous identity
– work cells	– milestone planning & control system	– delegative management style
– multipurpose transformation means	– limited process regulation	– few unwritten rules
– extensive production repertoire		– external orientation

277

relatively weak coupled self-organizing units are able to create new stabilities in new situations, without influencing the other units. In Mintzberg's terminology (1979) the organic structure resembles the 'adhocracy'.

The *innovative culture* consists of a heterogeneous identity within the different units, but there are multiple connections between the different 'thought worlds' (Dougherty, 1989). Meyer (1982) argues that organizations are more likely to adapt strategies that are more divergent from their previous strategies if they have a more heterogeneous organizational 'ideology'. This view is supported by Friedlander (1983), who argues that organizational learning in a 'reconstructive' mode takes place more readily where there is such heterogeneity. However, some connections in the form of a central direction are necessary; they define the conceivable limits of innovation. A too monotonous identity, on the other hand, leads to the disciplined ideological organization (Mintzberg & Waters, 1985).

The management style is based on delegation and improvisation, but not without some form of institutionalization (Selznick, 1957). It is often thought that an organization loses something (becomes rigid, inflexible, and loses the ability to innovate) when institutionalization sets in. But institutional leadership is particularly needed for radical innovations, which represent key periods of development and transition when the organization is open to or forced to consider alternative ways of doing things (Van de Ven, 1986). The strategic problem for institutional leaders is one of creating an infrastructure that is conducive to innovation and organizational learning. It is a mixed scanning approach (Etzioni, 1963); there is a long term broad vision and from this vision the organization goes step by step into the short term.

There are only a few unwritten rules, but they are not based on discipline dominance; exchange of knowledge and information between different disciplines is necessary for radical innovations (Kanter 1986). Participants can deal with a great proportion of ambiguity. Exceptions, that means violating the formal structure, are possible. Participants do not try to reduce the gap between formal and actual structure, by stressing the formal structure. In the more popular literature these 'violations of the formal structure' are often referred to in terms such as 'bootlegging' or 'lucky breaks' (Peters & Waterman, 1982).

The culture is externally oriented and very open; the resistance to signals which can threaten the existing idea-system is low, and results, in fact, in the adapting of the actual idea-system. Nevertheless, the external orientation is based on a long-term vision and idealization of the future (Ackoff, 1981).

The *deficiencies* of these organizational conditions of the S-entrepreneur are related, among others, to potentially serious problems of conflict of authority, unclear responsibilities, inadequate controls, lack of direction and shared ideology, and, consequently, greater scope for chaos and inefficiency.

The successful and unsuccessful A- and S-entrepreneurial organizations

The composition of the flexibility-mix and the organizational conditions were described for the A- and S-entrepreneur. It is important to understand that those are only two organizational configurations. With the use of the two dimensions of organizational flexibility, namely extensiveness of the flexibility-mix and the 'steerability' of the organization, four

Figure 8
Transitions in organizational forms in the entrepreneurial process

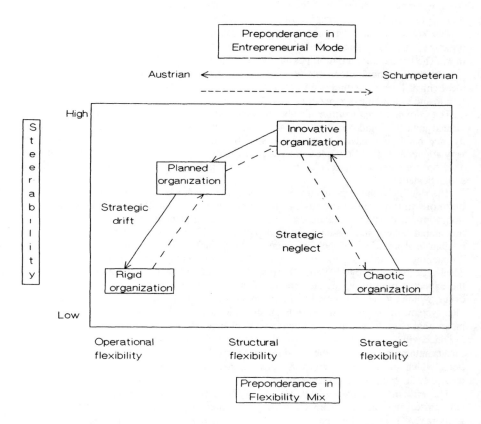

organizational forms can be distinguished: the rigid, the planned, the innovative, and the chaotic organization (see figure 8). The 'Planned organization' represents the successful A-entrepreneur, while the 'Innovative organization' stands for the successful S-entrepreneur. The four organizational types will be discussed briefly.

The *'rigid organization'* possesses a very small flexibility-mix and the steerability of the organization is low. The flexibility-mix, as far as it consists, is dominated by simple routines. The choice and variation possibilities are limited; improvisation is a taboo in this organization. The mature technology, the functionalized and centralized structure with many hierarchical layers together with an monotonous and narrow-minded culture results in a fragile and vulnerable organization.

The *'planned organization'* also has a limited flexibility-mix, but the composition is less limited than the 'rigid organization', and also the steerability is much higher. The flexibility-mix mainly consists of routines and specific rules and detailed procedures, which are very sophisticated and complex in nature. For every possible change the organization has developed a certain routine. Compared with the 'rigid organization' the mix is much more sophisticated.

The rigidity of this organizational form is not as much a result of the primary structure, but more an outcome of the strong process regulations of the structure, like standardization, formalization and specialization, and very detailed planing and control systems. Also, the shared beliefs and assumptions as a part from the culture give very little leeway for deviant interpretations of the environment. Dissonance with this idea-system is potentially threatening to the organization's integrity. This organizational form resembles the 'ideal-type' bureaucracy of Weber (Perrow, 1972). As long as there are no changes outside the expected repertoire, the steerability of the organization is high. However, if changes occur, which are not calculated in the planning repertoire and are threatening to the shared idea-system, the organization results in 'strategic drift'. By the notion of 'strategic drift' is meant that consciously managed incremental changes do not necessarily succeed in keeping pace with environmental changes (Johnson, 1988). These kind of changes only result in further attempts to perfect the standardization mechanisms and basic beliefs and assumptions, which are the very sources of inertia. Consequently, slowness of response is characteristic of the 'planned organization'.

The *'chaotic organization'* possesses a very large and extensive flexibility-mix, but is totally unsteerable. In this organization the possibilities of variation are unlimited; there is no anchorage. There are innumerable initiatives for innovation, but it is impossible to implement them. Administrative structures and some 'shared values' in the culture are missing. A lack of administrative stability is caused by 'strategic neglect' (Burgelman, 1983). 'Strategic neglect' refers to the more or less deliberate tendency not to pay attention to the administrative structure of the organization. As a result, those emerging administrative problems deteriorate from petty and trivial to severe and disruptive. In his study of new internal corporate ventures, Burgelman concluded that this administrative instability is exacerbated by the fact that there is no strong orientation, and there is still a lot of opportunistic behavior on the part of some participants of the venture. The range of possible procedures is so extensive and large, that it is very hard to make a choice. The decision-making capacity of the management strongly reduces (Scott, 1965). Decisions are delayed, while the situation requires a direct decision.

Finally, the *'innovative organization'* possesses a large and rich flexibility-mix and the steerability is reasonable high. A variety of innovation stimuli can be observed and also implemented with some supple adoptions within the existing structure (Ansoff & Brandenburg, 1971). The paradox between change and institutionalization or preservation is well managed here.

Trajectories within the entrepreneurial process

If, as our thesis suggests, the S and A opportunities do not exist in the same proportions at the different phases of the entrepreneurial process, then the composition of the two types of entrepreneurs in the organization, the flexibility mix, and the organizational conditions also need to vary in a corresponding fashion. That is, in the entrepreneurial process, the organization has to change its form to match appropriately with the dominant entrepreneurial mode of the opportunities which it chooses to address. On the basis of our organizational typology, different trajectories within the entrepreneurial process can be distinguished (see figure 8). As the dominant entrepreneurial mode shifts from the S to the A mode, the organization must change from the 'innovative' to the 'planned' form. In this process of change, the organization has to prevent itself from 'overshooting' and becoming a 'rigid' organization. Conversely, as the dominant entrepreneurial mode shifts from the A to the S mode, the organization must change from the 'planned' to the 'innovative' form. In this process of change, the organization has to prevent itself from 'overshooting' and becoming a 'chaotic' organization. The process leading in these opposite directions can each be conceived in terms of a trajectory in which the extreme positions are undesirable states characterized by organizational asymmetry. In other words:

1) The risks of the A-entrepreneurial organization is the transformation into the 'rigid organization' as a result of 'strategic drift'. The surplus of operational flexibility, consisting of simple routines, creates inertia in the form of a very mechanistic structure and a very narrow focused culture. The growing resistance to 'deviant' interpretations of the environment reflects a tendency toward 'overbalance' of the A-entrepreneurial organization.

2) The risk of the S-entrepreneurial organization is turning into a 'chaotic organization' caused by 'strategic neglect' The surplus of structural and strategic flexibility leads to unfocused actions, resulting in disconstructive ends. The lack of administrative structures and a sense of direction, shared beliefs and institutional leadership is characteristic of a tendency towards 'underbalance' of the S-entrepreneurial organization.

3) In order to survive an organization has to shift from the 'planned ' towards the 'innovative' organization and visa-versa. It is important to understand that the A- and S-entrepreneurial organization are different stages in a cyclical process. Mintzberg (1978) shows how organizations go through periods of strategy adjustment characterized by continuity, flux or incremental change, but also require more global changes. Greiner (1972) charts periods of evolution and revolution in corporate development. This is in line with the 'classic' of Burns & Stalker (1961), who concluded even then that the organic form was temporary because the necessary internal dynamics could not be sustained.

Conclusions and research implications

The entrepreneurial process, that is, the alternation of hegemony between the Schumpeterian and the Austrian entrepreneurial modes, creates significantly different situations, in response to which organizations have to alter their cultures, structures, and operational technologies over time, to become and/or to remain successful. The analysis presented above has sought to highlight two sets of transition. First, to become successful in promoting a Schumpeterian innovation, an organization has to rise from a state of initial chaos or disorganization. Second, to remain successful, organizations have to manage a dialectical process which requires them to transform themselves from an 'innovative' form into a 'planned' form, and then back from a 'planned' form into an 'innovative' form, to match the opportunities set by the changes in the dominant entrepreneurial mode over time.

The key question is how to manage this dialectic process between the A- and S entrepreneurial modes and their corresponding organizational forms. How would the organization be able to achieve such changes in its flexibility mix and its organizational conditions so as to enable it to be in tune with the needs and the opportunities of the situation, and what is the process involved? The management of changes in organizational structure, culture and operational technology to produce the appropriate flexibility mix corresponding to each phase of the entrepreneurial process is likely to become an increasingly important function as organizations begin to acquire a better understanding of the implications for organizational performance.

Notes

1. This flexibility audit has been used in a cross-sectional analysis of 7 organizations in The Netherlands. After that, the method was applied in 3 longitudinal case-studies: the Department of Commercial Accounts of the Dutch 'Postbank', the R&D Department of the 'Dutch National Gasunion', and the Production-unit Glass Bead Semi-Conductors of Philips Netherlands. This research project was made possible by the support of GITP management consultants, Nijmegen, The Netherlands.
2. It must be noted that even within Economics, the ideas of Schumpeter and the Austrian School have generally led a separate existence, and have proved difficult to integrate within orthodox, that is, neo-classical economics.
3. Systems theory is used here as an empirically vacuous theory; it helps us to order and to categorize complex phenomena.
4. This is in line with Block's (1986) assumptions about corporate venturing. He suggests that there are two distinct and equally important challenges to be resolved if venturing is to succeed. The first is the management of ventures. The second is the creation of the right context, structure and systems to foster entrepreneurship.
5. With the use of steering theory (De Leeuw, 1982) as a part from system theory, three forms of steering can be distinguished:
   - Routine steering (R): procedures to create flexibility, leaving the structure and goals of organization and environment intact.
   - Adaptive steering (A): procedures to increase flexibility, which result in a restructuring of the organization but without altering the organizational goals.
   - Goal steering (G): flexibility increasing procedures, which change the existing goals of the organization.
   Also, a distinction can be made between internal and external steering capacity.

- Internal steering (I) is directed at the organization itself, that is adapting to the environment.
- In the contrary, external steering (E) means trying to influence the environment, so that the organization is less vulnerable for changes in the environment.
  The foregoing means that the possible flexibility-mix consists of the following procedures <IR, IA, IG, ER, EA, EG> and that:
- operational flexibility stands for <IR, ER>,
- structural flexibility for <IA, EA>,
- and strategic flexibility for <IG, EG>.
6. The sub-dimensions which score on the technology dimension (routine vs. non-routine) are:
   - the way of producing (process, mass, batch, unit),
   - the physical production lay-out (line, group, functional, work station),
   - the means of transformation (specialized vs. multi-purpose),
   - and the operational production repertoire (limited vs. extensive).
   For a more elaborated discussion of those sub-dimensions see Volberda (1990,1991).
7. The different sub-dimensions which score on the head-dimension of organizational structure (mechanistic vs. organic) are:
   - type of structure (functional, divisional, matrix)
     grouping (function, product, client)
     levels (many, few)
     functionalization (high, low)
   - planning & control systems (high regulation, low regulation)
   - process characteristics
     specialization
     standardization
     education
     formalization
     lateral relations
     horizontal decentralization
     delegation
     participation
   For a more elaborated discussion of those dimensions see Volberda (1990,1991).
8. The different sub-dimensions of the head-dimension of organizational culture (conservative, innovative) are:
   - identity
     -communality (strong, weak)
     -scope (small, broad)
     -homogeneity (homogeneous, heterogeneous)
   - management style
     -leadership style (instructive, consultive, participative, delegative)
     -planning-approach (blue print vs. muddling through)
     -management attitude (routine, heuristic, improvisation)
   - unwritten rules
     discipline dominance (strong, weak)
     socialization (strong, weak)
     attitude formal-actual (unequivocal, unequivoeal)
     tolerance for ambiguity (low, high)
   - External orientation
     focus (short term vs. long term)

openness (closed, open)
planning attitude (reactive, inactive, proactive, interactive)
For a more elaborate diseussion, we refer to Volberda (1990,1991).

References

Aaker, D.A. & Mascarenhas, B (1984~), 'The need for strategic flexibility,' *The Journal of Business Strategy,* Fall

Ackoff, R.L. (1981), *Creating the Corporate Future,* Wiley, New York.

Ansoff, H.I. & Brandenburg, R. (1971), 'A Language for Organizational Design: Parts I and II,' *Management Science,* August.

Argyris, C. & Schon, D. (1978), *Organizational Learning A Theory of Action Approach,* Addison Wesley, Reading, MA.

Ashby, W.R.(1964), *An Introduction to Cybernetics,* Methuen, London.

Beer, S. (1985), *Diagnosing the system of organizations,* Wiley, New York.

Block, Z. (1985), 'Concepts for corporate entrepreneurs,' *Proceedings of the Texas A & M Business Forum,* January.

Burgelman, R. (1983), 'A Process Model of Internal Corporate Venturing in the Diversified Major Firm,' *Administrative Science Quarterly,* vol. 28, pp. 223-244.

Burns, T. & Stalker, G. (1961), *The Management of Innovation,* Tavistock, London.

Cheah, Hock-Beng (1990), 'Schumpeterian and Austrian Entrepreneurship: Unity within Duality,' *Journal of Business Venturing,* vol. 5, no. 6, November, pp. 341-347.

Child, John (1972), 'Organizational structure, environment and performance: the role of strategic choice,' *Sociology,* vol. 6, no. 1, pp. 1-22.

Clark, K (1985), 'The Interaction of Design Hierarchies and Market Concepts in Technological Evolution,' *Research Policy,* vol. 14, pp. 235-251.

Cohn, S.F. & Turyn, R.M. (1984), 'Organizational structure, decision-making procedures, and the adaption of innovations,' *IEEE Transactions on Engineering Management,* EM31, pp. 154-161.

Donk, D.P. van, Vries, J. de & Water, H. van de (1991), 'Towards a conceptual framework of the production function,' *International Journal of operations and production management,* vol. 13, no. 1, Forthcoming.

Dougherty, Deborah (1989), 'Interpretive Barriers to Successful Product Innovation,' Marketing Science Institute, *WorkingPaper,* Report No. 89-114, Cambridge, Massachusetts.

Eppink, D.J. (1978), *Managing the Unforeseen,* Dissertation, Administratief Centrum, Ermelo.

Etzioni, A. (1963), *A comparative analysis of complex organizations,* The Free Press, New York.

Friedlander, F. (1983), 'Patterns of individual and organizational learning,' in Srivastva (ed.), *The Executive Mind,* Jossey Bass, San Francisco.

Galbraith, J.R. (1982), 'Designing the Innovating Organization,' *Organizational Dynamics,* Winter, pp. 3-24.

Greiner, L.E. (1972), 'Evolution and revolution as organizations grow,' *Harvard Business Review,* July/August, pp. 37-46.

Gulick, Luther (1937), 'Notes on the Theory of Organization,' in I.L. Gulick & L. Urwick (eds.), *Papers on the Science of Administration,* Institute of Public Administration, New York, pp. 3-45.

Ham, J.C. van, Pauwe, J. & Williams, A.R.T. (1987), 'Flexibiliteit en stabiliteit vanuit individu en organisatie' (inflexibility and stability of individual and organizationn), in A. Buitendam (ed.), *Arbeidsmarkt, Arbeidsorganisatie, Arbeidsverhoudingen, Sociaal Beleid,* Kluwer/NVP, Deventer, pp. 74-90.

Hannan, M.T. & Freeman, J.H. (1984), 'Structural inertia and organizational change,'American *Sociological Review,* vol. 49, pp. 149-164.

Hofstede, G. (1980), 'Motivation, Leadership and Organization - Do American Theories Apply Abroad?,' *Organizational Dynamics,* Summer, pp. 42-63.

Hrebiniak, Lawrence G. & Joyce, William, F. (1984), *ImplementingStrategy,* Macmillan Publishing Company, New York.

Johnson, G. (1988), 'Rethinking Incrementalism,' *Strategic Management Journal,* September, pp. 75-91.

Kanter, R.M. (1988), 'When a Thousand Flowers Bloom: Structural, Collective, and Social Conditions for Innovation in an Organization,' *Research in Organization Behavior,* vol. 10, JAI Press, Greenwich, CT, pp. 169-211.

Kanter, R.M. (1983), *The change masters,* Simon & Schuster, New York.

Kieser, A. & Kubicek, H. (1978), *Organisationstheorien I und II,* Kohlhammer, Stuttgart.

Kirzner, I. (1985), *Discovery and the Capitalist Process,* University of Chicago Press, Chicago. Krijnen, H.G. (1979), 'The Flexible Firm,' *Long Pange Planning,* vol. 12, April.

Lawrence, P. & Lorsch, J. (1967), *Organization and Environment,* Harvard School of Business Administration Press, Boston.

Leeuw, A C.J. de (1984), *De wet van de bestuurlijke drukte* (nThe Law of Managerial Busynessn), Van Gorcum, Assen/Maastricht.

Meyer, A D. (1982), 'How ideologies supplement formal structures and shape responses to environments,' *Journal of Management Studies,* vol. 19, no. 1, pp. 45-61.

Minkes, A. & G. Foxall (1980), 'Entrepreneurship, strategy, and organization: Individual and organization in the behaviour of the firm,' *Strategic Management Journal,* vol. 1, no. 4, pp. 295-301.

Mintzberg, H. (1979), *The Structuring of Organizations,* Prentice-Hall, Englewood Cliffs, New York.

Mintzberg, Henry & Waters, James A. (1985), 'Of Strategies, Deliberate and Emergent,' *Strategic Management Journal,* vol. 6, pp. 257-272.

Perrow, Charles (1972), *Complex Organizations,* Random House (third edition), New York.

Peters,T.J. & Waterman, R.H. (1982), *In Search of Excellence,* Harper & Row, New York.

Quinn, J.B. (1985), 'Managing innovation: controlled chaos,' *Harvard Business Review,* vol. 63, no. 3, pp. 78-84.

Schroeder, Roger, Van de Ven, Andrew, Scudder, Gary & Douglas, Polley (1986), 'Managing Innovation and Change Processes: Findings from the Minnesota Innovation Research Program,' *Agribusiness,* vol. 2, no. 4, pp. 501-523.

Schumpeter, J.A. (1934), *The Theory of Economic Development,* Harvard University Press, Cambridge, Mass.

Selznick, P. (1957), *Leadership in Administration,* Harper and Row, New York.

Simon, H.A. (1960), *The New Science of Management decision,* Harper & Row, New York.

Starbuck, W. (1983), 'Organizations as Action Generators,' *American Journal of Sociology,* vol. 48, no. 1, pp. 91-115.

Steers, Richard M. (1975), 'Problems in the Measurement of Organizational Effectiveness,'Administrative *Science Quarterly,* vol. 20, pp. 546-558.

Thompson, J. (1967), *Organizations in Action,* McGraw-Hill, New York.

Trist, E., (1981), 'The evolution of sociotechnical systems as a framework and as a action research program,' in A. Van de Ven & W. Joyce (eds.), *Perspectives on Organizational Design and Behavior,* John Wiley & Son, New York, pp. 19-75.

Tushman, M. & Anderson, P. (1986), 'Technological Discontinuities and Organizational Environments,' *Administrative Science Quarterly,* vol. 31, pp. 439-465.

Tushman, M. & Moore, W. (1982), *Readings in the Management of Innovation,* Pitman, Boston. Van de Ven, Andrew H. (1986), 'Central Problems In The Management Of Innovation,' *Management Science,* vol. 32, no. 5, May, pp. 590-617.

Volberda, H.W. & Stelt, H. van der (1988), 'Flexibiliteit: een integrale managementbenadering' (Flexibility as an integral management approachn), *Bedrijfskunde, Journal of modem Management,* vol. 60, no. 3, pp. 250-256.

Volberda, H.W. (1990), 'Een Flexibele Organisatie als Voorwaarde voor Innovatie' (nA Flexible Organization as a necessary Condition for Innovationn), *M&O, Journalfor Management and Social Policy,* vol. 44, no. 3, pp. 215-242.

Volberda, H.W. (1991), 'Flexibility: The Paradox between Change and Preservation,' in Groen, AJ., *Vogelvlucht over en diepzee duiken in bedrijfskundig promotie-onderzoek,* Proceedings Dutch Junior Faculty Conference on management and organization, Eburon, pp. 230-248.

Part 7
Entrepreneurship and government policy

18 Towards an effective subsidizing policy

Hermann Frank, Gerhard Plaschka and Dietmar Rößl

Introduction

Increasing numbers of new ventures as well as increasing capital requirements ask for the question whether or not subsidies are useful. A variety of subsidies and bureaucratic obstacles have been questioning effectivity of subsidies for many years. Therefore, policy makers want to assure the usefulness of the financial resources they dedicate to business start-ups.

Since many researchers consider the 'regenerative power' of new ventures in an economy as an important factor, subsidies granted to new ventures are included in the objectives of policy makers (e.g. Szyperski, 1980, p.151; Pütz and Meyerhöfer, 1982, p.424). However, there are conflicting positions in the literature:

* On the one hand, it is argued subsidies are ineffective for the number of new business start-ups as well as their development and success.
* On the other hand, subsidies are considered to be an effective instrument for achieving the policy targets (e.g. Joos, 1987, p.404; Schiller, 1986, p.58).

A catalogue of policy targets in subsidizing new venture creation was developed by Joos (1987, pp.254; Schmidt, 1980, pp.144; Szyperski, 1980, p.151). Joos distinguished between competitive, structural, manpower and technology policy targets.

The objective of this article is to analyze the effectiveness of a new venture subsidizing program in Austria by the 'Bürges-Förderungsbank'. This body acts on behalf of the Austrian Ministry of Economics. The Bürges-Förderungsbank is the leading institution in subsidizing new ventures and spent approximately AS 7 billion in the last decade.

Usually a new venture gets a one-time non-repayable subsidy of 15% of a loan up to AS 2 million. On average, the subsidy is AS 100.000,-. The Bürges-Förderungsbank also offers guarantees for bank loans, whereby up to 80% of the loan is guaranteed. New ventures in specific areas (e.g. high-tech ventures) are also eligible to apply for subsidies at other institutions. Typically the Bürges-Förderungsbank subsidizes a 'normal' or 'average' private start-up company. Incorporated firms and founders older than 45 years cannot be subsidized.

Since many studies identify financial problems as very important in the start-up stage and in the future development (e.g. Mugler, 1986, pp.193), it can be assumed that subsidized ventures gain advantages over non-subsidized ones. It is often argued that most founders cannot cover their financial requirements on the capital market. Therefore, one elementary function of subsidies is to assist founders to overcome financial 'weaknesses' and their consequences. The logical consequence is that subsidizing institutions should have ideally a 'catalyst function' in a twofold way: At first, these institutions should promote new ventures with financial means. Secondly, these institutions should have different lending standards to new ventures than commercial institution with their rigid asset oriented lending standards.

The research question is to look in a first step if there is a difference among subsidized and non-subsidized ventures. An analysis of the Austrian subsidy system revealed that subsidized and non-subsidized ventures differ scarcely in respect of their development (Frank and Rößl, 1990). Therefore, in addition the question is asked if the current subsidizing policy/guidelines prefer a specific type of entrepreneur and/or if a specific type of entrepreneur is attracted by the current subsidy policy. As the analysis of differing variables leads to contradictory success effects, which are difficult to interpret (Frank and Rößl, 1990), we try to assemble these items to a typology. We employ the heuristical method of abstraction and simplification (Scheuch, 1989, p.78; Beier, 1973, p.202; Kirsch, 1971, pp.199) to evaluate the presumable development of these types besides the receipt of subsidies.

Frame of reference

Character of a heuristic frame of reference

Due to the lack of a comprehensive and consistent theory a frame of reference (Kubicek, 1977, pp.17) is used. It is applied as a methodological tool for integrating existing theoretical elements. The function of this frame of reference is to make our approach to the research object transparent and explicit.

A frame of reference approach reflects the 'processual character' of research. In this sense it focuses the data-gathering activities within the 'frame', but it is flexible in defining the categories suitable for the actual research project and in searching heuristically for relations between variables.

The frame itself has a preliminary character in respect of its theoretical elements and its comprehensiveness. The 'refinement process' of several frames of reference should finally lead to a comprehensive theory with high explanatory power.

Development of a frame of reference

The research design employed is based on a comparative analysis. Therefore, all theoretical elements of the frame of reference except the receipt of a subsidy are the same for both samples. This quasi-experimental research design allows the evaluation of the effectiveness of subsidies. Furthermore, in case the two samples do not differ in respect of venture development, an analysis of differences of the theoretical elements is possible.

Besides the *receipt of subsidies the person(ality)* of the founder and his/her *microsocial environment* are considered to be theoretically relevant (e.g. Plaschka, 1986; Klandt, 1984). Education, vocational training, job before business start-up, self-image, expectations in respect of the entrepreneurial career, knowledge of his/her line of business, jobs of parents and relations to acquainted entrepreneurs were used for the description and analysis of the founder.

The *'start-up position'* of a venture is of importance for its survival and future development (e.g. Plaschka, 1986; Birley, 1986). This factor was described by the size of the venture in terms of capital and employees, the time spent for the preparation of the venture creation and its perceived difficulties, entry barriers and the line of business.

The fourth theoretical element of the frame of reference deals with the *managerial behaviour* of the founder. A conscious application of certain management techniques and basic management knowledge is of relevance for the development of a venture (e.g. Frank, Plaschka and Rößl, 1989; Frank, Plaschka and Rößl, 1988). This element of the frame of reference aimed at considering the use of cost accounting, planning and planning horizon, perceived value of planning, goal setting and importance of growth goals and calling upon consultants in several management areas like finance, marketing, tax, etc.

Figure 1
Frame of reference

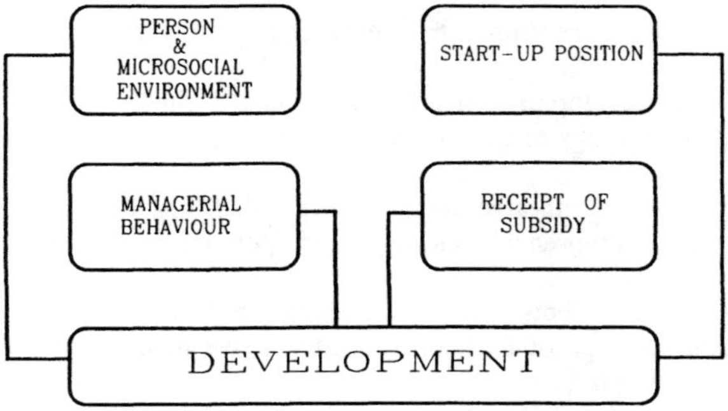

Sample and method

The study is based on a comparative analysis of a sample of subsidized and a sample of non-subsidized ventures.

A random sample of 777 business founders was drawn from founders who filled in an application form of the Bürges-Förderungsbank between 1979 and 1988 [1]. Each of these founders received a six page standardized questionnaire. The questionnaires were mailed in April 1989. For each venture the data from the application form and the data from the mailed questionnaire were linked. 276 questionnaires were returned and usable for data analysis (35.5% response rate) [2].

he population of non-subsidized ventures was based on listings of the Chamber of Commerce. Only ventures established between 1979 and 1988 were taken into consideration. Due to the fact that the majority of business founders receives some subsidies, a large sample of 1688 business founders was drawn randomly. This sample also included 288 founders who had applied for a subsidy at the Bürges-Förderungsbank but were rejected for formal reasons (e.g. the application was too late). The standardized questionnaire [3] was mailed to these founders in September 1989 [4]. 193 were returned and 109 questionnaires were answered by non-subsidized founders and were usable for data analysis (11.5% response rate, usable response rate of 6.5%).

Comparison of the two samples:

Both samples were compared regarding start-up year, type of venture creation (start-up or takeover of an existing venture) and type of industry. A comparison of both samples in respect of the start-up year revealed no statistical significant differences. The distribution regarding the type of industry shows a similar distribution as well: 28% of the subsidized (32% of the non-subsidized) ventures are manufacturers, 32% of the subsidized (29% of the non-subsidized) ventures belong to the trading sector and 40% of the subsidized (39% of the non-subsidized) ventures are in the service-industry.

Since there were statistical significant differences between newly established firms and takeovers [5] and due to the well-known differences in the development of these types (e.g. Hunsdiek and May-Strobl, 1986, pp.40) we analyze only newly established ventures.

Findings

We present our findings according to the following steps of arguments:

* we compare the development of subsidized and non-subsidized ventures
* to evaluate the findings of this step we look for further differences between the two groups
* in a third step we synthesize the results revealed to a typology of subsidized and non-subsidized entrepreneurs and try to incorporate it in existing typologies

Then we discuss the effects of subsidies as in the Austrian system which are traced back to the subsidized type of founder and, finally, we make some suggestions how to improve the subsidizing policy.

Subsidies and new venture development

In a first step we ask whether subsidized and non-subsidized new ventures differ with respect to their development. Politically, subsidies are mainly justified by the job creation they induce. Therefore, besides other factors like export sales, overall economic situation, etc. we use the increase in the number of employees as the main indicator for measuring the venture development.

In an overall evaluation we summarize that there are *no differences with respect to venture development.* Few differences even indicate that non-subsidized new ventures develop better.

As far as the subjective assessment of the firm and its development is concerned, there are no statistically significant differences. Only the sales growth expectations for the next year are higher for the non-subsidized ventures. In respect of objective factors we found that non-subsidized ventures are established at a larger size, but as the growth rates are the same, these ventures are larger also three years after foundation. Non-subsidized ventures are engaged in exporting more often and have higher export sales. The following table shows the results concerning the venture development of subsidized and non-subsidized ventures [6].

Typology-constituting differences

Besides the receipt of subsidies other factors influence the development. As the effects of subsidies could be concealed by other different factors, we search for statistically significant differences between the two samples.

As we focus on identifying a typology we do not discuss variables that are similarly distributed within the samples. The following table shows the statistically significant [7] differences:

Table 1

Development of subsidized and non-subsidized new ventures

test if significant at a 5% level	subsidized new ventures	non-subsidized new ventures
objective factors		
t-test	less employees at the start	more employees at the start
t-test	less empl. 3 years later	more empl. 3 years later
	similar growth rates	
X^2	export less often	export more often
t-test	lower export sales	higher export sales
	similar failure rates	
subjective factors		
	similar crisis probability	
t-test	sooner crisis occurance	later crisis occurance
t-test	lower sales growth expectations	higher sales growth expectations
	similar estimation of the firm's economic situation	
	similar estimation of the fulfillment of expectations	
	similar estimation of changes of founder's income	
	similar frequency of financial problems	

Table 2

Table 2

Differences between subsidized and non-subsidized new ventures

test	subsidized new ventures	non-subsidized new ventures
	1. person and microsocial environment	
t-test	age of founder is lower	age of founder is higher
X^2	poorer educated	better educated
X^2	more frequent vocational training	less frequent vocational training
X^2	former experience in the line of business	less experienced
X^2	believe that they have to work harder	do not believe this
X^2	more often supported by relatives	less often supported by relatives
X^2	being self-employed is not the only way of living	being an entrepreneur is the only imaginable way of living
X^2	perceive themselves to be well qualified	more critical self-perception
	2. managerial behavior	
X^2	location is a more severe problem	less severe problem
X^2	problems with public authorities	less severe problems
X^2	cannot explain his competitive advantages, the uniqueness of the business	can explain his competitive advantages
X^2	do not believe in the importance of concentrating on essentials	believe in the importance of concentrating on essentials
X^2	accounting is perceived as important	not perceived as important
X^2	more frequent financial consultancy	less frequent fin. consultancy
X^2	export less often	export more often
	3. start-up position	
X^2	less often in the field of manufacturing	more often in this field
X^2	more often in the field of tourism	less often in this field
X^2	not based on market opportunities	based on market opportunities
X^2	lower entry barriers	higher barriers

As the effects of subsidies could be concealed by these factors, the relation between these factors and the development has to be analyzed:

* As far as the age of the founder in the German literature [8] is concerned, no relationship between age and new venture success has been found (Klandt, 1984, p.222; Plaschka, 1986, p.82). But Brockhaus (1980, p.370) found significant differences [9], whereas Mayer and Goldstein (1961, p.101) found the opposite relation. Others draw their conclusions from the life-cycle concept and argue that there is a period between the age of 27 and 38 when one can make comparably free choices and ventures founded by persons of that age are more successful (Nathusius, 1983, p.39).
* The variable 'perceived location problems' is difficult to interpret because it cannot be defined whether these problems are real or not. In addition, the relation between location problems or rather the decision process on location and success have not been empirically verified (Mugler, 1986, p.241).
* Subsidized founders believe more often that they have to work harder in order to be successful. This orientation towards work could, on the one hand, be interpreted as a need for achievement that should foster new venture development (Klandt, 1984, p.355; Plaschka, 1986, p.147; McClelland, 1961). On the other hand, subsidized founders did not express that they liked to work harder and this would actually fit

into McClelland's need for achievement concept. All in all we do not think that this difference affects success.

* Subsidized founders do not think that separating essentials from matters of secondary importance in order to concentrate planning activities on the essentials is important for success. On the contrary, it was found that this ability discriminates between successful and non-successful founders (Frank, Plaschka and Rößl, 1989, Frank, Plaschka and Rößl, 1988) so that this difference should result in a poorer performance of subsidized ventures.

* Subsidized founders argue that knowledge of accounting techniques is important for venture success. On the one hand, this perception does not prove that their knowledge is really better, on the other hand, knowledge cannot be disadvantageous.

* Subsidized ventures are less often found in the field of manufacturing [10]. Generally spoken manufacturing firms tend to be more successful (Plaschka, 1986, p.103).

* As ventures usually use a bank for applying for the subsidy it is not remarkable that subsidized ventures show a higher frequency of financial consultancy.

* Vocational training has been identified as a success factor, therefore subsidized ventures should be more successful. Experience in the line of business has often been identified as a success factor (Plaschka, 1986, pp.167; Klandt, 1984, p.265), too, so that this factor should influence the venture's development positively.

* As far as education is concerned, diverse results are available. Hoad and Rosko (1964, pp.96) found a positive relation between the duration of education and success; Brockhaus (1980, pp.370) found a negative relation between the two factors, whereas Plaschka (1986, pp.98) found no relation between education and success (similar Collins, Moore and Umwalla, 1965, pp.80).

* Plaschka (1986, pp.152) found that the active support by the spouse is highly correlated with success, but no correlation has been revealed in respect of financial support by the spouse or relatives.

Due to the heterogeneous findings in the literature it is impossible to determine the probable development of the two groups based on the statistically significant differences between subsidized and non-subsidized ventures. So we try to synthesize the differences to a typology of founders as we hope that, by abstracting from confusing and contradictory details, these types can be interpreted more easily.

An emerging typology of subsidized and non-subsidized founders

Most of the subsidized ventures are founded without a clear definition of the market position and without creating specific competitive advantages. Due to the 'reproducibility' of these ventures a high degree of competition is the consequence.

From our perspective, the founder of a subsidized new venture can be characterized as neither market nor opportunity oriented business administrator with a tendency towards overestimating his/her own capacities. But in spite of his/her self-perception he/she does not show management profile [11], whereas the founder of a non-subsidized venture clearly states what he/she believes.

The perceived problems of founders of subsidized ventures are, generally spoken, less severe problems. They do not see the challenges and opportunities of a market-oriented venture creation. On the one hand, they perceive less entry barriers to the market, on the other hand, they cannot tell the uniqueness of their venture and do not pay attention to the market. So we think these entrepreneurs cannot be seen as an entrepreneur in the sense of opportunity managers (Stewart, 1989, p.11).

To distinguish between the founder of subsidized and non-subsidized ventures we call the founder of a subsidized venture a 'self-confident, experience-based administrator', whereas the founder of a non-subsidized venture can be characterized as a 'knowledge-based opportunity searcher'.

This differentiation fits quite well in Pleitner's typology. There is empirical evidence for classifying the founder of a subsidized venture as a 'buying-a-job founder', who has good vocational training, is experienced in his/her line of business and founds his/her own business to become self-employed. But this is not the risk-taking entrepreneur, who is following opportunities (Pleitner, 1984, pp.514), while the 'knowledge-based opportunity searcher' tries to more or less become a 'real entrepreneur' in Pleitner's typology.

To sum up we record that subsidized and non-subsidized ventures differ scarcely in respect of their development but show several differences in managerial behavior. Taking into account the literature on general management and entrepreneurship, the non-subsidized 'opportunity searcher' should perform better than the subsidized 'administrator'. As the latter is focusing more on operative matters than on essentials, opportunities and market challenges, it could be inferred that he/she should be less successful.

But we have to remember that research of success factors in the very early stage of the foundation process has not revealed conclusive results up till now and, therefore, a strategy based on experience and 'muddling through' applied in this period might work quite well.

Regardless of this question subsidies do not induce high growth rates in terms of employees or investments, at least in respect of the tape of venture that is subsidized by the existing system. Thus, subsidies are a questionable resource allocation mechanism from the point of view of pure growth.

Discussion and policy implications

If a subsidizing policy primarily intends to foster growth in terms of employees and if subsidizing programs are committed to an efficient allocation of financial resources, the political question is how to change the guidelines that not only this more or less unsuccessful type of venture is encouraged to look for subsidies and how to change the allocation mechanism so that this type is no longer favoured in receiving the subsidies.

From the results of this study the following suggestions regarding subsidizing policies emerge:

* Fewer new ventures should be subsidized with more money. If the receipt of subsidies were more attractive, also the 'real entrepreneurs' would apply for subsidies, and the allocation efficiency would increase, since 'real' entrepreneurs are more often in the field of manufacturing, which has a much higher growth potential than other industries.
* For the decision whether to subsidize a new venture or not in addition to the criteria of credit standing used by banks more qualitative data should be considered. The Austrian system of subsidizing new ventures is based on credit investigation by the bank which assists the founder in applying for the subsidy. So, in general, it is very likely that subsidies do not affect the granting of loans. As long as the 'rules of the

game' for getting money are quite the same for subsidized and non-subsidized ventures, the results will be similar.

* It must be secured that the non-repayable subsidy really broadens the room for financial manoeuvres and is not spent on debt rescheduling.
* The aims of the subsidizing policy have to be agreed upon and fixed. In many cases, the objectives of subsidizing are politically not clearly defined. For example, the Austrian system does not claim to favor special lines of business, but in fact ventures of the tourism industry have better chances to receive subsidies. Due to the mixture of formal guidelines, official, politically stressed aims and and 'informal' aims, the allocation effectiveness cannot be judged objectively.

Notes

1. This application form contains information on requested subsidy, legal structure of the venture, size, capital requirements, financial situation of the founder, etc..
2. 25 questionnaires could not be delivered.
3. This questionnaire contained the same questions which were used for the subsidized sample but included also questions of the application form.
4. 48 questionnaires could not be delivered.
5. Only 38% of the subsidized ventures, whereas 57% of the non-subsidized ventures are newly established firms.
6. These results were derived by t-tests as far as metric or interval scales were used and Chi-Square as far as nominal variables are concerned.
7. These differences are significant at a 5% level at least.
8. In order to exclude national particularities we primarily focus on empirical findings drawn from Austrian data.
9. The average age of successful founders is 23 years, and of non-successful founders 36 years.
10. As the definition of a line of business is rather broad so that a line of business includes a huge variety of businesses with different problems we do not believe that the economic sector is the appropriate unit for such an analysis.
11. He answers the questions concerning new venture management with a tendency towards middle-ranged items or by saying 'I do not know'.

References

Beier, U. (1973), 'Zur Anwendung heuristischer Entscheidungsmethoden bei der Bestimmung eines Konsumprogramms', *Zeitschrift für Betriebswirtschaft* vol. 43, no. 3.

Birley, S. (1986), 'The Small Firm - Set At The Start', *Frontiers of Entrepreneurship Research 1986*, Babson College.

Brockhaus, R.H. (1980), 'Psychological and Environmental Factors Which Distinguish the Successful from the Unsuccessful Entrepreneur: A Longitudinal Study', *Academy of Management Proceedings 1980*.

Collins, O.F, Moore, D. and Umwalla, D.B. (1965), *The Enterprising Man*, 3rd ed., East Lansing, Michigan.

Frank, H., Plaschka, G. and Rößl, D. (1988), 'Delegation and Information-Gathering Behaviour of Successful and Non-Successful Founders of New Ventures', paper presented at the *2nd workshop on Recent Research in Entrepreneurship*, Vienna.

Frank, H., Plaschka, G. and Rößl, D. (1989), 'Planning behaviour of successful and non-successful founders of new ventures', *Entrepreneurship & Regional Development* vol. 1, no. 2.

Frank, H. and Rößl, D. (1990), 'The Effects of Subsidies on New Venture Development', paper presented at the *13th Small Firms Policy & Research Conference*, Leeds University/Business School.

Hoad, W.M. and Rosko, P. (1964), *Management Factors Contributing to the Success and Failure of the New Small Manufacturers*, Michigan Business Reports, no. 44, Ann Arbor.

Hunsdiek, D. and May-Strobl, E. (1986), *Entwicklungslinien und Entwicklungsrisiken neugegründeter Unternehmen*, Schriften zur Mittelstandsforschung, Band 9, Stuttgart.

Joos, G. (1987), *Unternehmensgründungen aus wirtschaftspolitischer Sicht*, Frankfurt am Main.

Kirsch, W. (1971), *Entscheidungsprozesse, Band 2: Informationsverarbeitungstheorie des Entscheidungsverhaltens*, Wiesbaden.

Klandt, H. (1984), *Aktivität und Erfolg des Unternehmensgründers: Eine empirische Analyse unter Einbeziehung des mikrosozialen Umfelds*, Bergisch Gladbach.

Kubicek, H. (1977), 'Heuristische Bezugsrahmen und heuristisch angelegte Forschungsdesigns als Elemente einer Konstruktionsstrategie empirischer Forschung' in Köhler, R. (ed.), *Empirische und handlungstheoretische Forschungskonzeptionen in der Betriebswirtschaftslehre*, Stuttgart.

Mayer, K.B. and Goldstein, S. (1961), 'The First Two Years: Problems of Small Firm Growth and Survival' in Small Business Administration (ed.), *Small Business Research Studies*, no. 2, Washington D.C.

McClelland, D.C. (1961), *The Achieving Society*, Princeton.

Mugler, J. (1986), *Unternehmungen gründen und führen*, Teil 1, in Materialien des Instituts für Betriebswirtschaftlehre der Klein- und Mittelbetriebe, 3. Auflage, Wien.

Nathusius, K. (1983), 'Existenzgründung als Problem' in *Praxis der Unternehmensgründung*, 2. Auflage, Köln.

Plaschka, G. (1986), *Unternehmenserfolg: Eine vergleichende empirische Untersuchung von erfolgreichen und nicht erfolgreichen Unternehmensgründern*, Wien.

Pleitner, H.J. (1984), 'Beobachtungen und Überlegungen zur Person des mittelständischen Unternehmers' in Albach, H. and Held, Th. (eds), *Betriebswirtschaftslehre mittelständischer Unternehmen*, Wissenschaftliche Tagung des Verbandes der Hochschullehrer für Betriebswirtschaft e.V. 1984, Stuttgart.

Pütz, T. and Meyerhöfer, W. (1982), *Hemmnisse und Hilfen für Unternehmensgründungen*, Köln.

Scheuch, F. (1989), *Marketing*, 3. Auflage, München.

Schiller, R. (1986), *Existenzgründungen, Fördermaßnahmen und Ergebnisse: Beiträge zur Wirtschafts- und Sozialpolitik der deutschen Wirtschaft*, Köln.

Schmidt, K.-H. (1980), 'Die verteilungspolitische Bedeutung der Förderung von Existenzgründungen', *Internationales Gewerbearchiv* vol. 28, no. 3.

Stewart, A. (1989), *Team Entrepreneurship*, London / New Delhi.

Szyperski, N. (1980), 'Existenzgründungspolitik in der BRD', *Die Betriebswirtschaft* vol. 40, no. 1.

19 Incentives for the venture capital industry in Finland

Juha Auer, Kai-Erik Relander and Heikki Westerlund

Introduction

This descriptive, analytical study indicates, that as the environmental background elements vital to the development of the Finnish venture capital industry are not strong enough to support a competitive venture capital market in Finland incentives could be introduced.

Governments especially in several European countries have instigated venture capital activity by offering special incentives. This can be done in Finland as well. Direct incentives to the venture capital process often start with the authorization of venture capital investment vehicles by legislative action and thus recognizing the differing nature of their operations from other organizations in the financial markets.

Incentives can be allocated on three different levels: investors investing in venture capital, venture capital organizations and portfolio companies. Most of these incentives are fiscal, some are regulatory reliefs. Their use depends on the characteristics of the environment in different countries. Venture capital firms' investment activities can also be enhanced by reducing their risks or by improving their returns through government guarantee and co-investment schemes. Venture capital financing, in its institutionalized form, was born in the USA in the early 1960's and was introduced into Europe in the early 1980's. Important background elements have been the changes in the industrial structure in many industrialized countries and the resultant changed demand for industrial financing.

The most important environmental background elements vital to the development of a country's venture capital industry have been found to be the size of the technology sector, culture of entrepreneurship, financial markets for new companies and public policy incentives. Incentives can be allocated on three different levels: investors investing in venture capital, venture capital organizations and portfolio companies. Most of these incentives are fiscal, some are regulatory reliefs. Their use depends on the characteristics of the environment in different countries.

Venture capital firms' investment activities can also be enhanced by reducing their risks or by improving their returns through government guarantee and co-investment schemes. Approval to operate under a certain authorized status is often required in order to benefit from these incentives.

The most common structure to organize venture capital investing is a limited partnership structure, where the actual fund and the management firm are separate entities.

In general, incentive schemes have proved efficient in promoting the venture capital industry in individual countries, although some of them have become too bureaucratic for private venture capital organizations.

The Finnish venture capital industry is still in its infancy and common practices have begun to emerge only recently. The total capital under management as a ratio to the GNP is less than in Europe on average and special incentives for the venture capital industry do not exist so far. Most venture capital organizations are organized as corporations that invest their own equity and debt capital. This structure is too rigid for venture capital purposes. The efficient use of the Finnish limited partnership structure can be achieved through regulatory and legislative amendments.

Objectives and methodology

This exploratory study aims at defining the incentives that could be introduced in the Finnish venture capital industry as the environmental background elements vital to the development of a competitive venture capital industry are not strong enough.

The principal mean to obtain data on the USA, the United Kingdom, France and the Netherlands has been extensive literature analysis, articles and analysis of statistical material. The section on Finland is mostly based on the results of a questionnaire and structured interviews with Finnish venture capitalists. The aspects of taxation and the legal environment in Finland are mostly based on interviews with Finnish specialists.

The venture capital industry was examined starting from the most mature and sophisticated market, the USA, and then moving to the most important growing European markets, the U.K., France and the Netherlands. The development and environment in these three European countries were not analysed separately, but as a whole. The main reason for this was the somewhat common characteristics of these elements with respect to venture capital and the quite similar perceptions of the role of venture capital in these countries. The incentives established to encourage venture capital investments, however, differ between the countries, which has led to a wide variety of incentives. Incentives were therefore examined on a country-specific basis.

Finally, the development, environment and incentives regarding the venture capital industry are examined with respect to Finland. The results presented in this paper are mainly based on research projects on the venture capital industry initiated by the Finnish National Fund for Research and Development (SITRA) in years 1987-1990.

The venture capital environment

The development of the venture capital industry is effected by certain elements in the environment and the characteristics of these elements. First, there has to be enough opportunities for venture capital financing created by research and development activities (which contribute to size of the technology sector). Second, the attitudes found in entrepreneurial culture and thirdly the development of financial markets for new companies must permit venture capital firms to operate efficiently. Fourth, the public policy incentives are of great importance to the development of the venture capital market.[1]

Research and development activities

Technological innovation, is an important factor on the demand side of venture capital financing since technological innovation most often creates new potential high-growth markets. The fact that venture capitalists' investment preferences have traditionally been in technology-intensive businesses holds true not only in the USA, but also in other countries where the venture capital industry has emerged.[2]

The size of a country's technology sector is thus a significant factor in deciding whether that environment will support venture capital. The role of technology is critical because not only does it affect the size of the technical pool from which entrepreneurs emerge, but it also affects the size of the market for the kinds of products sold by high-tech companies, which are often bought by other high-tech companies.[3] The presence of large high-tech companies and their R&D activities for creating technology spin-offs, as well as government R&D expenditures, are also important.

The concentration of technology firms and research institutions around certain areas, in the form of e.g. science and technology parks, has been found to be a supporting element for venture capital. Not only does it promote cooperation between these firms, but it also creates a concentrated demand for venture capital and venture capital firms become located in these areas. The existence of well-developed venture capital networks provides incentives for entrepreneurial businesses. The availability of venture capital and such networks help attract entrepreneurs and technical personnel to these regions, creating a self-reinforcing cycle of new enterprise formation, innovation and economic development.[4]

Generally, venture capitalists invest in small business which intend to become large either in their specific market segment or in the marketplace as a whole.

Entrepreneurial culture

The chief criterion by which venture capitalists evaluate business proposals is the professional background and past achievements of the applicants, more than the mere content of their ideas or projects. Entrepreneurs choosing to start their own business primarily come out of existing companies, large or small, which they either started or in which they worked as employees. In the first case, the entrepreneur will have some form of track record of his ability to start a viable operation; in the latter case, the entrepreneur comes to the new enterprise with some history of how to keep a new company operating and moving toward larger market shares.[5] They may also have a proven management ability or a product idea and a desire to try it on their own. Other sources of new product and service ideas and entrepreneurs are science-oriented academic institutions and research laboratories. After a small business has reached the size of a large business, the entrepreneurial process recycles.

An appropriate entrepreneurial culture is needed to allow the entrepreneurial cycle to function. The availability of credible entrepreneurs depends on public attitudes towards entrepreneurial risk-taking and business failure/success. Entrepreneurs should be encouraged to create wealth (make money). If the risk element in entrepreneurial projects is not understood, failure may lead to loss of social status or at least deter a second attempt.

Attitudes towards and the attractiveness of self-employment among business and technical professionals are similarly important: these are influenced by the tradition of job mobility and security within these groups.[6] The culture-based degree of social and financial status awarded by society to the entrepreneur, who manages to find and promote practical applications for an original idea, vs. that awarded to the inventor, the intellectual, as a source of progress is also related to this.[7] In some countries, career advancement within large corporations is a more desirable path to business success. The benefits component of executive compensation makes the opportunity cost of leaving large business high.

On the other hand, capital is the catalyst in the entrepreneurial chain reaction; the perceived availability of risk capital is also a major factor in encouraging people to leave their secure jobs and become entrepreneurs.

Financial markets

In many cases unreceptiveness towards the outside ownership concept is indicated by relatively undeveloped equity markets.[8] Financial markets for SMEs and new companies, where firms do not have to meet the rigorous requirements of full stock exchange listing are particularly essential to the development of venture capital markets.[9] Not only is it important for venture capital firms to have an exit mechanism available to liquidate their equity positions in portfolio companies and realize their capital gains, but it is also important for successful venture capital-backed firms to turn to publicly-traded markets as a source of further financing for future development. In addition, the level of development and activity of financial markets for mergers and acquisitions is also of importance, as well as the tradition of the extent to which banks are allowed to take equity positions in companies; there might be less of an institutional difference between bank financing and venture capital financing.

The overall development of financial markets includes liberalization and diversification. Liberalization has the effect of allowing borrowers and lenders of financial capital greater flexibility in their choice of sources by way of domestic or foreign corporate or merchant banks, exchange dealers, brokers etc. Diversification is a critical background element for the development of venture capital markets.[10] It increases the choice available to those offering and seeking finance. It can be typified by the growth of markets in futures, options, company equities and major trading currencies, and is reflected by the types of institutions operating in these markets, as well as the products they offer.

Incentives

General incentives

The development of the venture capital industry is largely affected by the opportunities created for it by the surrounding environment. If market forces are not sufficiently strong, governments can instigate venture capital activity by offering special incentives. Many of these incentives are closely related to innovation policies in different countries, which in turn are closely bound up both with government's conception of its role in matters of economic policy and its overall policy as regards science and technology. These policies can be fiscal or regulatory and are usually aimed at removing impediments from the flow of funds within capital markets. They concern the investment activities of individuals and financial institutions, being allowed to place a part of their funds in riskier investments, taxation system and operation of the stock markets. Fiscal incentives limited narrowly to assisting venture capital formation and innovation in companies may be insufficient, when general personal and company taxation imposes levels of tax high enough to discourage entrepreneurs.

The role of public authorities in creating a climate favourable to innovation can be broken down into four main categories:

*providing adequate incentives for the entrepreneur
*providing adequate access to sources of science and technology, including foreign sources
*stimulating innovation in response to social needs
*maintaining and developing the vitality of the research enterprise.[11]

More specific measures in the field of R & D, education, and the development of industrial structures in order to stimulate this process fall into three broad categories:

*measures relating to investment in R & D and innovation
*measures relating to the acquisition and diffusion of knowledge and technical know-how
*measures relating to the general conditions of competition.[12]

From the US experience, it is known that any change in taxation of capital gains has an immediate and direct impact on venture capital funding.[13] In theory, funds will continue to flow into the venture capital industry until risk-adjusted rates of return between venture capital investments and other business investments are equalized at the margin. During period of high capital gains taxes, investors turn to lower-risk assets with a short-term horizon, since long-term profits may not be sufficiently greater than short-term profits to compensate the increased risk. Because venture capital firms invest in early-stage high-risk firms, they typically experience extraordinary gains on only a few portfolio companies. To compensate for the risks, investment losses and inadequate returns on the less successful portfolio companies, it is necessary to be able to liquidate stock in successful companies with an adequate after-tax return on investment.

High capital gains taxes may direct greater attention to current income among managers of small firms since the value of stock options may be significantly reduced. Founders of venture-backed companies may also demand a larger equity position to compensate for the higher capital gains.[14]

The treatment of incentive stock options has been found to be of importance to the venture capital industry. Young entrepreneurial companies in their formative years are often confronted with inadequate cash flow to attract the necessary skilled and professional talent. Talented managers and specialists who are in salaried positions with a career-oriented job have less of an incentive to abandon their secure jobs for highly risky endeavours. Being able to offer stock options and thus participation in the potential future success of the company to compensate for the risk is an attractive recruiting tool for these companies and venture capital companies. However, if stock options and capital gains are highly taxed, the marginal difference between existing salaries and bonuses vs. highly-taxed capital gains and stock options is insufficient .[15]

Favourable capital gains tax rates motivate investors to seek longer-term equity investments, raising the valuation of small growth companies; entrepreneurial activities are exerted because rewards are larger on stock appreciation and more people are willing to take risks starting new businesses.

Venture capital investment vehicles

The potential of venture capital firms to operate efficiently can be improved by several measures. At the outset, an efficient investment vehicle should be available for venture capital investments. These investment vehicles can be authorized by legislative action to form their own category. This is to recognize the differing nature of their operations from those of other organizations in the financial markets.

Authorization may involve the facilitation of the use of an efficient fund structure that it has not been possible to use for this kind of activity before due to unknown fiscal consequences and legal interpretation possibilities, or the law may not have permitted the use of this kind of structure in the first place.

Investment organizations that meet these criteria could be granted, within the framework of authorization, some relief in order to remove the unnecessary regulatory and tax burden placed on their operations, and incentives to make this kind of investing more attractive and channel investors' funds to venture capital activities.

The most commonly used structure to organize venture capital is a fund structure, where the fund and the firm managing the fund are separate entities. This structure is based on the US limited partnership structure and have been adopted by most developed venture capital markets.[16] It is likely that this kind of structure will also be proposed as a pan-European fund structure within the European Communities during the on-going integration process. The management firm has one or several funds under its management and it invests capital from these funds into investee firms. These funds may invest in parallel, or have different investment preferences. The funds have a fixed-term life, normally about 10 years, after which all investments have been exited, base capital and profits have been paid back to investors, and the fund is dissolved.[17]

Figure 1
Venture capital fund structure

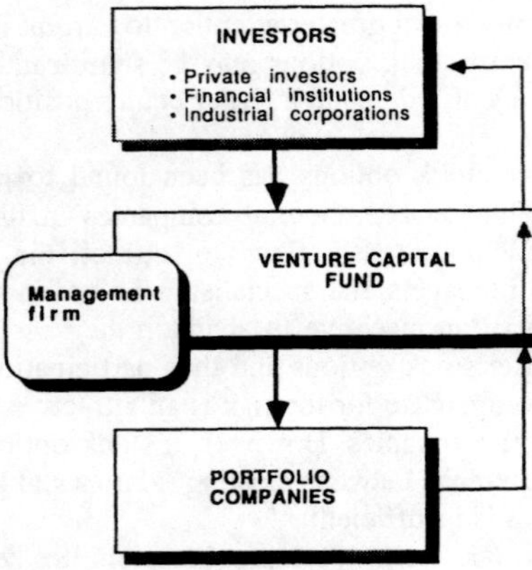

A management firm employs experienced managers who are familiar with the growth process of small businesses, and provides portfolio companies with assistance in most important strategic aspects. A management firm normally charges an annual management fee of 1.5-3% of the value of the fund. As an incentive, the management receives a bonus of typically 20% of the fund's profits. In addition to their initial capital contribution, investors get 80% of the profits.[18]

In structuring venture capital investment vehicles, the following objectives[19] are generally relevant, arising from the nature of venture capital financing:

- Investors must have limited liability
- The fund must be simple to operate
- The fund must be exempt or transparent for tax purposes
- The fund should be suitable for all kinds of national and international investors.
- It should be possible to incorporate a carried interest structure in the fund structure
- Ordinary management charges should be charged directly from the fund
- It should be possible for the investors to carry losses and profits back and forward.

Figure 2
Allocation of incentives in the venture capital process

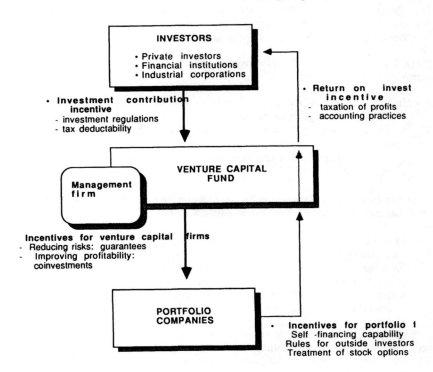

305

Allocation of incentives in the venture capital process

Three essential elements have to be considered in the venture capital process when planning on improving the fiscal and regulatory environment: investors investing in the venture capital market, venture capital organizations, and portfolio companies.

- In order to mobilize investors to invest in venture capital firms, special incentive schemes can be created, where the investor can deduct his investment in a venture capital fund, or part of it, from his annual taxable income.

In addition to an investment contribution incentive, investors also need some relief on their return on investment. Investment through a venture capital investment vehicle should not increase an investor's tax burden compared to direct investment.

- Dividends and interest received from venture capital investments could be tax-exempt if taxed at a lower rate in the hands of investors. More importantly, the capital gains from the liquidation of venture capital investments could be tax-exempt or taxed at a lower rate. In addition, investments in venture capital could be excluded from investors' taxable assets.

For the venture capital firm, incentives can be basically aimed at reducing their risks or improving their profitability.

- In order to reduce the risks attached to venture capital investments, guarantee schemes, where a government or semi-government organization guarantees part of a venture capital firm's investment, can be established. This can be extended to equity investments in particular. If an investment has to be realized with a loss, the guarantee organization would compensate a certain percentage of the loss to the venture capital firm.

Investments in early-stage technology companies have particularly proved highly risky, which has created a need for risk sharing partners.

- In order to improve venture capital firms' net return, a government or semi-government organization could participate via a co-investment in their investments. If an investment is successful, the government organization recoups its original investment plus a certain share of the profits. If the investment is lost, both parties lose their capital, but the private venture capital firm's loss is smaller than without the co-investor.

For the portfolio company, the scope of incentives can be broad and it is difficult to aim them directly at companies operating with venture capital firms. These incentives are likely to be more broadly connected with general policies to encourage new business formation, innovation and entrepreneurship.

Incentives more directly involved with venture capital firms concern the rules for outside investors and the self-financing capacity of companies.[20]

- Outside investors could be encouraged by making purchase of equity in SMEs more attractive. These measures could include taxation provisions favouring new equity, such as tax-exempt for new equity or deductibility from taxable income for such investments.

- Firms' self-financing capacity could be improved by tax-free periods in the early years or higher investment allowances. Fiscal incentives to undertake R&D activities are important. These should not only include tax deductibility of direct R&D expenditures, but also R&D-related expenditure such as social costs, consultancy manpower, writing down the value of patents and know-how, and depreciation of tangible property used for R&D purposes.[21]
- The improved treatment of stock options in order to attract key management and skilled workers to small firms. The owner of an incentive stock option should not realize any taxable income when the option is granted or exercised, but should be taxed on the disposition of the option stock.[22]
- Facilitating management buy-outs could be exercised by allowing deductions to individuals or companies for interest on borrowings to acquire shares of a business.
- Liberalizing the rules governing the ownership by a company of its own shares. This would enable the use of company buyback as a viable exit mechanism for venture capital firms.

Venture capital in Finland

Development of the venture capital industry in Finland

The venture capital industry in Finland is still in its infancy. Of the 19 organizations operating in the Finnish industry at the end of 1989, only three had been established before 1984. These organizations had a total capital of FIM 530 million under management. As a ratio to the gross national product, this is considerably less than the European average. Even though there has been some development in the last couple of years, the nature of the industry continues to remain rather unclear to entrepreneurs and investors, and its role in business development is not yet fully recognized. Common practices within the industry have not yet developed, and noteworthy cooperation between venture capital firms, e.g. in terms of syndication, has begun to appear only recently. It is also often difficult to distinguish venture capital firms from more development capital-oriented firms. [23]

The bulk of funds in the risk capital market in Finland is currently managed by large development capital companies that usually do not meet the definitions set for venture capital firms. Such development capital companies stress a majority equity position in more mature firms and seldom put a time-limit on their investment. They also often aim to reorganize the structures in certain industries by incorporating their portfolio companies. The industrial structure in Finland has permitted these kinds of operations and development capital companies have undeniably had an important role in developing and rationalising some industrial sectors.

The success of venture capital companies in the USA, as well as that of some of their European counterparts, led to the establishment of several such companies in Finland in the 1970's. Most development capital companies started in the spirit of orthodox venture capital idealism with minority investments in small growth firms, but soon found themselves concentrating on majority investments of a more permanent nature and on structural rationalization.

There have been many problems in venture capital financing in Finland:

- Future goals have often varied between the entrepreneur and the venture capitalists. It has proved difficult for a minority shareholder to influence the development of a business. Moreover, a minority stake is much more difficult to divest than a majority stake.
- The board of directors of venture capital firms have too often been peopled by the owners and financial backers of the company, instead of individuals with experience in managing and developing small businesses.
- Gains were often expected to materialize in too short a time and in order to avoid losses majority shareholdings were acquired. The long-term nature of venture capital investing has not been completely understood.[24]

Investee companies that were doing badly had to be rescued by a majority investment and the smaller number of successful companies needed a majority shareholder to safeguard their growth. A few development capital companies went public on the Stock Exchange and thus committed themselves to meet their investors' steady annual dividend requirements, which further hampered long-term minority investments. Some regional venture capital firms were also established in Finland. These quickly proved to have too narrow a base of investment opportunities, and bad investments had to be accepted. Regional economic development objectives are hard to match with financial return goals. The majority of these firms operate on a broader basis nowadays.

As in many other European countries the public sector became quite active in financing small and medium-sized entrepreneurial enterprises in the early 1970's. Public institutions are still by far the most important source of risk capital for Finnish SMEs. They provide financing mostly in the form of subordinated loans or grants. Direct equity investments form only a fraction of total investments and may even be forbidden for some institutions. The risk component of investments may be equivalent to venture capital investments, but financial return is not the primary goal and investors are mostly passive. These institutions include the Technology Development Centre of Finland (TEKES), the Regional Development Fund of Finland (KERA), the Ministry of Trade and Industry (KTM), the State Guarantee Board (VATA) and the Finnish National Fund for Research and Development (SITRA)

The venture capital environment

Research and development activities

Natural reasons for the slow development of venture capital in the early days included the small size of domestic markets and the relatively low level of research and development expenses in proportion to GNP. Consequently not enough high quality investment opportunities with sufficient growth potential have emerged. For example in 1971, Finland's R&D expenses were only 0.9% of GNP, which was several times less than in most developed industrial countries.[25] This can be partly explained by the fact that Finland's industrial structure has traditionally been weighted towards slow-growth, mature sectors, in which R&D expenses in relation to turnover are relatively low. Many large Finnish companies did not even have a separate R&D department or personnel in the

1960's and early 1970's. The government's share of all R&D spending in R&D-intensive high-technology sectors has also been less than in many other industrial countries.

Figure 3
Research and development expenses in Finland 1971-2000
Proportion of GNP

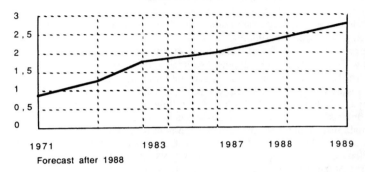

Source: Tilastokeskus 1989, Valtion Tiede- ja Teknologianeuvosto 1987

Table 1
Public research and development financing in various countries

| | Share (%) of public financing in 1987 of | |
	All R&D expenses	R&D performed by the industry
Italy	54	22
France	53	23
USA	51	34
Austria	49	..
Canada	46	11
Norway	44	19
Finland	38	5
West Germany	36	14

Sources: TKL 1989, 11

On the other hand, universities and research institutes have not sought to systematically transfer the technology/innovations they have developed to commercial markets. These institutions have only recently begun to encourage their employees to take entrepreneurial risks.

In the 1980's, policy questions concerning technology took priority in both the public and private sectors. Investment in R&D as a percentage of GNP has grown considerably, exceeding 1.7% in 1988.

309

In the 1980's, R&D expenses as a proportion of industrial turnover increased by 12-13% annually in real terms, which is one of the highest growth figures in industrial countries.[26] Investment in R&D activities by the private sector has grown more rapidly than investment by the public sector, and privately-funded R&D accounted for about 62% of all R&D expenses in 1987. It is the intention of the public authorities to maintain this 40/60 ratio in the future. One argument in favour of increasing the government's share of R&D expenses in Finland is the fact that even large Finnish industrial corporations are small by international standards. On the other hand, industry's R&D activities are still concentrated in a relatively small number of firms. One large corporation accounted for 15% of all private R&D in 1986.[27]

In order to boost transfer of technology, efforts have been made to increase industry's contacts with research and development sources in the 1980's. The most important vehicle for this has been the establishment of science parks in connection with universities and research institutes. The first science park in Finland - and the first one in Scandinavia - was established in Oulu in 1982.[28] This has been followed by six other science parks. There are some 250 firms located in these facilities and developments have been mainly encouraging.

The main instrument through which government R&D financing is channelled to private business is the Technology Development Centre of Finland, TEKES (Teknologian Kehittämiskeskus), which was established in 1983. TEKES financed R&D activities with about FIM 500 million in 1988, mostly in the form of risk loans and grants. Another vehicle for public R&D financing for private firms is Finland's National Fund for Research and Development, SITRA (Suomen itsenäisyyden juhlavuoden 1967 rahasto), which is a permanent foundation operating under the auspices of the Bank of Finland. The funds available for project finance amount to FIM 60-65 million annually. In 1988 FIM 44 million was invested directly in firms in the form of convertible and other loans.

The Science and Technology Policies Council of Finland set new goals in 1984 for increasing R&D investments. Under this programme the proportion of R&D expenses should reach 2.7% of GNP by the end of the 1990's.[29] It is expected that this increase will lead to the emergence of a significant number of innovations that will require both management expertise and financing to become successful in the marketplace.

Entrepreneurial culture

Although entrepreneurship is respected in Finland and the number of new business start-ups in proportion to the population is among the highest in the world (and consequently the number of bankruptcies) the country's entrepreneurial culture has not been particularly suitable for venture capital financing. Especially in the case of SMEs, the management and total ownership of businesses have traditionally been held by the entrepreneur/family, and the business skills of entrepreneurs have often been insufficient for managing fast growth.

The attitude has been one of 'do-it-yourself'. It is still not very common for entrepreneurs and venture capital firms to have the same goals e.g. in terms of growth and exit policies. Also, it is still quite rare for entrepreneurs to form a management team around one business idea rather than the idea being an extension of one individual's personality. There is no shortage of technologists capable of coming up with product ideas. The real need is for managers who can turn ideas into commercially viable products.[30]

Cooperation between firms is not especially well developed in Finland despite the small size of the market and the homogeneity of the population. In Japan, two-thirds of the production of large corporations is undertaken outside these corporations. In Sweden, 25% of the production of the engineering industry comes from sub-contracting agreements. In Finland, the corresponding figure is 20%.[31]

The availability of government grants and loans to SMEs as well as the important role of banks in financing all businesses, including SMEs, may also have contributed to the unreceptiveness of outside equity investors. It may be considered unusual that in addition to sharing the risks, the financier wants to share future profits.

The development and transition of saving behaviour away from passive deposits and debt securities to equity securities has also had an impact on business and entrepreneurial culture. The concept of separating management and ownership has become more acceptable and entrepreneurs have become more receptive to the participation of an active outside equity investor in the development of the firm. The new entrepreneurial culture is seen, for example, in the increasing popularity of entrepreneurship among the young and highly-educated people.

Changes are still required in order to improve utilization of the services offered by venture capital firms. Although some progress has taken place in the last two years, business plans are not yet widely used by entrepreneurs. This is partly due to the fact that the availability of venture capital on the one hand and the requirements of venture capital on the other, have not been fully recognized. In 1988, venture capital firms received on an average 60 business proposals from prospecting portfolio companies. Even though almost all venture capital financiers require a more or less formal business plan, only about 20% of the entrepreneurs have one available during their first negotiations with the venture capitalist. This makes the due diligence process even more time-consuming, which is also reflected in the relatively long time required for a funding decision (average 115 days).

Financial market

Until the early 1980's the capital market in Finland was strictly controlled. The availability of credit, both foreign and domestic, was regulated by the Bank of Finland, which also determined domestic interest rates. Finnish financial markets have traditionally been dominated by the banks. In 1980 bank deposits accounted for over 80% of the total amount of financial assets. The stock market was only of minor importance, with 13%.[32]

The financial structure of Finnish companies is clearly more weighted towards debt capital than in most other OECD countries. In 1987 the share of equity of all financial assets was only 28% on average.[33] There are two main reasons for this. Until the end of the 1970's, the inflation was high and devaluations were common. This made domestic loans attractive to companies. In addition, the use of borrowed capital was generously favoured in taxation. In the 1980's higher interest rates and slower inflation increased borrowing costs and risks. The need for equity financing increased.

Together with changes in the industrial structure, the capital markets have developed and liberalized in Finland during the 1980's. The stock market has expanded rapidly. By the end of 1988 the share of bank deposits had fallen to 40% while that of the stock market had risen to 22%.[34] The share of money market instruments had risen to 18% from zero in 1980. The market capitalization of companies listed on the Helsinki Stock Exchange, over FIM 130 billion in 1988, was 16 times higher than in 1980. The surge in stock prices can be attributed to several factors. Share prices were often undervalued compared to companies' asset values and corporate profits have risen rapidly. The business sector is also undergoing a restructuring process involving the ownership structure of companies. Economic growth has also been stronger in Finland than in OECD countries on average and private individuals have begun to redirect their savings.[35]

The liberalization process is also reflected in the increased internationalization of capital markets. Industrial firms can nowadays turn quite freely to international markets to raise capital. Regulations governing foreign property acquisition have been substantially eased for individuals as well as for institutions.

Along with liberalization, the capital markets also became more diversified in the 1980's. Increasingly specialized financing firms have emerged, in areas such as leasing and factoring. Trading in options and futures was initiated in Finland in May 1988.

No readily available exit mechanism for successful venture capital investments, e.g. a functioning OTC market has existed. The OTC market was established at the end of 1984, but it grew very slowly during the first couple of years, mainly because of a few unsuccessful firms among the first firms quoted on the list. The boom in the IPO market took place from the end of 1987 to the end of 1988, when the number of companies listed almost tripled. OTC-listed firms and firms seeking listing arranged 50 share issues in 1988, which raised a total of FIM 1.4 billion. The corresponding figure for 1987 was FIM 240 million.[36]

In recent years it has been difficult to persuade investors to make long-term illiquid investments in small firms, at a time when short-term investments in the Stock Exchange and real estate have been highly profitable.

Incentives

So far, there are no special incentives aimed at promoting venture capital in Finland. In 1984, however, a Development Capital Company status (Lex Sponsor) was enacted. A chapter was added to the Business Income Taxation Act which enabled the Ministry of Finance to classify companies under a special status for tax incentive purposes 'if the companies can be regarded as investors in industrial firms that are considered important to the economic life of Finland'. The decision is therefore totally administrative. Under this status, a company could receive dividends from portfolio companies tax-exempt without an obligation to redistribute them. Lex Sponsor was a temporary arrangement and was repealed at the end of 1988. Of the 18 firms studied, 6 had requested and were granted the status. The status was not considered very useful.

In other areas of legislation there are no regulations that specifically govern venture capitalists. Entrepreneurs and venture capital firms can, of course, enjoy the general tax incentives applicable at certain times. From 1984 to 1988 there was, for instance, a special research and development deduction granted to industrial firms. No fiscal incentives exist for financing with equity capital. Taxation of innovative firms does not differ from that of other companies. Certain incentives exist for companies investing in developing areas, but they apply to all kinds of businesses. Such incentives include favourable rates of depreciation for buildings, plant and equipment and reductions in assessable income.[37]

Investment vehicles

Venture capital corporations

All Finnish venture capital firms, with two exceptions, are organized as corporations which invest their own equity and loan capital. The corporation form is not flexible enough in its present form for practising venture capital financing. The long-term investment horizon typical of venture capital is difficult to carry out with the short-term profit requirements typical of the corporate structure. Venture capital firms organized in the corporate form normally require a steady cash flow to cover the expenses arising from the management services provided for the portfolio companies and possible interest payments on debt. Most Finnish venture capital firms therefore use a consulting fee, which is either annually fixed, bound to committed time, or to a portfolio firm's turnover or some combination of these, to remunerate their management services. Because of the double taxation of profits, the tax burden on investors increases compared to direct purchase of equity. The board of directors in venture capital firms is often relatively inexperienced with venture capital financing, which may easily lead to companies losing sight of their original business idea.

The structure of the Finnish venture capital limited partnership

Under the current law, there are two kinds of limited partnerships available: one under the Business Income Taxation Act and the other under the Income Taxation Act. In the former, gains are taxed partly at the partnership level. The latter is transparent in terms of profits. As the main function of the fund is to own shares in investee companies the first two venture capital limited partnerships in Finland have been considered not to carry on a trade and are taxed under the Income Taxation Act. The confirmation of the tax treatment requires approval from the Central Taxation Committee and can presently be granted for one year ahead.

The Finnish limited partnership structure meets the following objectives of an efficient fund structure:

- Investors have limited liability.
- The structure is simple to operate.
- The fund is transparent for tax purposes; all gains flow directly through to investors.
- A carried interest structure is incorporated in the fund structure.
- Management fees are offsetable against income arising from the fund.
- The fund is suitable for most domestic investors.

The management firm is the general partner which takes care of all the investment decisions and manages the fund. Investors are limited partners. Matters such as investment policy, life term, management expenses, carried interest can be defined quite freely in the management contract.

If a management firm does not have other business activities apart from the management of the fund, it will probably be treated as a consulting firm under the Income Taxation Act. If the management firm is taxed under the Business Income Taxation Act because of its earlier activities, this status is likely to remain. Confirmation of the tax treatment of the management firm will probably require the approval of the Central Taxation Committee.

The carried interest can be arranged basically in two ways: the managers can own partnership units directly or indirectly so that the management firm owns partnership units. In direct ownership it is likely that the Income Taxation Act will be applied. In indirect ownership taxation is likely to depend on the tax status of the management firm.

Under the Income Taxation Act the partnership can take advantage of the partial tax exemption for stock owned for more than five years. Investors, except for professional investors such as banks and insurance companies, can make use of this in their taxation. On the other hand, profits for investors such as industrial corporations are included in their external sources of income and it is likely that there are fewer ways of minimizing taxation. Profits to professional investors are included in profits from their other investment activities in which case there are several taxation minimizing methods available.

Defects in the limited partnership structure

The most significant defects in the limited partnership structure under the prevailing Income Taxation Act are:

" A limited partnership cannot offset losses from investments against profits other than those arising during the same tax year.
" A partnership unit is not considered a security. Thus investors are not able to use losses in their own taxation.

Defect arising from the laws concerning foreign ownership in Finnish businesses:

" Foreign investors' potential to participate in Finnish venture capital limited partnerships are essentially hampered. Under the prevailing laws, a foreign limited partner automatically turns the partnership status into what is referred to as a 'dangerous company'. Under this status the limited partnership cannot own shares in Finnish companies if 'full restriction' in an investee firm is in force. The ownership limit is raised to 20%, or at most to 40%, if an investee firm's articles of association permits this and it has been approved by the Ministry of Finance.

Other structures considered

In structuring the Finnish venture capital investment vehicle, three different organizational structures were considered:

" Corporation
" Unit Trust
" Limited partnership

Investors' limited liability and the distribution of profits automatically ruled out the use of unlimited companies, foundations and co-operative societies.

· As a venture capital fund, the corporation is substantially more complicated in terms of administration than the limited partnership. Problems concerning organizing the distribution of initial capital and profits to investors are seen as arguing against the use of corporations as much as actual taxation treatment.[38] Generally, even partial distribution of equity and reserves requires approval from the authorities.

However, it is possible for investors to have limited liability, if the fund does not guarantee loans for its portfolio companies in excess of its own equity capital. Investors' participation in the management of the fund's investments can be limited e.g. by the use voting and non-voting stock. To avoid the possible application of bankruptcy law in the event of the realization of substantial early losses before profits, stocks can be sold with a substantial premium so that capital and reserves are substantially larger than equity capital.[39]

Although the main operating principles of the unit trust structure under the Unit Trust Act of 1987 and the venture capital fund are quite similar, there are still substantial differences arising from their different roles as investment vehicles.[40]

- The main goal in unit trust operations is the avoidance of risks, which is carried out by efficient diversification of the portfolio in listed securities and other liquid investments without participating in the development of investments.
- Participation of foreign investors in the trust is prohibited.

According to 2 of the Unit Trust Act, activity in which the public is offered a possibility to participate in collective investments in securities, can only be carried out by authorized unit trusts or by subscribing shares of corporations having such activities.

Therefore venture capital investments, if adapted in this form, would require the enactment of a totally new law, which considering the size of the venture capital market would not be justified.

Discussions and implications

Venture capital financing, in its institutionalized form, was born in the USA in the early 1960's. During the last ten years the professional venture capital industry has developed rapidly in most of the world's industrialised countries. The most important background elements which have contributed to the growth of demand of venture capital financing have been the significant changes seen in the industrial structure worldwide. This has been witnessed by the decline of the traditional smokestack industries, the emergence of high-technology and service industries, as well as the growing importance of SMEs and entrepreneurship. These phenomena have given rise to a changing demand for industrial financing.

The most important environmental background elements vital to the development of a country's venture capital industry have been found to be research and development activities, entrepreneurial culture and attitudes towards entrepreneurial risk-taking and the development of financial markets, especially the existence of public stock markets for SMEs.

If these market forces are not sufficiently strong, governments can instigate venture capital activity by offering special incentives. Direct incentives to the venture capital process often start with the authorization of venture capital investment vehicles by legislative action and thus recognizing the differing nature of their operations from other organizations in the financial markets. The most efficient structure to organize venture capital has proved to be a fund structure, based on the U.S. limited partnership structure, where the fund and the management firm are separate entities.

Incentives can be allocated on three different levels: investors investing in venture capital, venture capital organizations and portfolio companies. Most of these incentives are fiscal, some are regulatory reliefs. Their use depends on the characteristics of the environment in different countries. Venture capital firms' investment activities can also be enhanced by reducing their risks or by improving their returns through government guarantee and co-investment schemes.

The USA has the largest and most mature venture capital industry. The public is very favourably disposed towards entrepreneurship and top executives for entrepreneurial high-technology enterprises and experienced venture capitalists are available. The level of R&D spending has traditionally been high and there are efficient links between the sources of R&D and industry. The financial market is very dynamic, as illustrated by an efficient stock exchange, a well-functioning OTC market and a tradition of company shares held by the public.

In the USA the growth of the venture capital industry has been seen as a private market response to the financial and managerial needs of new entrepreneurial businesses. This is also witnessed by the fact that it has been major tax and regulatory changes, most notably general taxation of capital gains and improvements in pension fund investment regulations, that have had the most important impact on the growth and development of the venture capital industry in the USA.

· The US approach to promoting industrial capital has concentrated on providing an overall economic climate favourable to investment and risk-taking. In addition to the Small Business Investment Company programme there are relatively few incentives aimed directly at venture capital. Direct government involvement is opposed by the US venture capital community. Individual states have provided tax incentives to regionally-based venture capital firms and permitted state pension funds to invest in venture capital funds.

Up until the late 1970's public policies in Europe favoured large firms, as opposed to the USA. During the 1980's, however, European governments' policies have increasingly focused on measures designed to stimulate the creation of new technology-based firms and venture capital, largely based on the US experience. The venture capital industry began to grow rapidly in Europe only after some countries introduced tax incentives and risk guarantee schemes. Secondary securities markets were also created for SMEs in many countries in the early 1980's.

Incentives in individual countries studied in this paper take different forms. In the U.K. the Business Expansion Scheme launched in 1983 provides individuals an annual tax deduction against their approved equity investments. In 1987 the use of a limited partnership structure as a venture capital fund was approved without any changes in legislation and nowadays it provides an efficient investment vehicle for venture capital.

The French government was the first in Europe to provide special incentives to venture capital firms. There are several authorized structures under which a firm can register to take advantage of tax incentives and guarantees. In the Netherlands a guarantee scheme was launched in 1981, which compensates half of a loss realised by an approved private venture capital firm. In addition to national incentives, the European Commission provides incentives for transnational co-investment arrangements, subsidies to seed investments, and training programmes for venture capital managers.

Most of the incentive schemes have proved efficient and have had an important impact on the development of the venture capital industry in different countries. The most significant drawbacks in some of these programmes seem to arise from government authorization and regulations, which in turn may lead to bureaucracy, and the sensitivity of these programmes to political moods. The SBIC program in the USA, for example, has lost popularity in recent years because of the above reasons and attempts have been made to partly privatize the programme. The BES program was initially very popular, but complicated regulations and the approval of tenency/shipping as BES investments (for political reasons) have significantly reduced funds raised by BES funds and prospectuses. In France the authorized venture capital investment vehicles are considered over-regulated and proposals have been made to limit the number of venture capital vehicles to two, while easing their restrictions on investment.

. There is no commonly accepted definition of venture capital in a single country, let alone worldwide. Furthermore, a definition that has been fairly widely adopted in the past may change over time. In the USA venture capital is no longer synonymous with investing in early stage technology-based businesses. It now encompasses a much broader scope of activity, including certain types of leveraged buy-outs, turnarounds and acquisitions. In Europe, this broader definition has applied since the industry started to develop in the early 1980's. US venture capital statistics do not usually include figures for specialist equity buy-out funds, which is commonly the case in Europe.

In Finland the venture capital industry is still in its infancy. In 1989 there were 19 organizations operating in the venture capital market. They managed a total capital of FIM 530 million, which as a ratio to GNP is considerably less than in Europe on average. The investments of Finnish venture capital firms have concentrated on expansion-stage financing in other than high-technology sectors. Investments have included many portfolio companies operating in traditional slow/medium-growth sectors which provide steady cash flow for the venture capital firm. The average size of investment is substantially smaller than in Europe on average.

The nature of the industry has so far been rather unclear to entrepreneurs and investors and its role in business development is not yet fully recognized by the public authorities. The activities of large development capital firms have further confused public attitudes towards venture capital firms. The industry has been characterized by a lack of common practices. Syndication between venture capital firms has only begun to emerge recently. The bulk of funds are managed by captive organizations and corporate venture capital subsidiaries. Banks have provided more than half of the pool of capital. Independent specialized venture capital organizations do not yet exist.

Research and development expenditure as a proportion of GNP has been small compared to most industrialized countries. Together with the small size of the domestic market this has made it difficult to find high-quality investment opportunities with sufficient growth potential. Universities and research institutes have only recently begun to seek to systematically attempt to commercialize their technology innovations.

Although entrepreneurship is respected in Finland entrepreneurial culture has not been particularly favourable to venture capital financing. There is a greater shortage of professional managers for fast-growing entrepreneurial businesses than of product/service ideas. The entrepreneurial culture has not been favourable to outside equity investors.

The financial markets in Finland have been undeveloped. Until the early 1980's the capital market in Finland was strictly controlled by the Bank of Finland. The financial markets have traditionally been dominated by a few large banks, which have also financed SMEs with loans. The securities market has been loosely regulated and the Securities Market Act came into force only in 1989. The public sector has also been quite active in providing SMEs with loans and grants. There has not been a public stock market available for SMEs, which could also have served as a viable exit mechanism for venture capital investments. The OTC market was established at the end of 1984, but did not really expand until 1987.

The changes in Finland's industrial structure during the 1980's, especially during the second half of the decade, and the simultaneous strong development of the capital markets have created a more favourable environment - and a need - for a venture capital industry. These changes have also had an impact on business and entrepreneurial culture. The concept of separating management and ownership has become more acceptable and entrepreneurs have become more receptive to active outside equity investors. The new entrepreneurial culture is seen, for example, in the increasing popularity of entrepreneurship among the young and highly-educated people. Since the mid-1980's, policy questions concerning research and development activities have taken priority in both the public and private sectors. Investment in R&D has grown considerably and should reach 2,7% of GNP by the end of 1990's. This level has been maintained by the leading industrialised countries.

No special incentives aimed at venture capital so far exist in Finland, unless the provisional (1984-1988) Development Capital Company status is considered as one. All Finnish venture capital firms, with two exceptions, are organized as ordinary corporations investing their own equity and debt capital. This structure has proved too rigid for venture capital purposes.

There is currently a lot of pressure from many sides to promote venture capital in Finland. By the time of writing, the legislative and regulatory amendment proposals presented in this paper have already been initially discussed by the representatives of the relevant authorities. The initial reactions have been encouraging and the idea as a whole has been well received.

The Ministry of Finance could make the best authorizing and supervising organization for venture capital firms. The ideal taxation treatment for venture capital limited partnerships would occur if profits were treated under the Income Taxation Act, and the Business Income Taxation Act followed for all other aspects. The advantages of the Business Income Taxation Act, most notably the carry forward provision for losses, are seen as hard to achieve, but not impossible. The Ministry of Trade and Industry sees no real hindrances for changing the treatment of foreign limited partners. This drawback may in fact be eliminated without any specially-tailored incentives for venture capital funds during the on-going amendments to the laws concerning foreign ownership in Finnish companies as a response to the European integration process. However, the legislative amendment process may take considerable time.

The launching of a guarantee scheme for private venture capital organizations has been initially negotiated with the State Guarantee Board. The reactions to this proposal have been encouraging. The State Guarantee Board has also thought of changing its role in this direction. The guarantee scheme initially discussed is similar to the one used in the Netherlands, but a totally unique model is also possible. It is likely that this scheme will be limited to investments in early-stage and/or technology-based firms. The failure of Mancon has raised some worries concerning the amendment proposals; Mancon played an active role in passing the Development Capital Company status in 1984.

It now seems that the Finnish venture capital industry will expand rapidly within the next few years, at least in terms of funds available. Several plans to set up venture capital funds have been initiated. One of these is quite large.

The discussion on incentives for the Finnish venture capital industry is stimulated by this research. Before major incentives presented in this paper are introduced, it is likely that the early-stage technology-based enterprises will be mainly publicly-funded. A guarantee scheme, if it materialises, might work as an incentive for private venture capital organizations and substitutes a part of public funding shortly.

Notes

1. Tyebjee, Vickery 1988, 125
2. Auer 1989, 23
3. Tyebjee, Vickery 1988, 125
4. Florida, Kenney 1988, 316
5. Pence 1982, 2
6. Preston, 1988
7. Tyebjee, Vickery 1988, 127
8. Tyebjee, Vickery 1988, 127
9. OECD I 1986, 15, Tyebjee, Vickery 1988, 128; EVCA I 1986, 14
10. OECD I 1986, 9
11. OECD I 1982, 150-151
12. OECD I 1982, 151-152
13. Premus 1985, 1920
14. Venture Capital Journal, Sept 1988, 1
15. Auer, 1989, 28
16. Auer, 1989, 28
17. Relander 1989, 11
18. Relander 1989, 12
19. Venture Economics I 1989, 65-66; BVCA 1989, 3; Business Research International, a seminar in London, May 1989, INFO EVCA, 2/1989
20. Gibb 1985, 60
21. OECD II 1986, 16
22. DHS 1988, 192
23. Westerlund 1990
24. Relander 1989, 117
25. Valtion Tiede-ja Teknologianeuvosto 1987, 7
26. Valtion Tiede-ja Teknologianeuvosto 1987, 32
27. Valtion Tiede-ja Teknologianeuvosto 1987, 32
28. Tunkelo 1988, 1
29. The Finnish Academy of Technology 1989, 11
30. Jussi Mykkänen
31. TKL 1989, 19
32. Malkamäki 1989, 7; Ollila 1988, Suomen Pankkiyhdistys 1989, 7-9
33. Suomi V. 2000, 1989, 54
34. Suomen Pankkiyhdistys 1989, 7
35. Malkamäki 1989, 9
36. Talouselämä 3/1989, 70
37. DHS 1988, 170
38. Jouko Kiesi
39. Jouko Kiesi, Hannu Niilekselä, Vesa Kumpulainen
40. Hallituksen ehdotus sijoitusrahastolaiksi 1986

References

Books

Auer, Juha; The Venture Capital Industry in the USA, Europe and Finland, SITRA 1990
Bigler Investment Venture capital. A perspective. Bigler investment management Co., Inc Hartford CT., 1983
Deloitte, Haskins, Sells Fiscal environment of, and (DHS) corporate vehicles for, venture capital inthe European communities. A study prepared for the Commission of the European Communities. Brussels,1988.
EVCA; Venture capital in Europe. 1988 Yearbook. Peat, Marwick, McLintock, London, 1988
The Finnish Academy; High technology from Finland 1989. of TechnologyThe Finnish Academy of Technology. Gummerus Kirjapaino Oy, Jyväskylä, 1989.
Gibb, John M. Venture capital markets for the regeneration of industry.North-Holland, Amsterdam,1985
OECD I; Innovation policy. Trends and perspectives. OECD, Paris, 1982.
OECD II; Venture capital: context, development and policies. Paris, 1986.
Pence, Christine C;. How venture capitalists make investment decisions. UMI Research Press, USA 1982
Premus, Robert; Venture capital and innovation. A study prepared for the use of the Joint Economic Committee, Washington D:C., 1985
Relander, Kaj-Erik; Venture Capital -toiminta ja kansainvälistyvä PKT-yritys, SITRA 1989
Suomen Pankkiyhdistys; Suomen Rahoitusmarkkinat. 1989
Suomi v.2000; Teollisuus 2000 visio, Kauppa- ja teollisuusministeriö, 1989
Tunkelo, Eino; Oulun teknologiakylä 1980-1988. Oulun Yliopisto, Oulu, 1988.
Teollisuuden Keskusliitto; Teollisuus ja innovaatiot. (TKL) Helsinki, 1989.
U.S. Small Business Administration I; Capital Formation in the States. Office of Advocacy. Washington, 1988.
U.S. Small Business Administration I; Small Business Investment Companies: Ithe SBIC program. Washington DC, 1988.
U.S. Small Business Administration III; The states and small business: programsand activities. Washington DC, 1986.
Valtion Tiede- ja Teknologianeuvostokatsaus; Tiede- ja teknologiapoliitinen 1987, Helsinki, 1987.
Venture Economics I; Structures of UK venture capital funds. Venture Economics, Ltd.London UK, 1989.
Venture Ecomomics III; Pratt's guide to venture capital sources. Venture Economics, Inc Ma, USA, 1989
Westerlund, Heikki; Venture capital-toimiala Suomessa 1989, SITRA 1990

Journals

Florida, Richard; Venture capital and high technology Kenney, Martinentrepreneurship Journal of Business Venturing 3, 1988, 301-319. Elsevier Publishing Co., NY, USA.
INFO EVCA; European Venture Capital Association.Various issues 1985-1989.
Mykkänen, Jussi; Käytännön venture capital-toiminnasta Suomessa, SITRA 1990

Malkamäki, Markku; Structural changes in the Finnish stock market: a trend towards efficient trading.
Tyebjee, T.; Venture capital in Western Europe.
Vickery, L.; Journal of Busines Venturing. No 3, 1988, 123-136.
Venture Capital Journal; Venture Economics, Inc. MA, USA. Various issues from 1986 to 1989.

Interviews

Kiesi, Jouko; Teollistamisrahasto Oy.
Kumpulainen, Vesa; Widenius, Sederholm & Someri Oy.
Niilekselä, Hannu; Widenius, Sederholm & Someri Oy.

Other sources

Esko Ollila; Venture capital in Finland. A speech. Sept 1988
Hallituksen esitys Eduskunnalle sijoitusrahastolaiksi sekä laeiksi eräiden siihen liittyvien lakien muuttamisesta. Helsinki, 1986.

Appendix

Legislative amendment needs

When considering the legislative amendment needs in favour of the use of the limited partnership structure, there are basically two options available:

- To propose changes in the tax laws and laws concerning foreign ownership in Finnish businesses.
  or,
- To propose changes in the limited partnership law.

The first way has the clear advantage over the second one since changes in the civil law have a tendency to be time-consuming, complicated and inflexible.

To accomplish the first alternative, the following measures can be taken:

1. Venture capital activities could be defined in legislation and the definitions could include at least the following broad definitions:
- Investment activities could concern only small and medium-sized enterprises that are not quoted on the Stock Exchange.
- Investments could be of a fixed-term nature and should be mainly minority investments.
2. If venture capital investments are made through a venture capital fund, these activities could be under the supervision of a public authority. The supervising organization could be e.g. the Ministry of Finance.

3. The Ministry of Finance could authorize venture capital status to funds that are considered to be venture capital funds. Under this status, funds should be granted certain reliefs in e.g. taxation.

A venture capital limited partnership could always be transparent with regard to gains and losses, as a limited partnerships under the Income Taxation Act. In addition, it should at the minimum be allowed to use the following advantage offered by the Business Income Taxation Act:

- Carrying forward losses from investments and using them in taxation, as is the case in any other business activities.

In addition, normally under the Business Income Taxation Act:

- Reserves and decreasing share value should be allowed and interest expenses be deductable from profits.

The last provisions may not, however, be important to venture capital funds.

- Foreign investors could be allowed to participate in Finnish venture capital limited partnerships. A limited partnership could be given equal status with the corporation form, in which case the foreign ownership limit would be 20% or 40%.
- Insurance companies' and pension funds' possibilities to invest in the venture capital market can be improved. This could be achieved by relaxing the regulations governing their investment activities to allow them to invest part of their funds, say 1-3%, in venture capital funds.

Part 8
Entrepreneurship and innovation/technology

20 Manager participation in innovation activities of small and medium-sized industrial enterprises

Liisa Hyvärinen

Introduction

This paper is a preliminary approach on the managers' participation in innovation activities of Finnish small and medium-sized industrial enterprises, SMEs. SMEs are very important for the economy of most of the EC and EFTA countries. For instance 99 % of the total number of Finnish industrial enterprises consist of SMEs. They employ 43 % of the total Finnish industry personnel (source: Central Statistical Office of Finland (1987, p. 13)).

The purpose of the paper is to examine the suitability of the input, output and impact aspect (presented e.g. in Hyvärinen (1990a)) in the individual level of SMEs' innovation activities, focusing on the managers' participation in these operations. The concepts of individual innovativeness and entrepreneurship will form the theoretical background of the paper together with the characteristics of SMEs.

In order to stay competitive in the long run in its existing markets or to be able to enter new markets, a firm has to develop and renew itself. In this study, the innovation activities of an enterprise are considered as operations aimed at developing new or improved products, processes, marketing means, markets, administration, financing and/or organizational changes. On their background there may be the knowledge arising from the research and science, technological possibilities to be taken the advantage of (technology push) or they may be aimed at satisfying demand on the market (market pull). The innovation activities of an enterprise can be external or internal. According to Central Statistical Office of Finland (1989), the Finnish industry spends about 3,3 milliard FIM in research and development in 1989. The proportion of SMEs is one quarter of it. Only 1 % of this investment is objected to the research and development activities outside the enterprises. Research and development, R & D, forms the core of internal innovation activities. Managers' participation in the innovation activities of their firms is essential especially in small and medium-sized industrial enterprises.

Innovativeness and entrepreneurship

The innovation behaviour of managers in the small and medium-sized industrial enterprises can be seen through the concept of individual innovativeness:

Innovativeness is the degree to which an individual is relatively earlier in adopting new ideas than the other members of his system. (Source: Rogers and Shoemaker (1971), p. 27)

The preceding view concerns the adoption and utilization of innovations. In an industrial enterprise the innovation activities consist to a greater extent of creation, development and adaptation of innovations. In his later work Roger (1983) defines innovativeness by taking the adopter categories and the aspect of an organization more into the consideration: Innovativeness is the degree to which an individual or other unit is relatively earlier in adopting new ideas than the other members of a system. (Source: Rogers (1983), p. 22)

For innovation Gartner (1990, p. 16), among others, uses the definition it being characterized by doing something new as an idea, product, service, market, or technology in a new or established organization. In this study the newness of an idea or created innovation in the relevant environment is utilized in examining the SME managers' personal output and impact as results of the participation in the innovation activities of their enterprises.

In Gartner's study (1990, p. 27), the experts defining entrepreneurship divide in two groups: The first one stresses the characteristics of entrepreneurship including the entrepreneur, innovation, growth and uniqueness, and the second group stresses the outcomes of entrepreneurship creating value, for profit, and owner-manager. This division to the entrepreneur's characteristics and the results of entrepreneurship is employed in this study in the form of SME managers' personal input and output in the innovation activities.

The concept of entrepreneurship will be utilized as a means to determine the individual characteristics, and through them the innovation behaviour of managers of SMEs, as input in the innovation activities. Ansoff (1984, p. 245) describes the entrepreneur being future oriented and concerned with changing the dynamics of the firm into the future. He seeks to enter new businesses and to diversify the firm, he sets new and challenging objectives. An entrepreneur is an imaginative creator of new futures, a willing risk-taker, and a divergent problem solver who creates new opportunities. In addition to that, Chell (1990) describes the typical entrepreneur being proactive i.e. initiative and attempting to control the events rather than simply reacting them, highly innovative in product or service, markets served, means of production and/or fixed asset investment, utilizing a variety of sources of finance, seeking opportunities to enhance the visibility of the company, becoming easily bored, pursuing of challenges, adventurous and an ideas-person, intuitive, creating situations which result in change, and often exploring new terrain.

Characteristics of SMEs' innovation activities

Typical for small and medium-sized enterprises, also in the industrial sectors, is the strong influence of the manager and the limited resources of all kind. This is the case also in their innovation activities.

Thom (1990, p. 182) claims the personal profile of entrepreneurs and managers being one of the dominant background instruments in promoting the innovations, together with communication and readiness to delegate. This concerns especially the small companies: The smaller and younger the enterprise, the closer the link between the enterprise and its manager. According to Docter, Van Der Horst and Stokman (1989, p. 52), the director of the company has a driving and significant role in the majority of innovation processes in SMEs.

Oakey, Rothwell and Cooper (1988) consider the internal R & D as the prime means of generating technical information in small firms. In SMEs, however, a separate R & D department or R & D budget are not common, and their innovation activities are seldom considered distinct from production or other operations of the firm. As substitutes and supplements to the internal innovation activities, SMEs often use external assistance and collaboration in research and development (sources: Mazzonis (1989, p. 65), Thom (1990, p. 189) and Hyvärinen (1990b, p. 432)), due to their limited resources. As an example it can be mentioned that the Finnish small and medium-sized industrial enterprises make one quarter of the total R & D investment, but two thirds of the investment in external innovation activities (source: Central Statistical Office of Finland (1989)). According to Oakey, Rothwell and Cooper (1988, p. 116) using customers or part-time internal R & D as sources of innovations does not require as much resources or commitment from the enterprise as the other forms of innovation activities. These last mentioned "simpler and easier" innovation strategies are the most common ones in SMEs. Customers generate typical ideas for product innovation projects. The suppliers of machines and equipment are frequently used as idea sources in production innovation projects. External experts are most often used in managerial or administrative tasks or in technological problem solvation of the innovation process itself.

The internal management of R & D is important in solving the problems both in gathering the adequate information for and during the innovation project as well as in putting it into practice. Most of these problems in SMEs are consequences of their limited financial resources, see e.g. Sexton and Van Auken (1982, p. 21 and 35), and Thom (1990, p. 183). The absence of systematic planning techniques and organization of management in general is also often signified as characteristic creature for small and medium-sized industrial enterprises. Consequently, the management of SMES' innovation activities is often inadequate, too. The management of innovation process can be divided in three sub-areas: managing technological resources, managing human resources, and administration including organizational management and operational guidance of the innovation project (sources: Vrakking (1990, p. 97-100) and McDonough and Pearson (1990)). The manager of a SME participates in all of them and needs additional knowledge form other persons. Technological skills mean having a good understanding of the relevant body of knowledge, stimulating the innovations and fostering the creativity of innovation team in advance.

McDonough and Pearson (1990) claim that higher technical skills of the leaders.

May somehow intrude the team's ability to exercise their own creativity. Human relations include providing of appreciation and encouraging the innovation team members to become involved in innovation activities, motivating the individuals to perform beyond their own expectations, and stimulating enthusiasm. The human relations orientation is a key factor in fostering the creativity and the team's willingness to take on new and unfamiliar technologies successfully. Administrative skills contain carrying out needed planning and scheduling, and handling the relations between the innovation team and other departments of the firm.

Managers' personal input, output and impact in innovation activities of SMEs

Forms of input, output and impact

The manager/owner and his/her efforts and attitudes towards the innovation activities form an essential part of the *input* to innovation processes of the enterprise. The manager often invests money in his/her firm. Besides that she/he also uses his/her educational and professional skills, ideas and time for innovation activities. The problem is that a SME director has to take care of a great many other things, too, and is therefore often unable to reserve sufficiently time for the development of innovations.

The personal output managers get from participating in the innovation activities of their firms and its impact are generally neglected when examining the results of industrial innovation activities. Patents, both applied and admitted, and various indicators based on economical performance of the enterprise are the most common means for measuring the output and impact of industrial innovation activities. They can be adapted to indicators for the individual dimension of innovation activities, too. Other forms for measuring the arising managers' innovations are the number of inventions and other renewals produced. As output from the participation in the innovation activities of his/her firm, the manager might also get a satisfying job in a firm of his/her own, and financial advantage and special rewards.

Data

The following empirical data is based on case-studies on 13 Finnish industrial SME managers. The data was collected by mailed questionnaires in winter 1989 and completed with personal interviews of the managers during the visits to the enterprises in autumn 1990. Three of the enterprises are in clothing industry and the rest in metal product manufacturing sector. 8 of the firms examined had less than 30 employees. They are considered as small enterprises in this study. Rest of the firms examined which employed up to 170 employees, form the group of medium-sized enterprises. Most frequently SMEs are defined as those employing less than 500 employees. Thus all the firms examined in this paper are considered as small ones in international scaling. In the following the enterprises in clothing sector will be examined as one group despite of their size differences since they operate in a very similar way as far as innovation activities are concerned. The metal product manufacturers will be divided into small and medium-sized ones because their innovation policies differed from each other. Because of the small number of managers included in the empirical part of this study, the results achieved can not be statistically generalized as such.

Input Analysis

The enterprises examined spend on the average 4 per cent of their annual turn over on various types of innovation activities. Three quarters of the total investment is spent on internal innovation activities, mainly concerning development of production and processes. Another important developing objective is products. Consequently, most of the arising innovations are connected to the processes, although product innovations are also quite frequent. The innovations are mainly incremental ones or new to the SME itself only. Very seldom the innovations are new to the market or the industrial sector SME is in. The average number of the personnel hired for innovation tasks solely is 1,5 per enterprise, including the manager as part-timer.

The average owner/manager of the examined Finnish SMEs works 54 hours per week. One quarter of it is spent on the development of the firm. Mainly this consists of the general management of innovation activities and generating ideas for the possible coming innovations. Taking part in actual innovation projects is less frequent among the managers, but when participating, the managers are responsible for the development of production processes and administration. This is obviously due to the SME managers professional background: Their experience mainly includes production tasks. The short administrative and marketing experience was generally achieved in the present company only. Other persons than managers are normally more responsible for the development of products and marketing. The managers are also, to a great extent, liable for gathering the needed information for innovation projects, see following figure.

Figure 1
Type of the tasks the managers participate in the development projects of marketing, production, products and administration, in addition to the general management of innovation activities and idea generation

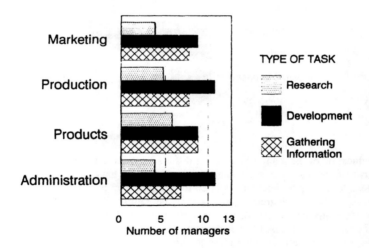

The small portion of basic research done in all four development fields is due to the limited time of the managers and the limited resources in SMEs. In fact they are the only persons to perform these kind of tasks in SMEs but rarely as the only job. The 'research process' is often going on in the manager's mind, simultaneously with two or three other things he/she has to take care of. In general, to find out what is going on during the day and as well as in the night in the mind of the manager for the development of their enterprise, is not easy to find out. However, it is a significant part of the basis of SMEs' innovations.

329

As a result of the comparison the three sub-groups of enterprises examined, it seems that the more employees in the enterprise, the shorter is the weekly working hours of the manager and the bigger portion of his/her is spent on the development tasks, see the figure below. Also in the types of tasks managers participate in innovation activities vary: In a bigger enterprise the manager does not anymore have to take part in all of the development tasks. The tasks managers usually, if possible, leave to the others include the actual development and lower level supervision of the innovation activities.

Figure 2
Managers' average weekly working hours

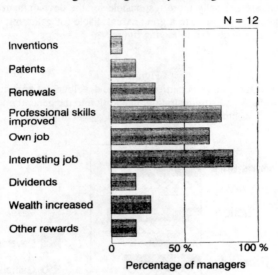

The education of the managers does not differ among the three enterprise groups examined. Most of the managers are technicians, engineers or have other corresponding institute/college level degree. Few have started to run their own business on vocational school background. University degrees are rare among the Finnish SME managers, too.

The professional experience of the managers seems to have some influence also on the origin of development ideas: Ideas for process and administration innovations generated by the managers are more usual than ideas for product and marketing innovations. The outside innovation idea sources proved to be important for the SMEs studied. Half of them regularly used outside experts, subcontracting connections and joint development projects in developing processes and administration as well as in gathering information for marketing operations. The main idea sources for development of marketing were, though, the enterprises' own marketing personnel and the actual market the enterprise is operating in. Own marketing personnel and surprisingly also the suppliers were the most frequent sources for new product ideas. The ideas for process development were most often sourcing to the new machines and equipment purchased, own production personnel and the markets. The development of administration is to a great extent dependent on the public recommendations, regulations and laws as well as on the ideas and suggestions of consultants. Between the three enterprise sub-groups examined there are only slight differences in the idea sources for various development targets.

The general personal attitudes of the SME managers were examined by using 5-scaled statements on willingness to take risks, attitudes towards new ideas in general, creativity in business, and determination in carrying out their plans. The statements (presented in Appendix 1) were taken from the studies of Khan and Manopichetwattana (1989a and 1989b), and Pitkänen and Vesala (1988). The results demonstrate these SME managers being willing to take risks (code RISK), see table 1. Moreover, they very much agree with the statement that new ideas make life worth while (code IDEAS). Concerning the need for creativity in business life instead of rational thinking only (code CREATIV) and attitudes towards trial of new ideas (code ATTINEW) earlier than others, these managers are more careful. The mean score values were 2,9 for creative thinking (CREATIV) and 2,5 for trying new ideas (ATTINEW) of the maximum 5, both with quite notable deviation. In carrying out the plans the managers have made (code PLANFUL) and realizing them without taking the others in concern (code PLANCONF), the managers are quite neutral.

Table 1

The statistical analysis of the answers of the
interviewed Finnish SME managers concerning their personal
attitudes towards risks and new ideas in general

Variable	Mean	StdDev	Minimum	Maximum	N
RISK	4.3	.6	3	5	13
IDEAS	4.7	.4	4	5	12
CREATIV	2.9	1.6	1	5	13
ATTINEW	2.5	1.2	1	5	13
PLANFUL	3.3	1.0	2	5	13
PLANCONF	3.2	1.2	1	5	13

Between the three groups of firms the only significant difference in the managers' attitudes was in taking others' opinions about new things into the consideration (code ATTIlNEW): The managers of firms in clothing sector were less willing to be the first ones to adopt new things than the managers of metal product sector.

On the basis of the above details there seem to be many suitable input indicators to be easily used as input factors also in individual level of innovation activities of an industrial enterprise, in the form of the usual approach.

Output and impact analysis

The following figure presents the frequency of managers' personal, i.e. not in the property of the firm, inventions, patents, other renewals, improved professional skills, getting an own and interesting job in this firm, dividends paid and otherwise increased personal wealth together with other personal rewards and received recognitions as results from participation in the innovation activities of their enterprises.

Figure 3
Managers' personal results from participation in innovation activities
of their enterprises

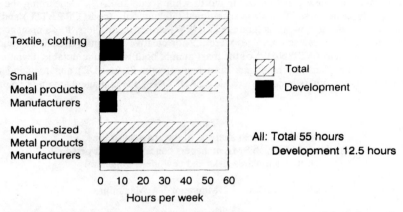

Nearly all of the SME managers studied were founders or owners of their firms. On the average, 64 % of the shares was owned by the manager. In spite of that, only a few of the managers had got dividends or other financial reward from their firm. The most frequent results achieved from participating the innovation activities of their enterprises, were improved professional skills and an interesting job in a firm of their own. Patenting was not common in the firms examined, neither were managers' personal patens. To some extent the goodness of this indicator is dependent on the industrial sector. Some managers had created other renewals, unsuitable for patenting, and got special personal recognitions from their home town or organization which were here classified as other rewards. Among the three subgroups of enterprises there were no differences in the frequency of various personal output of the managers.

As it can be seen on the basis of the above trials there seem to be very little suitable output and impact indicators which could be used as indicators of innovation activities of an industrial enterprise in individual level of managers. In addition to that the most frequent indicators adapted above which result to positive outcome can not quantified, for instance job satisfaction and improved professional skills. In this context the output and impact indicators adapted in the individual aspect approach the social view of organizational behaviour and the measuring of its results. In spite of this difficulty, it is possible to get more information of the innovation activities of SMEs by using the input, output and impact aspect provided that the output and impact indicators will be developed further.

Conclusions

Also the results of this small, exploratory study, show the strong impact of manager/owner on the innovation activities of Finnish small and mediumsized industrial enterprise.

In the Finnish SMEs examined the innovation activities are mainly aimed at developing production and process and strongly influenced by the managers. Due to their limited resources and the risk connected with internal innovation activities, most SME managers need external help to complete their knowledge in various innovation tasks.

The traditional input factors can easily be used also in individual level in the innovation activities. The results of this study present the managers' professional experience being the basis for the innovations ideas they generate and influencing also the type of the actual development projects the managers participate in most frequently. There are also development projects SME managers have to participate due to their position in the enterprises. The results also indicate the interdependence between a small firm and the personality of its owner/manager, who often is a risk-taking and ideas-person.

There are only a few suitable output and impact indicators to be used in the individual level of innovation activities of an industrial enterprise, in the level of managers. The results of this study indicate bigger importance for qualitative and social results than for the number of patents, inventions and innovations, as output the managers get by participating the innovation activities of their enterprises.

Provided that the output and impact indicators will be developed further, by using the input, output and impact aspect also in the individual level of innovation activities, it would be possible to get from a new aspect additional information of the innovation activities of SMEs.

Bibliography

Central Statistical Office of Finland (Tilastokeskus) (1987), *Yritys- ja toimipaikkarekisteri 1984* (The Register of Enterprises and Establishments 1984). YR 1987:4. Helsinki.

Central Statistical Office of Finland (Tilastokeskus) (1989), *Tiede ja teknologia 1989* (Science and Technology 1989). Helsinki.

Chell E. (1990), *The Characteristics of Entrepreneurs and Entrepreneurial Firms: A fresh approach.* Paper presented at Manchester Business School
Silver Anniversary Conference 'R&D, Entrepreneurship and Innovation',
on 10-11 July, 1990, Manchester, UK.

Docter Jaap, Van Der Horst Rob and Stokmnan Casper (1989), Innovation Process in Small and Medium-Size Companies. *Entrepreneurship and Regional Development,* Vol. 1, pp. 33-52.

Gartner William B. (1990), What Are We Talking about When We Talk about Entrepreneurship? *Journal of Business Venturing,* Vol. 5, pp. 15-28.

Hyvärinen Liisa (1990a), Innovativeness and its Indicators in Small and Medium-Sized Industrial Enterprises. *International Small Business Journal,* Vol. 9, No. 1 (Oct.-Dec., 1989), pp. 64-79.

Hyvärinen Liisa (1990b), Internal and External Innovation Activities in Small and Medium-Sized Industrial Enterprises. In: Karlsen Jan Irgens (ed.)(1990), *Proceedings of International Conference on Technology Transfer and Innovation in Mixed Economies,* Trondheim, Norway, 27-29 August 1990, pp. 425-435.

Khan Arshad M. and Manopichetwattana Veerachai (1989a), Models for Distinguishing Innovative and Noninnovative Small Firms. *Journal of Business Venturing,* Vol. 4, No. 3 (May 1989), pp. 187-196.

Khan Arshad M. and Manopichetwattana Veerachai (1989b), Innovative and Noninnovative Small Firms: Types and Characteristics. *Management Science,* Vol. 35, No. 5 (May 1989), pp. 597-606.

Mazzonis Danielle (1989), Small Firm Networking, Cooperation, and Innovation in Italy: Viewed by an Agency Engaged in Actions for Stimulating the Technological Upgrading of Industry. *Entrepreneurship and Regional Development,* Vol. 1, pp. 61-74.

McDonough E. F. III and Pearson A. W. (1990), *An Investigation of the Impact of Urgency on Project Performance.* Paper presented at Manchester Business School Silver Anniversary Conference 'R&D, Entrepreneurship and Innovation', on 10-11 July, 1990, Manchester, UK.

Oakey Ray, Rothwell Roy and Cooper Sarah (1988), *The Management of Innovation in High-Technology Small Firms. Innovation and Regional Development in Britain and the United States.* Quorum Books. Pinter Publisher Limited Great Britain.

Pitkänen Seppo and Vesala Kari (1988), *Yrittä jyysmotivaatio Kymen ja Vaasan lääneissä. Vertaileva tutkimus yrittäjyyteen ohjaavista tekijöistä.* (Entrepreneurship motivation in the Kymi and Vaasa provinces, Finland. A comparative study *of* socio-psychological backgrounds *of* entrepreneurship) Lappeenranta University *of* Technology. Department *of* Industrial Engineering and Management. Research Report 9.

Rogers Everett M. (1983), Diffusion *of Innovations. The Free Press. New York. 3rd edition.*

Rogers Everett M. and Shoemaker F. Floyd (1971), Communication of Innovations. A Cross-Cultural Approach. The Free Press. New York. 2nd edition.

Sexton Donald L. and Auken Philip M. (1982), Prevalence of Strategic Planning in Small Business. *Journal of Small Business Management,* July 1982, pp. 20-26.

Thom Norbert (1990), Innovation Management in Small and Medium-Sized Firms. *Management International Review,* Vol. 30, No 2, pp. 181-192.

Vrakking W. J. (1990), The Innovative Organization. *Long Range Planning,* Vol. 23, No 2, pp. 94-102.

Appendix 1

The statements to examine the personal attitudes of the interviewed Finnish SME managers towards risks and new ideas in general.

Risk is worth for taking if it brings along remarkable advantages. (RISK) (completely disagree (1) ... completely agree (5))

New ideas make life worth for living. (IDEAS)
(completely disagree (1) ... completely agree (5))

Creativity and inventions do not fit in business life where knowledge and skills are more needed. (CREATIV)
(completely agree (1) ... completely disagree (5))

One should take new things with reservation and wait for the others' opinions about them. (ATTINEW)
(completely agree (1) ... completely disagree (5))

If I make plans, I will definitely carry them out, too. (PLANFUL) (completely disagree (1) ... completely agree (5))

To put my plans into practice, I make sure they fit in with the plans of the others. (PLANCONF)
(completely agree (1) ... completely disagree (5))

21 Creating an entrepreneurial management system in large corporations: The STK innova case[1]

Birgit Helene Jevnaker

Abstract

How does an entrepreneurial management system come into being in existing mature companies? Based on a case study in a Norwegian corporation, this paper analyzes the development of a supportive sub-organisation for innovation and new ventures. The initiative and drive to pursue this opportunity was taken by a few individuals. The introductory process called for creative and untraditional solutions. The facilitation of internal entrepreneurship is discussed in terms of an entrepreneurial project.

Innovations - what to focus upon?

The focus of this paper is on how a new social *system* for stimulating innovation and internal venturing is created and implemented in large and "mechanistic"[2] corporations. Innovation can be bred in a surprising variety of organisations and by different strategies and alignments (Quinn 1985). Introducing a radically new system[3] with new strategy, methods and routines, may be seen as an innovative change by itself. Big business usually has 'big problems' fostering innovations and new ventures, particularly when the innovative effort stems from the "grass root" (Burgelman & Sayles 1986). Even if a corporation decides to go for an innovative change, it may be hard to implement. The purpose of this paper is to develop some tentative propositions about the creation of entrepreneurial management systems through an in-depth understanding of a large corporation.

Why address entrepreneurial management systems in a large corporation context? On the one hand, there is ample evidence[4] of barriers towards innovation in large corporations. On the other hand, large corporations do come up with new businesses and innovations developed internally (Quinn 1985, Burgelman & Sayles 1986, Kanter 1989). A possible answer to this paradox is the existence of *driving forces* behind innovations in large corporations. An interesting question is whether corporations could possibly speed up those driving forces and create more entrepreneurial environments in order to realise new opportunities? From a strategic management perspective, the problem is how corporate management can improve its capacity to deal with autonomous strategic behaviour. From an entrepreneurial business perspective, I would suggest that the problem is how to make a legitimate and good road for entrepreneurial venturing inside large corporations. An official, entrepreneurial management system may be one possible route (but not the only one) to cope with these challenges (Rothwell 1975, Quinn 1985, Burgelman & Sayles 1986, Kanter 1989). If an entrepreneurial management system is to be developed in large corporations, design and implementation of such systems have to be addressed.

In the creation of a new innovation-breeding system some obvious aspects are mobilization of slack resources and presentation of a visual environment - an easy identifiable "home" for the new type of effort. Large corporations may come up with these types of solutions, they often possess many necessary resources, for instance, a site and a few competent employees as resource persons. Not so evident is the development of an organisational policy and an effective management system to facilitate entrepreneurial behaviour. Sufficiently sensitive and versatile managerial practices are not easily 'installed' over night in a well-established hierarchic organisation (cf Kanter 1989).

I have chosen an exploratory empirical approach to address the question of how an entrepreneurial management system may be created in a large corporation context. Our knowledge of internal innovative and entrepreneurial forces in corporations is fairly low.[5] It is difficult to discover *any* company systems for breeding innovation, , other than the traditional laboratories and research and development departments.[6] This paper focuses on the creation of an official system intended to stimulate *employees* for entrepreneurial activities, not innovation management in general.

The issues discussed in the present paper are based on an exploratory case analysis of the effort in one corporation, Alcatel STK, a Norwegian corporation active in the fields of telecommunication and energy. The paper is organized as a trace of critical events and change agents over time. The single corporation approach allows an organisational in-depth focus of a fairly unique case[7] in the Norwegian setting. During the period 1984 - 1989 significant work was undertaken inside this mature corporation to develop a new system for innovation management: *STK Innova.*[8]

The paper analyzes the development effort inside one corporation from two perspectives; a) a programme implementation perspective and b) an entrepreneurial management perspective. The implementation perspective focuses on what happens (or does not happen) after some new policy or strategy is agreed upon. The entrepreneurial management perspective is a complementary perspective - to 'see' why radically new efforts may evolve despite many implementation barriers in large corporations. These perspectives highlight the critical factors and driving forces in how a corporation goes about implanting a new innovation-breeding strategy.

Programme implementation. To implement means to produce as well as to complete something: to carry out - effectuate activities in order to accomplish a formulated policy (Pressman & Wildavsky 1973), e.g. an innovation programme. In policy analysis it is practical for analytical purposes to separate the policy formulation phase from the imp-lementation phase.[9] The separating point is the decision on a new policy or strategy. Even if definitions carry on after the decision point, the decision - at least in formalized organisa-tions - may represent an important signal within the organisation (Offerdal 1978). The decision may legitimate as well as create a commitment for further design and implementation activities. The perspective is by no means a linear one, definition typically continues in the 'implementation' phase.

In implementation studies the notion of *change agents* often is important for facilitating and managing critical steps within, or transfers between 'phases' in the implementation of a new programme. This role concept is essential for two reasons:

(1) Failure to implement a new programme is typically more common than fulfillment (Pressman and Wildavsky 1973).

(2) A programme or policy is seldom 'finished' in terms of a planned and detailed implementation strategy.

These aspects make it a major challenge to carry out a new programme, especially when the programme is a departure from existing objectives and methods. The conception of change agents - or organisational entrepreneurs - may bring a better understanding of the driving forces behind discontinuous change in large corporations. Implanting a new system for managing innovation and internal venturing in a bureaucratic corporation, is probably not a 'normal adaptation'. It may be classified as an effort towards multidimensional or paradigmatic change (Sheldon 1980). The new system may involve a different "world-view", different values, skills and technologies. Such a system can easily be treated as an anomaly in a large well-established corporation. Creating 'disorder' from inside, may call for entrepreneurial management.

Entrepreneurial management. Literature on new business development and innovations commonly uses process models. The process is often broken down to certain analytical stages, which may be summarized in a definition phase and an implementation phase. However, Saren and Gorman (1987) emphasize that the process of innovation in large companies is more chaotic than these types of classification. They argue: 'The whole process is 'in there' somewhere, but it provides no insight into the kinds of processes and interactions taking place within and between stages... What seems to happen is that the *intrapreneur*, however he or she comes to be in that position, is charged with carrying the innovation right through to a commercial proposition' (p.393, my underlining).

Entrepreneurial activity may be necessary for successful implementation of a strategy or programme which is new and unfinished in a bureaucratic corporation. Entrepreneurship may be defined as a process by which individuals - either on their own or inside organisa-tions - pursue opportunities without regard to the resources they currently control. It is regarded as typical for the entrepreneur - or "intrapreneur" - 'to find a way' (Stevenson and Jarillo 1990). The explorative case study on which this paper is based, indicates that change agents typically found ways to establish a new channel for innovation and venturing. Therefore, the paper discusses facilitating mechanisms for innovation and venturing in terms of an entrepreneurial project itself. Some propositions are presented with reference to the definition and implementation of the STK Innova. What effects, if any, were experienced during the period 1985 - 1989?

Research design and methods. According to Yin (1984:20) a case study strategy has an advantage when a "how" and "why" question is being asked about a contemporary set of events, over which the investigator has little or no control. An exploratory case study design was chosen to investigate the approach of STK to innovation-facilitation. The STK Innova case was traced through a "snowball" method.[10] The main level of analysis in this study is the suborganisational level, i.e. STK Innova, but the discussion also reflect on other levels, such as the management level.[11] The investigation methodology is a qualitative one focusing on events, relations and processes. The case study questions were prepared in a short interview-guide including topics such as the background of initiating an 'intrapreneur' project, what information-sourcing or pre-investigations were made, what activities were planned or implemented, outcomes and experience perceived so far. The interviewing followed open-question and life-event techniques with probing. The data were collected by repeated *interviews* and dialogues with key or representative informants[12] during the period 1987-90. Hidden events - existing in all firms, in this case could be traced. A possible weakness of the data is that would-be entrepreneurs are not systematically interviewed, but spokesmen of blue-collar employees, trade union leaders, are interviewed more than once. The persons interviewed were partly selected because they were mentioned as important agents or "eye witnesses" in the implanting process (snowball method). All major actors were approached. In addition top mangers from different time periods were selected,9 senior managers served as useful key informants. Two change agents that stopped working for the corporation, shared their personal insights. Written *documents* such as internal decision papers, have been used extensively for suppliant data and for control purposes.[13] In case studies in real-life contexts one can never be sure to see the 'whole picture' and different interpretations exist. Drafting, communication and rewriting has been used in this case study, not so much to correct as to capture more of the critical pieces. When drafts are approved by change agents that feel comfortable with the analysis, at least higher confidence is reached. The time frame for the STK Innova case study is six years: 1984 - 1989.[14]

The STK innova case setting

Standard Telephone and Cable Factory (STK) was established in 1915 to meet the demand for electrical cables and conductors. Later, the company went into telecommunication equipment[15] and electrical household appliances. Two dominant owners have been present during the 75 year history of STK.[16] In the early 1980s the top directors of STK became concerned about a lack of innovativeness and a certain rigidity in internal operations. At the same time their products faced a tougher competition, especially on the domestic market for telecommunications.[17] The directors of STK, realizing a need for market orientation and restructuring, faced an administrative paradox: On one hand STK lacked a profitable renewal of its products and services. On the other hand, the corporation apparently had members with ideas and competence in technology-based areas. Due to the small scale of the new business project individual entrepreneurs at STK often experienced a lack of *attention* from the management.[18] The tradition channels apparently were not effective. For instance the product-idea committee had not inspired employees to come forward, and the ones that tried, were disappointed.

The directors' reflections coincided with a *spin-off* in 1984. A couple of engineers were disheartened after a time-consuming but successful innovation phase in an R & D project.[19] After which, none of the divisions of STK would take on the innovation, due to the high risk in an emerging market. Two engineers took the project out of STK and set up a new firm, eventually with some help from the "mother" corporation. That event was an important learning experience for some of the top directors. In this setting *STK Innova* evolved as a supplementary way to manage business ideas.

Innova - an evolving process

'Good ideas should not be locked in. Inside STK further development and sales were not given priority. Just to get the products through the production systems of STK was a considerable task.' (Two entrepreneurs; employees of the corporation STK until 1984).

'If you feel you are an entrepreneur or if you have a business idea that you cannot handle, then you are welcome to an information meeting on STK Innova.' (Invitation to employees of STK from STK Innova, April 1989).

The two statements from the case study in a Norwegian corporation, Alcatel STK Ltd. indicate that significant events have taken place in the 1980s inside this one corporation. In the following, two questions will be addressed:

(1) How (and why) did the STK Innova come into being?

(2) How was the new policy put into practice?

The first question is analyzed through an exploration of the initial phase, 1984 -1985, called the formulation or *definition* phase. In the 'preventure' period STK Innova was conceptualized and transformed from an idea to a project. The second question is investigated in the *implementation* phase, 1985 - 1989. During this period the STK Innova project was developed from an 'embryonic' business to a one-product business, followed by an expansion to a multiproduct (multiservice) business. Parallel conceptualization is used in Burgelman & Sayles (1986).

The definition phase

'The start was in fact a question of influencing the culture of STK,' the personnel director put it.

Motivations. Both managers[20] and employees of STK had perceived, experienced or articulated problems with organisational rigidity and a shortage of growth and renewal abilities in the corporation. The top directors wanted to change this profile -in light of more demanding markets. These critical issues were already put on the corporate '*agenda*' in connection with an ongoing transformation project inside STK. That project started up in 1983 and was expected to be finished in 1987; i.e. a time framing and focus that could allow for various initiatives and actions. Assisted by a consultancy firm[21] two dimensions were investigated: cost reduction and development/renewal activities. The new innovation system was triggered by this corporate transformation project, called "STK meets the Future".

How was the innova idea generated?

Inside STK spokesmen asked for a more proactive growth and renewal strategy combined with positive action, not only a cost saving project. The personnel director presented renewal ideas to the other top directors in a paper, entitled "Reflections on organizing for growth at STK". With reference to opinions amongst employees, middle managers and trade union representatives, the need for renewal *action* was promoted. The discussions inside the Transformation project concluded that STK had the available resources (e.g. professional competence), a market potential for growth, and management capacity to "do something". Some directors opposed the traditional way of operating: 'We are in a rut with respect to our limited product lines, and new businesses are random and without a strategy plan. There are many factors connected with market and technology that indicate that we must search for suitable forms to ensure corporate growth and our running operations' (Technical director of STK, in the document, STK 1984). These views were shared by the consultants active in the Transformation project.[22]

Initiative. In this corporate situation the personnel director seized the opportunity to suggest a new mechanism for innovation and entrepreneurship inside the corporation. By writing a paper setting out suggestions, he brought forward an action idea without committing top management too much. The action idea was embedded in his reflections on the state of the corporation and the ongoing transformation process. His paper, addressed to the top Administration, ended in a proposed model for a new line of business at STK; STK Innova. The "idea paper" also submitted suggested decision issues (conclusions) and procedures for further consideration.

The proposed mechanism was later conceptualized with the assistance of an external consultant already working for STK.[23] The intitiator was also influenced by other external contacts. The personnel director nurtured a varied set of personal contacts; with professionals, trade union representatives, politicians, business relations among others. Tushman and Scanlan (1981) have demonstrated that informational boundary spanning is accomplished only by those individuals who are well connected internally and externally. The STK Innova case material indicates that the personnel director at that time was actively communicating outside as well as inside the STK corporation.[24] The need for breeding innovations in new ways, was discovered through this networking.

From new idea to new concept

Who was active in defining a new system for innovation and internal venturing? The concept of Innova was created in a business/professional network, where the relationship between the external chief consultant and the personnel director seemed to be significant. The corporate background - or "climate" for the new innovation channel, should be considered in a broader context. For instance representatives from the different trade unions at STK had demanded renewal activities on several occasions.[25]

Key players and introductory elements. A small group of high status managers was change agents, in particular the personnel director. The decision strategy - how to seize the opportunity - was created mainly by this director.[26] His "idea paper" proposed the appointment of a small group, with the mandate to consider and elaborate upon the ideas and issues formulated. This step resulted in four papers which were collated with the first paper, in a report called *"Culture for Growth at STK"* (STK 1984). The coupling with the on-going Transformation project was visualized by the chosen title. The Culture for Growth Report included "STK Innova - a project proposal" with a tentative conclusive summary, and a proposed budget for a five year period. In this way, the top directors were prepared to give a starting signal - without involving too many actors or evoking existing corporate routines. Above all, the rigid investment decision system in the international mother corporation, ITT, was deliberately avoided by the originators of STK Innova. The new line of business was formulated as a 'strategic project', not a new company or a new investment plan. This ad hoc organisational form was chosen to introduce the practice of new experimental business activities, on a less strictly regulated basis.

In the definition phase both strategic linking as well as finding latent resources were important. The top directors got what they needed: a suitable decision material put into an appropriate context inside STK. The linking role was played by the personnel director who may be labelled an organisational champion: a person that understands the field of interest and strategies of the corporation at a particular point in time. According to Burgelman and

Sayles (1986:90) the organisational champion is able to relate the parameters and potential of a new venture persuasively to the ultimate goals of the corporation. Inside STK the personnel director at that time, played that role extensively in order to establish the STK Innova.

Concept-specification. The STK Innova idea was elaborated and the essentials were put down on paper by assistance of the entrusted chief consultant. Two objectives of STK Innova had been defined in the decision documents:

(1) generate practical business development; and

(2) contribute to a change-oriented culture at STK - in general, by its entrepreneurial climate, and by proactive use of that.

The core idea of business was formulated in the decision documents to the top directors: 'STK/Innova is a strategic line of business at STK which through own operations and/or economic and professional involvements shall develop, acquire or transfer new business opportunities inside or outside STK, and which is useful for the future business of STK' (STK 1984, chapt. 6). The documents stressed the interplay with the corporation in Innova's work, especially in those fields where the existing corporate lines of business/divisions did not want to operate or expand (cf. figure 1). In that way, the STK Innova may be seen as a new *channel* for innovation activities.

Figure 1
Idea and project development through STK innova

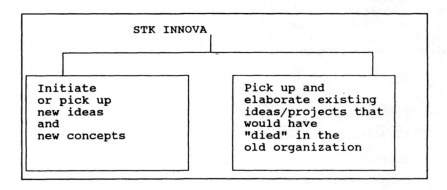

Innova was intended to detect and implement business potential. On what grounds were the new activities planned? The originators emphasized the human assets on the employee level:

-    would-be entrepreneurs with valuable ideas, and

-    competence resources of employees that could be applied in new settings and in new ways (STK 1984).

The competent employees were intended to be resource-persons for the would-be entrepreneurs. The entrepreneur was looked upon as more important than the venture idea.[27] This concept was proposed in the 'Culture for growth' report of October 1984, a report that was followed up by the establishment of STK Innova one year after - in September 1985. The time lag was attributed to several reasons. Other activities competed for key change agents' attention. In addition, according to two of the change agents, the Innova idea had to be "levered" gradually inside this corporation.[28] The decision to put STK Innova into force, is the separating point between the definition phase and the implementation phase. That decision was taken informally at the top management level.

The implementation phase

During the initial phase the Innova concept had been developed relatively independently of the corporate environment. When STK Innova was a reality, the new organisational unit became a starting point for further development and/or definition. As a matter of fact, the new channel idea was not fully defined into new services, processes or systems. More work was needed to complete and transform the concept into an ongoing business.

From embryonic business to one-service business

Means as well as resources for a set of activities had to be specified. Most significant, a *through-put* or appropriate technology (method) had to be developed in order to implement the new system. How did the STK Innova go about these challenges?

Policy measures and resources. The means of the STK Innova were developed according to its philosophy of entrepreneurship and business development. A mixture of individual means and infrastructural support was chosen (see textbox 3). The new innovation system tapped existing capabilities in new ways, such as using senior managers as supervisors for would-be entrepreneurs. New resources were pooled; information and know-how connected to market-driven innovations seemed to be most significant.

Figure 2
Available repertoir of measures, STK innova

POLICY MEASURES OF STK INNOVA

1. Unpaid leave (up to 2 years, return at own discretion).

2. Grant (e.g. salary during part of the granted leave).

3. Training programme (arranged during working hours with full salary).

4. Assistance from consultants (internal or external).

5. Assistance from mother organization (facilities, equipment, legal assistance etc).

6. Practical measures (e.g. localities).

7. Reward system (a. Originator given partnership in a new company: reward through value added in the company. b. Originator not part of the commercialization + evt. further development in an STK division: reward through a single cash payment or royalties after negotiation).

How were the activities of STK Innova financed? When Innova was established, the procedural systems of ITT dominated the daughter corporation STK. Capital investment was looked upon as a tricky matter, especially capital formation in other companies such as spin-offs. The formalized regulation had to be evaded, if possible, to avoid another "bottleneck" that could stop or put a brake on the new effort for growth and development.

Injection of capital to STK Innova was ensured through a separate financial company, *STK Venture Ltd.* The STK Venture was established August 1986 by a creative operation: A daughter company of STK (Brinchman) had already a 'sleeping' limited company with a capital base of NOK 200.000. This company was redirected to new objectives and received the new name, STK Venture. The transaction could be done without announcement beyond the circle that was already involved. In this way, initial 'seed money' was ensured. Organisational championing combined with a specific organisational form allowed this kind of implementation. A project is an ad hoc organisational form that may 'decouple' the project processes from the existing organisational routines and restrictions. STK Innova was allowed more freedom of action by the very initial definition of the sub-organisation.

In any bureaucracy, there is a great deal of freedom - only they don't tell you about that, you have to find them for yourself, according to an intrapreneur in a popular book on Intrapreneurship (Pinchot 1985, p 195). The literature on Entrepreneurship indicates that the entrepreneur wants to find the freedom factors himself.[29] The personnel director was the key person to find and to seize the STK Venture opportunity that was "open" inside the corporation. He also found other ad hoc solutions: The salaries of the first personnel of STK Innova were organised via the budget of the Personnel department. Other financial solutions were more difficult before the new venture company emerged. Two would-be entrepreneurs applied for financial help at STK Innova's door one month before the STK Venture was ready. The personnel director solved their urgent need for seed money by drawing a cheque on his personal account: NOK 105.000. That event was perceived by employees and it was retold as an anecdotal story.

Core technology. In the initial implementation phase of the new channel, the same consulting company, *INDEVO*,[30] headed by the entrusted chief consultant, played a partner as well as a supervisory role. The main methods of STK Innova, therefore, may be seen as a product of two elements: a) the consulting company with its main focus on management activities and b) the chief consultant's other experience in stimulating would-be entrepreneurs. In Norway, this consulting company had developed a new training programme for individual entrepreneurs, called the "Hairlifting" Programme. The main strategy of INDEVO, however, was to revitalize existing large corporations. These two types of influences in addition to internal influences, lead to slightly modified search and training methods used by the STK Innova. Later on, the training methods were further developed by the Innova managers.

An open search method based on self-selection[31] was used to get in contact with potential entrepreneurs. This search was called an *innovation campaign*. After presentation of ideas and further selection effectuated on a group basis, a training programme started. The objective was to help the would-be entrepreneur through a *process* where the necessary 'homework' and market testing should be effectuated as far as possible towards a commercialization of new products or services. The initial idea material should be refined through this process that normally should end in a presentation of a business plan as detailed and complete as feasible.[32]

From a one-service business to multiple services

Resources. Personnel during the initial phase of STK Innova were limited to 2 senior managers and about 1/3 of the working hours of the personnel director. Due to increased activities and reduced external consultancy assistance, more personnel were recruited from the STK corporation. In addition, ad hoc managerial and professional assistance was made available from the "mother" organisation, even though the mainstream activities had first priority. Due to slack resources and motivated personnel - finding it exciting to work for Innova, human capital was successfully reallocated to the new system. Most importantly, senior professionals were made available to create the new routines of the innovation-breeding system.

Activities. The first activity implemented by STK Innova, was the so called innovation campaign. Later on, this effort was reproduced as an annual activity together with the internal training programme in business development. In addition, other activities emerged, internally and externally, and they were taken on for different reasons. For instance consultancy work provided income to the Innova organisation. Externally, training seminars for would-be entrepreneurs were arranged in another large corporation as well as in a community-based setting. These activities probably prove the Innova concept as a legitimate way of operating. Eventually, project work for the mother corporation, Alcatel STK, was commissioned. In particular transfer of corporate projects of strategic importance, may be seen as an acknowledgement of the new innovation-breeding system. After which, the STK Innova evolved from a mainly one-service business to a multi-service company (see figure encl.). From promoting individual entrepreneurship through campaigns and training, the unit managed a group of activities.

Resource control. Personnel, technology and financing no longer represented acute problems, and business results were visible or ostensible (see next paragraph). However, the Alcatel mother company asked for a closer look on the STK Innova assets, in particular the investment pattern. Investment in new ventures afterwards was limited by Alcatel decision processes. This event also led to a new internal order of the innovation-breeding system: In late 1988 the STK Innova itself was transformed from a project to a separate company, by changing STK Venture Ltd. to Alcatel STK Innova Ltd.

STK INNOVA - which innovations?

What kind of results has Alcatel STK obtained, by organising a separate, formal device for innovation and business development, so far? As mentioned above, the STK Innova had two purposes: innovation/venturing and change-facilitation.

(1) Innovation/venturing

'If the survival rate of these new businesses is larger than 50%, STK will get a fair rate of interest from the input' (Senior manager of STK Innova (source: Bedre Bedrift no. 2, 1988). During the period 1985 - 89 Alcatel STK Innova has contributed to the establishment of 27 companies with more than 100 employees in total.[33] The effects seem to result mainly from extra-development efforts in terms of annual innovation campaigns and training programmes. Most of the products or services were developed in a fairly short time period, during the six months' training programme. In addition, three internal strategic projects are contracted with the mother company Alcatel STK. Bridging between corporation strategy and innovation networking is a resultant. The activities of Alcatel STK Innova are now on a self-sustainable financial basis.

A large portion of the new companies could be characterized as closely related to the Alcatel STK's lines of business and with a medium degree of innovative change. However, other types of businesses were created as well, such as a company arranging river rafting

ALCATEL STK INNOVA

Figure 3
Alcatel STK innova

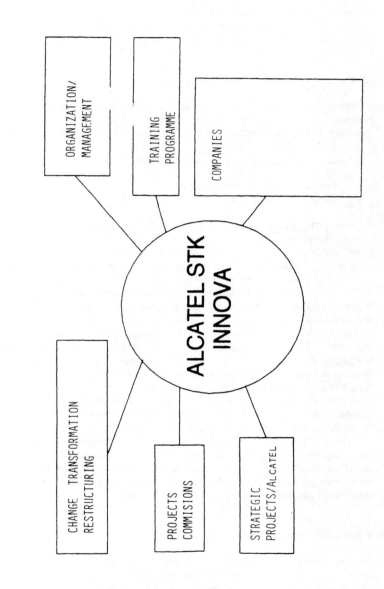

345

for tourists! Most of the new companies are more or less loosely coupled *spin-offs*[34] from the mother corporation. This result may be attributed to the fact that most of the "Innova projects" have been relatively small in comparison with the corporation's traditional focus on big projects. More importantly is that the new businesses probably were considered as projects of little strategic importance to Alcatel STK Ltd. There are exceptions: In fact the corporation bought back a project in business communication after an independent establishment externally.

(2) Creating a change-oriented environment

'We invited the employees to a business development seminar, but were first met by a concrete wall... Eventually, they saw that we were serious about it.' (Personnel, director, interview 21.09.1987). Innova has been approached by five different categories of users:
- rank and file of STK,
- corporate management and division leaders,
- personnel department,
- external would-be entrepreneurs and
- other interested parties.

Among the 3.000 employees of Alcatel STK in Oslo there were groups that did not contact the Innova office. The typical would-be entrepreneur seemed to be a male with some technical education combined with practice from the "middle" levels of the corporation.[35] Despite the positive opinions of trade union leaders towards action for renewal, the blue-collar workers and their trade union did not use the Innova opportunity before 1989/90. At that time, due to an excess labour situation on the shop floor, trade union representatives articulated the pressure for renewal in public as well as on a corporate basis. Six months earlier, blue collar representatives had expressed disapproval of the Innova concept. However, the knowledge of Innova's activities was fairly low at that time.[36] The opinions of the trade union representatives during different parts of the implanting process of the STK Innova, illustrate very clearly: Creating an innovative climate in a rigid corporation is indeed a complex process. Signs of change have been experienced in parts of the STK organisation, according to the management of Alcatel STK and STK Innova, respectively.[37] On a behavioural level certain signs indicate a change: 'Today the departments turn up and by themselves approach Innova, while this "amoeba" earlier was met with some reservation.'

The institutionalization of STK Innova as a daughter company indicated an acknowledgement on the corporate level. After the corporation lost a big contract in 1990, the change-facilitating aspect seemed to be enhanced. Innova took active part in the restructuring efforts - as an in-house consultancy, for instance restructuring of workshops in order to make them vital on an independent basis.

What can be learnt?

The case study has illustrated how a stimulating channel for innovations and venturing came about, and how it was put into practice in a large and rigid corporation. In the following, key elements in the development process will be highlighted and some practical and theoretical implications drawn with reference to this case study.

1. Initiators. The STK Innova did not arise as a deliberate, planned decision of the top level in the corporation. The entrepreneurial channel evolved from an idea to a concept, to

an experimental project, to an official system, to a daughter company. However, this evolvement was not 'self-generated' by ongoing processes. The new innovation concept had to be prepared and carried through by committed and skilled action by a few significant individuals: Boundery-spanning managers cooperated mostly in an informal manner in raising the issue on the top level.

Figure 4
Proposition 1: Initiators

Initiative for a new innovation channel typically come from boundery-spanning managers (not the top management or the first-line managers).

2. Key players and core processes. The processes by which these individuals developed the STK Innova, have been described in terms of two concepts: (1) an entrepreneurial activity, and (2) organisational championing. These kinds of activities and driving forces may "explain" why the Innova concept was successfully defined and implemented in a rigid organisation. Key change agents - especially an organisational champion - found the resources and the 'gates' inside this corporation to carry through "their" idea from the very initial phase right through to the implementation phases. Freedom factors apparently existed inside STK, but the development process did not lose momentum even if resources were not found immediately. The process was kept on the track by creative solutions.

Figure 5
Proposition 2: Key players and core processes

Establishing a new innovation channel are driven by organisational champions that mobilize existing visible and invisible resources and create conditions for continued support.

3. Central activities. The new personnel of STK Innova were recruited internally from the STK corporation, but their time and competence were used for new *purposes*. Reallocation of existing personnel to new purposes, as such, is a challenge to the hypotheses on the need for new personnel in radical innovations (Hage 1980, p 218-219). Evidence for the need for additional funds and for new technologies was found in the STK Innova case study. The processes by which these resources were provided, seemed to be different:
-    Conceptualization evolved through networking and 'meetings' as a more or less continuous search and design activity during the definition phase and beyond the pre-Innova stage.
-    Funding, on the contrary, was initially delayed, but later took advantage of the opportunity offered by the sleeping daughter company.
The relative importance of conceptualization in the STK Innova case, seems to be related with the mobilization of support (cf proposition 2). According to the former personnel director, support indeed had to be 'created'.

Figure 6
Proposition 3: Central activities

Defining a new innovation channel is more characterized by concept-development than technical or procedural activities. The latter is typically opportunity-driven to rationalize on entrepreneurial resources.

4. Meta-decisional processes. The start-up of STK Innova was characterized by *novelty* (new innovation concept, new objectives), *complexity* (new social system, new technologies) and *openendedness* (means, procedures, activities). Mintzberg et al (1976) defined this type of process a strategic decision process where 'groping' through a recursive, discontinuous process involves many difficult steps and a host of dynamic factors over a considerable period of time before a final choice is made (p. 250-251). In addition to Burgelman and Sayles thorough case study of internal venturing (1986), evidence from the STK Innova case study indicates: Some obstacles may be removed and some speedup may be achieved through organisational championing and entrepreneurial activities. In a corporate context mobilizing resources and opportunities in *new combinations* seems to be a challenging task, even though resources may be genourous (the slack hypothesis).

How are these 'new combinations' successfully developed? An organisational climate-explanation has been suggested as a moderating variable (Ekvall 1990). Another approach is to focus on loose *coupling*. Two systems that are joined by few common variables or weak common variables are said to be loosely coupled (Weick 1979, p 111). It looks like coupling and decoupling mechanisms were used by the key change managers to reduce formal and informal barriers to internal venturing. Evidence of decoupling, e.g. decoupling from ITT's red-tape: their investment decision system, indicate why untraditional solutions were consented. The activities of STK Innova were not implemented close to the basic lines of business in the corporation. Inside STK, the new innovation system emerged alongside the old organisation, which continued to exist (even though under some change pressure). The structural changes represented a *side-by-side overlap* in the existence of traditional and new ways of doing things. According to Sheldon (1980), the two systems must be buffered from each other, if change is to be successful. Physical, organisational and fiscal buffering are necessary. Failure to do this, inevitably leads to adverse consequences, Sheldon argues (p 67). The STK Innova was implemented from a separate innovation centre outside the Alcatel STK headquarter in Oslo. The fiscal and administrative practices were developed on fresh ground, although with some restrictions imposed later on. Innova leaders put market orientation and focus on entrepreneurial persons and facilitiating processes as important "world views". Invitation to would-be entrepreneurs, systematic preparation of a venture plan, market investigation or market entry under (some) supervision were new entrepreneurial practices in the corporation. However, the initiators as well as the managers of the new unit deliberately kept the Innova strategy compatible with the strategy of the mother corporation. This was effectuated through active communication to the top management of Alcatel STK and by meta-decisional strategies (decisions about decisions). The case material indicate that change agents behind Innova were concious about how and what kind of issues should be presented to different decision fora inside the corporation. Knowing how (informal and formal rules) and knowing who, seemed to be important. Both the first and the second top manager of Innova had practised lateral networking in former functions.

Figure 7
Proposition 4: Meta-decisional processes

The more radical the innovation-breeding system, the greater the need for managing loose coupling as well as interlocking behaviour during the introductory period.

5. Authorization. Decisions concerning Innova were taken at the top level inside STK, typically in an informal manner. These decisions to put STK Innova into force or transform its organisational form, may be seen as *responses* to definition activities. Were these top decisions important signals for the (further) implementation of Innova? I would say that the decisions were a signal for a stop or go-process. Without authorization,[38] the development process probably would have been more delayed or even easily stopped, since the driving forces were a few individuals - and one-two, only, as members of the top director group. As late as autumn 1990, the Innova organisation still was controversial, for instance among trade union leaders and divison leaders.[39] Innova's relationship of trust is based on top level support.

Figure 8
Proposition 5: Authorization

The more radical the innovation-breeding system, the greater the need for authorization and other supporting signals from the top management or board of directors.

6. Relational assets. Why were change agents capable of striking opportunity? STK Innova was conceptualized in a *relation* between the personnel director and the chief consultant from INDEVO. What they had in common, were a commitment to the systematic practice of innovation.[40] Based on the STK Innova case, we would like to add: Not only this shared commitment was significant, but their *shared and complementary knowledge*. The meeting between two experienced 'players' created something more than each of them probably could produce individually. An indication of this relational influence is that each of them attributed significant parts of the STK Innova formulation to the partner.

Figure 9
Proposition 6: Relational assets

The more radical the innovation-breeding system, the greater the need for shared and complementary knowledge in the development process in a rigid organisational framework.

7. Core competences. So, what did the originators share in the relationship? They shared assets that had been accumulated through operating transactions;[41]political skills, presentation skills, negotiating skills, creative (idea-generating) skills. Saren and Gorman (1987) suggest a skill 'package' as the reason why entrepreneurs may be capable of striking new opportunities, I would suggest a *personal* (Polanyi 1958) skill package:
* The entrusted chief consultant contributed the details of an entrepreneurial

mechanism; pieces of information from his long experience as a consultant and as a member of the INDEVO culture.

* The personnel director picked up the innovation channel idea initially from his external networking. His core competence, however, was his ability to take advantage of opportunities already existing in the large corporation and his ability to go beyond its current capabilities.

Finding 'a way' - also through what has been called an over-extension strategy (Itami 1987), is regarded as typical for entrepreneurial activities (Stevenson and Jarillo 1990). The core competence behind entrepreneurial activities, seems to be connected closely to mobilization of all sorts of *invisible assets* (Itami ibid): reputation, trust, political skills, networking abilities.[42] Some of the managers running the STK Innova business later on, seemed to make use of similiar skills in addition to professional skills (e.g. personnel, technical, marketing).

Figure 10
Proposition 7: Core competences

The more radical the innovation-breeding system, the greater the need for committed and skilled change agents. Core competences needed are multi-disciplined, but taking advantage of invisible assets is crucial.

The STK Innova has served to connect innovation and the market with respect to some kinds of products and services. The seven propositions suggested above, may seem to be important for the creation of a radically new innovation-breeding system. The innovation channel concept is not restricted to one corporation or to a Norwegian setting: It has already been diffused to a Swiss daughter company of Asea Brown Bovery. Identification of entrepreneurial individuals as driving forces for corporate innovation projects, has evoked a new interest.[43] The Innova concept is person-oriented, but not restricted to individual action. STK Innova brings together business proposals and individuals that exist in different parts of the corporation: A hotbed for innovation networking?

Practical implications

What can be learnt for practical purposes from this case study? Not all of the STK Innova case is as idyllic as it may seem. The complexity of creating a new social system in a routine-based organisation, should not be underestimated. Other corporations that do want to provide an official innovation system, should not only be aware, but think through the possible implementation problems that might exist in their corporation. In addition, it is recommended to search for driving forces - managers or management teams that are able to strike hidden opportunities and if necessary; go beyond the existing capabilities.

8. Learning processes. One problem is that a corporation has less knowledge than the sum of its employees and managers. Knowledge on innovative change may be especially difficult to produce, according to cognitive and bureaucratic theories. Still, a large and rigid company may learn to manage new and unplanned commercial activities in spite of learning barriers (Burgelman & Sayles 1986). How, then, can a large corporation learn (and unlearn)? In order to learn, mediating mechanisms may be required between internal

entrepreneurial activities, if any, and mature industrial corporations. These bridging mechanisms may be brought about by a proactive official innovation system. For instance the chief managers of STK Innova communicated up-wards directly to the very top in a confident manner.[44]

Figure 11
Proposition 8: Learning processes

The more radical the innovation-breeding system, the greater the need for speeding up learning processes in the corporation, especially on the top management level.

In the STK Innova case the top directors of Alcatel STK were eventually beginning to understand that a separate innovation channel had several advantages such as pushing embryonic business more effectively towards commercialization. It is indicated that learning on a top director level has taken place. Learning was probably obtained through a process of accumulated *enactments* (Weick 1979) of the STK Innova methods combined with its *visible* effects. One indication of learning is that the top directors decided to put some of their "own" strategic projects through the new channel. Another indication is that the chairman of the Board publicly proclaimed the advantages of large corporations helping would-be entrepreneurs: 'Excellent business projects disappear because nobody is there to keep them up when they are down' (Dagens Nringsliv 22.11.1988).

If neglect[45] is the problem, an official system may make a difference:

'But where will the funds come from, if they are not set aside? Where will the support be, if there are no official sponsors and allies? Where will the time come from, if the effort is not officially recognized outside of department priorities? What will be the incentives, if there are no special rewards?'(Kanter 1989:180).

Pieces of evidence from the pre-Innova period and later, indicate that an official system did make a noteworthy difference for would-be entrepreneurs inside this one corporation.[46] An official system may also speed up learning processes.[47] However, the STK Innova case illustrates that perception of an official innovation-breeding system may be biased or only eventually perceived by internal actors in a way that produce learning.[48] A possible implication is the need for dwelling-in[49] to really understand the functioning of a new innovation-breeding system.

9. Effort in time perspective. Many American corporations have supplied some sort of innovation-facilitating arrangement. One-fourth of the Fortune 500 companies had a formal new venture development department between 1965 and 1975, according to an estimation made by Norman Fast (Kanter 1989, p 180). His case studies of the evolution of a few of them showed that they rarely remained a viable channel for new ideas. Their fate was to disappear altogether in various ways, after a disappointing performance. According to Kanter (1989), an official system still makes a difference. However, the channels need to be dug again and again, the commitments renewed explicitly. In the STK Innova case, a top manager was appointed in 1988 in order to coordinate the emerging renewal activities. So far, the system has proved to be a continuous internal venture in promoting activity. An inherent managerial dilemma seems to be how to vitalize as well as balance between bottom-up and top-down activities - nurturing the needs of individual would-be entrepreneurs and catering the strategy interests of the corporate "mother".

Figure 12
Proposition 9: Effort in time perspective

The more radical the innovation-breeding system, the greater the need to vitalize the sub-system recursively.

This study indicates that it may be crucial to the results where the initiative is taken and who is responsible for managing an innovation-breeding programme. If the internal venturing effort is to be integrated in the "mother" company later on, it looks like a medium strong involvement from the mother corporation is suitable. Such an involvement evolves over time in a well-established corporation of the "mechanistic" type: The STK Innova, for example, was built up over a period of five years as a development device for internal venturing. A time-consuming introductory process, however, threatens a successful implementation. Someone has to fill the gap between initial commitments and numerous possible implementation problems (Pressman & Wildavsky 1973). In the STK Innova case, the major initiators in the definition phase also were key players in the beginning of the implementation phase. 'When you have taken the devil on your back, you had better carry him, too!', advised the top management. Later on, successors and fresh new players were added.

The more radical the innovation-breeding system, the greater the need for closing the gap between design and implementation. The initial corporate commitment should be follo-wed up by medium strong involvement combined with sufficient driving forces. Proposition 10: Closing the gap between definition and implementation

Theoretical implications

According to Stevenson and Jarillo (1990) there is a need to establish links between the fields of entrepreneurship and corporate management, if the large body of research in the former is to benefit the latter. This paper has focused on the introduction and first five year implementation of an entrepreneurial management system inside one corporation. The STK Innova case study indicated that not only understanding how best to nurture entrepreneurial persons and innovative ideas is important, insights into the well-established corporation are also paramount to introduce something new in an "old regime". But 'old theories' on implementation in a bureaucracy have concepts such as change agents, which could be vitalized by new theories on entrepreneurial behaviour which address the persons involved as well as the context.

I have deliberately used the term evolve rather than plan in presenting the creation of an entrepreneurial management system. However, the evolution of STK Innova did not happen without any reflections ex ante. An innovation-breeding *concept*, not ready-made but still 'half-prepared', seemed to be an important driving force in the evolution. An action-based and market-focused entrepreneurial training system was at the heart of the initiators' philosophy for the new corporate innovation channel. The STK Innova case, although rather successful, reveals that such a system is a fragile "mechanism", a device that may easily be stopped. The Mechanism-thinking is maybe not suited at all because it leads us to a machine-thinking. Since the introduction of 'newstream' in 'mainstream' business produces a lot of tension (Kanter 1989), is it better understood through the amoeba analogy? Something that does not have a fixed form and that is under continual pressure from the environment. Neither the mechanism nor the amoeba methaphor fits, the process is far more complex, proactive more than passive adaptation going on in those newstream systems that survive (cf Kanter 1989, p 219). As illustrated in the Innova case study, design and implementation tended to continue as *intertwinned activities* throughout the introductory process, even though a "go-decision" had been given. Design as well as implementation evolved as non-routine, creative activities. The management of such activities, then, seems to be a process that involves entrepreneurial skills as well as the creation of (continued) commitment.

Further research on driving forces behind innovative activities inside companies is needed to investigate more systematically the hidden events and managerial action that facilitates innovation and change - not at least in everyday life of a company (Burgelman & Sayles 1986) and on a more long-term basis. This case study indicates that organisational and 'entrepreneurial' knowledge to fill the gap between definition of a new innovation policy and its implementation, is crucial. Knowledge on creating innovative change, often seems to be invisible and tacit (Polanyi 1958). Through 'meetings' between skilled and committed players, adequate knowledge for entrepreneurial activities may be mobilized. Studying it, therefore, may require a closer focus not only on the individual knowing, but on relational knowing.

Notes

[1].The research was conducted by the author of this article, and it was financed by the Norwegian Research Council for Applied Social Science. The author wish to acknowledge Ingeborg Kleppe, Kjell Grönhaug, Torger Reve, Tor Fredriksen and Bengt Johannisson for suggestions and comments to an early draft of this article. Steve Dracup and Joyce Falkenberg used their spare time to comment on the English language. Tor Fredriksen also took part in the first field interviews. In particular, I wish to thank informants from Alcatel STK Ltd and INDEVO Ltd for valuable reflections. Lars Harlem, Sverre Tronsli and Sven J. Jacobsen should be mentioned, they shared with me personal insights on how to get things done in large corporations.

[2].The mechanistic/organic distinction was developed by Burns & Stalker (The Management of Innovation, London: Tavistock Publ. Ltd. 1961). A mechanistic organization typically has problems/tasks broken down into specialist roles, each sees tasks as distinct from tasks of the whole, precise definition of technical methods, duties, powers in each functional role, vertical integration within management (source: Kanter 1983, The Change Masters).

[3].A system is a set of interrelated elements, an open system is more than that: These elements make up a mechanism that takes input from the environment, subjects it to some form of transformation process, and produces output (D. Nadler and M. Tushman, A Model for Diagnosing Organizational Behavior, Readings in the Management of Innovation, Sec.ed., 1988). Business organisations - or sub-organisations - may be seen as open, social systems.

[4]. See Kanter (1989) for references.

[5]. See Special issue on Corporate Entrepreneurship of Strategic Management Journal, Volume 11 Summer 1990.

[6]. See for instance Myhre (1986) for information on Norwegian companies with innovation-breeding systems (Myhre, Terje, Intraprenørskap (Intrapreneurship), Diploma report, Department of Organization and Work Relations, The Norwegian Institute of Technology, 1986).

7. In the Norwegian setting the STK Innova is looked upon as a fairly unique corporate sub-organisation that is stimulating employees for new business development (own interviews with consulting firms; see also Myhre 1986, Ekvall 1990).

8. The new channel for innovation and entrepreneurship, was called STK Innova from the start. Later on, the name was changed to Alcatel Innova Ltd.

9. The same categorization is common in literature on business strategy: confer the two phases strategy formulation and strategy implementation.

10. Representatives from three consulting companies were interviewed, governmental officials in the Norwegian Regional Policy Administration were also contacted and relevant literature were searched.

11. The case study includes pieces of evidence from the trade union level, the management levels, the Research & Development department level and the venture project level.

12. So far, 18 persons have been interviewed, informants from the top director level, the STK Innova level, the Research department/Telecommunication division, Trade union level, Entrepreneurs/project or company level (three of the new companies that were located in sparsely populated regions). Some of the informants have been interviewed more than once, and follow-up telephone conversations have been conducted. Three of the key informants have read and commented on report drafts made by the author.

13. Annual reports, folders, administrative and decision papers, written speeches by managers, interviews in newspapers, internal documents such as documents prepared by managers or consultants, research reports by other researchers (Ekvall 1990 and a student report summary) and drafts made by the author of this article sent to key informants and commented by them, are used for control purposes. The response from one of the main change agents concerning a draft of this article, was that he found it exciting and correct, and he emphasized the detailed level of description, the historic perspective and the 'coupling' (of perspectives and evidence) as interesting.

14. The investigation started with exploring the initiation of the new innovation-breeding system. The case was completed by the transformation of Innova to a new legal form. The interviews and written documents were collected in the period 1987 - 1990.

15. The digital telephone exchanges, System 12, that STK has delivered to the home market, originated from an innovation made by the former foreign mother corporation of STK: the ITT.

16. The American multinational corporation, ITT, in the period 1930-86/87; and the European multinational, Alcatel NV, from 1986/87.

17. It is a well-known fact that after a long period of growth large corporations may experience a demand for consolidation, restructuring and renewal (Greiner, Larry E., Evolution and Revolution as Organizations Grow, Harvard Business Review, Vol. 50, nr. 4, p 37-46, 1972).

18. According to interviews with entrepreneurs and key informants inside STK.

19. The innovation effort resulted in a new apparatus for environmental monitoring. The R & D department could not do anything more to develop the project, they had already spent enough resources: The project leader had to recruit and train project personnel three times (!) during the development phase. A prototype had been tried out with success in the Hardanger mountain plateau (registerating meteorological data).

20. A few directors in different parts of the corporation, in the Personnel Department and in the Research and Development department, were concerned about the neglection of innovative ideas proposed by employees. They talked about the possibility of handling ideas or innovations developed by employees, in new ways. Source: Written speeches that some directors made at conferences, e.g. early in 1984. Personal interviews with

representative informants.

21. INDEVO Ltd, a multinational consultancy firm, originating from Sweden.

22. Source: Own interview with two INDEVO consultants that had participated in the transformation project at STK. Cf. also INDEVOs policy, formulated in their annual reports.

23. Source: repeated interviews with the former personnel director, the former INDEVO consultant and written documents.

24. Source: Personal interviews with trade union representatives, with the personnel director and his description of his activities, observation during two external conferences on business issues. The personnel director had earlier served as aä representative of the National Association for Engineers, and he is connected to influential political networks through kinship.

25. Source: Documents from the initial phase ("STK meets the Future", STK 1984) and personal interviews with two representatives from the blue-collar trade union, April 1989.

26. The former personnel director used these words himself in a dialogue after reading through our case report draft. Heä separated the decision strategy from e.g. STK Innova strategy (dialogue august 1990).

27. This philosophy of entrepreneurship was inspired by the ideas of the founders of the consulting company, INDEVO.

28. Source: The personnel director and one of the two senior managers that was recruited to STK Innova later on.

29. According to Bengt Johannisson (personal conversation).

30. Fee note 18.

31. At this stage in the process the STK Innova did not select ideas or employees/would-be entrepreneurs according to corporate strategy or other pre-venture principles. The personnel director was convinced that such selection would destroy the internal stimulating effect vis à vis the employees. This principle deviates from the selection principles used by the consulting firm in the "Hairlifting" Programme.

32. This method has many similarities with a process-oriented writing pedagogy.

33. In addition Innova has contributed to the establishment of new firms through activities outside the STK corporate setting.

34. Alcatel STK in January 1990 held a partnership in 10 companies, with a share ranging from one third up to 100 percentä (usually up to 49 pct). According to Innova policy, the entrepreneur should at least have 50 per cent of the shares. Then theä entrepreneur knows where the shoe pinches (feels the financial strain).

35. According to the management of STK Innova.

36. Interview 14.04.1989 with two representatives, thereof the chair person, of the blue-collar trade union at Alcatel STK, Oslo.

37. The personnel director summarized the results by 1987 in these pin-points:
- Innova has influenced the corporate culture;
- a number of employees of STK have approached STK Innova, applications that are generated by this business;
- Innova has given legitimacy to other ways of thinking organization. It means that the organizing pattern should fit the idea, not the other way around.
- STK has got a significant number of daughter companies or spin-offs. It has happened without much opposition from the top management or from the trade unions. This attitudal change is of great importance in connection withä restructuring. Trade union representatives are more relaxed concerning developmental processes now (1987),ä

"even partnership is discussed" (interview 21.09.1987). However, the personnel director was conscious about the difficulty of registerating impacts on a cultural level. Later on, the senior managers of the STK Innova have given other examples of attidual or behavioural changes.

38. Futhorization is common in strategic decision making (Mintzberg et al. 1976, p 259).

39. Information from the top director and from the leader of the blue-collar trade union.

40. Both of them expressed views and behaviour indicating such a commitment. This is a support for Drucker's notion of entrepreneurship as a committed activity for focused change (Drucker, Peter F., The Discipline of Innovation, Harvard Business Review, May - June 1985).

41. According to Itami (1987), valuable information assets are typically accumulated through business operations, it cannot be bought or stocked in a hierarchy.

42. Research by Howard Aldrich, Bengt Johannisson, Saren & Gorman and others indicate this suggestion.

43. Source: The former chief consultant of INDEVO Ltd, Asker. The importance of identifying persons rather than venture ideas in innovation efforts, was also emphasized by the top director of Alcatel STK, in an interview December 1990.

44. Own observation during visit at the STK Innova office.

45. In a Norwegian setting commercialization of innovations and new business embryos, is considered as a neglected but critical activity. Confer e.g. White Paper from the Norwegian Parliament on business policy, 1988-89.

46. Systematic information on the individual "intrapreneur" level is not available. Benefits that most of the internalä entrepreneurs have been offered, are: a free training programme arranged during working hours with full salary, assistance of different kinds and possibility to return to STK at their own discretion.

47. A survey (Susbauer 1973) of a large number of companies in the U.S. employing intracorporate entrepreneurship practices, found that companies which had initiated only formal programmes felt more positive towards their programmes than companies which had initiated informal programmes (regardless of the company size).Susbauer, J.C., U.S.ä Intracorporate Entrepreneurship Practices, R & D Management, Vol. 3, No. 3, 1973. Source: Rothwell (1975).

48. For instance the trade union representatives seemed to have changed their opinion towards STK Innova during the autumn 1989. This has happened in a situation where the Alcatel STK have decided to lay off a lot of employees due to lack of orders in the telecommunication businesses. However, learning may be the result of taking part in STK Innova's activities: an innovation campaign was arranged by the trade union of blue-collar workers and the STK Innova with support from the Alcatel STK.

49. Concept from Polanyi (1958).

References

Burgelman, Robert A. & Leonard R. Sayles (1986), Inside Corporate Innovation, The Free Press, N.Y.

Ekvall, Göran (1990), Idéer, organisationsklimat och ledningsfilosofi (Ideas, organisational climate and philosophy of management), FA-rådet, Stockholm.

Hage, Jerald (1980), Theories of Organizations, John Wiley & Sons, Inc., U.S.A.

Itami, Hiroyuki, with T. W. Roehl (1987), Mobilizing Invisible Assets, Harvard University Press, Mass. & London.

Kanter, Rosabeth Moss (1989), When Giants Learn to Dance, Simon & Schuster or (1990), Unwin Hyman Ltd., London.

Mintzberg, Henry, Duru Raisinghani & André Théorêt (1976), The Structure ofä "Unstructured" Decision Processes, Administrative Science Quarterly, Volume 21, No. 1,ä March.

Offerdal, Audun (1978), Kommunane som iverksettarar av statleg politikk (The municipalä authorities as implementers of public policy), Institute for Public Administration and Organization Theory at the University of Bergen.

Pinchot III, Gifford (1985), Intrapreneuring, Harper & Row Publishers, N.Y.

Polanyi, Michael (1958), Personal Knowledge, Routledge & Kegan P., London.

Pressman, Jeffrey L. & Aaron B. Wildavsky (1973), Implementation, University of California Press, Berkeley.

Quinn, James Brian (1985), Managing Innovation: controlled chaos, Harvard Business Review, No. 3, May-June.

Rothwell, Roy (1975), From Invention to New Business via the New Venture Approach.ä Management Decision 13,1.

Sheldon, Alan (1980), Organizational Paradigms: A Theory of Organizational Change. Organizational Dynamics, AMACON, a division of American Management Associations, Winter.

Stevenson, Howard H. & J. Carlos Jarillo (1990), A Paradigm of Entrepreneurship, Strategic Management Journal, Volume 11, Summer.

STK (1984), Culture for Growth, internal document of the STK corp.

Tushman, Michael L. & Thomas J. Scanlan (1981), Boundary Spanning Individuals: Their Role in Information Transfer and Their Antecedents, Academy of Management Journal, Volume 24, No. 2, p 289-305.

Weick, Karl E. (1979), The Social Psychology of Organizing, Random House Inc., U.S.A., Second Edition.

Yin, Robert K. (1984), Case Study Research. Design and Methods. Sage, Applied Social Research Methods Series, Volume 5.

22 Introduction of information technology to small firms: A network perspective

Mette Mønsted

Introduction

The introduction of information technology (IT) to small enterprises has not been unproblematic, which many aspects resembles that of larger firms. The reason for focusing specifically on small enterprises is that they lack in-house competence. The process and the diffusion of technology into small enterprises must thus be analyzed as a social process of interaction.

Small firms constitute approximately 85% of the Danish enterprises. The conditions for small firms of less than 20 employees are typically characterized by the lack of specialized expertise. As a group they are more dependent on external assistance than larger firms and most of them have to rely on external experts whose competencies they are unable to assess. Therefore, the decision making process and implementation of IT is a good case for analyzing the support of the network, the diffusion of a new technology and how the problems experienced by user groups are handled.

The aim of the study is not to evaluate the individual information system or configuration, but to assess how the implementation of IT is handled by small firms without 'in-house' expertise and how it changes the division of labour. In this perspective the network approach seems to be fruitful for interpreting the use of advisers and specialists.

The study on which this article is based is a part of a larger project on the IT field[1]. This article is based on interviews with 20 small and medium sized firms, up to 50 employees, within production and construction[2]. The firms selected are located around a provincial town of Western Zealand. Other interviewees are auditors, trade association officials inclusive of the Association of Authorized Public Accountants, and small IT suppliers in regional centers.

Small enterprises in a Danish perspective

The problems of introducing information technology in small enterprises may seem a very special issue. But the Danish industrial structure is dominated by what is considered very small enterprises in a European context. The enterprises with less than 20 employees constitute: 83 % in manufacturing, 96 % in construction and 97 % in retail (1983)(SE.1984-9).

The very small enterprises of less than 20 employees are qualitative very different from larger firms. They are most often *run by one owner-manager* who handles all the different roles of management.

The division of labour does not cater for specialists in all fields and the tradition seems to be to recruit mainly skilled laborers of the same skills as the owner. The generalized manager is the 'expert at hand', and he rarely has immediate specialists to draw on. Therefore, small firms are highly dependent on assistance and expertise from outside the firm (Mønsted, 1986). The typical owner-managers of small manufacturing or construction firms have skills and interests in technical issues related to the production. But *they often lack both skills and interests*, when it comes to *economic management*. Therefore, they are often highly dependent on persons who are qualified to deal with this issue, as for example an accountant in the firm, or external experts such as the auditor.

In some very small firms the owner also handles the accounts. But more often (in approximately 30% of the small firms) his wife assists him with office work. She is often responsible for the accounts, whether she is qualified as an accountant or not. The wives' backgrounds for doing this work are very different. Most of them, however, are not qualified as business administrators or book-keepers, they are trained on the job by the auditor. Firms with more than 10 employees more often employ a clerk who is in charge of administrative tasks as well as the book-keeping. But all major economic decisions are left with the owner.

Small firms relying on external experts are rarely able to assess their complementary skills properly. Therefore, co-operation with external experts is often based on personal trust and references from others. In order to avoid mistakes and to save time on searching for alternative information, small firms tend to build up networks of relative permanent relationships both through formal contacts, i.e. customers, suppliers, colleagues, and through informal relations, mostly friends, sports and sailing clubs, etc.(Mønsted, 1986, Friedman & Mønsted, 1988).

Motives for introducing IT

Small Danish firms within manufacturing and construction have, until recently, tended to let the auditor do most of the book-keeping, leaving only the cash book in the firm. Thus, the auditor to some extent functions as the external expert and service bureau.

The first introduction of administrative IT focused on the strong dependence on the auditor. The first systems were sold under the theme _save the auditor_, that is the introduction of IT in the firm would make the auditor redundant and thus pay for itself. However, this objective is not always easily obtained. The transfer of tasks from the expensive auditor to the firm may further the autonomy of the firm, but does not in itself make the firm more capable of dealing with financial issues.

Other motives for introducing IT have mainly been reference to other's opinion, and that 'this is the future, and you may just as well start it now', or 'the typewriter with a few lines of memory is more expensive than a PC so you may just as well jump into it'. However, the need for administrative systems in small firms varies. For many, the investment is not profitable in the way that it increases sales or profits. It may save time, but only after a long, and often very difficult introduction period implying much extra work.

The benefit of introducing an administrative system is not only the possibility of sending out invoices much quicker. It also qualitatively improves the firm's access to economic data. The latter implies that data, which were earlier left to the auditor, were not always available when needed for planning. Now, the firms working with administrative systems have immediate access to these data in the firm and can thus at any time produce figures for planning.

A large number of small firms are interested in introducing IT, but have difficulties in finding the financial resources. But well over half of the small firms do not have IT, and a considerable number of them do not want it either. The reasons stated are either that the investment is not directly profitable, or that they make few invoices, as for example sub-contractors, and thus do not feel the need at present. An often used argument is that a standard system cannot supply the customer with the personal service which is so important within their field.

The needs of the SMEs and the services offered by the suppliers

The suppliers saw the introduction of PC's into small firms as a chance to spread the technology and open up a totally new standardized market for IT. The suppliers, trade associations and auditors expected to penetrate rapidly into the market. However, the introduction of IT into small firms is different from that of larger installations where the requirements have been stated explicitly. Many of the small firms have not been able to specify their exact requirements and many salesmen have tended to sell much more comprehensive and complicated systems than required and to promise the customer 'a rose garden'. Furthermore, they have failed to give a realistic picture of the necessary amount of time to be spent on learning the systems. The first studies of the introduction of administrative IT in small firms revealed that the process had been extremely troublesome, and that some of the systems functioned poorly (Mønsted & Neergaard, 1986).

The needs of the SMEs can be divided into two fundamentally different types of situations:

a. The services demanded for the introduction.
The level of knowledge of IT in the firm is often very limited and the role of the 'IT specialist' is, together with the SME-owner/book-keeper, to specify the requirements often by using a mediator.

b. Service, maintenance and advice to firms using IT.
Once the small firm has introduced IT, and perhaps even has developed some internal expertise, the role of the IT specialist is much more specific and technical.

These are very different profiles of suppliers, and with the tendency of small enterprises to maintain already established service relations, they can not be expected to be well fulfilled both of them. How these demands are met varies much from case to case. The main difference seems to be dependent on whether the consultant is very technically minded and mainly concerned with the technology itself, or he/she is an advanced user of the software and hardware simultaneously with being acquainted with the issues to be computerized.

Earlier, the more technical consultants and sales persons were frequent and caused a lot of communication problems for first adopters. Today, the two roles can be combined as the software has become more self-instructive. But in many cases the 'techie' will expect the user to possess some basic knowledge of IT though he may not himself have much knowledge on the application area, for example accounting.

Currently there is a tendency for larger IT suppliers to combine the two roles and recruit people with different professional backgrounds related to the application area and then teach them the necessary IT to be able to deal with the customers. However, in many cases larger supplier firms are not very interested in servicing small firms which are thus referred to small suppliers. Therefore, the small supplier firms must, aside from the technical skills, also be able to communicate at different levels, understand the problems of the issues to be computerized and be capable of offering the necessary training during the introduction period. Thus integrating many aspects of computing in servicing small firms is demanding, but may be an opportunity for maintaining customers and securing the soundness of sales initiatives.

The decision to implement IT

The classical model of diffusion of innovation in Rogers innovation theory attributes great importance to the roles of information, early adopters and opinion leaders for a wide dissemination of the technology (Rogers, 1962, Rogers & Shoemaker, 1971). Therefore, the types of functions needed in the different stages of computerization change. The advanced users may need information and training that can only be rendered by a professional IT specialist. In the early phase, however, comprising few adopters, information, training, advice, and recommendations are very important to the dissemination of technology. During the actual decision process in the purchasing firm, there is a great need for psychological safety and different types of experienced users are often contacted for advice, also outside of the formal network.

Just as in other cases of new problems arising, small firm owners utilize their contact with colleagues, other consultants (e.g. auditors), and friends in order to find and assess relevant suppliers and relevant solutions. Most of them do not like the idea of being the first one to test out the technology, but will try to contact persons whose judgement they trust. The economic transaction of buying services and equipment is thus closely related to the evaluation by people trusted (opinion leaders), who are not financially benefiting from their choice.

Earlier research on small firms has shown, that the time span between the decision to have IT, and the decision of what to buy is very long (Mønsted & Neergaard, 1986). This long period is not spent on thorough assessments, but is characterized by preliminary examinations and much confusion. The possibilities are many, and frightening examples are plenty. The firm may well be stuck in this phase for a long time, unable as it is to evaluate the options and structures of the many and often contradictory information. The uncertainty is too overwhelming to get any overview to decide.

A recent study confirms this long time-lag from the first interest and information meetings with suppliers to the actual purchase and introduction of IT. The period is often more than six months and during this phase the different forms of network relations provide some help (Friedman & Mønsted, 1988). The informal network seems to be a way of screening the abundant amount of information from the suppliers, of finding relevant suppliers and of specifying some requirements.

The informal network is used to sort out information and limit the feeling of uncertainty to be able to act (Mønsted, 1990). This structuring is then based on other evaluations than the factual needs of the firm. More often by imitating solutions from 'nearly similar' firms. Another method to overcome this problem is a gradual and 'safe' introduction to IT may be to purchase a cheap 'bamboo' PC in order to become acquainted with the technology and its possibilities and hence better capable of defining the specifications and requirements to the 'real IT supplier'. This way of introducing IT has proved successful in a few cases, but it was very time consuming.

The implementation process

The early adopters were faced with many problems. Not only did they not have access to experience in their informal networks, but the first standard solutions were not very flexible. Thus the demand for programming expertise from the supplier specialists was evident. Also the technical problems were many: low capacity of hardware, poor or inadequate software, and functioning of the printer. This created a demand for technical computing services from specialists who, however, did not possess any expertise in accounting and were often incapable of understanding the requirements demanded. They were obviously much more *IT specialists, than support staff for new users*.

The marketed software has improved and thus the possibilities of getting good and more flexible standard software. Hence the demand for specialists has changed and eased the need for instruction. As the programmes and systems as such have improved and become more flexible, the technical demands to sellers are less. The ability to diagnose the combined problems of accounting, communication, and the technical solution becomes increasingly important for the competition between suppliers.

It is important to note that the small suppliers, who initially did programming, are now practically almost only into selling and instructing, and hardly do any programming today. This is now the domain of specialised software houses. The availability of software packages with built in user instructions open up new important aspects, as the user by following the instructions can learn how to utilize all aspects of the programme. Still, to do so some basic knowledge in and experience with IT is needed, but not at the level of a programmer -advanced users may well take over this function. The problems arise if other more technical services are needed for maintenance or developing special functions, then the real technical experts are needed.

Most systems implemented by small firms are related to simple accounting and invoicing tasks. Very few have installed more advanced systems for financial management, stocks or tenders.

The systems are fairly standardised but have undergone changes during the three years that the CHIPS research project has been focusing on the field and thus have improved considerably, especially in relation to the user support of the firm.

But introducing IT is not only a question of supplier-user relations, often it also involves other changes in the internal work processes, and thus in the skills needed. Furthermore, the division of labour between the firm and the external expertise is changed. Firms that earlier used the auditor as a service-bureau for book-keeping, most often handle the accounts themselves after having introduced IT. Thus, the process of computing is not only linked to the technology, but in many cases also to basic accounting problems.

In general the problems of implementation are due to the fact that information systems are not solutions in themselves, but rather a means to solve problems. Therefore, different types of expertise are required to convert them into something useful.

Mediators of IT to SMEs

If the introduction of IT to small firms is perceived as a diffusion process, the early stages could be described as situations, where the firms introducing IT are opinion leaders with special characteristics, and at the same time as situations characterized by few available specialists and standard solutions. The customized service mainly demanded in the beginning of the 1980's was too expensive for the small firms. In this phase, the large installations were the interesting markets for the suppliers, and small installations had difficulties in finding the service needed. The 'specialists' were interested in the technical aspects and were often incapable of communicating with the customer who had too little knowledge of the field to ask the right questions and specify his requirements. The probability of ending up with a satisfactory solution was small. There was every chance of the process being derailed by mistakes and problems.

With the introduction of the PC's in the mid and earlier 1980's the small and medium sized enterprises became an interesting market for the suppliers. Standard software was developed and a number of trade associations went into the field with the aim of diffusion of new technology by developing a better and easier introduction to IT for their members. The many problems and the felt need for introducing new technology, prepared the way for expanding the activities and engaging in the development of systems that met the specific needs of the members, as well as developing courses and a supportive structure for their members. (Boch, 1989).

The other perspective of diffusion is that IT is just a means and is sold as any other type of machinery. But 'the decision to change routines and formalize and standardize information processing may be much more difficult for the small firm, than the introduction of information technology itself' (Mønsted & Neergaard, 1986, s.161).

Thus, the introduction of IT not only gives access to new problem areas and involve new expertise, but it may also transfer job functions from an external expert to a non-expert in the firm. If this process is not supported, the result may easily be disastrous. It is no longer possible for the auditor to keep an eye on the liquidity of the firm and warn against crises due to lack of available funds.

The firm must be capable of handling the data, and time must be allocated to the process of learning how to computerize accounts. Furthermore, the users must thoroughly know the issues to be computerized - in most cases of small firms this means the principles of book-keeping. IT in itself is not a means to teach managers, secretaries or wives neither accounting nor book-keeping. The result is of course that technology is diffused, but the utility value remains very low. If the introduction is to succeed, it must be followed up by a learning process and supported by agents outside the firm.

The support structure of small enterprises during the introduction phase is different from that of large enterprises. Small firms often apply a combination of professional and non-professional advice and service (Friedman & Mønsted, 1988). The non-professionals are characterized by not possessing formal qualifications within the field, they have experience and may be rather advanced or even new users. During the phase of introduction it is most important to the SMEs that they can draw on somebody whose skills and judgement they trust.

The announcement of problems to colleagues, customers or suppliers provides access to alternatives or at least an important supplement to the IT supplier already picked. But it also tends to add to the IT specialists new groups, who have experience and may assist in a more 'private' or informal way. Some of these are real IT specialists employed as such. Others, however, have developed expertise themselves - as users of IT. Some of the early adopters of IT have had to develop certain skills, and even if this was not the purpose, they may be asked to play the role as specialists.

The group of people acting in the role of 'IT advisor' is heterogeneous and their reasons for entering the role are several. Some may only occasionally act in the role, as they happen to be around when problems arise, i.e. teen-age children, who diagnose the problem by applying the method of trial-and-error and often have more general computing experience -and perhaps the 'fearless approach' needed in the situation. Others are called among friends, customers or colleagues who have recently been through the problems themselves, and therefore know the trade.

The 'user specialists' have two important functions during the introduction phase. One seems to be related to recommendations on what supplier firms to choose, including specification of demands to the system, and in a few cases which system to choose. That is, the first search for advice seems to be related to: *Who to ask?* in order to avoid repeating the problems others have faced. This demands assistance from people who are both experienced and can translate the relatively vaguely defined problems of the application area, i.e. the needs of accounting and invoicing into technical specifications.

The other function is related to the availability of a resourceful person, someone who can act as 'trouble-shooter' when the system creates problems, and does not function as prescribed, or the introduction course or manual is not understood. Most of these problems are usually basic and simple and only require little knowledge and experience to be solved and may be solved by people with just slightly more experience.

The agents most often playing the role of mediator of IT are:

sales persons, auditors, consultants from trade associations, suppliers of courses, and from the informal network: friends and colleagues.

The more advanced trouble-shooters needed for more complex or technical problems are usually searched through the same network channels, and not only through the formal supplier.

Sales persons

From around 1986 the suppliers have very actively been trying to penetrate into the market of small and medium sized firms. In both 1987, and a follow up in 1989 and 1990, the interviewed firms told that they received telephone calls from suppliers or direct mail approximately once a week. Currently, sales persons seem to compete on their ability to communicate with and understand the needs of SMEs. An important criteria for recommending suppliers is the capacity to communicate to non-experts in a normal language, indicating the many problems experienced. Still, there seems to be a tendency to sell too comprehensive systems and to promise too much. The gap between what is demanded and the capacity of the system often gives rise to many problems in the small firms. The SMEs have often heard about the cheap solutions, and may insist on a cheaper solution, although it cannot meet the demands stated. The two parties inability to communicate and thus find solutions that meet the demands may very well constitute the basis for serious drawbacks. The sellers are often interested in getting a maintenance contract, but most SMEs find that this is too expensive and they expect the new machine to work perfectly without service.

The problems of communication are important for the understanding of SMEs' network of assistance. The support from the supplier may function satisfactorily and in many cases the 'hot-line' seems to provide good support. But there are several cases of errors or misunderstandings, and to solve these the firms often avoid the sellers and try to find someone else whom they feel they can rely on. When the existing support is blocked in some way, either because of lack of communication or because the supplier fails to meet the demands, the informal network is activated in order to find someone who can help solving the problems.

In the mid to late 80'es the suppliers have tended to exaggerate in promising too much service. The first customers refer to them because of the perfect 'hot-line', but if this is much used, the supplier is not generating income on this, and he will loose out economically or have to frustrate the expectations of the next customers.

There seems to be different expectations to the exchange, which may be the basis for failures, i.e. the culture of artisan responsibility versus that of high salaried technical service. Typically, the small firms try to find supplier firms which organizationally and culturally are similar to themselves. A series of suppliers have specialised in certain trade specific solutions, and tend to sell via recommendations of customers, thus using the collegial references and informal networks.

Another clear trend is the emergence of local supplier firms. Many of the small firms are located in the regional areas of Denmark whereas most large supplier firms are situated in the Copenhagen area or in the large regional cities. Thus, when problems arose, the small firms have often felt that the physical distance was too great and that it took too long time to get the necessary service. By choosing a local supplier they obtained both easier access to service and a better service, the latter because a local dealer is more dependent on his reputation.

Auditors

Originally, the auditors were reluctant toward IT, partly because of experiences from other countries, and partly because of the initial sales-arguments: 'save the auditor'. However, most of them seem to have changed their attitude and now support IT. The result is that they are asked for advice, and often assist in outlining the chart of accounts as well as training the person in charge of the book-keeping. Very often two parallel sets of accounts are made for the first three months, one is made by the auditor and the other one by the firm itself.

The auditors often seem to recommend the standard trade-association solution, where one is available. Or they recommend systems they work with themselves or happen to know from other clients. The increasing number of firms introducing IT has expanded the auditors' knowledge of systems and they may now be more inclined to recommend systems or suppliers, they know work well with other clients. The auditors are only to a surprisingly limited extent involved in the actual decision process or specification of requirements.

Trade associations

Several trade-associations decided that IT was an entrance to the future, and saw their role in developing a standard system for their members. This way they could both play a role in the diffusion of the new technology, and smoothen the road for the members into IT (see Mønsted & Boch, 1990).

A survey was carried out in the Spring of 1987 in order to identify how widespread the trade-association solutions were (Boch, 1987). 150 questionnaires were sent out, 70 were returned. However, other channels of information provides a few more, in all having 37 trade association solutions. Most of the trade associations' solutions were standardized programmes. A few trade associations had only consulting roles as mediators, to assist

366

with specification of programmes as well as recommending some of the acceptable ones (Mønsted & Boch, 1990).

Almost all trade-associations engaging in the development of trade-specific solutions to IT have chosen a supplier, who handles the direct contact with the member firms. The trade associations are to a varying degree financially involved in the IT solution with the IT supplier. They have seen the role of the trade association as important for the diffusion of the technology, for the development of suitable programmes for their members, and as an attempt to protect their members against the suppliers in the market. This is the only institution which defines itself as mediator of IT.

However, the close links to 'their own IT solution' imply that as a trade-association they can no longer be consulted for a neutral trade specific advice on this issue. The trade specific competence is biased to the one solution and their role becomes more like that of a supplier. One trade association, the plumbers, has changed this by loosening the close coupling of the trade to one supplier, thus discussing alternatives and evaluating the specifications more openly when involved in advice.

The trade associations that engaged in the market of IT apparently expected to obtain a kind of a monopoly of the solution offered to their members. Also, they expected a much more rapid diffusion of the technology. Actually most trade association solutions had a slow diffusion process, and have not spread much beyond 30% of the members. The exception is the Electricians' solution. Most associations estimate that the total percentage of members having IT is the double of those having purchased the trade association solution.

The trade associations went into the field of IT at a time when the PC had just been introduced (the early 1980's), and a time when the costs of developing software were very high. After a couple of years all of the trade associations' systems had to compete with other trade-specific systems which were being marketed. The maintenance and change of systems were difficult because it required large investments. For two of the associations that regularly supply the members with up-dated price diskettes covering all the item numbers of the stock, i.e. the electricians and the plumbers, this competition has proved to be serious as other suppliers and wholesalers are offering the same service at a lower price.

The most applied parts of the trade association solutions were pretty simple and had many standard alternatives. By the mid 80'es, it was difficult to see the rational need for a new development of a solution.

Most trade associations possessed very little competence within IT when they first started to engage in the issue and started to build a trade specific system. Thus, most members asking for advice were referred to the supplier with whom they had a contract. But right from the beginning all of the trade associations have emphasized the need for user-support, and they have established introductory courses in order to ensure a gradual and successful implementation of the IT solution. In the early phases this was only done by the computer firms, but the competitive situation has implied that more of the trade associations are involved in an evaluation and discussion of the systems. The trade associations have also expanded the range of courses and training offered, i.e. linking the courses in financial management and accounting to IT (as for example the association of painters). Thus the trade associations have been engaging more in the role of mediators and some of them gradually putting distance to the role of supplier.

Most trade association solutions recommend stock management as one of the modules of the package. With most small firms , this has proven very difficult. The work culture of construction workers or other skilled labourers is not bureaucratic on the registration of all small pieces used. The low acceptance of the importance imply, that there is a considerable gap between the registered and the actual stock. The stock registration however is one of the reasons for wholesalers to go into the competition of trade specific systems (plumbers). The offers of numbers of items as with the wholesalers, or modem-transfer of orders has been offered to secure permanent delivery relations. The diffusion of these systems, however, is very limited.

Suppliers of courses

The general system of evening classes also offers basic courses in programming and IT. Most of these are related to simple programming and the 'hands-on' experience rather than assessment of programmes. The courses offered both within the adult educational system and by suppliers provide an important source of information. They disclose some of the problems connected to IT and give the participants some practical experience and, as a side effect, offer the opportunity of establishing network contacts to skilled people and other users to draw on when necessary.

The users of IT in SMEs, who had participated in courses had very different experiences, and interviews with firms and institutions indicated that most of them spent much time after the course before they decided on a system. The experiences gained through the courses had made them aware of the many problems they might have to face and hence made them more cautious and careful customers. Some of the interviewees clearly stated that the courses were their only relevant source of information, which were not tied to any supplier or supplier interests and that they on the basis of this had felt encouraged to pursue the idea of introducing IT.

The trade associations' IT courses are closely tied to their own solutions. But IT is also introduced via other trade association courses, e.g. on accounting, financial management, tenders, and stock management.

Informal network - friends and colleagues

Naturally the early adopters of IT had very few experienced users to confer with and they were thus forced to rely on the sellers and IT people while simultaneously developing their own expertise. Very few of them knew anybody personally who was skilled in the field and whom they could ask informal assistance.

It has become increasingly important for SMEs to be able to draw on the experiences of colleagues and friends, both in relation to sorting out the abundant amount of information from the suppliers, to choose an appropriate supplier, and to secure assistance if the formal network fails to function. The firms interviewed during the last period of the survey (October-November 1988) had all used contacts among customers, colleagues or other suppliers in order to identify a reliable supplier firm. Some of the firms asked for the type of configuration, but the most essential question in the purchasing situation seemed to be the one of finding a relevant and reliable supplier.

Networks of assistance

The network approach seems to be fruitful for the study of how problems are tackled. Who are asked about what? Who are actually the 'trouble-shooters' within the field? The pattern is very complex and dynamic. The role of different formal support structures seems to have changed, and the quality of the systems provided also seems to have improved during the period studied.

A few cases illustrate some of the combinations of formal and informal structures of support connected to the decision to purchase and introduce IT:

a) A carpentry firm wanted to introduce IT. The standard trade association solutions were not feasible and the introduction was delayed. The son of the owner and one of his friends supported the idea and promised to assist in the introduction phase. The owner then decided to buy a cheap PC and gradually become acquainted with the technology, supported by this informal assistance. This way of introducing IT was time consuming, but offered a very safe process for the later larger system acquired.

b) A small electrician firm started attending courses at the technological information centre two years before introducing IT. The owner assessed the trade association solution to be too expensive. The version aiming at small firm had too small a capacity for his purposes and the large system was much too complex.

He attended courses offered by the trade association in financial management, discussed alternatives with colleagues and asked for their advice. Through an electrician colleague, he finally found a suitable system serviced by a very small consultancy firm.

Once the system is bought, a contact to a supplier is established. To supplement this a combination of formal and informal contacts may be drawn on when problems arise. The informal contacts are typical drawn upon if the formal supplier fails to meet the expectations of the firm:

c) A small electrical firm had also accepted an agency for a heat control systems. They had for a couple of years been working with a small IT accounting system. As the business developed, the capacity of the system became insufficient. They contacted the supplier of the system they already had and was advised to buy a larger system, which they did. However, the capacity of the hardware proved to be too low and the installations never functioned properly. The supplier firm had been paid and was very reluctant to render further services: A friend and customer (an auditor) of the owner learned about the problems and offered his assistance as he had experiences with the software. The problems were more complicated than he expected, but he referred to one of his friends, who was a skilled IT specialist and who managed to solve the problems.

To what extent a combination of formal supplier relations and more informal 'expertise' is used depends on the complexity of the problem, i.e. whether the defined problem implies both technical and accounting practices. In relation to some problems the supplier may be the only one asked. But with other types of problems, the information is checked or evaluated by others as well, i.e. friends, colleagues, or the auditor.

Concluding evaluation of IT in SMEs

From a strictly economic point of view it may not be neither very profitable nor rational for SMEs to invest in administrative IT. This is an argument often raised by some of the SMEs who do not want IT. Many SMEs have become hesitant after learning about the first adopters' difficulties. If the process of introducing IT is evaluated after the first six months there have been many failures. The overall experience is that it takes a long time to make the systems work satisfactorily. The use of software seems to be limited to for example book-keeping, accounts of creditors and debtors, and invoicing. Very few of the SMEs have introduced systems for financial management or stock management.

One indication of the problems of introducing IT may be deduced from a survey made by the steel employers' association (Jernet). One of the questions to new users of IT revealed the factors which the users found must be accomplished before the introduction of IT:

Table 1

Factors which need to be accomplished before introducing computers

Procedures and systems to be computerized must be organized properly	63%
Data discipline, chart of accounts and number systems	31%
Describe tasks, make analyses and set up system requirements	18%
Knowledge, training, attitudes	15%
	(Source: Jernet, 1984)

Many problems are created by the organisation's lacking capability of handling the important task of standardizing and systematizing data for IT. Many of these problems are often registered as IT problems, but they are actually caused by the firm's difficulties in bringing data to a standardized form and thus facilitate computerization.

What is actually characterized as a failure? If the machinery runs perfectly, the firms find the installation successful. But many firms discover shortly after the implementation that the capacity of the purchased system is too low, while others discover that the large and expensive system is only used for book-keeping. Some of the satisfied users will face problems later on. The apparently well fitting system may not be large enough or capable of coping with the complexity of tasks demanded later on. It is a classic problem of e.g. overloading the harddisk and unawareness of the problems this creates. If a large system is purchased and only a minor part of it is used, or if a small system that works well now, cannot be expanded when necessary, then it is worth questioning whether the solution is satisfactory.

Regardless of the many problems encountered almost all of those having introduced IT are satisfied once the installation functions, that is when they have overcome the long period of introduction. Some may not have an adequate installation, but they are happy to have just a limited amount of information in-house and to have overcome the introduction.

This may reflect the expectations to IT. In the early phase the expectations from the magic of IT were greater, but they seem to have declined, and many are satisfied if the system does not create too many difficulties and facilitates the book-keeping process. Some would not have bought IT, if they had known the problems and the vast amount of time required. But the general picture is one of relief: it works and a lot of tiresome routine work, which earlier burdened them during week-ends, has become easier to handle. The cash book and the making of the monthly or quarterly accounts were considered a burden, and many are now surprised how fast it goes.

The time saved may not be an argument for the profitability, as time often has no 'price' when the work is done by the owner or his wife. But once the burden of paper work is lessened, the evaluation of the time saved is very positive, though it cannot be calculated in terms of money.

The feeling of having relevant economic data within the firm is a general positive statement, whether or not the competence to use these data was present. This may well be a 'general statement', and it may reveal some mistrust in the auditors, and especially to the price of their services. Generally, the application of economic data is rather limited and primitive. Therefore, the criteria for good or bad solutions tend to become primitive and related only to whether or not it works. They do not comprise an evaluation of the unused possibilities of the system or of alternative solutions.

If the auditor is less used, also in connection with other issues than the book-keeping, then the change may be hazardous, as the occasions to discuss the accounts with a competent person disappear. The chance of having an early warning of critical trends may disappear too. It is imperative with such a system that the firm internally has economic expertise at its disposal or have access to a system where this service can be used at a fairly regular basis.

The decision process and implementation of IT in SMEs have often implied serious cultural clashes between sellers and 'techies' on the one hand, and the artisan culture of small firms on the other hand. The communication barriers are many and some of them resemble those of the large firms in the early phase of IT, but there are certain basic differences. Small firms cannot afford to employ an expert or buy customized software and are therefore continually dependent on a group of external consultants and suppliers, whose expertise they cannot really evaluate.

The combination of formal and informal networks seems to be important as a means to structure the first uncertain periods of seeking information. The combined network is developed to seek 'trouble-shooters': both to simple problems in the introduction phase and other parts of the network for the more complex technical problems.

The reliance on the informal network and basically non-professional assistance may lead to too much standardization and too large installations in order 'to play it safe'. The choice of configurations is more based on the imitation of other social network contacts than on a systematic evaluation of the possibilities in relation to the needs. This way of evaluating solutions and options seems to be fairly common also when evaluating consultancies, technical changes and marketing relations. The feeling of insecurity while having to decide in an area where the firm has no capacity or knowledge, is comforted by using the informal networks. That is, it may in some cases offer some kind of security against a total misinterpretation, but it does not provide professional evaluation of competencies.

Bibliography

Boch, Frans (1987): 'Trade Associations as Mediators of Technological Adaptation'. Institute of organization and industrial sociology, Copenhagen. CHIPS Working paper 1987-6. 1987.

Friedman, Andrew & Mønsted, Mette (1988): *'Purposive and Potential Networks in the Diffusion of Computer Systems to Small Firms'*. CHIPS working paper Jan. 1989-11, Copenhagen Business School, Copenhagen.

Jernets Arbejdsgiverforening (1984): *'Behovsanalyse blandt mindre virksomheder vedrørende informationsteknologi'*. Copenhagen.

Mønsted, Mette and Peter Neergaard (1986): EDB i mindre virksomheder. P.Neergaard (ed.): *'•konomisk Styring i mindre virksomheder'*.

Mønsted, Mette (1985): *'Små virksomheder i rådgivningssystemet'*. Copenhagen, Nyt Fra Samfundsvidenskaberne.

Mønsted, Mette (1990): *'Skills and overview in SMEs'*. Rencontres de St. Gallen. 1990.

Mønsted, Mette and Frans Boch (1990): *'Trade Associations as Mediators of Information Technology to Small and Medium Sized Firms'*. Copenhagen Business School, Cph.

Neergaard, Peter (1989): *'Microcomputers in small companies. Benefits achieved and problems encountered'*. Mimeo, Institute of Informatics and Economic Management, Copenhagen Business School, Copenhagen.

Neergaard, Peter (ed.) (1986): *'•konomisk styring i mindre virksomheder'*. Copenhagen.

Rogers, E and F.F. Shoemaker (1971): *'Communication of Innovations. A cross cultural approach'*. 2nd edition, New York.

Rogers, Everett M. (1962): *'Diffusion of Innovation'*. 2nd revisededition. New York.

SE-1984-9. Statistiske Efterretninger.

Notes

1. 'Computing History: Interdependencies, Power-strategies and Structures' (CHIPS).
2. 20 small enterprises, 5 supplier firms of IT to small firms, and 2 auditors were interviewed. Apart from this, trade association officials, inclusive of the Association of State Authorized Public Accountants, have been interviewed.